Religion and Political Modernization

Religion and Political Modernization

Edited by Donald Eugene Smith

New Haven and London, Yale University Press, 1974

Library of Congress catalog card number: 73–86917
International standard book number: 0–300–01730–8

Designed by John O. C. McCrillis
and set in Baskerville type.
Printed in the United States of America by
The Colonial Press, Inc., Clinton, Massachusetts.

Published in Great Britain, Europe, and Africa by
Yale University Press, Ltd., London.
Distributed in Latin America by Kaiman & Polon,
Inc., New York City; in Australasia and Southeast
Asia by John Wiley & Sons Australasia Pty. Ltd.,
Sydney; in India by UBS Publishers' Distributors Pvt.,
Ltd., Delhi; in Japan by John Weatherhill, Inc., Tokyo.

For

FATHER DANIEL J. DEVER

whose vision and initiative led to the

Institute for Religion and Social Change

Contents

Foreword

This volume brings together the papers prepared for a conference held in Honolulu in March 1971 to analyze the interaction of religion and politics in the transitional societies of the Third World. Religion is the central component of the traditional cultures of South and Southeast Asia, the Middle East, North Africa, and Latin America, and the interaction of religion with the processes of political modernization is a subject of fundamental importance.

It is clear that the major religious systems of this vast area—Hinduism, Buddhism, Islam, and Catholicism—are both influencing and being influenced by the political processes in their respective societies. It is also evident that the impact of religion on the processes of political modernization has both negative and positive aspects. On one hand modernization involves secularization, the process by which religious influence is reduced, but on the other hand religious values and perspectives can illuminate and clarify the objectives of planned social change. The essays in this book seek to analyze these complex interactions.

The conference that resulted in this book was the first to be sponsored by the Institute for Religion and Social Change, which came into operation in 1970. The Institute had its origin in the deep conviction that the world's religious and related philosophical value systems have a critical and creative role to play in imparting meaning and purpose to man as he strives to find solutions for the complex and perplexing problems of human development. The Institute is a research and conference center that seeks to understand the interaction of religion and social change, to discover how religion promotes or retards man's development, and through new perspectives to encourage constructive action.

The conference on Religion and Political Modernization was financed by a grant from the Juliette M. Atherton Trust of Honolulu, and we are deeply grateful for this generous support. I wish to express our sincere appreciation to all those who have supported us in this project, to the participants, and particularly to Professor Donald E. Smith for organizing the conference and editing the book. We are grateful to the East-West Center for placing at our disposal its excellent physical facilities and the services of its capable staff. We are very thankful to Miss Barbara Yamasaki, who ably and cheerfully typed most of the conference papers.

The Institute for Religion and Social Change hopes that this volume will help to bring the problems of religion and politics into sharper focus and stimulate further research and dialogue in this field.

Institute for Religion and Social Change   P. J. PHILIP
Honolulu, Hawaii   Director

PART 1

Introduction and Overview

1

Religion and Political Modernization: Comparative Perspectives

DONALD E. SMITH

Religion constitutes the core of the traditional cultures of South and Southeast Asia, the Middle East, North Africa, and Latin America. Throughout this vast area, to identify any particular society as Hindu, Buddhist, Muslim, or Catholic is to tell us a great deal about its character. Facts about basic geographic, demographic, economic, and other variables are of course essential to any adequate profile of the society in question. However, an understanding of the society's sacred symbols and values, and the ways in which these have been related to the social system, may well tell us more about behavioral predispositions than the per capita GNP.

While the relationship between tradition and change has now emerged as one of the central foci in studies of political modernization, the religious component of tradition (a very large part of the whole) has received relatively little attention. Despite the pioneering work of Max Weber, various factors, including the secularist assumptions of contemporary Western culture, have tended to relegate this problem to low priority. Most of the studies we now have were published in the last decade, and systematic comparative work (the central purpose of Weber's research) has only begun.

POLITICAL MODERNIZATION

There is as yet no single widely used definition of political modernization, but substantial agreement exists on some of the elements of a definition. Lucian W. Pye has identified three major themes running through many definitions: differentiation, equality, and capacity. Systems undergoing modernization become more *differentiated* in terms of governmental and political structures, place increasing emphasis on the *equality* of citizens in political participation and the allocation of benefits, and increase their *capacity* to bring about socioeconomic change.[1] In this book, we are concerned with important aspects of all three points: (1) *polity secularization,* the process by which a traditional system undergoes radical differentiation, resulting in separation of the polity from religious structures, substitution of secular modes of legitimation, and extension of the polity's jurisdiction into areas formerly regulated by religion; (2) *mass politicization,* the process by which mass participation in politics becomes the accepted norm and is substantially realized in practice; and (3) *developmental capacity expansion,* the process by which the polity increases its effectiveness in directing socioeconomic change.

Our purpose is to analyze the ways in which the religious factor is related to these processes of political modernization. Only in the first process, however, is the relationship with religion a direct one and here, of course, it is a negative relationship. Political modernization includes, as one of its basic processes, the secularization of polities, the progressive exclusion of religion from the political system. In the other two processes, the relationship with religion is indirect and partial, but positive. Granted that many secular forces and structures tend to promote the politicization of the masses, does religion also make some positive contribution to this process? The chapters dealing with religious nationalist movements, religious interest groups, and religious political parties suggest that under certain circumstances the religious factor can be quite significant in promoting mass politicization. Granted that many secular factors must be operative for the polity's developmental capacity to increase substantially, can a reformulated religious doctrine of development provide positive ideological support for the effort? The chapters dealing with this problem make it clear that such doctrinal reformulation is definitely taking place in the Third World, although in practical terms the impact of the new ideas may be marginal.

1. Lucian W. Pye, *Aspects of Political Development* (Boston: Little, Brown, 1966), pp. 45–47.

FOUR RELIGIOUS SYSTEMS

In this volume, we are interested in comparative questions, namely, the different ways in which the four major religious systems[2] are interacting with the three processes of political modernization. A number of the essays, however, deal with the problem in one society only; some are comparative in a limited sense, in that they deal with two or more Buddhist (or Muslim or Catholic) countries. The comparative perspective is suggested by the arrangement of the chapters, so that the relationships of the different religious systems to the process of secularization, for example, may at least be examined together. However, these features admittedly do not add up to a comparative study in the strict sense. A modest step in that direction, made here, is simply that of summarizing the findings of the fifteen authors within an explicitly comparative theoretical framework.

Some basic distinctions must be made as we examine the four religious systems. In the study of religion, many different classificatory schemes have been proposed, and each must be judged not as right or wrong but as more or less useful in relation to the specific object of the analysis. With respect to our purposes here, the analysis of religious systems in interaction with political processes, two questions are of paramount importance: (1) What *ideas* does the religious system provide about the course and meaning of history? (2) What *structures* link the religious system to the social system? [3]

In our analysis of ideas, we draw upon the familiar distinction between historical and ahistorical religious systems. In Judaeo-Christian-Islamic thought, history is a fundamental category. History began with the creation of the world, God intervenes in history through acts of self-revelation, history has meaning in the working out of divine purpose, and history will end with the ful-

2. Actually *five* religious systems are treated, for chap. 5 deals with the secularization conflicts that have challenged Orthodox Judaism in Israel. Other chapters, on the relationship between Judaism and politicization and on the religious legitimation of change in contemporary Israel, could have been prepared but for the limitations of space. The theoretical analysis presented here, however, relates only to Hinduism, Buddhism, Islam, and Catholicism.

3. This discussion summarizes the analysis elaborated in my *Religion and Political Development* (Boston: Little, Brown, 1970), especially pp. 1–10, 246–79.

fillment of that purpose. In ahistorical Hindu-Buddhist thought, on the other hand, history is viewed as endless, cyclical, and lacking in moral purpose. A golden age is followed by degeneration and decline, followed aeons later by regeneration and another golden age, as the next cycle begins. The fate of any particular society is inconsequential, for it is swallowed up in the vastness of the cosmic process.

In our analysis of structures, the primary distinction is between organic and church religious systems. Organic systems tend to equate religion and society; sacral law and social structure are at the heart of religion. Church systems, on the other hand, posit a structure that is within society but clearly separate from it; primary attention is given to the internal ordering of the church. This distinction cuts across the two major streams of religious evolution, for Hinduism and Islam are organic systems; Theravada Buddhism and Catholicism are church systems.

The essential nature of traditional Hinduism and Islam is found in the structures of caste and sacred law, respectively, mechanisms by which entire societies were integrated by divine regulation. The essential nature of Buddhism and Catholicism, on the other hand, is found in the church: the Sangha, or Buddhist order of monks, and the Ecclesia, or called-out assembly of Christians. Interestingly, the primitive meaning of both *sangha* and *ecclesia* is "assembly," a group that is set apart from the general society.

I can here only suggest, and treat in summary fashion, some of the important relationships between these characteristics of religious systems and the processes of political modernization with which we are concerned.

1. The church systems, because of their much greater attention to the development of ecclesiastical organization, are better equipped to respond to the whole range of problems posed by rapid social change: to oppose government-sponsored secularization efforts, to function effectively in politics through clerical interest groups and clerically led mass organizations, to reformulate their social doctrine and give it the stamp of ecclesiastical authority, and so on. Organic systems, with their relatively low level of ecclesiastical organization, respond much less coherently and effectively; laymen must undertake many of the tasks of resisting

ANALYSIS OF RELIGIOUS SYSTEMS

Analysis of Ideas

	Ahistorical	Historical
Organic	Hinduism	Islam
Church	Buddhism	Catholicism

Analysis of Structures

secularization, organizing political forces, and reformulating social doctrine.

2. In church systems, the raison d'être of the church is quite separable from functions of societal control. While a church can reach out to dominate the entire society (both Catholic and Buddhist churches have done this), the church continues to make sense religiously when the processes of secularization have stripped it of all its regulatory powers over society. The same processes, however, leave the organic religious system in considerable difficulty. Hinduism without a sacral social order or Islam without an operational sacred law faces a more fundamental problem of redefinition and with much weaker organizational mechanisms to attempt the redefinition, as noted above.

3. Historical religious systems have important advantages over ahistorical systems in attempting to develop religious ideologies of social change. Because the historical process is understood as being linear and fraught with transcendent meaning, the reinterpreters of Islamic and Catholic social doctrine can build convincing bridges to secular ideologies such as socialism. The underlying fact, of course, is that these religions share with Marxism a fundamentally biblical view of history.

THE SECULARIZATION OF POLITIES

Secularization is a complex process that can be analyzed further. I propose five analytically distinct aspects of secularization.

1. *Polity-separation secularization* refers to the institutional separation of religion and polity (church-state separation) and the denial of the religious identity of the polity (nonrecognition of a state religion or the religious character of the state). Government ceases to perform its traditional functions as promoter and defender of the faith.

2. *Polity-expansion secularization* involves the expansion of the political system into areas of society formerly regulated by religion. The polity thus extends its jurisdiction into areas of education, law, economic activity, and so on, which were subject to religious norms and structures in the traditional system.

3. *Political-culture secularization* refers to the transformation of values associated with the polity; secular notions of political community, the legitimacy of the polity, and the meaning of politics replace traditional religious notions in the thinking of many people.

4. *Political-process secularization* is the decline in political saliency and influence of religious leaders, religious interest groups, religious political parties, and religious issues; it also denotes the weakening of religious identity and ideology of the actors as a consequence of participation in the political process. For example, the waning influence of religious political parties and their increasingly secular orientation would both be manifestations of political-process secularization.

5. *Polity-dominance secularization* refers to a radical program of secularization by revolutionary regimes that recognize no area of religious autonomy. Their effort is to eliminate entirely the influence of religion from society or alter radically its content to bring it into line with official ideologies.

Polity-dominance secularization is a phenomenon limited to a few historical examples, but its significance is nonetheless considerable. The radical secularization attempted during certain phases of the French, Mexican, Russian, Turkish, and Chinese revolutions was based on a clear understanding of the stubborn capacity of religious systems to resist fundamental change.

The first four aspects of secularization, on the other hand, can be found to a greater or lesser extent in the recent experience of the vast majority of societies in the Third World. The first two (polity-separation and polity-expansion secularization) are largely initiated and implemented by governments committed to modern-ization, that is, by the efforts of westernized political and military elites. However, the third and fourth aspects (political-culture and political-process secularization) are not easily initiated and carried out by governmental policy. The state's control of the educational system, it is true, may effect the desired changes in the masses' values in the long run, but for decades to come traditional re-ligious understandings of government and politics will continue. Governments can of course ban religious political parties or the political activities of clerical groups, but in the absence of secular political values, these measures are effective only so long as coercion is applied.

The massive and prolonged use of governmental coercion in order to secularize the political culture and the political process is of central importance in revolutionary programs of polity-domi-nance secularization. Throughout most of the Third World, how-ever, the secularization of these areas of political life is a long-range process in which the possibly crucial factors will come not from the political system but from its environment. The general movement toward a world culture based in large part on human-ism, material values, science, and technology is gradually eroding all traditional world views.

The first four aspects of secularization clearly do not move to-gether at the same pace; events may not even move together in the same *direction*. As Fred R. von der Mehden has emphasized, a not uncommon phenomenon in South and Southeast Asia has been the *resurgence* of religious actors and issues in politics since inde-pendence, in some cases at the same time that governments have been implementing policies of secularization in other areas.[4] The political process becomes not more secular but more traditional-religious as lay and clerical politicians discover in religious symbols a powerful instrument for mass mobilization. Movements of re-ligious revival, merged with nationalism and promoted by those in power, may temporarily lead to the repudiation of the whole notion of a secular state.

It should be borne in mind, however, that this very political

4. I am indebted to Fred R. von der Mehden for his strong emphasis on this point, which was partly responsible for the development of the category "political-process secularization."

process in which the masses become involved is one of the major
components of our definition of political modernization. The
traditional-religious elements, that is, are in some sense contributing to political modernization, and this is the major theme
developed in the next part of this book. The history of the relatively more developed polities suggests that political-process secularization will prevail in the long run, for politics as a field of human activity makes sense in its own right and can function without traditional-religious props. Once a relatively high level of political consciousness is attained by the citizens, the political process
becomes self-sustaining.

Polity-separation, polity-expansion, political-culture, and political-process secularization are widely distributed phenomena,
and these processes continue to operate in the relatively more
developed as well as in the developing political systems of the
world. What we might call the classic model of secularization
would involve a traditional religiopolitical system that had many
centuries of relative stability before its disruption by the advent of
Western imperialism in the nineteenth century. The traditional
system, in which a divine king ruled a relatively static sacral society, collapsed with the imposition of a secular foreign government. The case of Burma, considered below, fits this model well,
but in other cases the historical pattern was quite different.

The analysis of the impact of secularization on Hindu society
and polity has naturally focused on the administration of British
India, to a lesser extent on the Hindu princely states that continued
throughout the British period, but primarily on the Republic of
India's efforts to implement the principles of a secular state. Leo
E. Rose's essay on Nepal, however, directs our attention to a state
that is the sole remaining Hindu kingdom. The monarch is not
only an "adherent of Aryan culture and Hindu religion" by constitutional requirement but, in accordance with ancient Hindu belief, is revered as an incarnation of the god Vishnu.

As the writer makes clear, the elements of traditionalism in
Nepal still far outweigh the processes of secularization. The
Himalayan kingdom escaped British rule, and its geographical
isolation served to limit cultural penetration by the West. But
Nepal is significant for what it tells us about how the process of
secularization reaches even relatively inaccessible societies and

about the particular points at which it affects a Hindu society most vitally.

I have classified the traditional Hindu religious system as organic in that it maximizes the equation of religion with society. In Nepal the subjects of the king are referred to collectively as "the four *varnas* and the thirty-six *jats* (castes)," suggesting a classical Hindu hierarchical social system. As Rose explains, there has been a gradual process of Sanskritization, by which diverse ethnic groups in the country have been incorporated in this hierarchical structure. From the fourteenth century down to 1963, successive legal codes (based on the ancient *Dharmashastras*) spelled out in ever greater detail the regulation of social life within and among the different castes. Assuming an inherent inequality corresponding to position in the caste hierarchy, the criminal law prescribed different penalties for the same crime for offenders of different castes. No Brahman could be executed, but all other castes were subject to capital punishment.

The new legal code promulgated by King Mahendra in 1963 marked a fundamental departure from all previous codes and completely ignored the caste-specific principle of justice found in the Dharmashastras. Equality before the law, the elimination of all high-caste privileges, the abolition of untouchability, the legalization of intercaste marriage, and other radical innovations are found in the new code. While full implementation is still far off, it is significant that such a basic reorientation of the formal rules of an entire society has met with such little overt opposition.

Despite the many traditional Hindu aspects of the Nepalese polity that remain, these legal reforms, which constitute an important manifestation of polity-expansion secularization, are most fundamental. In the Hindu organic system, polity-expansion secularization is crucial, for it goes to the very heart of the system and replaces sacral societal norms and relationships with secular ones determined by government.

Religious systems with highly developed ecclesiastical structures (church systems), on the other hand, are more importantly affected by polity-separation secularization. In church religiopolitical systems there are powerful ties between two structures, ecclesiastical and political, and church-state separation constitutes a fundamental break with tradition. In Theravada Buddhism the Sangha, the highly developed monastic institution, historically was closely linked to the governmental structure. In von der Mehden's essay on Burma and Thailand we find a most interesting comparison, for the former country underwent the secularization process under the disruptive pressure of foreign rule while the latter experienced it as a concomitant of modernizing indigenous rule, initially under Kings Mongkut and Chulalongkorn.

Polity-separation secularization in Burma was devastating in its effect, as the British deposed a semidivine monarch and severed the traditional links between Sangha and state. With its professed policy of religious neutrality (formulated originally in India), the British government refused to appoint a Sangharaja (head of the Sangha), and the ecclesiastical hierarchy above the level of the monastery gradually disintegrated.

If by the end of World War I the Burmese *polity* had become very secular, the *politics* of the following decades was largely informed by religious nationalism. Religious symbols, issues, and leaders (monks) played an important role in the politics of the 1920s and 1930s and again after independence, under U Nu (1948–62). On the whole, events moved, although not unilinearly, in the opposite direction from what I have described as political-process secularization. Ironically, by their refusal to support the traditional Sangha hierarchy, the British freed the monks from the monastic discipline that would have kept them apolitical, and the phenomenon of the passionately nationalist "political monk" emerged.

In Thailand the traditional links between state and Sangha have remained down to the present. Polity-separation secularization in institutional terms did not take place. However, King Chulalongkorn was anxious to strengthen the principle that secular and religious authorities should refrain from interference in each other's jurisdictions. Government continued to have the upper hand, but a large degree of Sangha autonomy was recognized. Monks were not permitted to engage in political activity, and in 1933 they were forbidden by law to participate in elections. This enactment not only underlined the secular nature of politics but also reaffirmed the *Vinaya* (code of monastic discipline), which forbade monks' meddling in the king's affairs.

The more subtle penetration of Western ideas and values, in

addition to the process of modernization under indigenous leader-ship, has permitted Thai society to change gradually without the upheavals that Burma has experienced. Thus far, however, these changes have all taken place within a strongly authoritarian frame-work, and the politics of mass participation has yet to evolve in Thailand.

It seems clear that certain aspects of secularization are facilitated by the nature of Theravada Buddhism as a church system. The clear-cut distinction between Sangha and society provided the potential basis for the broader distinction between sacred and secular. As we turn to Islam, however, we come back to a basically organic religious system. Islamic origins and continuing ideals stress the fusion of temporal and religious authority, which were institutionalized historically in the caliphate and a comprehensive sacred law (*shari'ah*).

The *ulama,* or religious scholars, acquired some of the char-acteristics of a clerical class, but on the whole they never de-veloped an autonomous ecclesiastical structure like that of the Buddhist or Christian clergy. Their organization, and whatever hierarchy existed, were generally dependent on the ruler, who employed them as legal interpreters and judges in shari'ah courts. The ulama also performed important educational functions, and al-Azhar, the famous mosque-university of Cairo, acquired great prestige and during certain periods exercised considerable auton-omy. That is, a church-like structure could evolve within a sacral society dominated by organic conceptions. By the same token, however, it could be attacked and even destroyed by hostile gov-ernments with a certain impunity, for the center of the religious system was elsewhere.

Daniel Crecelius' essay on the course of secularization in Egypt emphasizes the diverse agencies, motives, and ideologies involved in the process since the early nineteenth century. During the long reign of Muhammad Ali (1805–49) the ulama and their institu-tions were subjected to severe attacks by a government determined to modernize Egypt militarily and technologically. However, the ruler still acknowledged the supremacy of the shari'ah and made no effort to reform society as a whole. In the second half of the cen-tury polity-expansion secularization became an important trend, as Khedive Isma'il (1863–79) centralized his government's authority and expanded its functions in the areas of education and law.

In the first half of the twentieth century the liberal-nationalist elites articulated an ideology that substituted nation for *ummah* (Islamic community) as the highest political loyalty, popular sovereignty for divine sovereignty, and social reform for a static shari'ah-based society. As Crecelius cautions us, however, governmental policies and ideological pronouncements are not to be equated with the socioeconomic and political changes to which they point, and much of the traditional value system and behavior pattern continues in contemporary Egypt.

Crecelius sees the secularization of Egypt from the early nineteenth to the mid-twentieth century as basically a unilinear force that appeared to be heading toward a predictable goal. This process was continued for the first decade after the revolution of 1952, as Nasser nationalized the system of religious endowments (*waqf*), abolished the shari'ah courts, and largely secularized the al-Azhar university. Since 1962, however, the regime has made increasing use of Islamic symbols and legitimizing devices, particularly in its ideological formulation of Islamic socialism. The dynamic and creative force of the revolution appears to be spent, and the regime must revert to the traditional sources of legitimation.

In terms of the categories and definitions proposed above, I would interpret the 1952–62 period as one of polity-dominance secularization, in which a revolutionary regime conceded no area of autonomy to religion and sought to reduce radically its influence in society generally. The period since then must indeed be seen as a retreat to traditionalism, for the main *purpose* of government in denying the autonomy of religion now is not the secularization of society but the legitimation of a regime.

The state of Israel constitutes a unique case in the comparative study of secularization, for as Norman L. Zucker points out, the process is not associated with the disruption of an old society with a traditional religiopolitical system. On the contrary, "Judaism, for millennia, was a religion in search of a polity," and this was achieved only in 1948. However, traditional Judaic conceptions of law and society have survived and coexist uneasily and in frequent conflict with the secular Jewish nationalism of late nineteenth-century origin. In concrete terms, Israel's secularization conflicts frequently occur at precisely the same points as in other societies discussed in this book, particularly in relation to the political influence of the clerical establishment, religious law, and the definition of nationality.

Zucker emphasizes the fact that significant political-process secularization has *not* taken place in Israeli politics since 1948, and that between 12 and 15 percent of the electorate has consistently voted for the three religious parties. In the context of a multiparty system and coalition governments from which the religious political bloc has never been excluded, the secularists have frequently been frustrated in their efforts to modernize the polity further, despite the unquestionably European, democratic, and secular character of the basic structure. And, at this point, it seems clear that political-process secularization hinges on the gradual changes in value orientation that I have described as political-culture secularization.

Unlike Islamic law, with which it has important historical connections, Talmudic law developed in the absence of a corresponding religiopolitical system, and its statements concerning the body politic remained rudimentary. While the Agudah parties in contemporary Israel could grandly declare that "the Torah is Israel's constitution," the statement was more a pious aspiration than a concrete proposal. Nevertheless, the inability of the religionists and the secularists to reach agreement on the delineation of the religion-state relationship is the primary reason for Israel's lack of a written constitution to this day.

The secularization conflicts over the jurisdiction of religious law and the rabbinical courts in marriage, divorce, and other important matters closely parallel conflicts in Muslim (and for that matter, Catholic and Hindu) societies. It is interesting to note that Israel's Arab neighbors, which in most respects are more traditional, come closer to the model of modernity than Israel in this respect (the shari'ah courts were abolished in Egypt in 1955). As Zucker makes clear, the reasons for this are primarily political: the National Religious party in successive coalition governments, its control of the Ministry of Religious Affairs, and its support of the Chief Rabbinate. A most interesting and continuing controversy in Israeli politics concerns the relationship of religious faith and observance to Jewish nationality. As an ethnic religion Judaism faces this problem in a particularly acute form.

As noted in the essay on secularization in Latin America, the basic processes are similar to those in other parts of the Third World. The particular forms in which they have appeared, however, have been strongly influenced by three factors that are peculiarly characteristic of the Latin American tradition. First, the structure and ideology of the Roman Catholic church constituted a remarkably elaborate hierarchical organization ideologically committed to exercise extensive powers of regulation over society. Secondly, the regalist tradition of the Spanish and Portuguese empires, which has continued to the present in some republics, asserted in many critical areas the dominance of government over church. And finally, the phenomenon of anticlericalism in Catholic societies has been persistent and politically powerful; there are no close parallels in Hindu, Buddhist, or Muslim societies.

The Catholic church, then, had extensive organizational and ideological resources with which to oppose all forms of secularization, and in the nineteenth and early twentieth centuries these conflicts occupied a central place in the politics of most of the republics. The bitter anticlericalism that motivated many of the secularists made unlikely the development of church-state separation on the basis of mutual respect and goodwill, although this was achieved by Chile in 1925 after a long evolutionary process. But the polity-separation secularization proposed by the moderate president Arturo Alessandri was at first rejected by the archbishop of Santiago as "a public and solemn denial of God, a true and terrible national apostasy."

Half of the Latin American republics have separated church and state. Constitutional separation, however, is not necessarily the most important relationship to ascertain; the degree of autonomy exercised by the church is far more vital to its functioning. A high degree of church autonomy can be associated with both church-state separation (Chile) and church-state union (Colombia), and low church autonomy can be linked to both separation (Mexico) and union (Argentina).[5]

5. Ivan Vallier, *Catholicism, Social Control, and Modernization in Latin America* (Englewood Cliffs, N.J.: Prentice-Hall, 1970), pp. 33–36.

In the case of Argentina, the regalist pattern of state control of the church (in the appointment of bishops and other matters) continued until 1966. While the Argentine church received some benefits from its ties to the state, it paid a high price, for its fortunes were to some extent determined by the changing policies of successive regimes.

The low autonomy of the church in Mexico reflects not traditional regalism but a revolutionary program of polity-dominance secularization. The Mexican Revolution of 1910 dedicated itself during certain phases to radical attacks on virtually all aspects of traditional Catholicism in society. Since 1940, governmental policy toward religion has been much more relaxed, and a considerable degree of corporate religious freedom is exercised, but the anti-clerical laws have been ignored, not repealed.

Religion and Mass Politicization

In the traditional religiopolitical system, political participation was limited to a small number of individuals drawn from the royal family, the nobility, and the military, religious, and bureaucratic elites. Politics was centered in the royal court, and only under extraordinary circumstances (such as an insurrection) were large numbers of people mobilized for activity that could be termed political. Political modernization, as noted earlier, includes the changes in behavior patterns by which the masses are brought into the political process as participants on a more or less regular basis. Political modernization, in part, means the development of mass politics.

In the contemporary Third World, religion may contribute to the process of mass politicization by providing sacred symbols that acquire political significance. Clerical organizations, lay interest groups, and religious political parties find in these sacred symbols an important key to mass support, a key that their secular rivals in the struggle for power have denied themselves. The "use" of religion for the purpose of political mobilization can be manipulative, but it need not be. In many cases the projection of sacred symbols into the political arena proceeds from holistic world views which deny the sacred-secular distinction.

As suggested earlier, the process I am describing here moves in the opposite direction from political-process secularization. But the latter presupposes the *existence* of a political process in the modern sense, that is, the politics of mass participation. It is clear that in many cases a definite sequence is involved: religion helps to produce mass politicization and then declines politically as increasing numbers of participants come to perceive politics as a relatively autonomous area of human activity.

Religion is but one of the factors in mass politicization, and there is no desire to exaggerate its importance. Many secular agencies (political parties, labor unions, governments, etc.) and secular ideologies (nationalism, populism, Marxism, etc.) are also vying for mass support and mass participation under their respective banners, and in many cases their influence is clearly more significant. The religious factor is of special interest, however, for in contrast to these secular agencies and ideologies it is rooted in the traditional past and in the present consciousness of the large tradition-oriented segment of the population.

The five essays of this section explore different kinds of relationships between religion and mass politicization. The power of a sacred symbol to inspire a mass movement is most dramatically illustrated in the case of the caliphate agitation in Muslim India in 1920. Clerical hierarchies (Buddhist and Catholic), as part of the traditional power structure, were frequently unreconciled to the idea of mass political participation, and approached it warily. Clerical associations without hierarchical support (Buddhist, Muslim and Catholic) have frequently been more active in mobilizing the masses for political action. Laymen may take the leadership in representing religion in the political arena, particularly (as in the case of Hinduism) when the clerical groups are unorganized. Religious political parties (Hindu, Muslim, and Catholic) may be under either clerical or lay leadership, but the latter has tended to predominate and to establish its independence from clerical ties whenever possible.

The essay on "Gandhi, Hinduism, and Mass Politics" seeks to analyze the prominent yet elusive religious element in Gandhi's leadership of the Indian nationalist movement. The genius of Gandhi was that he could communicate simultaneously with both the Western-educated elite (from which most of his political colleagues were drawn) and the tradition-oriented Hindu masses. Differences in the interpretation of Gandhi have arisen in part from the fact that where the Western-educated saw political tactic, the masses saw spiritual manifestation.

The ambiguities of Gandhi as both a religious and a secular political leader may be summarized in four points. First we must note the important differences between institutional context and personal political style. As a leader of the Indian National Congress, Gandhi was part of an organization which on the whole, and especially when compared with nationalist groups in other countries, had maintained a remarkably secular orientation throughout its history. Gandhi's political style was at times characterized by highly traditional religious appeals, but he operated within a modern and secular organizational framework.

Secondly, Gandhi's political techniques such as fasts and *satyagraha* (nonviolent "truth-force") were understood by him and explained to the masses in terms of the Hindu concept of *ahimsa* (noninjury to living beings), the equation of nonviolence with Truth and God, self-suffering as a means of spiritual purification, and so forth. For the most part the agnostic Nehru saw in nonviolence no metaphysical truth but only an effective political technique, doubly compelling because there was no real alternative open to the nationalist movement.

Third, Gandhi's nonsectarian, universalist approach to religion (he read from the New Testament and the Qur'an as well as the Bhagavad Gita in his prayer meetings) led some to conclude, very illogically, that his leadership was secular after all. Gandhi's universalism, however, was based on unmistakably Hindu assumptions.

And finally, there is the question of Gandhi's own identity. The modern Hindu could point out that Gandhi himself was a Western-educated lawyer and that as a non-Brahman he had no ascribed clerical authority. In this sense a layman, Gandhi operated from a very different position than the political monks, ulama, and priests discussed in this book. However, this observation misses the point, for Gandhi was regarded by many millions of Hindus as the Mahatma ("Great Soul" or saint), as in fact an Avatar, an incarnation of the divine. Whatever his political colleagues saw in him, in a peculiarly Hindu way the masses saw in Gandhi an unquestioned manifestation of the divine, an avatar who called them to courageous political involvement and action.

Heinz Bechert's essay on Buddhism and mass politics underlines the importance of both monks and laymen in recent political mobilization efforts. For the Sangha in both Burma and Ceylon, the political activism of monks has been a divisive issue from the late nineteenth century to the present. The political monks' contention has been that the impact of Western imperialism on their societies has been so devastating that the Sangha, the traditional moral guide, has had to enter the political arena in order to restore Buddhism to its rightful place.

The monks have on occasion been quite effective in mobilizing the masses to attack the enemies of Buddhism, whether they be the British raj in colonial Burma, a westernized elitist government in independent Ceylon, or a Catholic dictator in South Vietnam. They have excelled in oppositional politics. It is not clear, however, to what extent mass politicization during crises contributes to the long-range patterns of political participation associated with modernization. From this point of view, religious political parties and other institutionalized forms of participation may be more significant.

The examples of U Nu in Burma and S. W. R. D. Bandaranaike in Ceylon have shown that the monks by no means enjoy a monopoly on the use of religious symbols in politics. Buddhist laymen could draw on the very old tradition of the ruler as a future Buddha, and U Nu was apparently convinced that his convening of the Sixth Great Council in Rangoon (1954–56) and his constitutional amendment making Buddhism the state religion (1961) assured him of this future status. Such issues undoubtedly made the political process relevant to the masses and drew them in as participants, although the reversal of the secularization process created other problems for political development.

Gail Minault's essay on Islam and mass politics examines the case of the Khilafat movement, which began in India after World War I. This extended anti-British agitation (1919–22) sought to prevent the dismemberment of the Ottoman Empire by the victorious allies, since the severance of the Arab provinces would deprive the caliph of Islam (the Turkish sultan) of temporal control over the holy cities of Mecca and Medina. The Khilafat (Caliphate) movement was thus directed to the preservation of the most sacred symbols of Islam: the cities of pilgrimage and, no less, the authority of the caliph as the religiopolitical head of the entire Islamic community (ummah).

That Muslims in India, thousands of miles from Constantinople, could be moved so profoundly by the threat to these symbols and mobilized in such large numbers for militant antigovernment activity is a dramatic illustration of the potency of religion in the process of mass politicization. The threat to the caliphate, of course, had to be explained and interpreted to the masses. Western-educated Muslim politicians such as the Ali brothers were anxious to make use of the issue, but they lacked the proper credentials and in fact were religiously suspect because of their secular education.

The ulama, on the other hand, were in a position to become effective political mobilizers and vigorously seized this role. Five hundred ulama signed a *fatwa* (a formal ruling on a point of Islamic law) that declared it religiously unlawful to cooperate with the enemy of Islam, the British government. The ban extended to education in government schools, service in the police and military, and payment of taxes. When the government confiscated copies of the document, Minault points out, the ulama argued that "since the *fatwa* was an abstract of God's orders, its proscription was a sacrilege." The ulama warned their audiences in town and village alike that Muslims who cooperated with the infidel government could expect nothing but the fires of hell throughout eternity.

In 1919 the ulama founded an overtly political party, the Jamiat al-Ulama-e-Hind, thus creating another link between Islam and mass politics. While the Jamiat's primary membership was restricted to the ulama, as its name indicates, its central purpose was to organize the ulama for more effective leadership of the community in all religiopolitical matters.

Lucy C. Behrman's essay on the Catholic priests and mass politics notes the evolution of the Chilean clergy's relatively progressive attitudes toward social change over the past half century and the important differences that remain within the church. The conservative priests of the early period emphasized Catholicism, authority, and hierarchy as the bases of the social and political order; mass political participation was therefore wrong in principle. However, as the electorate expanded, conservative bishops and priests had no option but to seek to influence the electoral process in the defense of Catholicism. They strongly supported the Conservative party and threatened the faithful with religious sanctions if they should dare to cast their votes for socialists or communists. Despite the great upheavals in Chile over the past decade, some of the clergy still maintain a basically conservative stance and nostalgically yearn for a return to the traditional Catholic society.

Other segments of the Chilean church, and particularly the Jesuit community, undertook a fundamental reconsideration of the church's relationship to social change and mass politics, and the term *Christian Democracy* (although not adopted until 1957) was significant for its recognition of the popular basis of political authority. Although led by laymen and independent of hierarchical control, the Christian Democratic party benefited immeasurably from the ideological and organizational support of the church.

While at the national level the Chilean bishops and the Jesuits of the Centro Bellarmino were close to the Christian Democratic administration of Eduardo Frei (1964–70), at the local level a new phenomenon emerged, the "people's priests." Eschewing the traditional paternalistic relationship by which the priest simply instructed his parishioners how to vote, the people's priests have emphasized *concientización,* the development of social and political awareness as part of a general orientation to self-reliance and problem solving. As Behrman points out, the declared objectives of the people's priests should not be mistaken for the results of their ministry, and their impact on the process of mass politicization must be regarded as a positive but marginal one.

Have Catholic political parties, with their predominantly lay leadership, been more significant in this regard? Harry Kantor poses this question in an essay that surveys the growth of Catholic parties throughout Latin America. He points out that there have been various kinds of parties that have claimed a Catholic ideological base or a role as ally and defender of the church. While the earlier Catholic parties were conservative and elitist, the Christian Democratic movement which emerged three decades ago accepted the principle of mass politics and sought mass support. However, thus far the Christian Democratic parties have achieved important electoral successes only in Chile, Venezuela, and El Salvador, and Kantor suggests that the 1970 defeat in Chile indicates that the movement has already seen its best days.

While Kantor grants that a continuing Catholic sentiment among a minority of Latin Americans can still be tapped politically, there are weighty factors opposed to any Catholic party in the long run. The church's aggressive political role in the past produced the reaction of violent anticlericalism, which is today as significant a component of Latin American political culture as Catholicism itself. A Catholic party must thus overcome considerable initial suspicion. Furthermore, to the extent that its concrete program approximates that of populist or socialist parties, its Catholic identity becomes blurred in the eyes of the faithful themselves.

Both Behrman and Kantor suggest that the impact of Catholicism on the development of mass politics has been ambiguous and marginal. The religious factor has been relatively more important in the mass politicization of Hindu, Buddhist, and Muslim societies. One of the basic differences between Latin America and Asia-Africa, which is fundamental to understanding the development of mass politics, is of course the pattern of imperialism-nationalism. For four and a half centuries Latin American rulers and ruled have shared a common Catholic faith. By contrast, nationalist struggles in Asia-Africa took the form of Hindu, Buddhist, and Muslim mass movements in opposition to Christian colonial governments.

THE RELIGIOUS LEGITIMATION OF CHANGE

It is clear that in traditional societies religious ideas performed an important integrative function by legitimizing the political, social, and economic system. Clerical groups legitimized royal power by elaborate ritual and inculcated the virtue of obedience in the masses. Religion was overwhelmingly supportive of the status quo. The question that engages us here is this: Despite their traditionally conservative role, can the major religious systems be reformulated to provide positive ideological support for largely secular political systems committed to rapid socioeconomic change? Can reformulated Hinduism, Buddhism, Islam, and Catholicism significantly reorient the motivation and behavior patterns of large numbers of people and help to mobilize them for the tasks of development?

The question is worth asking, for there is abundant evidence that the process of religious reinterpretation, which began in the nineteenth century, has been accelerated and intensified over the past two decades. Several of the essays in this section devote considerable attention to the content of reformulated religion, or religious variants of ideologies of change. But an examination of theological or ideological interpretations alone, while interesting in terms of intellectual history, does not take us very far toward an answer to the question posed above. The essays therefore reflect an equal interest in the ways in which these religious ideologies of change are related to sociopolitical movements and structures. The essay on Sarvodaya in India concerns an ongoing movement of social change, and the essays on Egypt and Peru suggest that religious ideologies are of some significance in legitimizing the developmental efforts of governments. Unfortunately, however, on the crucial point of the effect of the new ideas on individual and group motivation and behavior, our evidence is mostly impressionistic.

The four religious systems offer very different collections of raw materials for the development of religious ideologies of change. I have suggested above that in this regard the ahistorical-historical distinction is critical. Within both reformulated Islam and Catholicism there has been a repudiation of medieval timelessness and a rediscovery of the dynamics of the historical process through which divine purpose works itself out. Both of these systems draw upon a biblical notion of history, which in secular form also appeared in Marxism. History is a struggle impregnated with moral purpose, and this purpose has to do with justice among men. The formulation of Islamic and Catholic versions of socialism thus necessitate little ideological strain.

The ahistorical Indic religious systems, Hinduism and Buddhism, provide less adaptable raw materials for developing a convincing ideology of social change. There is no concept of a linear historical process from which ideological bridges to socialism can be built. Buddhism faces particularly difficult problems, for (unlike Hinduism) it also lacks a corpus of theoretical literature on problems of social organization, law, and polity.

That a concept of linear history is not the only basis for a religious ideology of change, however, is amply demonstrated by a consideration of the Sarvodaya movement in India, discussed in the essay by Miriam Sharma and Jagdish P. Sharma. Sarvodaya (literally, "welfare of all") is rooted in the largely Hindu sources of Gandhian thought, but it is explicitly labeled a social philosophy and movement that can be embraced by adherents of all religions or none. What Sarvodaya provides is (1) a vision of a communitarian society in which economic inequalities are drastically reduced, and (2) nonviolent techniques by which visible progress can be made toward the ideal. Vinoba Bhave ignored the massive superstructure of Hindu thought which for three millennia had legitimized the radical inequality of *varnashrama-dharma* (the sacral caste order) in order to assert an essential social egalitarianism based on man's spiritual nature. But he did not simply articulate a new social vision; the power of Sarvodaya was that by nonviolent means it actually began to *change* Indian society by redistributing land to the landless.

Bhave's appeals to the landlords contained no hint of coercion; he simply asked them to give one-sixth of their land to him for redistribution. The Hindu religious motifs were always present. In the past, he declared, devout men of wealth gave land to the deities who resided in temples, but in the changed circumstances of today it is now appropriate to give land to the landless, in whom God dwells. Lakshmi, the goddess of wealth, he reminded his village audiences, is the wife of Vishnu and the mother of all men, but the rich have usurped Vishnu's place and monopolized Lakshmi's bountiful provision, which was intended for all. The rich must therefore now share their land with the landless.

Fazlur Rahman's essay on the sources and meaning of Islamic socialism emphasizes the relatively long history of the theoretical discussion of the problem. The nineteenth-century leader Afghani first set the stage by criticizing the Marxist program of restructuring society on a materialist basis and pointed to the ideological resources of Islam itself for the promotion of socioeconomic reform. Other writers continued the discussion in the early decades of this century, and in the 1960s the notion of Islamic socialism gained wide acceptance in many parts of the Muslim world.

Capitalism was largely discredited in the eyes of Muslim nationalists because of its association with Western imperialism. Marxist atheism was equally unacceptable, and so the effort began to formulate an ideology that harnessed spiritual motivation to rapid social change. Rahman sees Islamic socialism as a genuine expression of and commitment to reformism, but he also perceives in it an element of apologetic, a defense of Islam against communism.

Rahman finds in modern Islamic socialist thought "an impressive and even moving array of ideas and symbols whose total impact and appeal is very strong." Verses from the Qur'an and tradition are quoted to show that the basic necessities of life must be made available to all by nationalization and that taxation (as in the institution of *zakat*) must be used to redistribute wealth more equitably. However, Rahman warns against the assumption that intellectual enthusiasm for Islamic socialism will quickly lead to real change. He sees significant economic development as closely tied to social change—education, family law reform, new attitudes toward work—and ingenious ideological constructs which demonstrate a tradition's essential modernity may lead to more complacency than change.

Guenter Lewy explores this problem of the Islamic legitimation of change through an analysis of the revolutionary regime that has ruled Egypt since 1952. Starting with a remarkably nonideological orientation, under Nasser's leadership Arab nationalism gradually emerged as a basic tenet of the regime, particularly in its application to foreign policy. Nasser seized the initiative in seeking to transform vague ideas and sentiments about Arab unity into concrete political reality. In the process of mobilizing mass support, however, his essentially secular nationalism drew increasingly on Islamic symbols of political community. The Islamization of nationalism proceeded by blurring the very serious theoretical differences between the traditional concept of Islamic community (ummah) and the notion of Arab nation.

If Arab nationalism was the most prominent idea in Nasser's foreign policy, Arab socialism was made the ideological basis for domestic policy beginning in 1961. Here too, Islam was quickly enlisted in support of the new ideological formulation. Arab socialism was sharply distinguished from Marxian socialism; the former was not only not opposed to Islam but actually derived from it. Nasser declared in 1964: "Islam is the first religion to call for socialism, the first religion to call for equality and the first to call for an end to domination and inequality."

Lewy points to the element of "pious fraud" in all such efforts at reinterpreting tradition. More serious in their practical effects, however, are the ambiguities created by using tradition to legitimize change. In Islam, precedent and tradition are highly valued, and the burden of proof rests on the innovator. Positive attitudes toward innovation, however, are the very spirit of modernization. Islamic symbols may be used to legitimize socialism, but in the process Islam as a whole may be confirmed, and traditional attitudes continue to inhibit change.

In his essay on the new Latin American Catholicism, Thomas G. Sanders points to a process of doctrinal reformulation that has been taking place within the church over the past decade and a half. Unlike Islam with its essentially organic relationship to society and low level of ecclesiastical organization, the structure of the Catholic church has impressive organizational resources to bring to bear on the problem of formulating an ideology of change. Sanders analyzes the documents of the 1968 Latin American bishops' conference as an authoritative statement of the new Catholicism's emerging consensus.

The consensus has evolved out of reflection on the earlier Catholic ideas and strategies of change. The Christian Democratic ideology and program in Chile was an imaginative attempt to marshal the church's resources on behalf of significant socioeconomic change. In part this built upon the church's traditional influence in society and sought to legitimate change by the use of papal encyclicals, pastoral letters, and institutions of "Christian inspiration" (labor unions, youth groups, political parties, etc.). The more radical Catholic movements, particularly in Brazil, allied themselves with Marxist groups and rather quickly lost whatever Catholic ideological distinctives they brought to the alliance.

The emerging consensus that Sanders finds in the 1968 documents suggests a much more modest role for the church in the transformation of Latin American society than the Chilean model posits. Accepting the reality of a secular-pluralist society, these documents indicate that the church is no longer seen as the dominant moral and legitimating institution of society but as one interest group among others. The church will motivate individuals to participate actively in bringing about change and, as an institution, will support the secular agencies striving for change. There is awareness that the church's contribution to the process of change is not likely to be a central one; nevertheless, the secular process of change itself has great *theological* significance.

The documents lay great emphasis on the theological understanding of history and on concientización, the process by which men become aware of their potential as participants in the process of change. The masses must become the agent of their own liberation. The church no longer offers a blueprint for societal reconstruction but exercises its prophetic function by condemning specific situations of injustice.

From the general doctrinal formulations of the Latin American bishops we now turn to a concrete situation, in which the church is providing legitimation to the Peruvian government's program of fairly radical change. As George W. Grayson, Jr., points out, the military junta that seized power in 1968 has developed a populist base and with strong church support has carried out far-reaching socioeconomic reforms. Grayson even suggests that "church-supported military populism offers a possible model for political development through institution building."

Following the agrarian reform decree-law issued by General Juan Velasco Alvarado, Peru's bishops declared that "every Christian must be committed to structural change, and fighting any selfish application of the law, will assure the full and effective realization of the reform process." Similar indications of church approval have followed the nationalization of the oil fields and the banking system, university reform, and other measures. Church-military cooperation has been highly visible in programs designed to provide technical assistance and public services to the residents of the slums that ring Peru's major cities.

Grayson points to certain similarities between the church and military in terms of middle-class leadership, authoritarian and hierarchical structure, trained personnel, and international ties. These affinities may provide the basis for close cooperation elsewhere in Latin America as well, at least wherever the two institutions are in substantial agreement on the urgency of socioeconomic change. However, the long history of church-state conflict cannot be ignored, and Grayson also cites recent cases of tension and conflict in Peru, such as the controversy over religious instruction in the public schools. In any event, the Peruvian experiment represents a most interesting model of the religious legitimation of change, and its progress will be watched closely by many.

PART 2

The Secularization of Polities

2

Secularization of a Hindu Polity:
The Case of Nepal

LEO E. ROSE

The Hindu kingdom of Nepal is situated high in the central Himalayas, straddling the strategic buffer area between India and Tibet. For several reasons, including its relatively inaccessible terrain, Nepal was better insulated from Western secular influences throughout the "colonial period" than most other Asian states. Secularization, thus, is a recent phenomenon, and one that has made only a tangential impact upon the Nepalese social and political elite at both the central and local levels. Nepal managed—with considerable difficulty—to maintain its independence throughout both the periods of Muslim and British rule in India (thirteenth to twentieth centuries). The isolation policy followed by the various hill principalities was considered essential not only to their political independence but also to the cultural and religious integrity of the area. Indeed, it was directed as much at the cultural as the political imperialism of India's alien rulers, and a strong sense of responsibility for the "defense of the faith" has imbued the elite of the area until very recently.

Complete isolation was impossible, of course, as there were unavoidable economic, political and cultural contacts between the central hill area, the Gangetic plain, and Tibet throughout this period. Indeed, Kathmandu's prosperity derived from its status as a major entrepôt, commercially and intellectually, between South and Central Asia. Nevertheless, the ruling elite in the hills was substantially successful in minimizing both the degree and content of cultural influences flowing into the hills. This was the case, incidentally, not only for the alien and potentially disruptive influences of Muslim, British, and Chinese origin but—and this is probably more important—for the influx of novel developments within Hinduism as well.

Nepalese Hinduism is an anachronistic curiosity in many respects when compared to that of northern India as it is far less infiltrated with accretions from external sources. Indeed, to many Hindus in Nepal, Indian Hinduism became suspect and Nepal was considered to be the last stronghold of orthodoxy and tradition. This was reflected in the stanza by an eighteenth-century Nepalese scholar: "During the rule of the Muslims, the land of the Hindus became greatly degraded; only this land of Nepal remained as pure as gold." [1] Nepalese of orthodox families even had to undergo purification ceremonies on their return from India, the motherland of Hinduism, although these were not as rigorous as those imposed after visits to Tibet, China, or the West.

Nevertheless, despite the relatively recent introduction of secularizing influences, there are two reasons why Nepal is a useful focus for a study of the process of secularization. First, the very immediacy of the insertion of secularizing factors into a society with strong and vigorous traditional institutions and values makes it easier to identify the sources of change and transformation than in countries that were gradually exposed to Western influences over several centuries. Furthermore, Nepal's status as the only traditional Hindu polity extant, in which Hindu social and cultural values are still closely interwoven with the political system, makes it a useful laboratory for the study of the interaction between modern secular influences and a highly stratified, traditional society. In Nepal the secularizing assault must be leveled against a wide variety of closely interlinked institutions and behavior patterns to have any concrete results as Nepalese social and political institutions have so far demonstrated a remarkable capacity to absorb change without themselves being transformed in the process.

At the outset, it would be well to raise the question whether Nepal is, in fact, a Hindu polity. If our enquiry were restricted to the Nepalese political elite and to certain key aspects of the polity, the answer would have to be in the affirmative—with some

1. Quoted in Surya Bikram Jñyawali, *Nepal Upatyakako Madhya Kalin Itihas* [Medieval history of Nepal Valley] (Kathmandu: Royal Academy, 1962), p. 69.

minor qualifications attached. The 1962 constitution, for instance, describes Nepal as "an independent, indivisible and sovereign monarchical Hindu State" and specifies that the king must be an "adherent of Aryan culture and Hindu religion." [2] Furthermore, the traditional term used to describe subjects of the present ruling dynasty—"the four *varnas* and the thirty-six *jats* (castes)" [3]—again would seem to imply the existence of a classical Hindu hierarchical social structure. But if that expression is really meant to apply to the entire population, then several non-Hindu, non-Indo-Aryan ethnic groups would have to be included, indicating that the term should not be interpreted too literally.

This problem in identifying the traditional religiopolitical system in Nepal stems primarily from the complexity of Nepalese society and the pragmatic accommodations that have been made over the centuries in evolving a viable political and social structure.[4] We will examine some of the more important components

2. *The Constitution of Nepal* (Kathmandu: Government of Nepal, Ministry of Law and Justice, 1963), pp. 2, 10.

3. Presumably at one time the reference to 36 jats had a practical basis, but it is not possible from sources available to me to enumerate these or even to be sure the term encompasses only caste Hindu groupings. The 1854 legal code, for instance, includes one clause that states: "The Shastras as well as the laws permit the men of the four varnas and the thirty-six jats to marry their younger and elder sisters-in-law." *Shree Panch Surendra Bikram Shah Dev ko Shasan Kal ma Baneko Muluki Ain* [The legal code formulated during the rule of King Surendra Bikram Shah Dev] (Kathmandu: Government of Nepal, Ministry of Law and Justice, Law Books Management Committee, 1965), 1 : 444–45. The wording is ambiguous but could be interpreted to imply that the 4 varnas and the 36 jats were exclusive entities and that the latter referred to groups outside the varna system. No doubt the group of old Nepalese historians who are well grounded in the traditional literature on Nepal could answer this question immediately, but they have not concerned themselves with it in their writings—probably because they assume their audience knows the answer already.

4. The literature on this subject is very limited. Most of the anthropological studies conducted so far in Nepal have been limited to a single ethnic community or region, and few attempts have been made as yet to fit these into a comprehensive national social structure. One pioneering study in this respect is Dor Bhahadur Bista, *The People of Nepal* (Kathmandu: His Majesty's Government, 1967). Probably the most thorough attempt to analyze intercommunity and intercaste relations is that of Baburam Acharya, *Nepal ko Samkshipta Vrittanta* [A short account of Nepal] (Kathmandu: 1966), particularly pp. 127–51. I must admit, however, to have been more confused than enlightened by certain sections of this study, primarily because the Acharya was writing for an audience that he assumed would be better informed on certain fundamentals than myself.

of Nepalese society and observe how these fit into the religiopolitical system. It should be noted that similar groups are also present
in India, but in much smaller proportions to the majority community.

The identification and characterization of the ruling elite
throughout most of Nepal is a relatively easy proposition; the vast
majority (until relatively recently at least, when ethnic-based elites
began to emerge) are descendants of migrants from India claiming
Brahman (priestly) or Kshatriya (ruler-warrior) caste status. Their
values are those of orthodox Hinduism as prevalent in northern
India in the fourteenth century. They are almost exclusively
Saivite in ritual terms, with the Pashupati sect, in which the Himalayas play a major role, given particular emphasis. Shankaracha-
rya was probably the last of the great Hindu reformers in terms of
their Hinduism. Some tantrik influence is evident, but Vaishnav-
ism (particularly of the *bhakti* variety) has never been widely influential except within the Newar community in Kathmandu valley. The reform Hindu movements of the nineteenth century,
such as the Arya Samaj or the Ramakrishna Mission, also made
little impact on this hill area elite.

Another subcategory, closely related to the ruling elite both
historically and in their religious and social structure, are the
Khas, Indo-Aryan migrants of good caste status from the hill
areas to the west of present-day Nepal. One element in this group,
the Tagadharis, are accepted as Kshatriyas by the higher castes and
are entitled to wear the sacred thread. But another category,
known as *Matawalis* (or drinkers of alcoholic beverages), are assigned a more ambivalent position at the bottom of the Kshyatriya
varna—for example, the Khattri-Chhettris.[5] Both groups, however, spread throughout the hill areas of Nepal in which rice production is feasible (i.e., up to about 8,000 feet) and played important roles in the establishment of the numerous Hindu-ruled
principalities in the western hills. They still constitute the major

5. This distinction between Matawalis and non-Matawalis (as well as between
enslavable and nonenslavable Matawalis) among the middle- and lower-caste groups
is of vital importance to their duties and privileges under the various legal codes.
As far as I know, this kind of distinction between caste groups is not found in India,
at least under this terminology.

element in the Nepal army, although rarely at the very top level of command.

The large majority of the population of Nepal, however, belongs to a wide variety of other social groups, organized either along ethnic, tribal, or caste lines. Perhaps 20 percent of the population are relatively recent migrants from northern India, most of them of middle- or lower-caste status, who are concentrated in the plains area (the Terai) at the foot of the hills. In contrast to the political elite in Nepal, the Hinduism of this group has been strongly influenced by the reform Hindu movements in India and the secularization of the social and economic system in adjacent areas across the border.

Another important community in education, commerce and administration are the Newars of Kathmandu valley. Historically, the Newars were a community comprised of Buddhists but ruled by Hindu dynasties for more than a millennium. A gradual Sanskritization[6] process has long been operative among the Newars, and indeed the first Hindu-based social and legal code in the hills was introduced by a Newar ruler, Jayasthiti Malla, in the fourteenth century. The synthesis of Hinduism and Buddhism is well advanced in this community, with the former assuming the dominant position in the past two centuries.

Perhaps two-thirds of the hill population of Nepal is of non-Indo-Aryan and non-Hindu origin. Some of these communities have also been heavily Sanskritized in the past few centuries by their high-caste Hindu rulers and Brahman priests, but the process is not yet completed. The social and religious values of these ethnic groups are obviously a cultural mixture; their Hinduism can scarcely be classified as orthodox although the trend is in that direction. Several of the more isolated ethnic groups or more recent migrant communities from Tibet have only been lightly touched by Sanskritization, although the initial stages of this process are also evident among them. All of these groups constitute a problem in terms of national integration but one that

6. Sanskritization is used here essentially in the sense employed by M. N. Srinivas, involving the acceptance of Brahmanic practices on such questions as pollution, marriage, dining, etc., and the gradual absorption of the Brahmanic world view on proper social relationships.

is receding in importance in some vital respects under the impact
of nationalizing and socializing forces. Nonetheless, the Sanskritization process is only partially completed, and Nepal is still very
much a pluralist society in social and cultural terms.

SANSKRITIZATION AND MODERNIZATION

Political modernization in Nepal should not be perceived as a
recent phenomenon or one that is solely the consequence of
"westernization" but rather as a process of change that has been
underway for at least several centuries. The principal hypothesis
argued here is that the modernization of the Nepalese polity and
society has been, at least until very recently, the consequence of
Sanskritization rather than secularization and that both are still
dynamic aspects of social and political change in that country.
Secularization has significantly affected only a comparatively small,
if vital, part of the Nepalese population. Sanskritization, on the
other hand, is still underway on a massive scale throughout much
of Nepal, although in some areas it has occurred concurrently with
the initial stages of secularization.

The argument relating political modernization to Sanskritization is based, of course, upon certain preconceptions about the
former term in non-Western contexts. In using the concept in this
essay, I shall restrict my definition of political modernization to
the expansion (planned or otherwise) of political, economic, cultural, and social interrelations between divergent groups within
specified boundaries (i.e., the nation-state) and to the evolution
of institutions and processes of communication within this context that make a more complex polity and society viable.

What, then are the preconditions for modernization under this
limited and very specific usage of the term? The first, of course,
is the movement from primordial (tribe, ethnic group, or caste,
in Nepal) to broader units of association and identification—an
essential stage in what is usually referred to as national integration.
As employed here, however, the term does not necessarily emphasize the emergence of a strong centralized authority replacing
all other intermediate units of association. The Indian term "unity
through diversity" has been the subject of much derision, particularly from Westerners who all too often have a narrowly centrist
concept of integration, but it may well be a more viable approach

to the problem of national integration in societies such as India and Nepal (and perhaps all of southern Asia) than the central-dominant theme.

Despite this reservation, modernization does nevertheless involve some degree of standardization of social, economic, and political norms, at least to the point where behavior and value patterns are not so divergent as to make routinized interaction impossible. Modernization also probably has to include some broadening of participation, on either an individual or group basis, in the broader social-political structure. This is not being argued on a value basis (e.g., democracy as a preferential governmental form) but rather on the assumption that an expanded communication system necessarily involves more interaction on either group or individual levels. The rationalization of the economic system, for instance, is probably strongly dependent upon the broadening of participation at all levels of society and not just on the introduction of economic reforms, no matter how radical in objective and content. This is fully understood in communist societies where economic change and massive politicization (along carefully prescribed lines) are integral parts of the theoretical approach, but it is also probably true for democratic, authoritarian, and even traditional Hindu polities as well.

Using this definition of the term, I would contend that Nepal had advanced substantially in the direction of modernization long before secularization made an appearance and that this was accomplished largely through the gradual Sanskritization of society in the central Himalayas. Until about the fourteenth century, what is now the Nepal hill region, including Kathmandu valley, was politically a "tribalized" area in which boundaries were usually drawn on ethnic-cultural lines. It was the input of high-caste Hindu refugees from the Muslim invasions of India, who scattered all over the lower hill area, that basically changed the situation. Previously, there had been no unifying links within this region that made a broader, multicommunal polity feasible. The migration of high-caste Hindus and their intermarriage with local elites throughout the hill area constituted a new factor of great political potential. By the sixteenth century, virtually all of the hill principalities in the central Himalayas were ruled by these refugee families claiming Kshatriya caste status. Moreover, they ruled over polities composed of several ethnic communities, thus commencing the process under which the narrowly drawn ethnic boundaries were gradually broken down. Without the previous Sanskritization of the ruling elite throughout this area, and their acceptance of a common value system, it is doubtful whether it would have been possible to absorb these local elites into a centralized administrative and political system under the Gorkha dynasty in the late eighteenth century.

Furthermore, Sanskritization also had the general effect of transforming the forms—if not necessarily the extent—of participation in social and political processes from a tribal-ethnic base to cross-community lines of communication. The tribal system may have been more egalitarian than the new political system based primarily upon familial and caste factors, but it was also more parochial and exclusivist. It is interesting to note, for instance, that during the period in which political parties were legal in Nepal (1951–60), the political organizations were either multicommunal or, more frequently, based on family, regional, or caste affiliations. The few attempts to organize parties on strictly ethnic lines met with little success. Since Nepal is still a society in which ethnic identification continues to be very strong, this was indeed unexpected. The reasons are unclear, but perhaps the fact that cross-communal lines of communication had been long established *before* the introduction of democracy was one decisive factor.

Much of the base for a relatively rapid modernization of Nepal's political, social, and economic system, thus, had been laid long before secularizing influences were introduced into the country, and this is attributable primarily to the gradual but effective Sanskritization of the central hill area over the past millennium. While it is obvious that some aspects of the traditional polity in Nepal are obstacles to further change and innovation (and these are the subject of attack from both Western-educated Nepalese and Westerners), the positive role of Sanskritization in effecting changes in the past should not be ignored, nor should its potential for the future be underestimated. The assumption that this is the age of secularization may have some basis in fact, but under prevailing conditions in Nepal it would be foolhardy for any Nepalese regime not to continue to make use of both Sanskritization and secularization in the effort to integrate and modernize the polity.

So far I have focused on the modernization process in the period prior to the introduction of secularizing influences into Nepal in the first half of the twentieth century. Despite the best efforts of the Rana family regime prior to 1951 and some reservations on this subject within the Nepalese government thereafter, it was not possible to immunize the society completely from the rapid process of change and transformation occurring in the surrounding areas. Space limitations prevent the consideration of such secularizing influences as the introduction of Western-style educational institutions, the proliferation of cinemas and newspapers in urban centers throughout the country, and the annual mass movement of Nepalese from the hill areas into India in search of employment at certain times of the year, although these are obviously important to the total secularization process.[7]

I now turn to a discussion of three major areas in which the process of secularization is at work in Nepal. While in many respects the continuity of tradition in Nepalese society impresses the observer more forcibly than the phenomenon of change, significant secularization is also taking place. I shall consider this process in relation to law, bureaucracy, and monarchy.

THE SECULARIZATION OF LAW

The important role played by legal codes in the standardization of values and behavior patterns in Nepal since the fourteenth century has already been noted. These codes, which in every instance up to 1963 were the products of Brahman advisors to Hindu rulers, were based as far as possible upon the *Shastras* (the principles of social and political organization in a Hindu polity) and particularly upon a later, abbreviated version of the *Manusmriti* (Code of Manu), which prescribed the maintenance of a rigidly hierarchical caste structure as the primary duty (*dharma*) of a Hindu monarch. Rather ironically, during the past five hundred years at least, it has been only in Nepal that Hindu principles of law have been so broadly and literally applied, for the Hindu princely states in India had to adjust their legal systems to conform to the concepts of justice and law of their alien Muslim and British rulers.

7. See John Hitchcock, "Some Effects of Recent Change in Rural Nepal," *Human Organization* 22 (Spring 1963): 75–82.

Even in Nepal, however, concessions had to be made in the legal codes to the traditional practices of the non-Hindu tribal and ethnic communities in the central hill area, but always until 1963 within an increasingly Sanskritized framework. The code introduced by King Rama Shah of Gorkha in the early seventeenth century, for instance, prescribed detailed social regulations for only the higher-caste Hindus and virtually ignored the non-Sanskritized social groups that constituted a large proportion of his subjects at that time.[8] The 1854 legal code introduced by the progenitor of the Rana family regime, Jang Bahadur Rana, went much further in the application of Shastric principles in that it contained nearly a hundred pages of incredibly detailed provisions regulating social relations both within and between all of the different caste, ethnic, and tribal communities in Nepal.[9]

The regulation of intergroup relations became increasingly stricter—in the Shastric sense—in each of the later editions of the legal code. Separate sets of rules were provided for each caste subcategory within the social system—Brahmans, Rajputs, Tagadharis, Matawalis (enslavable and nonenslavable), and untouchables—as well as for such tribal and ethnic communities as the Newars, Gurungs, and Limbus. In most cases, the laws regulating relations _within_ a group were based upon its own customary practices, while those that applied to intergroup relations strongly reflected Shastric concepts of responsibility (maintenance of prescribed caste functions) and pollution (rules on contact with members of other castes). Under these principles, the punishment prescribed for the same illegal act—for example, adultery with a person belonging to a different social category—became increasingly severe for perpetrators further down the Shastric-defined hierarchical scale. A Brahman who committed adultery with a woman of a lower caste was liable to pay a smaller fine than a man from a caste below that of the woman. Brahmans enjoyed another special privilege in that they were exempted from capital punishment for any crime in accordance with the strict prohibition against the

8. See Surya Bikram Jñyawali, _Ramasah ko Jivan Charita_ [A biography of Rama Shah] (Darjeeling: 1933). This book and his _Nepal Upatyakako_ contain summary accounts of the Rama Shah code. See also Yogi Narahari Nath, _Itihas Prakash ma Sandhi Patra Sangraha_ [A collection of treaties in the illumination of history] (Kathmandu: Itihas Prakash, 1968), pp. 684–85.

9. _Shree Panch Surendra . . . Muluki Ain_, 1 : 444–87, 2 : 491–526.

"killing of a Brahman" in the Hindu scriptures. All other castes were subject to capital punishment and for a wider number of crimes as we look down the social scale.

The 1950–51 revolution that overthrew the Rana family regime introduced a democratic political system into Nepal. This, however, was not reflected in the revisions of the legal code introduced between 1952 and 1955, which retained the Shastric base and differed little in spirit and form from its predecessors except that the range of caste-determined punishments was narrowed for certain violations.[10]

The new legal code promulgated by King Mahendra in 1963, on the other hand, marked a complete departure from precedent as it introduced a fundamental change in the character of the Nepalese legal and judicial system. All discrimination between groups, including the prescription of different sets of responsibilities and punishments in accordance with caste status, was abolished, thus nullifying the Shastric base that had underlain all previous codes.[11] Under the 1963 code, every citizen of Nepal is entitled to equal treatment before the law, and the special privileges of the higher castes are no longer supported in the code. There has even been one instance in which a sentence of capital punishment was imposed and implemented upon a Brahman, although under what would appear to be a unique set of circumstances.[12]

Why was this total innovation in the legal system introduced? Certainly it was not because of irresistible internal political pressure, for the legal code had never been an issue of any significance in Nepalese politics; nor was it because of international disapprobation since the outside world was both unaware of and disinterested in Nepal's legal code. Two factors would seem to have been of some importance. First the law ministry, which had the responsibility for revising the legal code, was by 1960 staffed

10. *Muluki Ain* [Legal code] (Kathmandu: Government of Nepal, 1952–55), in particular, part 5, pp. 1–152.

11. *Muluki Ain,* 1963 ed. Not all of the Shastric tradition was abandoned, however. The ban on the slaughter or maltreatment of cows, for instance, was retained virtually intact in the 1963 code.

12. The prisoner in this case belonged to a Terai caste of recent origin in Nepal whose claim to Brahmanic status is sometimes contested by the Nepalese hill Brahmans.

mostly by younger Nepalese who had received their legal training in Indian institutions or the "Western-style" law college in Kathmandu. Their education had been primarily structured along modern Indian lines and the essentially egalitarian legal principles of modern India and the West. Their approach to revision of the legal code presumably reflected their legal training, and it would have been only on direct instruction from the governments of the day—the Nepali Congress cabinet (1959–60) or King Mahendra (after December 1960)—that they would have retained the Shastric base for the legal code. The democratic-socialist Nepali Congress would never have agreed to that; King Mahendra, for quite different reasons, found it politically expedient to assent to the changes for it contributed to his image as a reformist, innovation-minded ruler at a time his regime faced internal challenges from within the educated elite community.

In any case, as might be expected, social behavior in Nepal is changing much more slowly than the prescriptive legal rules. Intercaste marriages are now legal, for instance, but are still a rarity and the object of substantial social disapproval when they do occur. The government, moreover, is extremely cautious in implementing some of the potentially controversial provisions of the new code in order to avoid antagonizing the still strongly entrenched traditionalist elite groups. Indeed, both officials and the public often tend to act as if the legal code had not been changed. Discrimination on the basis of untouchability has been officially abolished and the concept of pollution by touch is no longer enshrined in the law. But some premature efforts by the Kathmandu untouchable community to exercise its rights by worshipping at temples previously open only to caste Hindus were officially "discouraged" on the grounds that such actions were "prejudicial to the social customs and traditions of others" [13]—that is, the high-caste Hindu views on pollution. Nonetheless, the new legal code constitutes one of the most significant formal steps in the direction of secularization in Nepal and one that will become increasingly controversial as previously disadvantaged groups begin to agitate for compliance with both the spirit and the letter of the law.

13. *Gorkhapatra,* 6 December 1963.

THE SECRETARIAT: SECULARIZED STRUCTURE, TRADITIONAL ETHOS

The traditional administrative institutions in Nepal, as developed under both the Shah rulers and the Rana family regime in the 1770–1951 period, were deeply imbued with the ethos of a traditional Hindu polity. Kautilya, the master Indian political theorist of the ancient period, would have enthusiastically endorsed both the form and the operating principles of the Nepalese administrative system. We do not know whether the Nepalese practitioners of the art of statecraft had been exposed to Kautilya's *Arthashastra,* but his guiding principles were certainly fully understood, both in domestic politics and in the conduct of foreign affairs in Nepal. This, more than any other single factor, would seem to justify Nepal's identification as a traditional Hindu polity.

Hierarchical status, and the privileges and responsibilities attendant thereto, were rigorously defined within the Nepalese administrative system, even to the point of determining the size of the guard force to which the *durbar* (court) of each high official was entitled. Certain offices were held on a hereditary basis by a particular family over several generations, and subinfeudation of subsidiary posts in this department to "client" families was also a common practice—an administrative variation of the *jajmani* system characteristic of rural Hindu intercaste relations.

The conspiratorial approach to palace politics, so intrinsic to the spirit of the *Arthashastra,* was also an integral part of the Nepalese administrative system. The very concept of the institutionalization of political relations in routinized forms was a totally alien concept; a political leader—when out of power—conspired on an extrasystemic basis rather than maneuvered within the system. The *sawals* and *ains* (rules of procedure) prescribed for each department reflected this spirit, and the basic operating principle of any sensible administrator—other than the man at the top— was to avoid assuming sole or even primary responsibility for a decision or policy. The main objective of an official was the protection and advancement of the interests of his family and its various client families within the accepted hierarchical frame of reference.

Developments after the 1950–51 revolution have led to major

changes in the secretariat's organizational structure, with a modernized administrative system as the stated goal. A number of foreign advisors in public administration have been brought in at various times to assist in this project, while several Nepalese have obtained advanced degrees in this discipline in Western educational institutions. An "O and M" (operations and methods) department was established in 1956 to give guidance to administrative reorganization and to prepare new procedural manuals (sawals) for the departments. A civil service commission was established and instructed (but not empowered) to apply the principle of appointment to official posts on the basis of merit. Thus, most of the attributes of a secularized administrative system have been introduced: an organizational chart of the secretariat and the legal definition of departmental roles and functions in the procedural manuals would warm the cockles of the heart of even the most finicky and ethnocentric Western expert in the field.

And yet, even a limited exposure to the Nepalese secretariat would soon impress an observer with its strongly traditional, nonsecularized character in actual operation,[14] and this despite the fact that most of the officials at the upper level are relatively young men educated in Western-style schools from which they emerged as strong advocates of innovation and modernization. The sawals may have been revised to fit a modern (i.e., westernized) conceptual framework, but the standard operating procedures in most departments are still very similar to those of the prerevolutionary period.

It would be wrong, perhaps, to underestimate the long-term impact of the structural changes that have been made or the insidious influence of the younger, well-educated officials, but it is also readily apparent that success in the secretariat is still largely dependent upon such traditional factors as diluting decision-making responsibilities, building up a clique based upon client relationships, and, most important of all, coming from one of the small number of families that have always provided the personnel for the upper level of the secretariat. It is possible that the changes introduced in the administration in the name of modernization

14. For a description of administrative reorganization in Nepal see Mangal K. Shrestha, *A Handbook on Public Administration in Nepal* (Kathmandu: Government of Nepal, Ministry of Panchayat Affairs, 1965).

are so totally alien to Nepalese values and accepted behavioral patterns as to be unworkable, at least under existing conditions. Astrological technicians may no longer play as critical a role in decision making as in the past, but the planning technicians—working on no more reliable a data base—have taken their place, and it is highly doubtful that this constitutes a significant advance toward secularization or the rationalization of the decision-making process.[15] In other words, secularization in form but not in fact is the probable destiny of traditional polities such as Nepal for some time to come, and this should never be confused with modernization. At the same time, the retention of traditional institutions but the redefinition of their functions and roles in the polity, as is also happening in Nepal, should be recognized as vital aspects of the modernization process.

SECULARIZATION OF DIVINE KINGSHIP

The royal house of Nepal, tracing descent from a famous Rajput ruling family of Rajasthan, has been staunchly orthodox in defining its own status and duties and in its acceptance of the traditional Hindu conception of kingship. This not only obligates the dynasty to uphold the principles of *Dharmashastra* but also endows the ruler with certain superhuman qualities. In the Nepalese context, and this would seem to be a direct derivation from traditional Rajput conceptions of kingship of the pre-Muslim period, the monarch is considered to be a manifestation of the god Vishnu and is honored as such on several religious festivals involving the entire population of Kathmandu.[16]

The political relevance of this religiopolitical status is difficult to analyze in specific terms not only in contemporary Nepal but even in the period when Hindu orthodoxy provided the theoretical foundation for the entire polity. It has not, for instance, secured the monarch against deposition or even assassination, as the history of Nepal amply demonstrates. There is the possibility, however, that this is one factor that helps explain

15. Aaron Wildavsky, "Why Planning Fails in Nepal" (Unpublished manuscript, 1971).
16. For a useful analysis of the traditional Hindu conceptualization of kingship see Charles Drekmeier, *Kingship and Community in Early India* (Stanford: Stanford University Press, 1962).

the reluctance of the Rana family, which held a monopoly of
political and military power in Nepal from 1847 to 1951, to
depose the Shah dynasty and place a member of their own family
on the throne.[17] Under the Ranas, the kings were deprived of
any role in the political process and played only an honorary role
in such diplomatic functions as the reception of the new British
resident to the Kathmandu court. They were isolated in the royal
palace (on steadily diminishing revenues) and were kept out of
public view almost entirely. Indeed, it was usually only on those
occasions in which the king's presence was required for religious
festivals that he was allowed to make a public appearance before
the general populace. Without this tradition, the status of the
royal family might well have declined even further during the
Rana period. Public memory of the existence of the family would
have faded, for even the monarch's coronations were celebrated as
relatively private affairs and the name of the ruler was not even
attached to public documents, at least during the latter phase of
the Rana period.[18]

It is difficult to determine the extent to which the people of
Nepal, many of whose absorption of traditional Hindu conceptions is still very limited, accepted the Sanskritic tradition of
monarchy and the attribution of superhuman qualities to the
king. In this respect, however, it should be noted that most of
these ethnic communities have been ruled by Hindu dynasties
for at least several centuries. The response of the populace to the
late King Mahendra on his several tours of the kingdom over a
period of sixteen years would seem to indicate that there is a
wide acceptance of the sanctity of the king's status and that a
higher form of *darshan* is obtained from his presence than that

17. Jang Bahadur Rana, the protagonist of the Rana regime, was suspected (and
with considerable justification) of holding such ambitions. But his approach to the
situation was classically Hindu in conception. He first had himself granted (by the
reigning Shah ruler, who was his puppet) the status of maharaja of two small
principalities in Nepal, thus attaining in his own right the attributes of kingship
within the Hindu tradition. The next step, the deposition of the Shahs and his
own accession to the throne, thus, would have been no different than the Shahs'
replacement of the Mallas on the Kathmandu throne a century earlier.

18. A Nepalese acquaintance, whose early schooling in Kathmandu coincided
with the last decade of the Rana regime, remarked on one occasion that his teacher
asked the class the name of the reigning monarch of Nepal and only two or three
of his fellow students could provide the answer.

of even the most respected political leader. Whether this attitude conforms to accepted Hindu concepts of kingship is relatively incidental to the political significance of the popular acceptance of the legitimacy of the king's status and his right to rule. The Western-educated political activists and intellectuals in Kathmandu may scoff at this incredulous acceptance of an archaic ethos by the people, but they cannot ignore it in making their own political calculations. Even the communists never openly questioned (though they have debated) the constitutional provisions that stress the traditional Hindu character of the monarchy except in the immediate postrevolutionary period (1952–56) when the party was illegal.

A more intriguing question, and one that defies confident analysis, concerns the late king's own perception of his religio-political status. In interviews with journalists he referred to his status as a manifestation of Vishnu in a rather lighthearted, almost disparaging manner, but this may have been with a particular audience in mind. Mahendra had a very traditional Hindu education (he was denied a Western-style education by the Ranas and was always suspicious—or perhaps envious—of his subjects who had had this experience), and his tutors were primarily Brahmans of orthodox tradition. His poetry, several volumes of which have been published, are filled with traditional Hindu symbolisms and syllogisms, and it may not be irrelevant that many of his earlier poems (i.e., before nationalist requirements intruded) were in Sanskrit rather than Nepali.

Under Mahendra, the monarch's participation in religious festivals was maintained with a strict adherence to established forms and proprieties. Even on his visits to the more prestigious Hindu temples in India, the king was due, and received, special honors. Whether King Mahendra participated in these various religious-based ceremonies primarily for political reasons (e.g., reminding the Hindu public of India that he was the *only* independent Hindu ruler) or as a devout, tradition-minded Hindu could be a matter only of conjecture, but we certainly cannot dismiss the latter possibility.

What does all this mean as far as King Mahendra's conceptualization of the role of the monarchy under objective conditions? Was this a factor, for instance, in his reluctance to accept the role of a constitutional monarch as defined under the 1959 constitution and the substitution of a new constitution in 1962 that made the monarchy the fulcrum of the entire polity? There is no doubt that King Mahendra defined a very different role for the monarchy than any of his predecessors (and particularly his father) since the eighteenth century, with his attempts to establish direct communication with his subjects through walking tours of the country and through direct involvement in the governance and administration, even to the point of acting as his own prime minister on occasion. To Mahendra, a passive role for the crown would seem to have been considered as tantamount to a dereliction of duty, and the direct leadership of the monarchy in the achievement of broader national integration and economic and political innovations, within the framework of Nepalese traditions, was a categorical imperative. His speeches constantly emphasized royal responsibilities. The terminology used was often in the modern idiom, but the spirit was dharmashastric in its fundamentals.

I would conclude that King Mahendra modernized the monarchy, but he by no means secularized it, and it will only be his successor, educated in a totally different environment, who may move in that direction. In view of the crucial importance of the crown in the Nepalese polity, a strongly traditional monarch will be a constant deterrent to secularization in other spheres as well, although probably the most he can be expected to do is neutralize some of its effects.

This brings us back to one of my original hypotheses, namely, that modernization in Nepal will occur within a framework of limited secularization and that this polity, while constantly changing, will be more notable for the persistence of traditional Hindu values and behavior patterns. But in the Nepalese context, in which new, supposedly modern institutions are sometimes essentially traditional in operation while traditional institutions are in some cases demonstrating an unexpected adaptive capacity, it is often difficult to distinguish persistence from change, modernization from a stubborn adherence to the past.

3

Secularization of Buddhist Polities:
Burma and Thailand

FRED R. VON DER MEHDEN

Burma and Thailand constantly offer fascinating possibilities for comparison. Apparently similar on so many levels—size, population, religion, custom and tradition, agricultural base, and geopolitical relationship to powerful neighbors—they display distinct differences at the same time with regard to colonial experience, levels of violence, reactions to the outside world and political-economic ideology and practice. This chapter seeks to analyze one element of seeming similarity and actual variation, Thervada Buddhism, and most particularly the secularization of the Burmese and Thai polities during the past century.

In this study I want to elucidate three points that the two cases illustrate: (1) The secularization of the polity may not develop a concomitant secularization of politics and in the colonial experience may lead to the politics of religious nationalism. (2) Secularization need not be a unidirectional development. (3) As scholars we should assess more carefully the functional differences, if any, between religion and ideology when discussing forces such as secularization.

TRADITIONAL BUDDHIST RELIGIOPOLITICAL SYSTEMS

It is first necessary to establish the base point from which secularization developed in Burma and Thailand. Prior to the final British occupation of the Burmese Kingdom both countries were Buddhist states in theory, although differing somewhat in practice and organization. In both the king was considered "divine." He was considered the protector of the Sangha and religion. Organizationally, this meant that in Burma a lay official, the

Mahadanwun, was responsible for support of the Sangha while in Thailand it was the Krom Dharmkara, or Department of Religious Affairs, although in both the monastic communities had considerable autonomy.[1]

The two countries differed considerably, however, with regard to the political role of the hierarchy. In Burma the "royal chaplain," the Thathanabaing, although the head of the hierarchy, was primarily a palace figure and, as such, close to the king. According to Harvey, he advised on various state issues, led revolts, and even acted as regent.[2] Traditionally, a new king appointed a new Thathanabaing, showing the personal relationship between the two. In Thailand the Supreme Patriarch was appointed by the king after consultation with the Sangha and held office for life. Secular control of the Sangha was in the hands of the Department of Religious Affairs and the patriarch was in charge of spiritual needs of the Sangha, not of the king. Normally eschewing political interference in secular matters, he embodied the greater separation of church and state found in the Thai system. Yet in both states the hierarchy of the religious orders fell under the final control of the monarch, and the king's ultimate legitimacy depended on Buddhist and Brahman ceremonies, the doctrine of royal divinity, and his exalted role as protector of the Sangha. By tradition he and his advisors were expected to be Buddhist. One final point of contrast between the two nations was toleration toward other religions. Partially due to the character of leaders and partially due to international political pressures Thailand proved to be significantly more tolerant of non-Buddhists.

It was at the local level that Buddhism was central to the populations of both nations. The "monastery" was the center of the religious, educational, and social life of the village. The Sangha provided social control, supported the existing monarchical system, educated the males in traditional religious and social practices, advised the village on a variety of secular matters, and gen-

1. See the excellent dissertation by Kasem Sisisumpundh, "Emergence of the Modern National State in Burma and Thailand" (University of Wisconsin-Madison, 1962). See also Fred Riggs, *Thailand: The Modernization of a Bureaucratic Polity* (Honolulu: East-West Center Press, 1966), pp. 65–109, and John Cady, *A History of Modern Burma* (Ithaca, N.Y.: Cornell University Press, 1958), pt. 1.

2. G. E. Harvey, *History of Burma* (London: Longmans, 1925).

erally acted to maintain order and social cohesion within the society.

In viewing the development of secularization in the two countries from these base points, we can note three more or less distinct historical periods within which we can analyze this process, the forces that impinged upon it, and its ramifications. Until the 1930s there developed in Burma a secularization of governmental structure and policy against a backdrop of religious nationalism, while in Thailand there was a gradual erosion of religious values under an indigenous leadership that maintained the outward trappings of the religious state. The following decade saw the emergence of nationalists who differed in their perception of the role of religion in the state. However, control of the power structure for a time was in the hands of those who sought to use religion for nationalist secular ends or chose to emphasize only secular goals. Finally, the bulk of the postwar era has again shown the divergence of the two polities as Burma was ultimately led by its monk-politician, U Nu, to the establishment of a Buddhist state, only to be toppled by a secular revolutionary military elite. Meanwhile Thailand returned to its gradual evolution toward secularism with little effort to advance any one policy in the area aside from maintenance of national cohesion through emphasis on the three symbols of king, Buddhism, and Thai nation.

SECULARIZATION IN BURMA

The approximately fifty years following the final collapse of the Burmese kingdom illustrate sharply the differences that colonial rule made in the secularization process in Burma, in contradistinction with her neighbor. It can be argued that the varied policies of the Burmese and Thai kings prior to the 1880s laid the foundations for the different paths the two nations took and that westernization inevitably meant increased secularization. However, British colonial rule must be given credit for the distinct pattern that developed in Burma, and the lack of European occupation is the key variable in explaining the Thai experience. Most particularly, Christian British domination must be examined if we are to explain the anomalous situation in which the Burmese polity became secularized while Burmese politics became emphatically religious in tone. This contrasts with Thailand's unique maintenance of independence and general separation of religion and politics.

In the Burmese case, colonial rule brought a greater secularization of the polity in a variety of rather obvious ways. Buddhism no longer had an official role in the governance or legitimation of the state. Although some efforts were made to maintain the Sangha hierarchy, at least around Mandalay, the character of the British occupation, which took the country piecemeal, broke the discipline and organization of the monastic community.[3] During the colonial period no unified religious command was successfully formulated, the first tentative success coming only with the Japanese occupation during World War II. Meanwhile, the British maintained an officially neutral attitude toward religion and, unlike their Dutch counterparts, refused even to establish a department of religious affairs within the government apparatus. Thus, a fractionalized Sangha operating within a religiously neutral polity no longer had its traditional advisory and legitimizing role.

Secondly, religion was not considered a prerequisite for office within the British raj and, in fact, Buddhists found themselves deprived of previously held positions. The colonial service was headed by the Christian British with the aid of three non-Buddhist elements: Indians who were employed in a variety of services from policemen to members of the professions; Anglo-Indians and Anglo-Burmans who were important in customs, post, and transportation; and hill tribes who dominated the military through most of the period of colonial rule. Reasons for choosing these non-Buddhist elements were secular in nature: they could be trusted more than the more nationalist Buddhists, they were more familiar with the British colonial system, and they had a secular education. As well, some Buddhist nationalists followed a plan parallel to that of their Islamic Indonesian counterparts in sporadically supporting noncooperation and refusing to join the civil service.[4]

3. Fred R. von der Mehden, *Religion and Nationalism in Southeast Asia: Burma, Indonesia, the Philippines* (Madison: University of Wisconsin Press, 1963), and Donald E. Smith, *Religion and Politics in Burma* (Princeton: Princeton University Press, 1965), pp. 43ff.

4. For Indonesian nationalist policy see von der Mehden, *Religion and Nationalism*, pp. 74ff.

This decline in the percentage of Buddhists in government service was in turn related to the secularization of a major monopoly previously held by the Sangha—education. Colonial government and modern technology found little use in the products of traditional monastery education with its emphasis upon Pali and scripture. Burmese youth who saw a future in the Western system, no matter their dislike of European domination, found it necessary to turn to Christian missionary and secular schools. Not only were the new religions of science and modernization not taught within the physical and spiritual confines of Buddhism, but more often than not they were learned from Christian missionaries. Under this dual Western and colonial impact, enrollment in monastery schools sharply declined, falling from an average of fifty to sixty in 1885 to ten and fewer less than four decades later.[5]

Finally, British rule managed to break the whole pattern of legitimization in Burma. As noted, the religious hierarchy was dismembered by the three-tiered character of the British occupation, leading to a breakdown in the organization and discipline of the Sangha. But this was only part of a process that saw the elimination of the monarchy, the destruction of former patterns of local authority, and the exchange of foreign for indigenous economic leadership. Ultimately a structure was formed having little or no roots in the past, no traditional legitimacy—a system toward which the Burmese could feel neither familiarity nor loyalty.[6]

This collapse of legitimacy paralleled the expected challenge to traditional religious values from modernization. New demand patterns were initiated as religion, the family, and subsistence agriculture no longer encompassed the entire life of the villager. Greater mobility, and particularly the movement of significant portions of the population into new rice lands in the delta, tended to fragment traditional relationships. Commercial agriculture and growing debt, which in turn brought social and political instability, brought the Burmese into patterns of European law and control. New forms of education, amusement, and employment

5. *Report of the Committee Appointed to Consider and Report upon Buddhist Religious Instruction for Buddhist Pupils in Vernacular Lay Schools under Buddhist Management* (Rangoon: Government of Burma, Government Printing Office, 1931).
6. See Fred R. von der Mehden, *Comparative Political Violence* (Englewood Cliffs: Prentice-Hall, 1972).

left traditional legitimizing forces at all levels all but destroyed, and major new economic forces swept both rural and urban areas.

While the political and social structure and official ideology was in the process of being secularized through colonial administration and Western influences, this very secularization under nominal Christian leadership led to the instillation of religion into the political process through the nationalist movement. Reacting against the non-Buddhist nature of the regime, the westernization of education under missionary auspices, perceived insults to the faith, and a felt decline in the moral character of society under the impact of Western values, Buddhist political and religious leaders gave the nationalist movement a religious tone that continued into the 1930s and in some aspects even later.

Politics in Burma during the first forty years after the fall of the kingdom displayed the Janus-like character of religious nationalism in Southeast Asia. On the one hand, structures and methods became European in character as political parties, colonial assemblies, urban councils, and elections became the arenas of disputes, and strikes, demonstrations, newspapers, noncooperation, and petitions became the tools of political action. However, both these structures and tools were initially used by groups and individuals to achieve goals heavily influenced by religious values. The Burmese political actors themselves were primarily Buddhist laity and members of the Sangha.[7] During the first three decades of this century this combination, working through the Young Men's Buddhist Association, General Council of Burmese Associations, and similar nationalist organizations, participated at one time or another in all of these arenas and used the full panoply of Western political weapons to fight three aspects of secularization noted by Donald E. Smith—polity-separation, polity-expansion, and polity-transvaluation secularization.[8]

In the area of separation the demand was for the return to

7. It should be noted that there is continuing controversy as to the percentage of religious personnel actively involved in nationalist activities of this sort.

8. Smith, *Religion and Political Development*, pp. 84–123. (In chap. 1 above this analysis has been altered somewhat. "Polity-transvaluation secularization" is now called "political-culture secularization," and a fourth aspect, "political-process secularization," has been added—ED.)

the monarchy and religious state, both somewhat idealized as time passed. Secondly, attacks were made on the expansion of Western education to the detriment of religious education in particular, while continued opposition was declared against efforts to substitute Western values for traditional Burmese precepts.

SECULARIZATION IN THAILAND

The process of secularization in Thailand displayed a significantly different development from that of Burma as the result of three basic factors. First and foremost, Thailand remained independent under a Buddhist monarch and with indigenous leadership. The nation's overall homogeneity, when combined with the absence of any necessity for the colonial practice of ethnic divide and rule, kept Thais governing Thais except in outlying regions of the kingdom. Changes that did take place were neither abrupt nor illegitimate and secularization proceeded gradually under the impetus of indigenous leadership and somewhat controlled Western inputs into the system. With the maintenance of the monarchy at the top and indigenously reformed local government below, authority was recognizable and legitimacy became based upon Buddhism, king, and country (or Thai people). The ultimate result was that politics did not revolve around differences in religion and race between ruler and ruled, Buddhism never became a major political issue, and the Sangha remained largely unpoliticized.

Secondly, the commercialization of agriculture and the movement of Thai farmers into new lands were slower and more controlled in Thailand, leading to greater political and social stability. High crime rates and the breakdown of authority, which were so prevalent in the new lands of Burma, did not have their parallels in the delta region of Thailand. Differences can be seen in the large-scale alienation of land that took place in Burma by the third decade of this century as against the Thai case, where this process escalated in the central plains only in the 1960s.

Finally, Thailand was fortunate in having rulers who were prepared to reform the system gradually, changing laws, structures, and ideas slowly from the top and retaining—even reinstituting— outward ties between the monarchy, Buddhism, and the ongoing political system.

Against this background secularization in Thailand revolved around two developments. The strong Thai kings, Mongkut and Chulalongkorn, set about to rationalize and westernize Thai custom and organization under internal pressure to eliminate those things (including aspects of Buddhism) which were in conflict with Western science and external pressures to modernize in order to defend the kingdom from European imperialism.[9] In the area of law Chulalongkorn set about to establish modern codified laws in a variety of fields from crime to commerce and in the process deposed the previous primary position of the rules of the dharma. He also set out to reorganize the Sangha, laying out the principle that secular authority should not interfere with the religious and vice versa, while recognizing the continued need for governmental support of the Sangha. He also introduced the view that monks should not partake in secular elections, all of which laid the foundation to the political, if not financial, separation of church and state in Thailand. Finally, Chulalongkorn officially declared that there would be toleration of other religions, an act that helped free politics from religious controversy.

Succeeding regimes clarified this trend toward secularization, although the movement was not without reversals. Due to conflict over the possibility of a foreigner taking the throne, in 1924 the Act of Royal Succession declared that only a Buddhist could be king. In 1933 it was officially promulgated by law that monks could not participate in elections, and the following year monastic lands were declared to be public property as part of the movement away from the absolute monarchy. The Revolutionary Constitution, formulated after the 1932 coup, read, "The King shall profess the Buddhist faith and is the upholder of religion," at the same time promising that "every person is entirely free to profess any religion or creed and to exercise the form of worship in accordance with his own belief. . . ."[10]

Secondly, the combination of Western influences and the pressure of Thai leadership weakened the power and prestige of the

9. Sisisumpundh, "Modern National State," pp. 76–92, 239–42, and Riggs, *Thailand*, pp. 97ff.

10. Quoted in Kenneth P. Landon, *Siam in Transition* (New York: Greenwood Press, 1968), p. 208.

Sangha in education and social influence, particularly near urban centers. Rationalist religious thinking, originally developed under the leadership of Mongkut and lay thinkers, weakened the monastic orders, while the same influences that brought a decline in monastery education and traditional morality in Burma were prevalent in Thailand in the years prior to World War II. However, it should be noted that religion remained an important element in education, although no longer monopolized by monastery schools. Buddhism was taught in state schools, religious books were part of the curriculum, and monks at times preached in class to both Buddhist and non-Buddhist. This does not mean that the Sangha remained entirely free from politics, as the political instability following the overthrow of the absolute monarchy in 1933 brought small, sporadic attempts by some monks to enter the political process. However, tradition, hierarchical discipline, and strong government action kept such activities to a minimum.

Transition, Disruption, and World War II

By the mid-1930s both states had moved toward secularized polities, one through colonial occupation and the other through a combination of elite decisions and the more subtle influence of westernization. At the same time, reaction to foreign-dominated secularization in Burma brought religious nationalism, while in Thailand gradual change under indigenous leadership kept religion largely out of the political arena.

The succeeding period was one of transition as internal political pressure and Japanese expansion changed the pattern of the previous forty years. In Burma young nationalists began to justify their activities on the basis of secular ideologies of nationalism, democracy, and Marxism while attacking the role of the Sangha in politics. Older politicians in their turn began to use members of the Sangha and religious issues more to further their own political careers, and charges of political opportunism on religious questions became prevalent. The Sangha for its part became more divided as older leaders became distressed by political activities of younger, more militant monks. As a result the bulk of the Sangha withdrew from political activities although a section of the younger monks remained active and even took part in violent demonstrations such as the anti-Indian riots of 1938.[11]

The Japanese occupation of Burma from 1942 to 1945 saw the temporary end of the absolute division between church and state in Burma. The Japanese, although not fully realizing the differences that lay between Buddhism as practiced in Burma and Japan, were anxious to employ their common religion to fortify cooperation between the two countries. The Burmese wartime "dictator," Dr. Ba Maw, although European and Christian educated, desired to strengthen his regime by emphasizing traditional values. He copied many attributes of the monarchy in his own manner of dress and court activity, while reinstituting historic traditions such as the "Sacred Soil of Shwebo." For the first time in almost fifty years the Sangha came under the protection of the state and was reorganized under a unified body. Thus, Ba Maw, a leader personally influenced by the old monarchy, began a return to some of the outward aspects of the religious state. However, his short period of power, followed by the interregnum of secular rule during the postwar government of Aung San, did not allow sufficient time to institutionalize these changes. While it cannot be argued that Ba Maw laid the foundation to the religiously oriented ideas promulgated by U Nu when he took power following Aung San's death, he did provide the transition from neutral colonial rule to a Burmese government with a desire to reinstitute some elements of sectarianism.

Meanwhile, in Thailand the Revolution of 1932 had initiated the institutionalization of a number of changes in the relationship between church and state. The end of the absolute monarchy and formulation of the Constitution defined the roles of the king and Sangha, as previously noted. The ensuing political instability, combined with the social and political impact of the depression, loosened traditional bonds within the population and minute sections of the Sangha became involved in politics. Of greater importance to our subject, the end of the absolute monarchy meant that succeeding civilian and military governments no longer based their power on traditional symbols of legitimacy. The old order

11. For the role of monks in the riots see *Final Report of the Riot Inquiry Committee* (Rangoon: Government of Burma, Government Printing Office, 1939).

was further weakened by the resignation of the king, the education of his under-age successor abroad during trying times, and abortive efforts by the traditionalists to overthrow the new authorities.

In the process of legitimizing their rule, the new Thai leaders turned to nationalism and economic and social reform, while the military provided the ultimate foundation of power. General Pibul Songgram, in the years following his ascension to power in 1938, was the most active organizer of Thai nationalism as he attempted to institute his own version of Thai fascism. His "National Ideology" was copied from the Japanese and praised the nation and warrior rather than traditional religious values.[12] While emphasizing the Thai race, the new ideology also attempted to introduce specific features of Western culture and dress. However, Pibul's efforts, like those of Ba Maw, ended with the Japanese defeat.

DIVERGENT PATHS OF POSTWAR DEVELOPMENT

The postwar period introduced a new political era in Southeast Asia, particularly among the newly independent states in the region. For Burma the years following the end of the world conflict were traumatic ones bringing independence, assassinations, a generation-long civil war, and economic and social disruption. In the sphere of church-state relations the immediate policy was one of Marxist-oriented secularism promoted by those around the "father" of independence, Aung San. The constitution of the new republic was not what prewar Buddhist nationalists would have hoped as it recognized only the "special position of Buddhism as the faith professed by the great majority of the citizens of the Union."[13] In spite of the choice of the deeply religious U Nu as premier following the assassination of Aung San in 1947 there was little immediate movement toward changing this concept.

U Nu was, however, desirous of moving the country in the direction of greater sectarianism and his personal efforts to instill greater religious content into politics was to become one of the

12. Walter Vella, *The Impact of the West on Government in Thailand* (Berkeley and Los Angles: University of California Press, 1955), pp. 386–87.
13. *Constitution of the Union of Burma*, section 21.

dominant themes of the next fifteen years. More than once he articulated his belief that most major state problems could be solved through greater attention to Buddhism, although he was often vague as to how its principles were to be applied. In fact, by his very religious bearing he was able to give an aura to government that was quite different from his secular predecessor. As one foreign observer noted, U Nu stood "unique among the world's statesmen, by his unparalleled piety and the embodiment of the ideal of Rajarsi, the ruler who is also a sage." [14] He thus became defender and promoter of the faith and began to fulfill the role of religious leader hoped for among the religious nationalists of the 1920s.

U Nu did take certain positive steps toward inculcating Buddhism into Burmese society. One of his first efforts was to convene the Sixth Great Buddhist Council of 1954, which he used as a vehicle for religious revival. The succeeding years saw programs to revive the sagging discipline and organization of the Sangha and to help train the monks in Pali and scripture. Religious symbols were given prominence and Buddhist relics were brought to Burma with government blessing, pagodas were restored, abortive efforts were made to place Buddhist as well as Islamic and Christian education into state schools, and public Buddhist and *nat* ceremonies attended by government functionaries were widely publicized. U Nu thus followed a multifaceted campaign to lead Burma toward his ultimate aim of a religious state.[15]

The Buddhist state was finally promulgated in 1961. This is not the place to analyze the political infighting that took place in the process of establishment. However, the character of that system does give a point of reference as to how far the Buddhist state had evolved three-quarters of a century after the fall of the monarchy. Without detailing every aspect, we note the following major elements.

1. Buddhism was declared the state religion.
2. The government was to protect, honor, and promote Buddhism, its teachings, practice, and enlightenment.

14. Quoted in von der Mehden, *Religion and Nationalism*, p. 96.
15. For an excellent analysis of the role of U Nu see Richard Butwell, *U Nu of Burma*, rev. ed. (Stanford: Stanford University Press, 1969).

3. The state would aid in building pagodas and hospitals for the Sangha.

4. Buddhism was to be taught in the schools and in the future schools could be established in monasteries if practical.

5. Various holidays were established and other ceremonies legitimized.

6. Government officials need not be Buddhists.

7. A further amendment guaranteed freedom of worship to religious minorities.[16]

The last two points caused considerable debate and anger among more militant younger members of the Sangha who desired a more all-embracing system, while religious minorities and military leaders opposed its implementation.

There was not sufficient time to test the full impact of the new Buddhist state as within less than a year the military under General Ne Win overthrew U Nu's civilian regime and established a secularist, Burmese-Marxist-oriented polity. The thoroughgoing housecleaning by the military of all aspects of the previous system involved the elimination of the Constitution and all laws giving special privileges to any one religious group. Instead there was formulated a secular, socialist doctrine that, while referring to the spiritual needs of man, did not mention any one faith and was highly eclectic in origin.[17] More than that, the military moved to diminish the influence of the Sangha, which was the last legal organized group that could offer opposition to the new regime. In the succeeding twelve years there have been numerous clashes between military men and the Sangha and the Ne Win regime has continued its secular policies. Thus, Burma moved back to a doctrine more compatible with the desires of those who, under Aung San, led the nation to independence.

The postwar period in Thailand has displayed no major changes in the long-term trend toward secularization. It remains a Buddhist state under the leadership of the king and Supreme

16. See Fred R. von der Mehden, "Rise and Fall of the Buddhist State in Burma," *Southeast Asia,* vol. 1 (1971), and Smith's excellent chapter on the Buddhist state in his *Religion and Politics in Burma,* pp. 230–80.

17. *The Burmese Way to Socialism* (Rangoon: Government of Burma, Information Department, 1962).

Patriarch, although there have been developments that have given new directions to the relationship between religion and the body politic. Marshal Sarit, uncontested ruler for five years after achieving power in 1958, was particularly interested in employing traditional values, symbols, and institutions to strengthen his regime and integrate Thai society against the dangers of both increased modernization and encroaching communism. Under his direction the Sangha was reorganized in 1962 to strengthen the power of the hierarchy and centralize administration and discipline. Closer administrative ties were established between the Department of Religious Affairs and the Buddhist orders, and local religious autonomy was diminished.[18]

Sarit also set out to propagate the king as symbol of the nation by attaching him to traditional activities such as the Royal Barge ceremony and emphasizing his person through the media and education. Other ceremonies were also reinstituted to provide pageant and traditional legitimacy to the polity. In the words of Yoneo Ishii, "Sarit thought that national integration must be strengthened to realize national development. To attain this goal he planned to start with fostering the people's sentiment for national integration through the enhancement of traditional values as represented by the monarchy and Buddhism." [19] This effort to reinforce the regime through the monarchy and Buddhism continued during the following decade until now the very attractive royal family is a power in itself and has become an institution almost invulnerable to domestic attack.

Similar to the Burmese military, the Thai government has also attempted, on a smaller and less systematic scale, to use religion against communism. Circulars, speeches, sermons, and articles have been employed to show how communism is opposed to the three treasures of king, Buddhism, and country. Yet, this activity has been low-key and elements within the government have been cautious in using the Sangha as propaganda tools or as communicators of development in insurgency areas. The examples of politically oriented monks in Burma and Vietnam provide instruc-

18. Yoneo Ishii, "Church and State in Thailand," *Asian Survey* 8 (1968): pp. 869–71.

19. Ibid., p. 869.

tive examples to those who desire the limitation of popular political activity.

While these governmental programs tended to somewhat reverse the official secular policies that followed the 1932 coup, the process of modernization in Thailand has probably more than overcome this change at the popular level. The postwar era has been one of extensive social and economic change in the kingdom as communications have opened large, previously isolated areas. Comparatively few villages are without radios and even remote sections occasionally see mobile film units. Thais have also become highly mobile and recent surveys show considerable movement of peasants to and from urban centers.[20] Western amusements, material goods, and ideas have begun to take the place of more traditional and parochial influences. Studies show that villagers now seek essentially secular outputs from the government, such as roads, water, education, and health and the monastery has become only one, albeit often the most important, purveyor of ideas and formulator of standards. In Bangkok-Thonburi the impact of Western culture is even more pervasive and traditional values more vulnerable to attack.

A COMPARISON OF SECULARIZATION PATTERNS

There remain two tasks, an assessment of where Burma and Thailand are with regard to separation, expansion, and transvaluation (political culture) secularization and an analysis of the two polities based upon the three points noted in my introduction: secularization of the polity versus politics, unidirectional secularization, and functional comparability of religion and secular ideology.

Polity-separation secularization. Burma has followed a zig-zag course from complete separation of church and state combined with vigorous religious nationalism during the British period through a tentative renewal of church-state relations under Ba Maw to the victory of the AFPFL secularists at the end of World War II. Then under the leadership of U Nu, who in Donald E.

---

20. A variety of studies have been made of village attitudes on these subjects by Toshio Yatsushiro for USOM/Thailand, 1965–68.

Smith's words "assumed the role of the traditional Burmese king as patron and protector of Buddhism," [21] the nation moved toward a closer ideological and organizational alliance between Buddhism and the state, culminating in the short-lived establishment of the Buddhist state in 1961–62. Since 1962 the military regime has officially supported the separation of church and state and declared its own philosophy of Burmese socialism, which owes its intellectual antecedents to a variety of ideological currents including Buddhism and Marxism.

Thailand has displayed a steadier course which, while divesting the king of some earlier powers, has always maintained the organization and, with one brief exception, the ideology of the religious state. Today there is officially no separation of church and state administratively and the king remains protector of the faith. At the same time there has been a clear political separation, and the Sangha and religious issues have normally been kept out of the political arena.

Polity-expansion secularization.   Burma has gone through two major radical cases of polity expansion during the British occupation and the coup of 1962. It was only for short periods during the two decades following the government of Ba Maw that the state tentatively sought to support organizations and activities previously aided by the old monarchy. However, even during that period the educational, social, and political functions of the Sangha had been badly eroded. In the Thai case, the government continued to support the Sangha administratively, financially, and, to an extent, ideologically, but secular law and education had largely supplanted traditional prerogatives prior to World War II.

Polity-transvaluation (political-culture) secularization.   This is a more difficult problem. Certainly it can be argued that during the colonial and postcoup eras of Burma the official foundations of legitimacy and political culture were neutral with regard to religion and that both Ba Maw and U Nu attempted to give the state a renewed religious dimension and to legitimize programs through reinforcing traditional values. It is also obvious that,

21. Smith, *Religion and Political Development*, p. 262.

except for the short post–1932 coup period, Thai Buddhism has been an essential ingredient in legitimizing the regimes in power and the king has been both a national and a religious symbol.

What is more difficult is an assessment of the popular culture, particularly as Western values and the goods and services of modernization have begun to make inroads into Thai and Burmese society. To what extent do Thais and Burmese still believe that it is necessary to be a Buddhist in order to be a national? To what degree have Western values supplanted traditional patterns of thought and influenced action in both rural and urban Burma and Thailand? The degree to which traditional religious values may influence a particular decision of a specific individual must remain obscure, although the fact that change has taken place is clear. We have no way of judging these and other questions in post–1962 Burma and there is not sufficient data to make more than superficial commentaries in the Thai case.

To conclude this paper, three hypotheses will be considered.

1. In a colonial situation secularization of the polity by the occupying power will tend to increase the religious content of politics when there is a high degree of indigenous religious homogeneity. The Burmese case in particular shows that polity secularization can initiate high levels of religious nationalism, which can result in demands for the reversal of a secularization process perceived as an adjunct of colonial policies. Polity secularization may thus be but a catalyst to the major political theme of the system —religious nationalism.

2. Secularization need not be unidirectional in terms of formal governmental arrangements or national ideology, although secularization of the society may be basically unidirectional as the result of the process of westernization. In both the Burmese and Thai cases government policy oscillated, the Burmese more radically, as to the degree of secularization of the formal polity. Contemporary Asian politics tends to be deeply influenced by charismatic rulers and the particular position of a leader such as Pibul, Sarit, Ba Maw, U Nu, or Ne Win can be the essential ingredient in determining what the "constitutional" relationship will be between church and state and what attitude the government or party will hold toward propagating a religiously oriented ideology. On the other hand, it can be argued that the inevitable process of

modernization tends increasingly to limit his options in the direction of desecularization. In neither Burma nor Thailand will it ever be an easy task to return to education in its traditional mold, to put the Wat back in its former near monopolistic position in the village, or to blot out the multitude of modern material demands of the westernized urban dwellers.

3. In most basic functions there are few differences between polities with fundamental affinities toward major religions and those with systematic secular ideologies. Both function to legitimize the state and provide a basis for national integration or, where there is conflict, group identity. Both supply reference guides to orient the believer to issue positions, and both offer the bases for recruitment. In Almond and Powell's terms, "the ideology provides an inflexible image of political life, closed to conflicting information, and offers a specific explanation and code of political conduct for most situations." [22] This is an excellent description of one type of traditional religious polity.

It is therefore arguable that while the secularization of religion has brought a breakdown in that faith's ability to be the final legitimizer and arbiter of the society, this may be just part of an ongoing process in which new ideologies are occupying the functions formerly held by religion. In Burma we may thus be seeing a perhaps abortive effort to copy the successful communist attempt to *desecularize* Russian and Chinese life and to propagate another "religion."

22. G. Almond and G. Powell, Jr., *Comparative Politics: A Developmental Approach* (Boston: Little, Brown, 1966), p. 61.

4

The Course of Secularization in Modern Egypt

DANIEL CRECELIUS

Secularization has been identified as an integral part of the modernization process, yet the great majority of studies on modernization in the Middle East have concentrated on but two aspects of secularization as it has affected traditional Islamic society. These themes have been the separation of religious institutions from those of the state, or to put it another way the differentiation of political and religious functions, and the ideological response of the *ulama* (learned men of religion) to the spread of Western ideas and institutions.[1] Studies on Islamic reform have been largely confined to the attempts of a mere handful of religious reformers, such as Jamal al-Din al-Afghani, Muhammad Abduh, Rashid Rida, and Hassan al-Banna (all, incidentally, associated with Islamic reform in Egypt) to restructure or reinterpret traditional Islamic thought and practice. Emphasis has been on their conceptual systems rather than on the impact of their ideas on society. Few studies have in fact dealt with the realities of socioeconomic change on the religious institutions and still fewer have attempted the difficult task of evaluating the secularization of the Islamic polity.[2]

1. Two examples of the first approach are the outstanding studies by Bernard Lewis, *The Emergence of Modern Turkey* (London: Oxford University Press, 1960), and Niyazi Berkes, *The Development of Secularism in Turkey* (Montreal: McGill University Press, 1964). Among the studies on the ideological response of the ulama are Malcolm Kerr, *Islamic Reform: The Political and Legal Theories of Muhammed Abduh and Rashid Rida* (Berkeley and Los Angeles: University of California Press, 1966), and Charles C. Adams, *Islam and Modernism in Egypt* (London: Oxford University Press, 1933).

2. Gabriel Baer has virtually pioneered the field of social history in modern Egypt. Among his works, see in particular *Egyptian Guilds in Modern Times* (Jerusalem: Israel Oriental Society, 1964), and *Studies in the Social History of Modern Egypt* (Chicago: Chicago University Press, 1969).

This chapter will attempt to trace the course of secularization in modern Egypt, to evaluate its quality as well as its impact, and to suggest some reasons for the course that relationships between religion and the state have taken in revolutionary Egypt. Before statements on these topics can be made, however, it is essential to review the relationship between religion and the state in traditional Islam.

THE TRADITIONAL ISLAMIC RELIGIOPOLITICAL SYSTEM

The separation of religious and political institutions or functions has been achieved with far less conflict in the Muslim Middle East than it has in the Christian West. But results of that separation have been far more disastrous to the Islamic religious institutions than to the Christian ones. Part of the explanation for this lies in the nature of the traditional relationship between religion and the state in the two religious communities.

Traditional Islam represents a system that Donald E. Smith classifies as organic, one in which religious and political functions are fused.[3] Christianity is characterized in his scheme as a church model, one in which there is a close alliance between two distinct institutions, between government and church. The separation of the two institutions in the church model is not necessarily disastrous for the religious institution since it can exist apart from the state. The same cannot be said of religious institutions in the organic religiopolitical model.

Islam is a revealed religion, hence the community (the *ummah*) is divinely ordered and guided, Allah's desires being revealed to mankind in the sacred Qur'an and the *sunnah* (traditions) of the Prophet. The sum of Allah's commands and prohibitions, most of which had to be deduced from the Qur'an and the sunnah through the devices of consensus (*ijma*) or analogy (*qiyas*), forms the corpus of the sacred law, the *shari'ah*. In theory the shari'ah provides guidance for every aspect of the life of both the individual and the community, which of course includes the state. The best Islamic society was that which could live as closely as possible to the ideal society outlined by the regulations and the principles of the shari'ah. The ulama who devoted their efforts to the knowledge and understanding of the shari'ah and other religious sciences

3. Smith, *Religion and Political Development,* p. 7.

interpreted Allah's commands and prohibitions for the community; the ruler, whether caliph or sultan, was charged with insuring the application of the sacred law in the community. In theory the ruler and the state were subject to the law, hence subservient to those who were responsible for interpreting it. The only sovereignty was that of Allah and all legislation received divine sanction when enunciated by the ulama.

Despite the fact that religious and political functions might be fused in an organic state, a clear differentiation of function somewhat akin to what we know in the West may yet develop. Already in early Islam such a differentiation between the political and the religious was apparent. It became the function of the ulama to preserve, study, interpret, and propagate the sacred law and religious principles through their teachings, and it fell upon the state to defend and apply the sacred law, insuring that the community would make the greatest approximation possible of the ideal Islamic society.

The organic unity of religion and state was particularly symbolized in the institutions of the shari'ah, education, and the caliphate or sultanate. In reality, the ruler dominated the learned men of religion, who usually gave way to the superior force of the military commanders, for the ulama did not attempt to *wield* political power so much as to *manipulate* it, hoping to influence state and society through their teachings and pious conduct. As Gibb and Bowen have written in their classic study:

> The first essential function, then, of the religious institution was to indoctrinate all ranks of society (including the members of the ruling institution) with habits of thought and principles of action and judgment in conformity with its ideals. The second was to raise up and maintain a body of scholars and teachers who would by their learning safeguard the principles upon which the religious institution was founded, and by their manner of life win the respect and affection of the people.[4]

This traditional self-view the ulama held of themselves as advisers, not rulers, has characterized the Sunni concept of the rela-

---

4. H. A. R. Gibb and Harold Bowen, *Islamic Society and the West* (London: Oxford University Press, 1957), vol. 1, pt. 2, p. 81.

tionship between religion and the state to the present. Recognized spheres of influence were ultimately differentiated for each socio-political group, but the just ruler was expected to consult the ulama on all matters of the law in its broadest aspects. The ulama had become the legitimizers of political power, the arbiters of social conduct, even the molders of economic policy.

The unity of religion and the state was maintained no matter how wide the political gap between ulama and rulers, and the ummah was always divinely guided, no matter how far society might stray from the ideal, as long as the rulers recognized the superiority of the shari'ah and gained the approval of the ulama for their actions. The ulama thus continued to act as the final arbiters of what was pleasing (legal) or reprehensible (illegal) but were often forced to compromise in the face of the superior power of their rulers. They therefore continued to define the limits to which law and custom could accommodate innovation or deviation from the ideal. As long as the state recognized the theoretical supe-riority of Allah's law the ulama condescended to stretch the tolera-tion of that law to remarkable limits. The preservation of this traditional "veto" power has remained one of the fundamental de-mands of contemporary ulama in their debate with secularists over the relationship of religion and state in modern Islam.[5]

Islamic scholars often remark on the seeming autonomy of such religious institutions as the corps of ulama, the law, education, or the dervish orders. It appears, however, that religious autonomy in traditional Islam was largely a function of the sociopolitical or physical distance of the religious institutions from state power. Autonomy even varied within an institution, depending on the re-lationship a particular level of any institution maintained with the state. Much of the difference in autonomy between the dervish orders and the ulama is to be explained by the stronger and more frequent relations, both formal and informal, that the ulama main-tained with the military elites. Likewise, village ulama were not subjected to the ideological tests that the higher ulama and the

5. Leonard Binder remarked that the ulama sought to reestablish their traditional prerogatives in the constitution that was to be written for Pakistan after partition from India: "The core of this agreement was contained in the provision empower-ing the Supreme Court to invalidate all acts of the legislature which are repugnant to the Qur'an and the Sunnah." *Religion and Politics in Pakistan* (Berkeley and Los Angeles: University of California Press, 1961), p. x.

state might jointly apply to those ulama serving in courts, mosques, or schools in urban centers. The higher ulama in particular had far less opportunity to develop political or ideological autonomy than those of lesser rank because of the very close social, economic, and administrative ties they maintained with the state. In eighteenth- and early nineteenth-century Cairo, for instance, popular insurrections against unjust governments were more frequently led by ulama of the districts or of lesser rank than by the recognized religious leaders who held high positions within the religious hierarchy.[6]

Sunni Islam was totally dependent upon the state in its battle against unbelief. The higher ulama, working through institutions supported by the state, strove mightily to defend their interpretations of religious truth from Shi'ah formulations or the excesses of popular religion. They sought to impose their system of belief upon the ummah and the state through the application of the sacred law and the indoctrination of the masses through example and learning. The latter was imparted through a vast system of *kuttabs* (the primary school of the Muslim community) and *madrasas* (the college-mosque). Heresies, superstitions, and unbelief were thus held in check by the law and combatted through the spread of education. The military rulers, too, found the law and education useful means by which to control the polity, especially since Sunni ulama preached obedience to the ruler as one of their fundamental political principles.

The educational concern of the ulama in traditional Islamic history was generally limited to matters religious. Their virtual monopoly over education and the interpretation of the sacred law should not blind us, however, to the antagonistic political relationship that existed between them and their military rulers. Not only were the ulama themselves subservient to the state in terms of political power, but the religious institutions that were the very wellspring of the vast influence they possessed were also dependent

6. I have argued elsewhere that the higher Egyptian ulama ought rightly to be considered part of the ruling elite in the late eighteenth century, rather than mere intermediaries between government and society, as so many works on the subject characterize them. See "The Emergence of the Shaykh al-Azhar as the Pre-Eminent Religious Scholar in Egypt," forthcoming in the commemorative volume of the 1,000th anniversary of the city of Cairo, to be published for the U.A.R. Ministry of Culture by Akademie Verlag, Berlin (GDR).

upon the state for support and sustenance. The great mosques, the numerous madrasas, even the *takiyahs* (dervish "monasteries") of the community were built and maintained at state expense and had their functions supported through an annual allotment by the state or by the alienation of lands or revenues (once again usually donated by the state or higher officials of the state) in the form of *awqaf*.

The organization of the legal system, too, was considered within the proper domain of the state, though it remained the function of the ulama to determine the content of the law. The state therefore organized the judicial hierarchy and appointed judges within the system. The state could likewise choose to enforce or abandon certain prescriptions or interpretations, as it did in the ninth century when it changed direction on questions posed by the Mu'tazilites. Likewise, a new regime might attempt to change significant segments of the belief system of the ummah. In Egypt, for instance, the victory of the Fatimid forces in A.D. 969 meant the eclipse of Sunni teaching and the imposition of a Shi'ah interpretation. For this purpose the great mosque school of al-Azhar was originally founded.[7] Shi'ah Islam in turn gave way to Sunnism when Salah al-Din al-Ayyubi wrested Egypt from the last Fatimid ruler in A.D. 1171. After a brief period of decline al-Azhar became the bastion of Sunnism in the Middle East as a result of the support given to it by the revived Sunni state.

The traditional Islamic state appeared as both patron and master of the legal and educational institutions of Islam. It was imperative, in a state or society ordained by God, that religion and the law be dominated by the state. Nor did the ulama or the dervish orders remain totally outside state control, for it was also necessary for the religious state to force a minimum degree of religious conformity on all levels of society and upon all social institutions. My own research has indicated that in late eighteenth-century Egypt even the heads of native religious structures such as the dervish leaders, muftis, and the Shaykh al-Azhar could not claim or maintain their positions without the approval of the state. All, moreover, had to submit to the discipline of the ruling Mamluk-

7. The *nizamiyah madrasas* that spread across the Middle East in the 11th century can likewise be seen as an attempt by the Sunni state to propagate through educational institutions a particular interpretation of Islamic "truth."

Ottoman military elites. Society, moreover, was virtually abandoned by both the state and the higher ulama to heterodox beliefs and practices, to superstition and ignorance.

I have dealt at some length with the realities of the political relationship between religion and state, between ulama and military-political leaders, in order to emphasize the dependence of religious structures upon the state. Though they may be characterized as having an organic relationship, their relationship was not a balanced one of equals. If this analysis is correct, it will help to explain a phenomenon to which I would like to return at the end of this chapter, being a topic seldom dealt with by studies on modernization in Islam. This is the determination by some of the revolutionary Islamic states to forge a new relationship between religion and state, a relationship in which the state is totally dominant over religion, one in which the state, not the ulama, assumes the chief responsibility for the reinterpretation of Islamic thought and in which the state makes every effort to utilize religious symbols and principles to reach the religious masses with the message of Islamic socialism.[8] Religious institutions, having been differentiated from those of the modern state over the course of a century or more, are once more drawn into a close, though completely subservient, relationship with the revolutionary state.

THE FATAL BREAK

The reign of Muhammad Ali Pasha (1805–49) marks the beginning of the differentiation of political and religious structures in modern Egypt. His decisions and programs have in fact largely determined the course that secularization has taken over the last century and a half in Egypt.

The first and most abrupt move toward the differentiation of religion and state came in the attacks Muhammad Ali made against the political influence of the ulama. Between 1809 and 1813 he deposed those among the higher ulama who opposed him, assumed the right of the government to appoint or depose all the leading *shaykhs* who comprised the native religious elite, abolished the *iltizam* system of tax-farming and seized the revenues of the *awqaf*

8. Smith identifies this as the dominance of the polity over religious beliefs. See *Religion and Political Development*, p. 86. I will have more to say on this point later.

khayriyah (pious foundations alienated in perpetuity) that supported religious institutions and their functions. By stretching his hand over the dervish and guild leadership, over provincial and village heads, and by providing a loose administrative framework for their organization, Muhammad Ali increased the control of government over these semiautonomous structures to limits unknown before his reign. But above all, he departed from traditional principles of Islamic government by refusing to accept the advice and mediation of the ulama in the councils of state. The acts of political terror perpetrated against the ulama by Muhammad Ali and his son Ibrahim Pasha generally silenced the voices of the ulama in the highest councils, but they did not keep them from privately opposing the reforms of the new regime. Despite their unwillingness to accept the many reforms he now introduced, Muhammad Ali found ways to impose the hated innovations (*bid'ah*) within a limited governmental circle.

The regime's attacks upon the political influence of the ulama and its seizure of most of the revenues that sustained the vast system of schools, mosques, takiyahs, and ceremonies of the religious community had a terrible effect upon the religious institutions in Egypt. Deprived of most of their revenues and ignored by the new regime, religious institutions entered a period of rapid and continuous decline. Numerous kuttabs fell into ruin during Muhammad Ali's reign, and by 1875, when Ali Mubarak Pasha made his famous survey of mosques and schools, decay was widespread. "The majority of the schools," he reported, "have become mosques." [9] He also noted that there were no more salaries for ulama, except at al-Azhar, and that many mosques, unable to support the personnel necessary to sustain public services, were turned into occasional meeting places for small groups of dervishes. The very function of many mosques and schools had therefore been abandoned. Other institutions such as the guilds and the dervish orders experienced a similarly disastrous century of decay.

The ulama found it inadvisable to challenge Muhammad Ali once he insisted upon imposing his will upon them. The best they

9. Ali Mubarak Pasha, *Al-Khitat al-Tawfiqiyah al-Jadidah* (Bulaq: 1887), 1:87. Of 95 madrasas that he mentions in vol. 6, 23 were in ruin, 2 were inactive, 34 were functioning, 25 had become *zawiyah*s, and 41 had become mosques. The total is more than 95 because some madrasas fit more than one category.

could do was to attempt to limit the scope of the modernizing trends their pasha now set in motion or through their own tactics to surround, isolate, and eventually suffocate the hated innovations. It was difficult, though, to oppose successfully the introduction of new practices or organizations at the level of the state, where the pasha was supreme. Muhammad Ali did not openly challenge the traditions and concepts of the ulama nor totally abandon the basic concepts of Islamic government. He recognized the supremacy of the shari'ah and continued the bald charade of consulting the ulama and gaining their official approval for his programs, even if this meant forcibly securing a necessary *fatwa* (legal opinion) from an unwilling *alim* of the second rank. Above all, he made no attempt to challenge their control of religious education, the law, or their moral dominance of society.

One of the key relationships between the ulama and the military elite, between religion and the state, was nevertheless missing from the new pattern of relationships being forged by Muhammad Ali. Where once the military elites had respected the ulama, patronized their activities and institutions, solicited (and generally obeyed) their counsel, and made them virtual partners in government, the new regime saw them as obstacles to modernization, rivals for power, and teachers of ideas, attitudes, and practices that were responsible for the social, economic, and intellectual backwardness of the nation. They and their teachings were increasingly seen as major factors in the military weakness of Muslim states.

The strategy that each side adopted in the struggle to modernize appears in retrospect to have greatly facilitated the institutional modernization of the state and to have permitted the substitution of one belief system for that of another among a small segment of society without totally disrupting traditional socioeconomic institutions and beliefs in general. Early modernizers such as Muhammad Ali felt they could borrow just the "cutting edge" of Western civilization without disturbing society's basic equilibrium. Modernization was felt to be a simple operation of grafting onto traditional society a narrow range of Western borrowings, in particular a new military organization, discipline, and technology.

Muhammad Ali therefore made no attempt to modernize society in general. The many innovations he introduced into Egypt were meant solely for the aggrandizement of the state, particularly its

military arm. The factories he founded produced items essential
to the military, such as weapons, ammunition, and uniforms. The
schools he established were military schools. Even the famous
medical college, which was placed, like so many other new programs, under the direction of an infidel, was meant to train medical
specialists for the armed forces alone. The pasha's programs, the
new techniques, the new skills, and the institutions he introduced
therefore were to benefit only a small segment of society clustered
around the military-bureaucratic institution of the modernizing
state.

Despite the necessary public approval the higher ulama were
obliged to give to the pasha's innovations, they joined the rest of
their corps in maintaining an unrelenting hatred for and opposition to virtually all the new programs. The ulama were powerless
to halt the introduction of these changes at the level of the state,
where even their own theories told them the ruler was supreme,
but their public opposition successfully confined the reforms
within a narrow governmental circle.

The results of this mutual policy have been disastrous for the
ulama, for their institutions, concepts, political influence, and self-
image in particular, and for Islamic society and its belief system
in general. Having usurped their former revenues, curbed their
political influence, and destroyed their inner cohesion, the regime
abandoned all religious institutions to their own devices. Deprived
by their alienation from the government of necessary financial support, the ulama saw their institutions fall into a physical decay and
intellectual stupor from which they have not yet recovered. The
policy of permitting innovation at the level of the state, while trying to block its spread to society, moreover, appears very much like
permitting the introduction of a virus into one part of the body
and then working frantically to contain its spread to other parts.[10]
The strategy of isolation is therefore responsible for the wide cul-

10. Uriel Heyd noted that in the Ottoman Empire the higher ulama helped to
write and implement the sultan's reform programs. But their strategy of participation had the same result as the Egyptian ulama's policy of isolation. Heyd wrote,
"Retrospectively, the support given by the high ulema to the policy of opening the
Ottoman Empire to European secular ideas and institutions seems a suicidal policy
from the point of view of the interest of their corps." "The Ottoman 'Ulema and
Westernization in the Time of Selim III and Mahmud II," *Scripta Hierosolymi-
tana* (1961): 76.

tural and political gulf that now exists between the still relatively small modernized sector of society organized around new institutions and concepts and the vast majority that still clings tenaciously, but in bewilderment, to traditional beliefs and practices. The latter remains organized around dead or decaying socioeconomic institutions and continues to follow an impotent religious leadership adhering to outmoded concepts and practices.

Though most of Muhammad Ali's actual reform programs disintegrated in the decade of the 1840s, the essence of secularization survived. While his military factories and armed forces were dismantled, his schools closed, and his state monopolies abandoned, the spirit of reform continued to guide the policies of a small elite bent upon further modernization. Secularization during the first half of the nineteenth century was confined largely to the expansion of nonreligious functions by the government, the growing centralization of authority, the casting adrift of religious institutions, and the creation of the skeletal institutional framework of a modern state bureaucracy. Secularism appeared to make no penetration of society's beliefs or institutions and remained confined to a handful of reformers intent upon borrowing only a narrow range of Western military technology or bureaucratic practices. Yet secularization seemed to break through the barriers thrown up against it and to overwhelm Egyptian state and society in the latter half of the century. Secularism was expressed, not merely as a changing set of institutional relationships, but as a coherent ideology and style of life.

THE TRIUMPH OF SECULARISM

The second half of the nineteenth century appears to be the key period of secular gestation, for it is the period when socioeconomic change developed the momentum to destroy the equilibrium of Egyptian society and when new institutions, concepts, and elites coalesced to form the basis of a modern state and society. All systems by which Egyptians ordered their lives were profoundly affected during this period by four factors: the frenetic attempts by Khedive Isma'il (1863–79) to make Egypt "a part of Europe"; the extensive activities of a vastly enlarged foreign community that founded new businesses, opened modern schools, brought Western technology, and introduced new habits, values, and attitudes; the policies of a reforming British administration that controlled Egypt after 1882; and the efforts of a modernizing native elite. The course of secularization was now largely determined by three interdependent forces, the continuing trend toward the expansion of government functions and the centralization of authority, the disruptive nature of socioeconomic change, and the spread of Western political concepts among the new political elite.

The trend toward institutional secularization begun by Muhammad Ali continued as the government expanded its functions and centralized its authority. It was not always disruptive of the rhythm of traditional institutions because much of the government's expansion was into areas of only marginal concern to the religious community or into entirely new areas such as public health and sanitation. Ultimately, however, the evolution of a state bureaucracy performing a wide range of nonreligious functions developed an inertia of its own that impelled the state to seek control of *all* institutions and to perform functions normally left to religious groups.

Isma'il was the first ruler in modern Egyptian history to attempt to revive decaying religious institutions. He made a modest effort to bring order to the chaos within al-Azhar's educational system, gave lavishly of revenues and lands to reinvigorate the dervish orders, supported public religious ceremonies, and sought to make structural changes in the organization of the shari'ah courts. But all his programs, and those of succeeding regimes, no matter how well intentioned, have been viewed by the ulama as a threat to their remaining political and economic influence and have been successfully blocked or deflected by the stubborn defense they have made of their positions.[11] Because education and the law together form such an indispensable part of the institutional and philosophical framework of any society, the struggle between modernists and conservatives for their control has been particularly intense and drawn out. Though they suffered the gradual secularization of other areas, the ulama made successful stands to safeguard the autonomy and content of religious education, shari'ah law, and *waqf*.

11. See my article, "Non-Ideological Responses of the Egyptian Ulama to Modernization," in Nikki Keddie, ed., *Sufis, Saints and Scholars* (Berkeley and Los Angeles: University of California Press, 1972).

Finding it impossible to impose reform upon the ulama, Isma'il returned to the policy of Muhammad Ali by creating entirely new institutions to duplicate the functions of the religious ones still under the control of the conservatives. Secular law codes slowly took their place alongside shari'ah law, secular court systems (consular, minority, and mixed) increased in number, and modern schools belonging to the state or to religious and/or national minorities began to compete with the kuttabs and madrasas. Over the course of the next century these institutions gradually expanded their functions at the expense of traditional institutions until the scope of the shari'ah was reduced to personal status law (marriage, divorce, inheritance, etc.) and the kuttab-madrasa system had fallen to a secondary status behind the secular system of primary, secondary, and university schools developed by the state and the non-Muslim minorities.

The duplication of functions and institutions permitted reformers to work around the opposition of conservative forces, but it led to a painful cultural bifurcation in all fields. Two societies, the one modernizing around imported institutions and concepts, the other clinging tenaciously, but often in bewilderment, to traditional values and habits, were now locked in constant competition. Two societies touching at every point but having virtually nothing in common now coexisted alongside one another. The result was cultural chaos.

Religious institutions might resist the expansion of governmental functions and the imposition of central authority from without, but the force of socioeconomic change from within was completely shattering the cohesion of Islamic state and society. As Manfred Halpern points out, socioeconomic change was generating forces *outside* traditional systems, forces over which the ulama had no control.[12] Once these forces gained enough momentum to penetrate the traditional systems, they sundered the links that had bound the various elements of Islamic society together for centuries. One by one, the institutional, economic, social, psychological, and ideological links that bound together such institutions as the sultanate, guilds and dervish orders, kuttab-

12. Manfred Halpern, *The Politics of Social Change in the Middle East and North Africa* (Princeton: Princeton University Press, 1963), pp. 15–24.

madrasa education, and the shari'ah were loosened or lost altogether as socioeconomic change began the inexorable transformation of Egyptian society. While the ulama saw modernization as
the imposition by government of administrative reform, the spread
of a foreign belief system, or the diminution of their own influence
and successfully defended their own institutions from infection,
socioeconomic change was rapidly destroying the intricate pattern
of relationships upon which their own influence, functions, and
concepts were dependent.

The same forces that were destroying the ideological, social,
economic, and institutional bases of traditional society were slowly
giving birth to a new combination of forces. Entirely new social
groups emerged to perform a vast range of skills not found within
traditional society. The lawyers, doctors, journalists, novelists,
professional politicians, engineers, and others, themselves both the
product of socioeconomic change and the chief motive force for
further development, now challenged the political, intellectual,
and social leadership the ulama had always enjoyed and forced
them ever farther away from the center of the political arena.

Socioeconomic change also gave impetus to secularism in the
changing attitudes, values, beliefs, habits, even in the dress and
style, of the modernizing urban social groups. Secular ideas and
attitudes found their way into literature, formed the basis of new
fields of study, were popularized in a burgeoning native press and
taught in modern schools and courts. Secularism even found expression within Islamic reformist circles when such modernists as
Muhammad Abduh tried to relocate the boundaries between religion and science, between reason and faith.

The twin goals of the emerging social and political elites, nationalism and liberal reform, were explicitly framed on the basis
of secular principles derived from the West. The liberal-nationalists developed the same disdain that Muhammad Ali had shown
for the ulama and conservative religious beliefs and practices, but,
unlike Muhamad Ali, they were willing to contest the control of
religious institutions with the ulama, to challenge their concepts
and interpretations in open debate, and to engage them in a struggle for the moral and cultural leadership of the masses. Though
they expressed clear secular principles, it would be wrong to call
the liberal-nationalists antireligious; many, such as Sa'd Zaghlul

and Taha Husayn, were themselves the product of the Azhar system. They realized that only the state could impose reform upon the ulama and their institutions and therefore sought to gain political control over them in an effort to revive them, not to destroy them, for they felt religious principles ought rightly to continue to form the moral basis of society. It was the successful defense that the ulama made of their institutions and beliefs that forced the state to develop secular institutions alongside the unreformed religious ones while continuing to gain control over the latter. This drive by the liberal-nationalists to subject the Islamic educational, legal, and charitable institutions to state discipline and control is of no less importance for the emergence of a modern national state in Egypt than is the struggle to obtain complete independence from England, but it has unfortunately not enjoyed as much study as the latter.

By concentrating on the emergence of Western political theories and institutions, Western scholars have had a tendency to exaggerate the pace of socioeconomic change in modern Egypt, assuming that socioeconomic change was racing hard on the heels of ideological and institutional change. Though traditional society was beginning to show signs of disintegration, modernization had transformed only a very small segment of urban Egyptian society.

In his annual report for 1899, Lord Cromer, the British resident, offered a sobering reminder that modernization remained confined to a small, socially prominent minority clustered in Cairo and Alexandria. Discussing the crucial field of education, he remarked that the total number of students in schools under state direction was only 7,735. Against that figure he offered an estimate of 180,000 students enrolled in approximately 9,000 kuttabs spread across the country. Al-Azhar alone contained more students than all the state-directed modern schools and remained the only "university" in Egypt.[13] Cromer also estimated that 91.2 percent of males and 99.4 percent of females in Egypt remained illiterate.[14] All other statistical indexes would indicate that secularism had made little headway in Egyptian society.

13. The Dar al-'Ulum, which opened in 1872, was a preparatory school for teachers. The secular university and the modern school for judges were not opened until 1907–08.

14. *British Sessional Papers*, vol. 112 (1899), pp. 1003, 1007.

Gabriel Baer's many studies on Egyptian social history also offer a counterbalance to the studies on Egyptian ideological or political change. In one study he concludes that

> the contact with Europe and the economic and administrative development in the nineteenth century changed only partly the life and organization of Egyptian society. The traditional family and religious community remained intact and the position of women in society did not change. Neither wealthy Egyptians nor the lower classes acquired the mentality of an industrial society. The social change brought about consisted almost entirely in the destruction of the traditional socio-economic framework: the dissolution of the tribe and the village community, the disappearance of the guilds, and the abolition of slavery. Most of these developments occurred during the last two decades of the century. But the creation of modern groupings, such as modern parties or labour trade unions, was left for the twentieth century.[15]

Despite the limited scope of socioeconomic change, a secular political theory, derived entirely from the West and resting on the concepts of constitutionalism, consultative or representative government, nationalism, and popular sovereignty, evolved in the latter part of the nineteenth century and gained rapid acceptance among the emerging social groups. The separation of the Ottoman Empire into independent national states in the aftermath of World War I marks a significant turning point in Islamic political history, for it signals the triumph of radical political concepts over classical Islamic ones. Together, these concepts laid the basis for a secular state.

Nationalism redefined the community in terms totally inimical to classical theory by substituting in place of the universal ummah or the dynastic empire a greatly reduced entity composed, not of Muslims and *dhimmi*s (non-Muslims having protected status, but unequal rights and duties), but of men of all faiths sharing a common citizenship, equal rights, and common duties. As understood by those responsible for giving nationalism articulation, many of

15. Gabriel Baer, "Social Change in Egypt: 1800–1914," in P. M. Holt, ed., *Political and Social Change in Modern Egypt* (London: Oxford University Press, 1968), p. 160.

whom were themselves of the Christian or Jewish minorities, nationalism has been a powerful secularizing ideology in the Muslim world by eliminating altogether emphasis upon the religious bonds holding the polity together.

By far the greatest blow to the classical theory of the Islamic state was the acceptance of the Western concept of popular sovereignty as the basic organizing principle of the new national state. In his review of the attempt to create an Islamic constitution for Pakistan, Leonard Binder remarked that "Islamic legal theory does not recognize the authority of any human legislation." [16] Yet the modern national states that emerged claimed the right, based on the popular sovereignty of the nation, to organize their own affairs and make their own laws.

The popular will was expressed in the written constitutions, and the legislation that flowed from the newly established parliaments was legitimized not by the ulama (who in general obstinately opposed the flood of reforms now legislated by the liberal-nationalists) but by secular politicians claiming to speak in the name of the popular sovereignty of the nation. Though they did not totally abandon the classical concepts, their actions virtually replaced the sovereignty of God with the sovereignty of the people and raised the national state to the level of divinity.

The emergence of national states based on Western political institutions and theories was a remarkable triumph for the liberal-nationalists and secured the victory of secular principles at the level of the state. The liberal-nationalists, finally in control of the government, now sought to complete the modernization of Egyptian state and society by pushing reform into all areas. But first they had to gain control of the bases of their own state.

A continuous battle was fought between the ulama and the liberal-nationalists over a myriad of fronts. Issues such as the liberation of women, the freedom to think and write as one chose,[17] and a host of other questions involved the ulama in constant po-

16. Leonard Binder, "Pakistan and Modern Islamic Nationalist Theory," *Middle East Journal* 12 (1958): 48.

17. One of the most obnoxious powers the ulama enjoyed was the right to censure the writings of Azhar graduates. A board of conservative ulama was able to "try" holders of Azhar certificates and to stop the publication and distribution of their work. The three most famous cases of censure involved Taha Husayn, Ali Abd al-Raziq, and Muhammad Bakhit.

litical conflict with their modernizing government. The ulama showed little willingness to depart from traditional political theories or even to understand fully the new political concepts that formed the ideological basis of the modern state.[18] They let pass the opportunity to brand the concepts of popular sovereignty and nationalism as totally reprehensible to Islam, have instead held stubbornly to the classical theory of the Islamic state, whose major institution (the sultanate-caliphate) no longer exists, and have faithfully kept up an implicit criticism of nationalism by teaching that the only true unity is that of the universal ummah of believers.

Despite the recalcitrance of the ulama, the drive by the liberal-nationalists to create a modern state and society in the image of the West was giving great impetus to the force of secularization. Politics was the first area to approach almost complete secularization. The state was organized around secular institutions on the basis of Western political thought. Political parties, parliaments, and an expanding national court system had usurped virtually all the remaining political functions of the ulama and forced them into headlong political retreat after independence. Religious principles and practices were under constant attack, liberal-nationalists denied the ulama the right to "interfere" in the affairs of government, and few serious attempts were made to derive political concepts or to legitimize economic or social policy, administrative reform, or foreign policy by reference to religious principles.

The liberal-nationalists continued to borrow almost exclusively from Western thought, maintained a determined confidence in the superiority of a Western belief system and its appropriateness for Egyptian society, and kept up constant pressure on and criticism of traditional concepts, beliefs, and practices. Though they strove mightily to impose reform upon the ulama, even employing the weight of government legislation against them, they failed in their

18. In a remarkable little book Muhammad Ali Gharib revealed that he was with other students at al-Azhar when someone rushed into the courtyard and announced that students were striking in the streets. He and his companions, all of them villagers, were surprised, he reported, because they did not know what "strikes, revolution or independence" meant. They knew only that the British occupied their country. See *Azhariyat* (Cairo: 1962), p. 37.

attempts to reform awqaf, Islamic education, or shari'ah law or even to subject Islamic institutions in an unambiguous manner to central authority. It nevertheless appeared only a matter of time until Western beliefs and institutions would totally displace Islamic ones and Islamic society in Egypt would accept the separation of politics and religion as the West had done. Secularization appeared to be a unilinear force heading toward a predictable goal.

The Retreat from Secularism

Liberal-nationalism had not yet achieved its secular goals when the Revolution of 1952 introduced a radical new factor into the Egyptian political equation. Now the trends toward the differentiation of function and the centralization of authority that had been set in motion by Muhammad Ali were brought to a speedy conclusion as the Free Officers created a highly centralized authoritarian state around their Revolutionary Command Council, the executive committee of the revolution.[19] Religion posed an immediate and dangerous political problem for the Free Officers because of the power and appeal of the Muslim Brotherhood (al-Ikhwan al-Muslimun), a broadly based religiopolitical organization of a fundamentalist nature that was making a serious bid for power behind the banner of Islamic revival.[20] A brief period of flirtation between the Free Officers and the Brotherhood ended in the unsuccessful attempt by the latter's extremist arm on the life of Abdel Nasser in 1954. The subsequent destruction of the Ikhwan organization was no less a rejection by the new leaders of its fundamentalist ideology and programs, which the majority viewed as disruptive and antimodern, than of its politics. Its elimination permitted the revolution to subject all religious institutions to the discipline of the state and to develop its own solutions to Egypt's complex religious and cultural problems.

19. An interesting study of the manner in which the military penetrated all institutions in Egypt is Anouar Abdel-Malek, *Egypt: Military Society,* trans. Charles Lam Markmann (New York: Random House, 1968).

20. Published studies on the Ikhwan movement include Richard P. Mitchell, *The Society of the Muslim Brothers* (Ann Arbor: University of Michigan Press, 1970); Christina Phelps Harris, *Nationalism and Revolution in Egypt* (The Hague: Mouton, 1964); Ishaq Musa Husaini, *The Moslem Brethren* (Beirut: Khayat's, 1956), and J. Heyworth-Dunne, *Religious and Political Trends in Modern Egypt* (Washington, D.C.: privately printed, 1950).

Waqf had been the first of the remaining semiautonomous religious institutions to fall under the complete control of the state. It had been seen by the new regime as inextricably intertwined with the general question of land reform, and following suggestions proposed by the liberal-nationalists in the debate of waqf reform in the 1920s, the state announced in 1952 the abolition of all personal religious foundations (*awqaf ahliyah*). Existing family foundations were to be distributed among their beneficiaries and the creation of new ones was prohibited. In 1953 all public religious foundations (awqaf khayriyah), except those whose supervisors (*nazirs*) were their founders, were placed in the hands of the Ministry of Awqaf, which was assigned broad new powers to administer their revenues in the best interests of the state.[21] Since then the government has also ordered the registration of the remaining awqaf of a mixed (*mushtarakah*) variety preparatory to their being transferred to the administration of the ministry.

The revolution also developed a radical solution to the questions concerning shari'ah law. The confusion that had characterized Egypt's legal structure since the days of Muhammad Ali was ended dramatically in 1955 when the regime suddenly announced the abolition of all religious courts, including those of the minority communities. As of 1 January 1956, shari'ah and other courts were to be absorbed into the secular state system. Henceforth a single system of courts would apply a unified code of laws, a code in which religious statutes would cover only the area of personal status.

The last remaining bastion of autonomous clerical (and Islamic) power was finally breached when the regime imposed upon al-Azhar a sweeping reorganization of its educational system in 1961.[22] The reform reduced the Shaykh al-Azhar to the position of a mere figurehead, placed al-Azhar's various administrations into the hands of laymen appointed by the government, reformed its cur-

21. For a careful study of waqf reform in modern Egypt see the chapter on this subject in Baer, *Social History of Modern Egypt*, pp. 79–92.

22. For a study of how the regime approached the problem of reform for al-Azhar and an analysis of the reform law see my article "Al-Azhar in the Revolution," *Middle East Journal*, Winter 1966, pp. 31–49. One of my subsequent articles reports the failure of the reform to have the desired effect upon the traditional core of religious studies within the university or upon the ulama; see "Al-Azhar: A Millennium of Faithfulness to Tradition," *MID EAST*, April 1970, pp. 34–41.

riculum, and added four modern (secular) faculties. At the same time as the announcement of the Azhar reform the government opened a withering propaganda attack against the ulama in the nation's press, a campaign whose aim was not only to make it difficult for them to mount a defense of their institution by throwing them off balance but also to silence them completely, to drive them from the political arena, and to wrest from them the control of religion itself. Among other things the ulama were accused of medievalism, obstructionism, and obscurantism, and of the formation within Islamic society of a religious aristocracy, or priesthood. Even President Nasser joined in the personal attack upon them by declaring:

> Of course the shaykh does not think of anything except the turkey and the food with which he filled his belly. He is no more than a stooge of reaction, feudalism and capitalism. At that time some shaykhs were trying to deceive us with fatwas of this nature. From the beginning, Islam was a religion of work. The Prophet used to work like everybody else. Islam was never a profession.[23]

Perhaps the most telling charge leveled against the ulama was that their inability to reform their own institutions or to make religious ideals compatible with modern science or conditions was turning the nation away from Islam and bringing into question the validity of the Prophet's revelation. Herein lay the seeds of the regime's evolving activist religious policy, for implicit in this criticism was a rejection of liberal-nationalism for its heavy reliance upon a belief system derived from the Christian West and its banishment of religion and religious principles to the domain of private concern. The military leaders were moving toward a religious solution that had eluded the ulama, Islamic reformers such as Muhammad Abduh and Rashid Rida, the Ikhwan, and the secular liberal-nationalists.[24]

23. Cited in Crecelius, "Al-Azhar in the Revolution," p. 42.

24. The resignation of Western-trained scholars to the growing control by the state is reflected in a statement by Mahmud Hubballah: "Yet, the state that controls the sinews of life has the right, when it wishes, to interfere in religion itself, which becomes dependent upon the wish of the state." "The Challenge of Modern Ideas and Social Values to Muslim Society," *Islamic Literature* 11 (1959): p. 35; cited in Crecelius, "Al-Azhar in the Revolution," p. 37.

The high-water mark of the secular tide was reached in 1962 in the debate on the Charter, the document that was to be Egypt's blueprint for future development. Not wishing to give prominence to conservative religious forces or ideas, the revolution refused to submit to the vociferous demands by the ulama to have the Charter designate Islam the religion of the state.[25] But even as this secular tide reached its highest point, a new wave of antisecular force was beginning to crest. The revolution reversed itself when in 1964 the constitution designated Islam the state religion. Islam remains the religion of the state in the new constitution of 1971.

The revolution has sought to achieve cultural unity no less than institutional unity, for it has viewed social and cultural problems just as seriously as those of a political nature. Liberal-nationalism had spent its strength by the 1930s as Britain's refusal to grant Egypt true independence, growing disillusionment with corrupt democratic institutions, and continuing poverty and social injustice led Egypt's intellectuals to reconsider their former support of rationalism and secularism. P. J. Vatikiotis has observed that

> such leading modernists as Taha Husayn, Muhammad Husayn Haykal, and Mahmud Abbas al-Aqqad, were, by the 1930's, already in hasty retreat from their earlier positions of secular liberalism and the adoption of European culture. Their reverential studies of the early fathers of the Islamic Community smacked of frantic and solicitous apologia for their earlier rationalist-secular attacks upon religion and its cultural heritage. A romantic proclivity for the epic quality of early Islam now became a major characteristic of their writings.[26]

25. The Charter was in fact to mention Islam only once. When it referred to religious matters it spoke in general terms such as the following: "The eternal spiritual values derived from religions are capable of guiding man, of lighting the candle of faith in his life and of bestowing on him unlimited capacities for serving truth, good and love. In their essence all divine messages constituted human revolutions which aimed at the reinstatement of man's dignity and his happiness. It is the prime duty of religious thinkers, then, to preserve for each religion the essence of its divine message." *The Charter* (Cairo: U.A.R. Information Department, 1962), p. 85. The Charter also stated clearly that the revolution would not bow to religious pressure. "The freedom of religious belief," it read, "must be regarded as sacred in our new free life."

26. P. J. Vatikiotis, *The Modern History of Egypt* (New York: Praeger, 1969), p. 323. In a perceptive article Ibrahim Abu-Lughod commented on similar antisecular trends throughout the Arab world in the decade of the 1950s: "Retreat from

This trend has carried right through the revolution.

In considering the antisecular tide that has swept over republican Egypt, we must understand the background and psychology of the Free Officers themselves. Many of those who formed the inner ruling clique around Nasser were, like him, of rural backgrounds, men whose first views were shaped by religious training. Some, including President Sadat, were (and remain) men of deep religious conviction, though their views have not always coincided with those of the ulama of al-Azhar. It was thus natural for them to seek the solutions to Egypt's problems in their own culture rather than in further emulation of the West. The Charter of 1962 marks a clear turning away from total reliance on the West and begins a search for native cultural roots, for it acknowledges that "the real solutions to the problems of one people cannot be imported from the experience of another." [27]

The revolutionary regime took an important first step toward reviving the power of religion in 1954, when, after a Meccan pilgrimage by its leaders, Egypt founded the Islamic Congress in partnership with Pakistan and Saudi Arabia. The work of the congress was quickly paralyzed by political disputes among the three governments, but Egypt, sensing the importance and potential of such an organization, proceeded to create its own Supreme Council for Islamic Affairs. Under the astute direction of a former army major the council has achieved great success in the short period it has been in operation. Among its more important activities is the publication of a highly respected monthly journal, *Minbar al-Islam,* which in my view has become a leading voice of religious reform in the Muslim world. It is significant, moreover, that the most important articles dealing with the reinterpretation of Islamic principles are consistently written by lay intellectuals, such as university professors. Among the most prominent contributors is Hussein al-Shafi'i, a vice-president of the U.A.R., who has a monthly article in the journal.[28]

The regime has not been hesitant to use religious symbols and

the Secular Path? Islamic Dilemmas of Arab Politics," *The Review of Politics* 28 (October 1966): 447–76.

27. *The Charter,* p. 42.

28. An analysis of this trend appears in my article, "Die Religion im Dienste des islamischen Staatssozialismus in Ägypten," *Bustan* 3 (1967): 13–20.

reinterpreted Islamic principles to legitimize its revolutionary programs. "This policy was strengthened," wrote Morroe Berger, "as the regime seemed to recognize more and more that Islam remained the widest and most effective basis for consensus despite all efforts to promote nationalism, patriotism, secularism, and socialism." [29] Besides offering its own interpretations of Islamic tradition, the regime solicits from the ulama formal legal opinions (fatwas) on the entire range of its activities, including birth control, land reform, nationalization, scientific research, foreign policy, and social affairs. The most serious attempt to date to use Islam for the benefit of the regime has been the erection of a socialist ideology on the basis of reinterpreted Islamic principles.[30] All this has made religion once again an important factor in the politics of the nation, but it is the regime, not the ulama, that inevitably introduces Islam into political debate.[31]

As Libya and Egypt continue to draw closer together, the religious character of Libya's dynamic Mu'ammar al-Qaddafi is having a growing impact on Egyptian attitudes and policies. Qaddafi's positive avowal of Islam and his active defense of traditional values and customs are reviving hopes that traditional Islamic principles might yet form the basis of a modern "Islamic" society. Libya's religious policy has also forced President Sadat to adopt a more conservative religious stance in Egypt, for there can be no doubt that many Egyptians look upon Qaddafi as a new champion of Islam in the battle against secularism, westernization, materialism, and atheism.

The very essence of a secular state appears to be missing in Egypt today. It occurs to me that the absence of religious issues in po-

29. Morroe Berger, *Islam in Egypt: Social and Political Aspects of Popular Religion* (Cambridge: At the University Press, 1970), p. 47.

30. The *Minbar al-Islam* contains the single most important attempt by a group of writers to lay out the major concepts of a socialist ideology drawn from Islamic principles. See my "Die Religion in Ägypten."

31. Berger writes, "The danger to religious autonomy in Egypt does not lie in the advent of secularism. The religious establishment has long ceased to aspire to real political control; it has accepted secularism in fact if not in principle. But because religious beliefs and loyalties continue so strong among the people, avowedly secular holders of power are themselves unwilling to be fully secular even though they proclaim themselves socialists and revolutionaries. Controlling all the nation's institutions, it is they who connect religion with poiltics by using it in domestic and international affairs." *Islam in Egypt,* p. 128.

litical debate, the withdrawal of religious groups from the political arena, and the clear separation of religion and politics constitute the true essence of secularism. It is difficult to agree with Donald E. Smith's assertion that the dominance of the polity over religious beliefs, practices, and ecclesiastical structures in itself is a form of secularism.[32] It is not the institutional *relationship* between religion and state (whether or not the polity dominates the religious structure) that is important, nor even who introduces religious considerations into political debate, but the character of the *issues* themselves that constitutes the essence of secularism. Secularism of necessity therefore demands the ability by the individual and the state to make that subtle psychological distinction between religion and politics, to be able to accept willingly a public sphere where rational, secular concepts and principles are dominant and a private sphere where religious principles prevail —to be able, in short, to know what to render unto Caesar and what to render unto God.

Most studies on the process of modernization or secularism recognize the necessity for *all* systems by which man lives, the psychological and intellectual no less than the political or economic, to undergo transformation.[33] We do not find this change in Egypt, whether at the level of the state or society, except among a small, sophisticated minority. Traditional beliefs, practices, and values reign supreme among Egypt's teeming village population and among the majority of urban masses. The ability of sufism to survive as such a widespread movement, among educated middle and upper classes no less than among the lower ones, ought to give caution to those who might be tempted to exaggerate the extent of secularization in modern Egypt.[34] The political force and in-

32. Smith, *Religion and Political Development*, p. 86.

33. Halpern, *Politics of Social Change*, and C. E. Black, *The Dynamics of Modernization* (New York: Harper & Row, 1966), refer to the necessity of changing one's psychological system. Smith, *Religion and Political Deevelopment*, pp. 113–18, refers to this process as polity-transvaluational secularization.

34. During many nights in attendance at sufi dhikrs in Cairo in 1969 and 1972 I was struck by the middle-class backgrounds and dress of the dervishes I met. College graduates such as lawyers, pharmacists, bureaucrats, teachers, doctors, bankers, even members of the secret police and generals of the army participated in the ceremonies with deep devotion and/or fervor. Citing an incredible story revealed by Mohamed Hassanein Heikal in his daily *al-Ahram*, the *Los Angeles Times* of 4 June 1971 reported that former General Mohamed Fawzi and former Interior Minister Sharawi

tensity of such movements as the Muslim Brotherhood indicate that even urban, educated middle classes continue to be swayed by traditional symbols and the promise of a resurrected Islamic government. Secular concepts have thus made little headway in Egypt. Even the ulama, though they mouth the phrases of Arab nationalism or Islamic socialism, remain unalterably opposed to any ideology that seeks to divide the religious unity of the universal ummah or is contrary to revealed truth.

The use of religion by the revolutionary regime does little, therefore, to spread views on the separation of politics and religion among the masses. Nor does the regime directly challenge the private religious views of its citizens. It has not entirely eliminated the kuttab, where many Egyptians receive their first educational experience by the rod of a traditional shaykh, nor does it prevent the dervish orders from playing a prominent role in the public religious celebrations that mark the nation's major holidays. On the contrary, it supports their participation by providing funds or equipment for *mawlid*s (celebrations of saints' birthdays) or *dhikr*s (the dervish ceremony of worship).

Morroe Berger has also observed this failure on the part of the revolution to complete the secularization process. He notes that

> the military regime's denial of political influence to the ulama is not secularism. . . . Secularism means separation of church and state and the latter's supremacy; it does not call for the state's control of the intimate details of religious teaching or the harnessing of religion to the purposes of the government of the day.[35]

The regime continues its reform of Islamic institutions, such as al-Azhar and waqf, while at the same time using them for its own political purposes. Even personal status law, which many regarded as the unchangeable heart of the shari'ah, has been revised by the

---

Gomaa participated in spiritualist seances. "The general called on the spirit of a dead sheik to find out the best time for attacking Israel, it was stated." Such a story indicates that policy decisions of the highest importance might not be made entirely on a rational basis. Indeed, I have noticed a seemingly pervasive spirit among Egyptians that some sort of divine intervention, such as the shaykh's advice in this case, will overcome Israeli technology, organization, and military power.

35. Berger, *Islam in Egypt*, p. 128.

regime. Polygamy, for instance, has been made exceedingly difficult, and women have been given a vast range of new liberties, including the right to initiate divorce proceedings.

None of the Islamic institutions in Egypt has retained its traditional form. The sultanate-caliphate has disappeared altogether,
the ulama have lost their monopoly over the interpretation of
Allah's law and education, institutions such as waqf or the shari'ah
have been radically changed, and classical religiopolitical concepts
have been rejected or seriously reworked. Yet for all this change,
Egypt remains an Islamic state, secular in part, but nevertheless
preserving the one vital link that connects state and society to
God. Even as it changes the shari'ah in a drastic manner and
expands the sources from which legal principles can be drawn, it
does not repudiate the *theoretical* primacy of the shari'ah and continues to argue that *shar'i* principles govern the ummah.

Western scholars have generally considered the secularization of
Islamic law to have been almost completed and point to the state's
changes in the personal status codes as the final destruction of the
shari'ah. Yet the crucial *theoretical* link between the state and the
sacred law remains. Modern Muslims have generally taken offense
at the tendency by Western scholars to view the process of legal
reform as one of gradual disintegration of shari'ah law. In a
caustic criticism of this tendency Abdallah L. Tibawi wrote,

> On the one hand they allege that Islam is too "rigid" and ad-
> mits of little change in its system. On the other, when far-
> reaching changes are made in the application of Islamic law,
> those same advocates miss no opportunity to point out that
> such changes undermine the shari'ah.[36]

The modern Egyptian state has regained control of religious
institutions and religion in the manner of some of the classical
Islamic states. It assumes responsibility for religious interpretation,
determines what role Islam will play in political life, and or-
ganizes the religious life of the nation. This leads us to question
whether any Islamic state will formally sever the final link (the
sacred law) between God and man and whether religious institu-

36. Tibawi, "English Speaking Orientalists," *The Muslim World* 53 (July 1963):
p. 202.

tions can be cut fully loose from the state in a system where previously they were bound together in an organic relationship. The continued use of religion by the modernizing state will seriously retard the clear separation of religion and state into private and public spheres and may adversely affect the evolution of an unambiguous rational spirit in Egypt.

5

Secularization Conflicts in Israel

NORMAN L. ZUCKER

Judaism, for millennia, was a religion in search of a polity. In this respect it differs dramatically from the other religions considered in this book. Nonetheless, because Judaism is integrally related to the new polity of Israel, like the older societies with traditional religiopolitical systems, Israel also faces secularization conflicts. Throughout the Dispersion of the Jews the concepts of exile (*galut*) and redemption and return to Zion (*geulah*) memorialized the glories of past nationhood, reconciled the Jew to his circumstance, and foretold an elusive golden future when there would be "the end of the days" and the Children of Israel would dwell again in their rightful land. The internal religious apotheosis of the Land of Israel coupled with the external realities of persecution and harassment to produce a unique form of Jewish nationalism that culminated in the modern secular-directed Zionist movement of the nineteenth and twentieth centuries and the ultimate establishment of the state of Israel in May 1948.

With the creation of Israel, the Jewish people for the first time had to face the problem of how Judaism, as a communal religion, could operate within the framework of a modern, democratic state. During their Dispersion, Jews had never been confronted with the problem of adapting Jewish law to the exigencies of an autonomous, industrialized, secular state. Religious law had prevailed within the confines of the ghetto, and there were few areas in which religious law was inadequate to the needs of the community. With the emancipation from ghetto existence and gradual assimilation into the various bodies politic, operative religious law, no longer subject to rigid communal enforcement, became

This chapter was written with the assistance of Naomi Flink Zucker.

voluntary. The emancipated Jew in the Diaspora had a choice. He could choose to abide by either secular practice or religious law or, in the vast majority of cases, to evolve according to his own conscience and personality an accommodation of the two. But such accommodations are more easily made by individuals than by governments, and with the creation of the state of Israel, the problem was magnified.

Secularization conflicts, more than any other topic in Israel's polemic ideological atmosphere, tend to be argued in extreme terms. At issue are different belief systems. Orthodox Judaism provides for total regulation of society. All temporal acts have spiritual relevance and must, accordingly, conform to a strict religious code of law that is subject to rabbinic interpretation. Religious issues are not "private" matters affecting only the rabbinate and the observant; they are of primary public concern because they involve claims of legitimacy that are dependent on the state for action and enforcement. The nonreligious Jewish Israeli and the minority of non-Jewish Israelis are affected too, and the issue of religion in a free society is raised. Religious issues frequently become political issues because of the Israeli political system, which has nourished religious parties.

IMPACT OF THE RELIGIOUS POLITICAL PARTIES

Israel's Knesset, a 120-member unicameral assembly, is elected from the country at large (i.e., a single national constituency), on the basis of proportional representation. Any party polling 1 percent of the countrywide vote is entitled to seats in the Knesset. Growing out of the Knesset is the cabinet, which under the leadership of the prime minister acts as the executive or government. Proportional representation, a history of party ideological doctrinairism, and a relatively stable distribution of the electorate's allegiance among the various parties have encouraged multipartyism which, in turn, has required coalition government. The largest party, Mapai, has never had a clear majority in the Knesset and has been forced to acquire coalition partners.[1] Accordingly, to date,

1. Mapai, the largest and most pluralistic of all Israeli parties, has always been the principal party in the government. In the 1965 Knesset election Mapai and another secular left party, Achdut ha-Avodah, ran as an electoral alliance under the rubric Alignment. After the Six-Day War, Rafi, a splinter party from Mapai,

all long-term Israeli governments have consisted of coalitions led by Mapai or by the Mapai-dominated Israel Labor party (ILP) and predicated on the inclusion of the National Religious party (NRP).

The NRP, the largest and most theologically moderate of the three religious parties, has been included in the coalitions, not because the leading party agrees with its theological stance, but for purely partisan reasons. The NRP has been used by Mapai-ILP to act as a buffer between the competing pulls of the secular right and left parties and to protect its own programatic objectives from the erosion of secular coalition compromises. The NRP thus acquired a position of strategic leverage and, despite the fact that it has never commanded more than twelve Knesset seats, enjoys a position of political importance disproportionate to its actual strength. As a coalition member, the NRP has acted to move Israel closer to its conception of a Judaic state. The NRP has had the assistance in this of the two smaller ultra-Orthodox religious parties, Agudat Israel and Poale Agudat Israel. While all three religious parties want Israel to become theocentric, they differ in emphasis and approach.

The National Religious party is an outgrowth of the Mizrachi (an abbreviation of Hebrew words meaning "spiritual center") movement founded by European Jews in 1901 to infuse the spirit of Orthodoxy into secular political Zionism. Mizrachi organized as a political party in Palestine in 1918 as

> that party in Zionism which strives for the upbuilding of the Jewish national home . . . on the basis of Israel's religious traditions in the belief that the Land of Israel was not intended to be merely a dwelling place of the Jewish people but also the abode of the Jewish spirit. The party's synthesis of its philosophy is well indicated in its slogan: the land of Israel for the people of Israel on the basis of the Torah of Israel.[2]

---

merged with Mapai and Achdut ha-Avodah under the name Israel Labor party. In 1969, prior to the Knesset election, Mapam, still another secular left party, joined the Israel Labor party in an electoral alliance. For a discussion of party fusion and faction, and other points developed in this chapter, see Norman L. Zucker, *The Coming Crisis in Israel: Private Faith and Public Policy* (Cambridge: M.I.T. Press, 1973).

2. Joseph Dunner, *The Republic of Israel: Its History and Its Promise* (New York: McGraw-Hill, 1950), p. 131.

In 1922, some industrial workers and farmers, dissatisfied with the conservative economic attitudes of the body, split and formed Ha-Poel ha-Mizrachi party (the Spiritual Center Workers party). Ha-Poel ha-Mizrachi stressed a program that integrated Orthodoxy, socialism, and Zionism and established Orthodox collective farms and cooperatives in an attempt to counteract similar activities undertaken by the secular Zionists. For Israel's first election in 1949, the two Mizrachi parties joined in an electoral alliance with the two ultra-Orthodox Agudat Israel parties, under the rubric United Religious Front. In the two subsequent elections, in 1951 and 1955, the two Mizrachi parties, unable to agree with the two Agudah parties, ran together as an electoral alliance under the name National Religious party. In 1956 the two Mizrachi factions formally fused and retained the name National Religious party. With the exception of the 1965 election when it dropped slightly to a low of eleven Knesset seats, in all other elections following the merger (1959, 1961, and 1969) the NRP has won 10 percent of the Knesset membership, twelve seats.

More rigidly Orthodox than the Mizrachi factions are the Agudah parties. Agudat Israel (Union of Israel) was founded in Europe in 1912 and is the organizational home of those ultra-Orthodox who are willing to participate in the Israeli political process. Agudat Israel believes that

> the aim of the party is to enable the Jewish people throughout the world to live according to the principles and practical precepts of the Torah, eternally in force for the public life of the Jewish people, and directing the life of the individual as far as that is connected with the former.
>
> . . . The party works towards the goal that the Jewish State should be based on the laws of Torah.[3]

In the prestate period, Agudat Israel opposed Zionism and the Mizrachi movement and did not participate in the organizational life of the Jewish community in Palestine (*Yishuv*). This reluctance to join with other parties was based on the belief that cooperation with irreligious elements would compromise their Orthodox Torah position. Agudat Israel conceived of national reconstruction

---

3. L. Berger, ed., *The Israel Yearbook: 1969* (Tel Aviv: Israel Yearbook Publications Ltd., 1969), p. 307.

mainly as the building of theological seminaries (*yeshivot*). After the creation of the state, Agudat Israel changed its position and agreed to participate in the political process.

Poale Agudat Israel (Workers of the Union of Israel) is the labor wing of Agudat Israel. It was founded in Warsaw in 1922 with the object of counteracting the antireligious and un-Orthodox sentiments and practices among the workers. In 1934, Poale Agudat Israel began to establish rural villages in Palestine on the principle that the Messiah would come only if his chosen people merited redemption in the Holy Land. The political aim of the Poale Agudat Israel, like that of its parent body, "is the transformation of the State of Israel into the Torah State which bases its constitution, legislation, and the manner of life of its residents on the written Torah and tradition." The essential difference between the parent body and its labor faction is that Agudat Israel stresses relations of man to God and concentrates its attention on the study of religious literature to prepare for God's redemption, while the worker party's approach is more activist: God's intention will be realized by human exertion.

Agudat Israel and Poale Agudat Israel ran together as the Torah Religious Front in the elections of 1951, 1955, and 1959, receiving five, six, and six Knesset seats. In 1961, 1965, and 1969 they ran separately; Agudat Israel won four seats in each election and Poale Agudat Israel won two.

The hold of the religious parties on a segment of the electorate has been significant. The percentage vote for the combined religious parties has been 12.2 percent in 1949, 11.9 percent in 1951, 13.8 percent in 1955, 14.6 percent in 1959, 15.4 percent in 1961, 13.9 percent in 1965, and 14.7 percent in 1969.[4] (However, religious sentiments are more widespread than straight electoral patterns show; observant Jews also vote for some of the secular parties.)

WRITTEN CONSTITUTION OR TORAH STATE

The first major secularization struggle that took place in Israel occurred over the basic issue of a constitution. In many respects

---

4. Zucker, *The Coming Crisis*. See also Ervin Birnbaum, *The Politics of Compromise: State and Religion in Israel* (Rutherford, N.J.: Fairleigh Dickinson University Press, 1970), pp. 317–18.

the deliberations over the question of a written constitution were a microcosm of the religion-state problem and a foretaste of secularization conflicts that would subsequently agitate Israeli political life.

The debate over the constitution took place during the period of the Provisional Government and later during the first Knesset. Under discussion were a draft constitution and the overall question of whether or not a written constitution should be adopted. Arguments for and against were heated and emotional. This was understandable, for at stake were basic values and symbols, the structuring of practical political and economic power, and the determination of a secular versus religious conception of Israeli nationality. Certain issues continually cropped up, particularly those relevant to the central question: To what extent should the constitution of a Jewish state be of a specifically Jewish character?

Secularists argued bitterly against any attempt to impose a religious way of life on the country. Specifically, they felt that the preamble of the draft constitution had too strong a religious cast. They also felt that Jews, as well as Christians and Muslims, were entitled to the assurances of freedom of conscience, and civil marriage, therefore, should be allowed.

The religious camp was divided in its viewpoints. Some religionists were in a quandary; they readily admitted the desirability in modern society of the draft constitution's provisions regarding female equality and the abolition of the death penalty, but they could not reconcile these provisions with traditional Jewish law. The Mizrachi members believed that the constitution should take a positive stand on Judaism, but unlike the Agudat members they avoided the claim that the law of the Torah was the only legitimate law. The Agudah representatives were negative about the entire concept of a written constitution. For them it would be adequate to declare: "The Torah is Israel's constitution." However, if there had to be a written constitution, it should provide for "the centrality of the Torah in the state's existence." And finally, there were those ultra-Orthodox, not present, who refused to recognize the legitimacy of a secular Jewish state. The Natore Karta sect, the most fanatical of all the ultra-Orthodox, refused to recognize the existence of the state because it had not been established by the Messiah. Noncooperation and nonrecognition were the watchwords. The Natore Kartaites would not even concern themselves with such irrelevancies as a constitution.

There were many practical problems arising out of the concept of a "Torah Constitution." Judaism does not have a political philosophy dealing with the modern democratic nation-state. Talmudic law originated in the land of Israel and developed in the Diaspora, where the Jews had little need to concern themselves with the ordering of a body politic. Consequently, talmudic political concepts were rudimentary and ideas such as constitutional limitation, checks and balances, separation of powers, and presidential or parliamentary structure are unknown in talmudic law.

The constitutional controversy appeared to be irreconcilable. It was contributing to national acrimony and deflecting energies from the pressing tasks of national survival. Accordingly, Prime Minister David Ben-Gurion, who had favored a written constitution during the Provisional Government period, switched positions and forcefully pushed for the postponement of its adoption. The Mizrachi representatives, who earlier had seen no disaccord between their religious views and the possibility of a written constitution, now yielded to the pressure of the more extreme rabbinic leaders of the Agudat Israel and took the position that a written constitution was undesirable at that time. Now they argued that Israel's constitution was to be a bridge between the Jewish past and the Jewish future and must reflect the singular Jewish *volksgeist*. Furthermore, the "Ingathering of the Exiles" was not complete—the constitution should reflect the will not of a few but of all.

The central question of the role of religion in a modern Jewish state deadlocked the Knesset. Any resolution of the issue offensive to either the secularists or the religionists would be no resolution, for a *Kulturkampf* was certain to follow. To resolve this dilemma a compromise resolution was introduced. Under the compromise motion the Constitution, Law, and Justice Committee was directed to prepare a draft constitution that would be constructed, article by article, in such a manner that each article in itself would constitute a fundamental law. Each article would then be brought before the Knesset, as the committee completed its work, and all the articles together, when adopted, would comprise the constitution. This compromise was adopted and debate over the constitution terminated. The principle that the state should have a written constitution was accepted, balanced by the potent hedge that the document would be neither imminent nor comprehensive. For the time being, fundamental laws were to be adopted individually.[5]

The Basic Laws envisioned by the 1950 resolution were slow in coming. A decade passed before the first Basic Law was enacted, in February 1958. Entitled "Basic Law The Knesset," it consolidated legislation previously adopted concerning, primarily, the election and functions of the Knesset. Three other Basic Laws have been adopted: one dealing with the state's lands, another relating to the office of the president, and a third dealing with the government as the state's executive authority. For some, the creation of a constitution by installments has been a disappointing experience. Some important areas, particularly civil liberties, have no established guidelines. To rectify the existing constitutional situation, attempts to reconsider the problem of the constitution were undertaken in the mid-1960s, and in 1967 a Knesset constitution subcommittee was charged with the task of preparing a draft constitution. But some salient facts remain. Despite the considerable criticism of the existing constitutional system, the political process functions successfully. Furthermore, the very same issues are present today that restrained the constitution makers during the Provisional Government and the First Knesset and postponed the completion of a codified constitution. Despite more than twenty years of statehood, a change in the population matrix, and the rapid increase in the number of *sabras* (native Israelis) born after the attainment of statehood, Israel is no closer to a constitutional religion-state definition than it was when the issue first came to the fore. The partisan polemics surrounding religiopoliti-

5. Emanuel Rackman, *Israel's Emerging Constitution: 1948–1951* (New York: Columbia University Press, 1951). Yehuda Leo Kohn, "The Emerging Constitution of Israel," in Moshe Davis, ed., *Israel: Its Role in Civilization* (New York: Harper and Brothers, 1965), pp. 130–45. "Constitution of Israel: Proposed Text," *Jewish Frontier* 16 (1949): pp. 4–9; Amnon Rubinstein, "Israel's Piecemeal Constitution," in G. Tedeschi and U. Yadin, eds., *Studies in Israel Legislative Problems* (Jerusalem: Hebrew University, 1966), pp. 201–18. For Ben-Gurion's argument why a written constitution should be postponed see David Ben-Gurion, *Rebirth and Destiny of Israel* (New York: Philosophical Library, 1954), pp. 363–80.

cal issues are no less strident, the passions no less fiery, and the righteousness of the militant secularists and religionists not at all diminished with the passage of time.

In the avoidance of a Kulturkampf, state and religion have been neither wedded nor divorced. A secular state has been established; but, given the presence of the religious parties and the open-endedness of the compromise, "private" religious questions will continue to be "public" in character. In the words of Chief Rabbi Yitzchak Ha-Levi Herzog, the "synthesis of democracy and theocracy" is still to be worked out. The result of the constitutional compromise has been the continuation of coalition politics. The basic religion-state relationship will be defined in the future through the political process.

RELIGIOPOLITICAL MODUS VIVENDI

In the more than two decades since the debate over the constitution, the pressure tactics employed by the religious parties have been abetted, sometimes, by a feeling of nationalism springing from religious tradition and a common ethnic and cultural heritage shared with the secularists. As a result, the following organizational and legal relationships between the state and Orthodox Judaism have come about.

1. The Chief Rabbinate, the local religious councils and religious committees, and the Ministry of Religious Affairs are the monopoly of Orthodox Judaism and are supported by the state.

2. The legal system delegates to the rabbinate's religious courts exclusive jurisdiction in marriage, divorce, and certain aspects of personal status.

3. The state promotes Orthodox norms through the passage of various discrete legislative acts having a religious relevance.

The Chief Rabbinate is the institutionalized Orthodox religious authority. It interprets Jewish law (*halakhah*), supervises and certifies rabbinical ordination, certifies rabbis to teach in religious state schools, controls the training of religious judges, licenses religious scribes and circumcisers, and enforces dietary regulations (*kashrut*). (It is the Chief Rabbinate's power to determine the validity of a rabbinical degree that enables it to monitor marriage, divorce, dietary regulations, etc.) The religious authority of the Chief Rabbinate, however, is not absolute. The ultra-

Orthodox follow their own leaders and do not necessarily accept
the jurisdiction of the Chief Rabbinate. The Ministry of Religious Affairs, a secular bureaucracy closely associated with the religious parties (primarily the NRP), works closely with the rabbinate and actively promotes Orthodox Judaism. The ministry is
responsible to the Knesset for the general administration of the
rabbinical courts and holy places. Working with the rabbinate
and the local religious councils, and in the smaller localities with
religious committees, the ministry helps finance talmudic acad-
emies and contributes money toward the building and maintaining of synagogues. The local religious councils and religious committees, as their names imply, deal on the local level with a variety
of public services of a religious nature. They sustain the general
services of the rabbinate and rabbinical courts. In addition, for
fees, they supervise ritual slaughter, issue certificates of kashrut,
and register marriages and divorces. Fees alone, however, cannot
support the councils and committees, and financing is provided
by the national and local governments.

The minister of religious affairs, a political official, plays an
important role—which may have far-reaching political and theological overtones—in the ordinary administration of his office
and in the process by which the two chief rabbis and the Supreme
Religious Council are elected. A neutral or hostile minister, potentially a possibility if a strong secularist-oriented government
ever achieves a solid power base, could attempt to either neutralize or hamper state support to the rabbinate. To date, however, the ministry has acted to enhance the power of the Orthodox, particularly since 1961 when Dr. Zerah Warhaftig of the
National Religious party, an able exponent of his party's principles and objectives, became the minister of religious affairs.

This alliance between established Orthodoxy and the state has
been in contradiction to the foundations of the state. Israel's
Proclamation of Independence guarantees freedom of religion and
conscience. But it became necessary for the cabinet to issue a
statement reaffirming religious liberty.[6] The Chief Rabbinate and
the Ministry of Religious Affairs have officially refused to rec-

6. For a discussion of some of the problems besetting Reform Judaism in Israel
see Mendel Kohansky, "Reform Judaism Meets in Israel," *Midstream* 14 (1968): pp.
54–61.

ognize Judaism's Reform wing and have an uneasy relationship with Conservative Judaism. The Orthodox argue that Conservative and Reform Judaism were responses to Judaism's minority status in a Christian setting and that they therefore have no place in a Jewish state. It is paradoxical that in a secular state, the Orthodox rabbinate has attained establishment status and now so jealously guards its position that Conservative and Reform Judaism have to look to the government and the courts for protection of their rights.

THE RABBINATE, RELIGIOUS LAW, AND THE STATE

One of the ways the established rabbinate attempts to maintain and extend its privileged position is through its control over dietary supervision. Two specific controversies in the area of dietary regulations are illustrative. When Zim Israel Navigation Co., Ltd., a government-supported corporation, announced its intention of having both a kosher and nonkosher kitchen on its flagship, the S.S. *Shalom,* the Chief Rabbinate threatened to revoke the certificates of kashrut of *all* of Zim's vessels and the NRP threatened to resign from the coalition and precipitate a cabinet crisis. After much bickering and cries from the secularists that they were being denied dietary freedom of choice, the *Shalom* sailed the Atlantic with only a kosher kitchen. The Chief Rabbinate was less successful, however, when it tried to prevent a regional abattoir, Marbek, from marketing its meat as kosher. The Rabbinate maintained that for meat to be kosher it had to be ritually slaughtered in the locality where the meat was to be consumed. Most people saw this contention as a device on the part of the Rabbinate to protect the fees of the religious councils. Unable to work out slaughtering arrangements with the Rabbinate, Marbek employed an ultra-Orthodox Natore Karta rabbi to supervise ritual slaughtering and certify the meat as kosher. The Rabbinate, incensed that a nonestablishment rabbi was being used to thwart them, withdrew certificates of dietary purity from shops and supermarkets that carried Marbek's meat. The withdrawal of certification affected not only meat but all products sold. In response, Marbek's management went to the secular courts and requested an order nisi requiring the Chief Rabbinate to show cause why it refused to undertake kashrut supervision at

the abattoir. The Supreme Court ruled it was competent to hold
hearings on the order nisi. Marbek requested that the Court
make the order nisi absolute because, they alleged, the Rabbinate's refusal to give them a nationwide kashrut certificate was
based on grounds other than halakhah. The attorney general,
whose presence attested to the importance of the case, stated that
in his opinion the rabbinate was within its legal right to base its
decisions on halakhah, but the High Court certainly had the
power to determine whether or not the Rabbinate was basing its
decisions on halakhic principles. When the Court published its
rationale for holding the Chief Rabbinical Council subject to its
jurisdiction, it pointed out that the Rabbinate exercises its public
functions by state law, and therefore, in the absence of a Knesset
declaration to the contrary, its acts are like those of any other
public body in that they are subject to High Court surveillance.

The Rabbinate was now faced with a problem. They were
respondents to a court order, and if they refused to appear in
court, the order could be made absolute. If they refused to comply, that is, to supervise kashrut at Marbek, the High Court could
then issue a contempt of court citation against the Rabbinate.
The possibility of a clear-cut confrontation between the High
Court and the Rabbinate loomed but never came. A compromise
was arrived at out of court. Marbek was allowed to market its
meat as kosher. The Marbek incident was a successful challenge
to the right of the Rabbinate to withhold or revoke certificates
of kashrut in order to compel obedience. In addition, the secular
court strongly articulated its right of judicial scrutiny of certain
of the Rabbinate's acts. An important step in the process of secularization had taken place.[7]

The rabbinical courts have exclusive jurisdiction primarily in
matters of marriage and divorce. But the secular authorities impose penal sanctions when a person refuses to comply with a
rabbinical court ruling. In other areas of personal status, rabbinical courts enjoy concurrent jurisdiction with civil courts, but
only by option of all the litigants. Moreover, there has been
circumscription by the Knesset of religious law (frequently over

---

7. Succinct summaries of the *Shalom* and Marbek incidents are given in Morris
Fine and Milton Himmelfarb, eds., *American Jewish Yearbook 1965* (New York:
The American Jewish Committee, 1965), pp. 463–64.

the objections of the religious parties). This circumscription has taken place in particular in areas where religious law is anachronistic. For example, the Marriage Age law, the Women's Equal Rights law, the Guardianship law, the Succession (Inheritance) law, and so on are all secular incursions that restrict, in some manner, traditional religious law.

Other restrictions on the rabbinic courts have come from the civil courts. Izhak Englard, in a scholarly and perceptive assessment, has summarized the existing situation:

> The division of jurisdiction between the rabbinical and civil courts is an unending source of friction. The rabbinical court considers its authority, according to the view of Halakhah, to be extremely wide. The civil court, which has residuary jurisdiction in all matters, sees in the rabbinical courts a special judicial system with limited powers as defined by law. In interpreting the laws defining the jurisdiction of the rabbinical courts the tendency of the civil courts has been, as appears from the reported decision, to narrow the jurisdiction of rabbinical courts by means of strict interpretation of the law. The High Court of Justice exercises general supervision over the application of the rules of "natural justice" in the proceedings of the religious courts, and takes meticulous care that they should not go beyond their jurisdiction as specified by law. The secular view thus wins out whenever there is a conflict.[8]

Although the Supreme Court has asserted its right of judicial scrutiny over some of the Rabbinate's acts since 1953, the Rabbinate has exercised exclusive jurisdiction over marriage and divorce and other limited aspects of personal status such as maintenance and alimony. The Knesset's decision to eliminate civil marriage and divorce and give them to the officially recognized religious communities was a significant gain for the religionists. Secularists opposed abandoning civil marriage and divorce as a matter of principle. Other opposition was directed not so much to the principle of religious marriage and divorce but to the fact

---

8. Izhak Englard, "The Relationship Between Religion and State in Israel," in Tedeschi and Yadin, *Israel Legislative Problems*, pp. 269–70.

that religious law in this area of personal status has created a
number of specific hardship situations. (For example, under religious law a descendant of a priestly family may not marry a
divorcee; remarriage is often difficult for a woman whose hus-
band's death is suspected but not proven; and the custom of
levirate marriage may be invoked.) Supporters of the religious
marriage and divorce legislation, however, were not confined only
to the religionists. Support also came from a large cross-section
of the population who believed that religious marriage and divorce would serve as a means of preserving and unifying the
Jewish people.[9]

Another aspect of secular-religious controversy is illustrated by
the Dayyanim law. When the Dayyanim law, which deals with the
qualifications, appointments, independence, tenure, and other ad-
mininstrative aspects of rabbinical judges, was passed by the
Knesset in 1955, there was violent debate surrounding it. The
debate centered on the proviso that the rabbinical judges (*dayyanim*), before taking their seats, had to swear allegiance only to
the state of Israel and not to the laws of the state. (Judges in
civil courts are required to swear allegiance to the laws of the
state of Israel.) In arguing successfully against an amendment to
the Dayyanim law that would have required dayyanim to pledge
allegiance to the laws of the state, a representative of Agudat
Israel summarized the feelings of many of the religious when he
stated that where a law of the state conflicted with a religious
law, the dayyan must follow the religious law.[10]

The role of the rabbinical courts within the Israeli legal system
is only part of the total law and religion picture. The very character of Israel's evolving legal system has been enmeshed in an
attempt to answer the root question: What is the role of Jewish
law in a Jewish state?

After the creation of the state, the Provisional Council enacted
a reception statute that incorporated into the laws of Israel a vast

9. For comments and details on the debate over civil marriage and divorce see
Joseph Badi, *The Government of the State of Israel: A Critical Account of Its
Parliament, Executive, and Judiciary* (New York: Twayne Publishers, 1963), pp.
253–54; Eliezer Goldman, *Religious Issues in Israel's Political Life* (Jerusalem: Mador
Dati, 1964), pp. 74–80. Badi's view is prosecular; Goldman's view, proreligious.

10. Englard, "Relationship Between Religion and State," p. 261.

body of jurisprudence that was operative at the time of independence. There were components of French law, Ottoman law, English law, and the religious law of the resident recognized communities. The decision of the Provisional Council to carry over the prevailing legal system was the only practical one at the time. However, the diversity and complexity of the often conflicting legal philosophies, along with the desire to have a legal system responsive to the needs of the new Jewish polity, spurred the movement for an up-to-date, comprehensive system of Israeli law. But, much like the constitution—and for many of the same reasons—the Israeli legal system is evolving piecemeal. Progress is occurring slowly, and at present the legal system is far from homogeneous.

The demand that Jewish law serve as a basis for the Israeli legal system comes from both religious and nonreligious segments of the population, although the desire to incorporate halakhah has come primarily from the religious sector. Some of the Orthodox believe that absorbing halakhah into the legal system would be an intermediate stage in the evolution of Israel into a Torah state. At the same time, many of the nonreligious are willing to see elements of Jewish law incorporated into the fabric of Israeli society. They consider Jewish law a vital ingredient of their cultural heritage and a means of emphasizing the historical continuity of the Jewish people with the Land of Israel. But, though halakhah has many positive aspects—it is adaptable, flexible, and most importantly, humanitarian—these are counterbalanced by very substantial negative aspects. Halakhah is, in many respects, inadequate to the needs of a modern technological society. This is so because, paradoxically, with the emancipation of Western Jewry, the judicial activity of rabbinic courts declined, and halakhah developed substantive lacunae, a circumstance that cannot be tolerated in a viable legal system.

There are also important philosophical problems associated with attempts at any large-scale or total incorporation of halakhah into the Israeli legal system. Can halakhah retain its inspired origin if it is incorporated into the legal system by the legislature? Is this not secularization of divine law? Is not the very act of selective reception a denial of the sanctity of halakhah, which must be accepted in its totality? Can halakhah ever be reconciled with a secularly based Jewish state? For the Orthodox purist, the answer is simple and direct: The divinity of halakhah cannot be compromised; its primacy cannot be denied. Its inclusion into the Israeli body politic as a shared, selected element is a purely political activity having no relevance to theology. Halakhah will prevail when, and only when, Israel becomes a truly Jewish Torah state effectuated through God's divine intervention in the form of messianic redemption.

This position, however, is not shared by most of the religious population. The objections raised by the theological purists are bypassed by most of the religious population, who place a religious interpretation upon the creation of the state. The historical reality of the state of Israel and all its secular apparatus can be explained by them as the beginning of redemption. Man must work toward a perfect Torah state, and the vehicle for such work is politics. Selective incorporation of halakhah is a small step in the right direction.

Notwithstanding the rationale, the confluence of the religious and nationalistic ideological streams has had practical results. There has been the enactment of Jewish content into the legal system. The Ministry of Justice maintains an adviser on Jewish law who actively tries to incorporate, where possible, principles of Jewish law into all draft legislation submitted to the Knesset. The present situation has been delineated by Menachem Elon, one of Israel's leading authorities on Jewish law. Elon has written:

> Jewish law has been a considerable source of legislation by the Knesset and . . . resort or reference to it was a matter of some regularity in the various legislative processes. How far it has formed the basis of such legislation varies from subject to subject. In criminal and public law it does so to a limited extent. In civil law its contribution is greater and in family and succession law considerable. We do not infer the fact that a given law is based upon Jewish principles merely because its content embodies such principles but also because the different elements that operate in the legislative field—the Government and its representatives and the Knesset and its members—emphasize specifically in the Explanatory Notes to Bills and in the course of debate in the Knesset that

the source of an enactment falls within the Jewish Law. Although in point of law the statements made in the Explanatory Notes and in the Knesset are not binding upon the courts in construing any particular law, in point of jurisprudential and historical truth such statements indicate the source from which it is drawn, and it is to be presumed that the courts are fully conscious of the fact when they interpret that law. . . .

There are, however, many other Laws which do not rest on Jewish Law. There are various reasons for this. One of them certainly is the degree of preparedness of Jewish Law on a particular topic but our investigations have shown that this reason is far from being decisive. At times provisions contrary to Jewish Law have been enacted in the clear knowledge and acknowledgment that the Knesset is not prepared to accommodate itself to one or other given principle.[11]

In short, religion-state conflicts in the legal system have been resolved by the compromises inherent in the operation of the political system.

In addition to legislation applying to the rabbinical courts, political accommodation, aided by its sometime ally, nationalism, has also been responsible despite secular opposition for Knesset passage of various discrete legislative acts having some religious relevance. By a series of piecemeal steps, Orthodoxy, to some extent, has been incorporated into the Israeli body politic. The Days of Rest ordinance prescribes the Sabbath and the Jewish festivals as nonworking days. The Kosher Food for Soldiers ordinance, as its name implies, guarantees kosher food to military personnel. The Jewish Religious Services Budgets law and amendment provide for state funding to the Orthodox through the religious councils. The Anatomy and Pathology law recognizes religious objections to dissection. The National Service law grants concessions to religious women. The State Education law establishes an education system in which the state supports a network of religious state schools run by the Mizrachi and subsidizes the "recognized" ultra-Orthodox schools of the Agudat Israel. The

11. Menachem Elon, "The Sources and Nature of Jewish Law and Its Application in the State of Israel," *Israel Law Review* 4 (1969): pp. 138–39.

Pork Prohibition law makes the raising of pigs illegal throughout the country except in certain centers of Christian population.

THE "WHO IS A JEW?" CONFLICT

Recently, the Knesset opted for the religionists' view in the "Who is a Jew?" conflict between Jewish religious nationalism and emergent Israeli secular nationalism. The "Who is a Jew?" debate involved several phases. In the first phase, Israel Bar-Yehudah, a secularist-oriented minister of the interior, issued a directive in March 1958 to the offices of the Registry of Citizens that touched off a storm. This directive was intended to introduce some consistency into the registration of Israeli residents, who carry identity cards on which are listed "religion" and "nationality." The minister's directives allowed each person to be registered in accordance with the information given by him or by his parents. This meant that if a non-Jewish woman declared in the registry office that she was Jewish, she and her child would be so registered. The NRP representatives to the cabinet reacted sharply to the directive, charged a violation of the status quo set by the coalition agreement, and demanded a discussion. The resultant interministerial discussions, however, did not fundamentally alter the situation and the following instructions were issued by Bar-Yehudah's office in regard to

> Any person declaring in good faith that he is a Jew and is not of another religion. . . . If both members of a married couple declare that their child is Jewish, this declaration shall be regarded as though it were the legal declaration of the child itself. . . . The registering official need not be concerned over the fact that according to the law of the Torah (in case one of the parents is non-Jewish) the child has the same status as its mother. . . . The parents' declaration that their child is Jewish suffices to register him as Jewish.[12]

The implications of this directive were clearly unacceptable to

12. Baruch Litvin, comp., and Sidney B. Hoenig, ed., *Jewish Identity: Modern Response and Opinions on the Registration of Children of Mixed Marriages* (New York: Phillip Feldheim, 1965), p. 314. This book gives a comprehensive account of the first phase of the "Who is a Jew?" controversy.

the religious ministers, and they resigned. According to the instructions anyone, no matter what his faith, could identify himself as Jewish for purposes of national identification. The secularists argued that since the register had a civil and not a religious purpose, religious criteria for determining Judaism were not relevant. The Orthodox refused to accept this reasoning, and the NRP ministers resigned from the cabinet. Ben-Gurion needed the leverage of the religious ministers and looked for a way out of the deadlock. Despite a committee being set up, the question of "Who is a Jew?" for identity card purposes was not resolved until after the 1959 elections. Coalition stability once again required the presence of the NRP. The NRP returned to the cabinet in exchange for the Ministry of the Interior. The NRP minister immediately issued new instructions to the registrars defining a Jew as "a person born of a Jewish mother who does not belong to another religion, or one who was converted in accordance with religious law." The Orthodox viewpoint prevailed and so ended phase one.

Phase two began in November 1962 when the judgment in *Oswald Rufeisen* v. *the Minister of the Interior* was handed down by the High Court. The Court in a 4–1 decision upheld the validity of the interior minister's definition of a Jew as "a person born of a Jewish mother who does not belong to another religion." The "who" clause was at odds with some rabbinic dicta which held that a converted Jew remains a Jew. On the basis of these dicta, Oswald Rufeisen, more commonly known as Brother Daniel, a Jewish convert to Christianity, applied for the right of automatic citizenship under the Law of Return. The majority denied Rufeisen's petition, holding that the term "Jew" as used in the Law of Return had a secular meaning and was not identical with the religious meaning of the term "Jew" as used in the Marriage and Divorce law. Another step in the direction of defining Israeli nationalism had been taken and phase two of the "Who is a Jew?" issue concluded.[13]

The third phase involved the Shalit case and its legislative aftermath. Benjamin Shalit, a Jew born in Haifa, married a non-

13. The Supreme Court. *Judgment: High Court Application of Oswald Rufeisen v. The Minister of the Interior, State of Israel* (Jerusalem: The Ministry of Justice, 1963).

Jewish woman. The couple considered themselves "nonbelievers" and attempted to register their children in the population registry as being Jewish by ethnic affiliation. The minister of the interior refused to register the children as Jewish by ethnic affiliation because the mother was Gentile and under religious law, in the absence of conversion, the children could not be considered Jewish. Shalit appealed to the courts to have his children registered as Jewish by nationality. The High Court was now faced with determining if Jewish nationality in its ethnic connotation was identical with Jewish religious affiliation. The link between Jewish religion and Israeli secular nationalism was at issue. For the secularist it was possible for the child of a non-Jewish mother to embrace Jewish nationality and identify historically and emotionally with the Jewish people, religious criteria notwithstanding. For the religionist, Jewish nationality was impossible without Jewish religious identification. The Court tried to sidestep the issue by suggesting to the cabinet that the entry "nationality" in identity cards and the population registry be abrogated. This the government refused to do and the Court had to face the issue. In January 1970, by a 5–4 vote, the High Court ruled that the minister of the interior had to register the Shalit children as Jewish by nationality even though their mother was Gentile.

The court's ruling in favor of a secular concept of Israeli nationality unleashed a furious protest from the religionists. The NRP ministers threatened to defect from the coalition unless legislation nullifying the Shalit decision was forthcoming. The government agreed to the religionists' demands and, after several stormy Knesset sessions, the Knesset passed legislation overthrowing the Shalit ruling. Henceforth Israeli nationality was officially tied to Jewish religious criteria. Another aspect of the religion-state definition had been resolved. The issue, however, remains far from settled as there still remains the problem of conversion. Conflict can be expected between the religionists, who insist that conversion according to halakhah can only be performed by Orthodox rabbis, and others, who argue that an acceptable conversion can be performed by rabbis who are not recognized by the established rabbinate.[14]

14. *High Court Ruling in "Who is a Jew?" Case* (Pamphlet reprinted from the *Jerusalem Post*, 25 January 1970).

PROSPECTS FOR SECULARIZATION

Specific secularization conflicts, like the conversion dispute, will certainly continue to agitate the Israeli political process. The existence of the religious parties alone is sure to guarantee this. Should a coalition be formed without any of the religious parties, thus sharply diminishing their bargaining power, the fact that they represent a not inconsiderable segment of the population will assure the continuance of religiopolitical conflicts. As long as the rabbinate remains in its preferred position, there will be conflicts of authority with the secular government and with Reform and Conservative Judaism. Further, the Orthodox rabbinate is likely to fight any attempts at its disestablishment or the attenuation of its powers. But secular circumscription of the rabbinate has begun in the courts and will not abate. Nor will the secular government permit the rabbinate to push its positions too far. Significantly, a number of the Orthodox have come to recognize that the organized rabbinate has become a political interest group, in derogation of the rabbinate's spiritual mission. Within Orthodoxy itself, a movement has begun for the depoliticization of the rabbinate.

Although the primary culture of Israel is secular, and the polity has never derived its legitimacy from religion, nevertheless it has sought to buttress its emergent nationalism by affirming, wherever possible, Judaic roots and customs, thereby interweaving strands of secular nationalism with theological nationalism. The attainment of complete secularization in Israel is going to be difficult and, given the unique fusion of Judaism with nationhood and the historic experience of Judaism as a communal religion throughout the Dispersion, perhaps impossible.

6

Patterns of Secularization in Latin America

DONALD E. SMITH

The general processes of secularization in Latin American polities and societies are similar to those taking place in other parts of the Third World and can be analyzed in the same terms. However, the distinctive features of the Latin American reality are no less important and have powerfully influenced the patterns of secularization. In this essay I shall first analyze the elements of Latin American uniqueness and then relate these to the five general processes of secularization discussed in chapter 1.

LATIN AMERICAN DISTINCTIVENESS

Generalizations about Latin America are notoriously vulnerable, but I refer here to basic sociological and historical facts that, on one hand, are generally true of all Latin America and, on the other, have no close parallels elsewhere in the Third World. Three sets of factors are of fundamental importance: (1) the structure and ideology of the Roman Catholic church, (2) the continuing regalist tradition of church-state relations, and (3) the phenomenon of anticlericalism.

The unique character of the Catholic ecclesiastical organization requires little comment. It is perhaps sufficient to remind ourselves of Max Weber's inclusion of the Catholic church, along with the modern European state, in his short list of "distinctly developed and quantitatively large bureaucracies." [1] The hierarchical and authoritarian nature of the church structure, which emerged early in its history, permitted certain kinds of relationships with political authority and society that were not found in the non-Catholic

1. H. H. Gerth and C. Wright Mills, eds., *From Max Weber: Essays in Sociology* (New York: Oxford University Press, 1958), p. 204.

world. While Buddhism also developed a church system, the Sangha hierarchy did not exist apart from royal appointments and had no authoritarian orientation.

Combined with this highly organized Catholic church structure was an ideology that claimed large areas of social, economic, and political life as the church's legitimate sphere of influence and legislative competence. The church claimed exclusive rights in the fields of education and the regulation of family life, and it developed an impressive system of canon law, which on various subjects governed laity as well as clergy, and the judicial machinery (ecclesiastical courts) to enforce it. To continue the comparison suggested in the previous paragraph, while the Sangha did in fact enjoy a monopoly in the field of education, there was no comparable Buddhist ideology of social control.

The Catholic church, with its well-organized, authoritarian structure and ideology of extensive temporal powers, could be understood as a "state within a state" by its defenders as well as by its enemies. The church had impressive organizational and ideological resources to be mobilized in the struggle against the forces of secularization, far greater than those of the Asian religions. By the same token, the church presented a far more concrete and visible target for secularizing movements and regimes: this was a key factor in the emergence of the uniquely Catholic phenomenon of anticlericalism.

The regalist tradition of church-state relations constitutes the second major factor. Regalism was the system under which the Spanish and Portuguese kings dominated the church in their respective colonies in the New World.[2] The rights of royal patronage were so extensive as to deny any autonomy whatsoever to the church. In the appointment of bishops, the demarcation of dioceses, the disciplining of the clergy, the collection of tithes, and other vital matters, the king exercised absolute authority. No communication from the pope reached the church hierarchy in America without the king's permission.

This general pattern of royal promotion and control of religion was of course also found in Hindu, Buddhist, and Muslim religiopolitical systems, but for the most part it broke down under the

2. Harry Kantor elaborates on this point at the beginning of his essay, see chap. 11.

force of Western imperialism. Latin America, however, did not experience a century or more of imperial rule by powers professing religions different from that of their subjects. The independent republics that emerged out of the Spanish Empire in the early nineteenth century insisted that the right of patronage, or control of the church, was "one of the inalienable prerogatives of sovereignty."[3] The political leaders of the new states, for the most part, fought tenaciously to establish and exercise this right. Historically, of course, the claims to national patronage were well founded; if the republics inherited the sovereign powers exercised by the former empire, control of the church was undoubtedly one of them. The national patronage, however, introduced serious complications in church-state relations and profoundly influenced the subsequent course of secularization.

The heart of the matter was that the Spanish and Portuguese kings, and their viceroys and other officials, shared a basic value system, Catholicism, with the church hierarchy and clergy. During the colonial period there was a high degree of ideological consensus in the ruling elites of the church and state. Royal control of the church was virtually complete, but the church still prospered in terms of material wealth and temporal influence. After independence, however, the stage was set for radically new conflicts stemming from the use of the patronage by secular, anticlerical governments to attack the church and reduce its influence in society.

The phenomenon of anticlericalism must be accorded a prominent place in any analysis of secularization in Latin America or elsewhere in the Catholic world.[4] Anticlericalism is a persistent intellectual tradition and political posture of hostility to the influence of the clergy in political and social affairs—and frequently to church dogma as well. Anticlericalism has its intellectual roots in eighteenth-century rationalism, particularly in the work of Voltaire, and became closely associated with liberalism, nationalism, and later socialism in the nineteenth and twentieth centuries. Anticlericalism is a sustained tradition that has lost its ideological

3. Frederick B. Pike, ed., *The Conflict Between Church and State in Latin America* (New York: Alfred A. Knopf, 1964), p. 13.

4. See J. Salwyn Schapiro, *Anticlericalism: Conflict Between Church and State in France, Italy, and Spain* (Princeton: D. Van Nostrand, 1967).

fervor only in recent decades. It is associated only with Catholicism; there are no significant parallels in Protestant, Islamic, Hindu, or Buddhist history.

As suggested above, there have been different levels of opposition to the church in the ranks of anticlericals. All have agreed in their opposition to the political power of the church, and for most the curtailment of this power meant separation of church and state. This was not invariably the case, however, for as we have seen, the regalist tradition suggested other means of restricting church power. Beyond the sphere of government and politics, most anticlericals have also opposed the influence of the church in other areas of society—education, culture, economy, the family, and so forth. Some have gone further, to attack Catholic dogma itself, and have condemned that belief system as irrational, antiscientific, obscurantist, and inimical to all modern progress. As these anticlericals have viewed their societies, it was impossible to tolerate Catholicism as a set of purely private beliefs held by individuals, since it was precisely the church's control over the thinking of the people that formed the foundation of the clergy's temporal power. The most radical anticlericals have always insisted that neither state nor society could be free from clerical control, or at least clerical ambitions, until the majority was free from Catholic dogma.

We must now analyze the processes that were so deeply affected by the church's structural-ideological character, the regalist tradition, and anticlericalism.

POLITY-SEPARATION SECULARIZATION

The leaders of the young Latin American republics looked to the United States for models, and many features of their constitutions reflected this influence. In the matter of religion, however, the earliest fundamental laws were staunchly traditionalist, recognizing the Roman Catholic religion as the sole and exclusive faith of the state and explicitly rejecting the principle of religious liberty. In the early decades after independence the small political elite in most countries divided into proclerical conservatives and anticlerical liberals. While in the United States a vigorous religious pluralism provided much of the pressure for church-state separation, in Latin America the struggle was between proclericals

allied with the church hierarchy and anticlericals of Catholic
background. While the liberals professed the principles of religious liberty, this was usually not thought to apply to the autonomy of the Catholic church.

Colombia (then called New Granada) was the first Latin American republic to separate church and state, in 1853. The crucial
provision of the act was the state's abandonment of the traditional
rights of patronage: "all intervention of the civil, national, and
municipal authorities will cease in the election and presentation
of all persons whatsoever for the provision of ecclesiastical benefices, and in all and any matters relating to the exercise of the
Catholic cult or any other professed by the people of New
Granada." [5] The ownership of churches and cathedrals was at
first vested in the resident Catholics of the respective parishes and
dioceses, but two years later the local churches were granted
juridic personality to own property. The clear intention was to
accord the church a large measure of autonomy—"a free church
in a free state," to use Cavour's later formula. In 1861, however,
a fiercely anticlerical dictator came to power: the clergy were subjected to severe state regulation, the Jesuits were expelled from
the country, convents and monasteries were suppressed, and bishops were imprisoned and exiled. Anticlerical extremism thus converted the initial process of polity-separation secularization into
one of polity-dominance secularization in which church autonomy
was completely lost. These policies continued until the return of
the conservatives to power in 1884.

In Chile a more moderate course was followed. The *reformas
teológicas* of the 1880s secularized cemeteries, instituted civil
marriage, and almost succeeded in separating church and state.
However, the proponents of separation wisely adopted a strategy
of gradualism. The Radical party failed in another attempt in
1906, but the issue was kept alive and strongly supported by most
Chilean intellectuals. With the election of Arturo Alessandri to
the presidency in 1920, the stage was set for the final resolution
of the controversy.

In a speech to the Senate, Alessandri emphasized the spiritual

5. Cited in J. Lloyd Mecham, *Church and State in Latin America: A History of
Politico-Ecclesiastical Relations,* rev. ed. (Chapel Hill: University of North Carolina
Press, 1966), p. 122.

essence of religion, which was solely a matter of the individual conscience and which by its very nature was unsuited to union with the coercive powers of the state: "This is what I fervently desire for my fatherland: the Church, religious communions of whatever dogmas and beliefs, dedicated exclusively in their action to the sphere of consciences, the peculiar and proper sphere of the spiritual order; the neutral and equalitarian State, without privileges or exceptions, giving an example of respect for all consciences, and upholding the guarantees which in religious matters, as in everything, correspond equally to all inhabitants." [6] The historic Roman Catholic church, however, was not easily reduced to this purely spiritual influence, and the Catholic teaching on church and state, reaffirmed in the encyclical *Immortale Dei* (1885), had explicitly rejected the principles that Alessandri praised. Hence it was not surprising that the archbishop of Santiago condemned the proposed separation as "a public and solemn denial of God, a true and terrible national apostasy." [7] But the separation was nevertheless achieved by constitutional means in 1925, not only without bloodshed but with considerable mutual understanding and respect, and the archbishop was able to reconcile himself to the fact, if not to the principle, of church-state separation.

In addition to Chile, the best example of constitutional separation of church and state with high church autonomy are found in Brazil (since 1890) and Uruguay (since 1919). Disestablishment of the Catholic church has also taken place in Cuba, Ecuador, Guatemala, Honduras, Mexico, Nicaragua, and Panama, but in a few of these countries (particularly Mexico) state interference in the church and outright persecution of religion during certain periods have been prominent phenomena. As Vallier has emphasized, the autonomy of the church is a crucial variable: a high degree of church autonomy can be associated with both church-state separation (Chile) and church-state union (Colombia), and low church autonomy can be linked to both separation (Mexico) and union (Argentina).[8]

6. Excerpts from this speech are found in Donald E. Smith, ed., *Religion, Politics, and Social Change in the Third World: A Sourcebook* (New York: The Free Press, 1971), p. 46.

7. Smith, *Religion, Politics, and Social Change,* p. 47.

8. Vallier, *Catholicism, Social Control, and Modernization,* pp. 33–36.

POLITY-EXPANSION SECULARIZATION

Separation of church and state was a cherished goal of the nine-teenth-century liberals but provoked intense controversy every-where and furthermore was burdened with ambiguities stemming from the regalist tradition. Other religious issues seemed clearer, particularly those in which the church exercised functions which, as the liberals saw it, rightly belonged to the modern state. Polity-expansion secularization is the process by which the state con-solidates its sovereignty at the expense of church structures in law, education, and other areas of social control.

The early nineteenth-century church exercised the power of taxation through the imposition of the tithe, which was collected by the civil government. The tithe was abolished in Venezuela as early as 1834, although it was then provided that the clergy were to be paid from the public treasury.[9] Efforts to suppress the tithe succeeded in most of the republics by the end of the century, and regardless of whether state appropriations to the church were sub-stituted, the principle that the state had the exclusive right to levy taxes was firmly established.

The church maintained an extensive system of ecclesiastical courts, and the *fuero* (privilege) exempted clerics from the juris-diction of the regular courts. With their own judicial system, the clergy constituted a separate and privileged class. The liberals gradually succeeded in abolishing the fueros in almost all the Latin American republics. Lauding this action in Mexico in 1856 a historian of the time wrote: "No more fueros! . . . Equality for all citizens! Perfect sovereignty of the temporal power!"[10]

The secularization of law meant the enactment of civil mar-riage laws, which undermined the church's control over this vital area of social life. Not only was the Catholic sacramental mar-riage no longer the sole legal form; in some cases the civil mar-riage contract was given exclusive legality, so that the religious ceremony had no legal effect and hence was optional. Some coun-tries went on to provide for absolute divorce, that is, with the right to remarry, thus rejecting the church canon law which on

9. Mecham, *Church and State*, p. 100.
10. Ibid., p. 361.

this subject remains unchanged today. During the 1880s, a decade that saw more anticlerical legislation than any other throughout Latin America, various states took over the administration of the records of vital statistics. Formerly, parish priests recorded births, marriages, and deaths, and this function gave them great influence in matters of litigation such as inheritance.[11] The secularization of cemeteries was also carried out in several countries, thus depriving the church of its power to coerce individuals by threatening to deny them burial in consecrated ground.

The secularization of education was another liberal objective and has proceeded with varying degrees of success. In general, the basic secularization of the public schools, that is, freeing them from church control, has been effectively carried out, although various states make provision for religious instruction during or after school hours. However, the church's freedom to manage schools of its own has led in some cases to an impressive expansion of the Catholic educational system, while the state system lagged behind. In Colombia, for example, three-fourths of the nation's academic secondary schools are now operated by the church, and the Catholic church still claims thirty universities throughout Latin America, some of high academic standards.[12] Of the major areas considered in this discussion of polity-expansion secularization, Catholic influence today is strongest in the field of education.

POLITICAL-CULTURE SECULARIZATION

The secularization of the intellectual and cultural life of the upper and middle classes began much earlier and penetrated more deeply in Latin America than in other major areas of the Third World. In most Hindu, Buddhist, and Muslim societies, the secularization of intellectual life was a consequence of late nineteenth-century foreign rule, and the secularized component of the elite culture consisted of Western ideas and values transmitted through European languages. Latin America, on the other hand, was markedly affected by the Enlightenment by the latter part of the eighteenth century; while the sources of the ideas were for-

11. Ibid., pp. 214, 255.
12. Ibid., p. 137.

eign, these were quickly assimilated and transmitted through the Spanish and Portuguese languages.

The Enlightenment challenged the philosophical edifice of scholasticism based on sacred authority, and in the late eighteenth century the universities turned their attention from theological speculation to mathematics, the natural sciences, medicine, and engineering. It is noteworthy that the movements to overthrow the sterile scholasticism of the time were in some cases led by prominent prelates of the church. One did not have to be an atheist in order to assert the preeminence of reason and science in the solution of practical problems.[13] However, no new, over-arching system of Catholic thought emerged to synthesize the old and the new. A secular intellectual tradition emerged and in succeeding generations strengthened its independence from Catholic influence. As Victor Alba has noted, with the exception of the recent Christian Democratic movement, "intellectual and religious life have had no interrelation, despite the existence of Catholic universities and the church's control of most private schools." [14]

Nineteenth- and twentieth-century literary and artistic works have reflected remarkably little of the Catholic heritage.[15] Some of the important themes of literature have concerned national or Latin American identity, but the religious component of this identity has received scant attention. Even the assertion of a superior Latin American spirituality (Arielism) has had little to do with Catholicism.

In this analysis of political culture the emphasis is on the ideas and values of the relatively small number of people—from the upper and middle classes—who have in fact made the political history of most Latin American countries. Of this small group particular attention must be given the *pensadores*, the men of ideas, whose impact on politics has frequently been great. The first freely elected president of Venezuela was a novelist whose works exposed the misery and injustice of the city and the countryside;

13. German Arciniegas, *Latin America: A Cultural History* (New York: Alfred A. Knopf, 1967), pp. 286–94.

14. Victor Alba, *The Latin Americans* (New York: Praeger, 1969), p. 348.

15. See Jean Franco, *The Modern Culture of Latin America: Society and the Artist* (New York: Praeger, 1967).

many artists and intellectuals have entered politics, directly or indirectly, by the same avenue of social criticism.[16] And despite the frequently sterile nature of ideological conflict among Latin American intellectuals, the zeal for ideas remains. As Frank Bonilla suggests, "ideology has remained central because society has always been trying to transform itself—to locate the source of its chronic malaise and generate courage to take some pre-scribed cure." [17]

Liberalism, with its many variations of theme and emphasis, constituted the most important cluster of ideas from independence to the 1860s. As previously noted, liberalism was associated with anticlericalism, moderate or extremist, since the authority of the church was regarded as an obstacle to individual freedom. From the 1860s to the turn of the century, positivism was the dominant school of social and political thought. Based on Auguste Comte's developmental theory of history (theological, metaphysical, and positive stages), positivism reinforced anticlericalism and provided support for the view that secularization was absolutely essential to social progress.[18] Positivism was the stage in which the premises and methods of science would be applied to all the problems of society. In the twentieth century, Marxism, nationalist populism, and Christian Democracy have been the most important ideological currents.

At the level of the pensadores, then, the dominant ideas of Latin American politics have had a notably secular character from independence to the present. There are two qualifications that must be added to the generalization: the continuing but declining tradition of the conservative Catholic pensador and the much more important Christian Democratic movement. From 1810 to the present, of course, Catholicism has not been without articulate defenders from the ranks of clergy and laity alike. Compared with

16. German Arciniegas, "Intellectuals in the Politics of Latin America," in Cole Blasier, ed., *Constructive Change in Latin America* (Pittsburgh: University of Pittsburgh Press, 1968), pp. 164–65.

17. Frank Bonilla, "Cultural Elites," in Seymour Martin Lipset and Aldo Solari, *Elites in Latin America* (New York: Oxford University Press, 1967), p. 241.

18. See Miguel Jorrín and John D. Martz, *Latin-American Political Thought and Ideology* (Chapel Hill: University of North Carolina Press, 1970). On positivism, see Leopoldo Zea, *The Latin American Mind* (Norman: University of Oklahoma Press, 1963).

the liberals, positivists, and socialists, however, the impact of their *ideas* has been slight. A right-wing Catholic nationalism was articulated in Argentina early in this century, emphasizing that "the higher values of life would have to be protected through a system of authoritarianism that was to be the political manifestation of a hierarchical social structure." [19] This intellectual tradition was marshaled in support of Perón in the mid-1940s, but it was withdrawn when it became clear that he was more interested in generating political power through mass mobilization than in maintaining a hierarchical society and was unwilling to make Catholicism the dominant element in Argentine nationalism.

Traditional Catholic thought has little in common with some of its twentieth-century reinterpretations. In the work of Jacques Maritain, democracy and pluralism replaced authority and hierarchy as key concepts. Maritain and the social encyclicals have been the basic sources for the ideological development of Christian Democracy since 1945, strongly reinforced by the new impulses generated by Vatican II. The Christian Democratic movement is highly significant in that after two centuries of intellectual defensiveness and retreat, a radically changed Catholicism has been able to reassert itself and seize the initiative politically. However, it is possible that the Frei government's six years in power in Chile (1964–70) have already marked the peak of the movement. We must also consider the possibility that its Catholic ideological distinctives have been so diluted by pragmatic politics and an emerging humanist consensus that we may well speak of the secularization of Christian Democracy.

Historically, the strongest political commitment to Catholicism has been associated with the large landlords, for reasons that are obvious, yet this class also has proved vulnerable to the secularization process. At the bottom of the social hierarchy, the peasantry demonstrates a basic religiosity, although this frequently has little to do with the doctrinal and sacramental Catholicism of the church. The masses, urban as well as rural, have only begun, and only in a few countries, to move into active political participation.

19. Fredrick B. Pike, "South America's Multifaceted Catholicism: Glimpses of Twentieth-Century Argentina, Chile, and Peru," in Henry A. Landsberger, ed., *The Church and Social Change in Latin America* (Notre Dame, Ind.: University of Notre Dame Press, 1970), p. 55.

With the exception of the Christian Democratic party, all of the movements that have had some success in politicizing them—populist, trade unionist, socialist—have been of secular orientation.

POLITICAL-PROCESS SECULARIZATION

This is the process by which overt political activity becomes increasingly secular, religious issues become marginal to politics, the clergy ceases to be politically influential, and religious political parties decline. The Latin American pattern is that from the early decades of independence, religious issues and church hierarchies *increased* in political importance and (with many variations from one country to another) began to decline only in the twentieth century. By World War II the decline was readily apparent in many republics. Catholic-oriented political parties generally followed the same pattern, but in the postwar period the Christian Democratic party has emerged as a vigorous and effective protagonist, especially in Chile and Venezuela.

The Spanish empire in America was on the whole a well-integrated religiopolitical system in which the church hierarchy had a recognized and established position. Officials of state and church occasionally came into open conflict with each other, but the more characteristic form of politics was the maneuvering for advantage close to the center of power. Regalism in the empire, as noted previously, established beyond any possibility of challenge the subordination of church to state. Independence from Spain and the instability of the new republics enabled church hierarchies to assert a more independent political role, which in some cases proved to be a formidable one.[20]

Religious issues in the nineteenth century were at the center of politics. The great questions over which debates and wars were waged were precisely those of polity-separation and polity-expansion secularization. These conflicts have now, on the whole, been resolved, and with their resolution one of the major motives of clerical intervention in politics has been eliminated.

Until little more than a decade ago, the Catholic church tended regularly to support conservative dictatorships such as that of

20. Pike, *Conflict Between Church and State*, p. 13.

Pérez Jiménez in Venezuela and Rojas Pinilla in Colombia. The church partnerships with both these leaders eventually turned into enmity and opposition. Over the past decade, however, the church has increasingly abandoned support for regimes that offered little more than anticommunism and a few political favors for the church. Increasing attention is being given by the bishops to the national problems of socioeconomic change and development, correspondingly less to questions of the church's institutional self-preservation. Less inclined now to influence elections by telling the faithful what parties to vote for or against, the church has shifted the emphasis to broader questions of social justice and social change.

POLITY-DOMINANCE SECULARIZATION

The process of polity-dominance secularization is one in which the political system not only repudiates its traditional connections with religious institutions and takes over many of their functions of social control, but it goes on to secularize society by seeking to destroy or radically alter religion itself. Extreme methods of coercion are used by the government, for it is deemed necessary to secularize the political culture and the political process rapidly. In polity-dominance secularization the religious system is left with little or no autonomy. It can be objected that since the state is still deeply involved in religious matters, this is really not secularization.[21] However, the *objective* of the revolutionary regimes that have pursued this policy is the key factor; their aim is a secular society, even if the means involve extensive temporary intervention in religious matters.

The Mexican Revolution, and the governments that have acted in its name since 1910, provide the clearest example of polity-dominance secularization in Latin America. Many of the anticlerical enactments of the Revolution revived laws of the nineteenth-century movement known as the Reform. On the eve of the Reform, which began in 1855, the church owned over one-third of the land in Mexico; its vast wealth was easily translated into other forms of temporal power. Led by Benito Juárez, Valen-

21. Daniel Crecelius takes this position in his essay on Egyptian secularism. See chap. 4 on "The Retreat from Secularism."

tín Gómez Farías, and Miguel Lerdo, the Reform abolished the ecclesiastical courts, separated church and state, nationalized church property, secularized cemeteries, instituted civil marriage, secularized education, suppressed monasteries, and imposed severe limitations on the activities of the clergy. The upheavals generated by the Reform included a savage three-year war in which the government was opposed by a military-clerical alliance and the clerically inspired intervention of the French under Archduke Maximilian.

The coup of 1876 led by Porfirio Díaz was the beginning of a long dictatorship in which the laws of the Reform gradually fell into disuse and were forgotten. The church recovered much of its social, economic, and political influence during Díaz's thirty-four years in power, so the situation that faced the men of the Revolution in 1910 was not too different from that which the liberal reformers had attacked in 1855. Indeed, in the crucial area of education, the church's role was far greater than in the earlier period.

During the Revolution's harshest periods of anticlerical attack, the Catholic church was permitted no internal autonomy whatsoever. The constitution of 1917, in addition to restoring the key provisions of the Reform, gave the state legislatures the exclusive power to regulate the number of priests to be permitted within their respective states. The state of Tabasco, for example, authorized six priests for the entire territory.

The failure of the Reform revealed the limitations of governmental action, no matter how determined, in seeking to effect social change without broad-based changes in attitudes and values. Nineteenth-century liberalism offered no guidance as to how governmental power could be used to change people's values and was, in fact, fundamentally opposed to any such attempt. New ideological currents, especially socialism, made the men of the Revolution more aware of the nature, problems, and possibilities of cultural change.

Defending the anticlerical and antireligious policies of the Revolution, one official noted that the modern Mexican state "no longer circumscribes its functions to the creation of law, but on the contrary extends its actions much farther and embraces all matters connected with economic, political, and cultural administration, and . . . has set for itself as one of its specific objects, the extirpation of fanaticism." [22] It was necessary for the state to intervene in "guiding the consciousness of the masses" in accordance with scientific knowledge, attacking "those superstitions and falsehoods that darken the soul of childhood." The ideals of freedom, equality, and human dignity, the principles of the Revolution, would replace the traditional Catholic value system that had enabled the clergy to dominate society for centuries.

In introducing a new educational plan in 1934, General Plutarco Calles declared: "It is necessary that we enter into a new phase of the Revolution which I shall call the psychological revolutionary period; we must enter into and take possession of the minds of children, the consciences of the young, because they do belong and should belong to the Revolution. . . . It is absolutely necessary to drive the enemy out of that entrenchment where the clergy has been, where the Conservatives have been— I refer to Education." [23] The constitution was amended to provide for "socialistic" education, and in a number of states teachers were required to make an ideological declaration in which they professed atheism and vowed to endeavor to destroy the Catholic religion.

By 1940, however, the Mexican government's hostility to the church had run its course, and church-state relations have gradually been normalized since then. Many of the legal restrictions on the church are no longer enforced, although they have not been repealed. The Revolution achieved one of its primary objectives in that the church no longer exercises much influence in temporal affairs. Religious faith continues to be important in village life but is not subject to political mobilization, and the ideals of the Revolution have indeed become a significant component of popular consciousness at all levels.[24] A logical con-

22. Emilio Portes Gil, *The Conflict between the Civil Power and the Clergy* (Mexico City: Government of Mexico, Ministry of Foreign Affairs, 1935), p. 4; excerpts found in Smith, *Social Change in the Third World,* pp. 50–51.

23. Cited in Mecham, *Church and State,* p. 406.

24. "There is some evidence . . . that the continuing impact of the Revolution explains part of the attachment to their political system that Mexican respondents manifest. Respondents in Mexico were asked if they could name some of the ideals and goals of the Mexican Revolution. Thirty-five per cent could name none, while the remaining 65 per cent listed democracy, political liberty and equality, economic

comitant of Mexico's serious commitment to the development of a democratic polity has been a drawing back from the quasi-totalitarian aims of "thought control" expressed in the earlier period.

---

welfare, agrarian reform, social equality and national freedom." Sidney Verba and Gabriel A. Almond, "National Revolutions and Political Commitment," in Harry Eckstein, ed., *Internal War* (New York: The Free Press, 1964), p. 229.

PART 3

The Role of Religion in Mass Politicization

7

Gandhi, Hinduism, and Mass Politics

DONALD E. SMITH

The thesis of this essay is that religion constituted a major and indispensable link between Gandhi as a political leader and the Indian masses. It is widely recognized that one of Gandhi's greatest political achievements was the transformation of Indian nationalism from an elite into a mass movement. My argument is that religion, and specifically Hinduism, was a primary vehicle of this mass politicization.

Gandhi himself spoke with great frankness about his mixing of religion and politics. He noted in his *Autobiography*: "I can say without the slightest hesitation, and yet in all humility, that those who say that religion has nothing to do with politics do not know what religion means." [1] And, even stronger, his statement in 1922: "For me there is no distinction between politics and religion." [2]

The definition of "religion" was obviously a crucial point, and to define the word in terms of moral philosophy or universal spiritual principles, as Gandhi frequently did, was to settle the problem satisfactorily for most Indian intellectuals. It is clear, however, that Gandhi's great effectiveness as a mobilizer of the masses lay in his appeal to specifically *Hindu* ideals, values, and symbols. [3]

1. M. K. Gandhi, *An Autobiography, or the Story of My Experiments with Truth,* 2d ed. (Ahmedabad: Navajivan, 1948), p. 615.

2. Quoted in Lloyd I. Rudolph and Susanne H. Rudolph, *The Modernity of Tradition* (Chicago: University of Chicago Press, 1967), p. 158.

3. For a comparative study of religion in relation to revolutionary mass movements, see Donald E. Smith, "Religious Revolutionaries of the Third World: Gandhi, Gandhians, and *Guerrilleros,*" in Paul F. Power, ed., *The Meanings of Gandhi* (Honolulu: University Press of Hawaii, 1971), pp. 135–52.

In emphasizing the religious character of Gandhi's mass appeal, I do not wish to ignore other aspects of his leadership. Many writers have commented on the great complexity of Gandhi's personality and work, and part of this complexity stems from the fundamental fact that he was both a political and a religious leader. As a practical politician he labored assiduously on the organizational details of the Indian National Congress, for he fully understood the need for organized effort to achieve political goals. It is also true that some of the symbols he used to good effect in mass political appeals were secular. His campaigns of public burning of foreign cloth, the glorification of the *charka* (spinning wheel), and the wearing of garments made from home-woven cloth (particularly the white "Gandhi caps") were powerful political symbols by which millions of Indians came to identify with the nationalist movement. My argument, however, is simply that secular organization and secular symbols alone are inadequate explanations of Gandhi's mass appeal; the religious element was central—and indispensable.

The study of the relationship between Hinduism and mass politics in Gandhi's leadership of the nationalist movement touches some sensitive areas in Indian thinking, even a quarter-century after independence. As Father of the Nation, Gandhi's place in history is secure, and yet the question remains: Did not Gandhi, despite his religious universalism and dedicated efforts on behalf of communal unity, lend such an overwhelmingly Hindu appearance to the movement as to discourage Muslim participation and thus strengthen the separatist tendencies that ultimately led to the partition of India? M. A. Jinnah and other Muslim League leaders repeatedly characterized the Indian National Congress as a Hindu organization; the charge was unfair in important respects. But in politics, symbols and "image" are of great importance, and those communicated by Gandhi could hardly be described as secular. The relationship between the Hindu and the universal aspects of Gandhi's religion is an important point that must be clarified. In the following analysis I shall consider Gandhi's four religious roles and relate them to his political leadership.

THE ECLECTIC RELIGIOUS LEADER

I begin by noting that various prominent aspects of traditional Hinduism were important components of Gandhi's religion. Religious eclecticism and universalism formed the basis for Gandhi's efforts to reach out and enlist the political support of members of other communities. It is important to remember, however, that his eclecticism was based on unmistakably Hindu assumptions.

Gandhi declared in 1921 that he regarded himself as a *Sanatana* (orthodox) Hindu and related this to his firm belief in *varnashrama dharma,* the sacral hierarchical caste order of society. He emphatically rejected untouchability but long defended the regulations that prohibited caste interdining and intermarriage. His views on caste restrictions gradually became more liberal, but he never rejected the fundamental idea of *varna* as the ordering principle of society. Gandhi had a deep-seated belief in rebirth and the law of *karma,* which operated to produce the appropriate moral consequences of deeds performed in previous existences. He regarded cow protection as a central tenet of Hinduism.[4]

Gandhi's eclecticism and universalism were no less prominent aspects of his religion. In 1928 he declared: "After long study and experience I have come to these conclusions, that: (1) all religions are true, (2) all religions have some error in them, (3) all religions are almost as dear to me as my own Hinduism. My veneration for other faiths is the same as for my own faith."[5] In his daily prayer meetings Gandhi had readings from the Qur'an, the New Testament (he was particularly fond of the Sermon on the Mount), and other scriptures as well as from his beloved Bhagavad Gita.

While Gandhi was acutely conscious of the elements of distinctiveness in the various religious traditions and proceeded in part by embracing them all, at a deeper level he sought to define the "Religion of Truth" that transcended them all. Gandhi's "Religion of Truth" had to do with self-suffering, nonviolence, and

4. See J. T. F. Jordens, "Gandhi's Religion and the Hindu Heritage," in Sibnarayan Ray, ed., *Gandhi, India, and the World* (Philadelphia: Temple University Press, 1970), pp. 39–56.

5. Quoted in Jawaharlal Nehru, *The Discovery of India* (New York: John Day, 1946), p. 365.

ethical action (we shall consider it more fully later). While he sought to establish some connections between *ahimsa* (nonviolence) on one hand and Christianity and Islam on the other, the interpretations were awkward and strained. To a considerable extent the same was true of his efforts to establish nonviolence as the *core* of Hinduism, but as a Hindu working within his own tradition he stood in a long line of religious reformers who had functioned by a process of highly selective emphasis and reinterpretation.

One problem with Gandhi's universalism was that it refused to take seriously what orthodox Muslims and Christians said about *their own* religious traditions. In stating that "all religions are true," Gandhi simply affirmed what an ahistorical, pluralist, and relativistic Hinduism had always taken for granted, namely, that doctrinal and ritual differences exist only at a lower level of reality. The Rig Veda proclaims: "Reality is one; sages speak of it in different ways." But orthodox Islam and Christianity were rooted in particular, allegedly historical events of divine revelation to man. To many Hindus it has seemed a mark of intolerance that orthodox Muslims and Christians should refuse to accept the place offered their traditions within this Hindu framework.

Gandhi dealt sympathetically with the problems of the Muslim minority arising out of threats to their distinctive traditions, particularly in the case of the Khilafat movement, which he vigorously supported.[6] But it is quite clear that he regarded this crisis primarily as an opportunity to cement Hindu-Muslim unity rather than as an issue of intrinsic religious importance.[7] The Indian Muslims' deep concern over the fate of the Turkish caliph's domains placed them in an anti-British posture, and strong Hindu support for their demands, Gandhi reasoned, would go far toward creating a united nationalist movement. The Khilafat movement, which began in 1919, failed to achieve its objectives, and its disintegration coincided with serious new outbreaks of Hindu-Muslim conflict. In 1924 the Turks themselves, under

6. See chap. 9, "Islam and Mass Politics: The Indian Ulama and the Khilafat Movement."

7. Hafeez Malik, *Moslem Nationalism in India and Pakistan* (Washington, D.C.: Public Affairs Press, 1963), p. 283.

the leadership of the secularist revolutionary, Kamal Ataturk, abolished the caliphate.

Hindu-Muslim unity was an objective that Gandhi pursued relentlessly throughout his more than thirty years in Indian politics. His opposition to the creation of Pakistan was, characteristically, based on religious premises. "Partition means a patent untruth," he wrote.

> "My whole soul rebels against the idea that Hinduism and Islam represent two antagonistic cultures and doctrines. To assent to such a doctrine is for me denial of God. For I believe with my whole soul that the God of the Qur'an is also the God of the Gita, and that we are all, no matter by what name designated, children of the same God." [8]

One of the great peaks of Gandhi's moral leadership came near the end of his life when he strove mightily, by fasts and by the power of his presence, to stop the communal bloodshed unleashed by partition.

SOUL-FORCE MOBILIZER

Satyagraha (literally, holding fast to truth, sometimes translated as truth-force or soul-force) was Gandhi's political technique of nonviolent moral pressure. Developed as a form of resistance to British rule, Satyagraha was first tested in India in 1919. It was a method by which Gandhi and his followers created confrontations with representatives of the imperialist government, publicly defied their authority as unjust, and reacted nonviolently when subjected to physical attack. Organized on a mass scale, satyagraha became a political technique of compelling dramatic power.

For Gandhi, to be sure, it was far more than an effective political technique and stemmed from his profoundest religious and ethical beliefs. He regarded his "experiments in the spiritual field" as the source of whatever power he demonstrated in politics. And satyagraha derived from Gandhi's conviction that Truth "is the only correct and fully significant name for God," and that ahimsa and self-suffering are the means to Truth. "[W]ithout

8. M. K. Gandhi, *To the Hindus and Muslims* (Allahabad: Law Journal Press, 1942), p. 428.

ahimsa it is not possible to seek and find Truth. Ahimsa and Truth are so intertwined that it is practically impossible to disentangle and separate them. . . . Nevertheless, ahimsa is the means; Truth is the end. Means to be means must always be within our reach, and so ahimsa is our supreme duty. If we take care of the means, we are bound to reach the end sooner or later." [9]

While the concept of ahimsa was a very ancient one in Indian thought, Gandhi's interpretations sought to locate it at the very center of Hinduism. The historical distortions thus produced were considerable, for on one hand ahimsa was far more central to the Jain and Buddhist traditions, and on the other, important aspects of Hindu thought were diametrically opposed. Thus, animal sacrifices were a part of Vedic religion, the Gita provides a clear moral justification of killing when done dispassionately as part of one's dharma, and the whole tradition of the Kshatriyas (the ruler-warrior caste) knows nothing of ahimsa. Nevertheless, Gandhi's impact has been so great, from the 1920s to the present, that many Hindus have been thoroughly convinced that nonviolence is at the heart of their religion.

Gandhi was deeply convinced that the close connection between Truth (God) and ahimsa meant that satyagraha was in line with, and undergirded by, cosmic forces. The whole force of the universe supported the *satyagrahi* in his search for truth by nonviolence. Many of his closest colleagues in the Congress did not share his religious and metaphysical views but were attracted to satyagraha because it was a program of vigorous action involving mass mobilization. The older strategies, constitutionalism and terrorism, had both failed, and Gandhi's mass movement shook the British Raj in an unprecedented manner. Nehru recalled in his autobiography:

> We were moved by these [Gandhi's] arguments, but for us and for the National Congress as a whole the non-violent method was not, and could not be, a religion or an unchal-

9. M. K. Gandhi, *From Yeravda Mandir: Ashram Observances,* 3d. ed. (Ahmedabad: Navajivan, 1945), p. 8; quoted in Joan V. Bondurant, *Conquest of Violence,* rev. ed. (Berkeley and Los Angeles: University of California Press, 1965), pp. 24–25. In this work Bondurant presents a careful and comprehensive analysis of Gandhi's ideas and actions related to satyagraha.

lengeable creed or dogma. It could only be a policy and a method promising certain results, and by those results it would have to be finally judged. Individuals might make of it a religion or incontrovertible creed. But no political organization, so long as it remained political, could do so.[10]

The accounts of the great satyagraha campaigns can leave no doubt as to both their moral grandeur and considerable political effectiveness. At the height of the 1930–31 movement, hundreds of thousands of satyagrahis all over India moved in disciplined nonviolent action to defy the government. In some of the campaigns, wave after wave of peaceful volunteers offered themselves unresistingly to be brutally beaten by police and then arrested. The overall political effect was to create a politicized population in determined opposition to British rule.[11]

What Gandhi *said* and *did* in the field of mass politics was certainly important. Behind his mass appeal, however, was what Gandhi *was,* or at least what he was perceived to be by the masses. It is to this aspect of his impact that we now turn.

The Mahatma—Hindu Saint

Unlike the political monks, political ulama, and political priests discussed elsewhere in this book, men whose effectiveness in the realm of mass politics depended in part on the prestige of clerical status, Gandhi occupied no such position within the Hindu religious system. To begin with, as a non-Brahman he had no ascribed religious authority. Gurus of various devotional (*bhakti*) sects, it is true, were sometimes of nonpriestly caste, and Gandhi was influenced by the bhakti tradition, but he did not travel this path to religious leadership. He had no special training in religious subjects, and his study of religion was pursued privately in conjunction with his "experiments with truth." By formal training in England and by vocation, Gandhi was a lawyer.

As a religious figure Gandhi did not need clerical status, however, for he was regarded as a Mahatma ("Great Soul" or saint) and was himself an object of veneration. In one sense Gandhi had

10. Jawaharlal Nehru, *Toward Freedom* (New York: John Day, 1942), p. 82.
11. For descriptions and analyses of five campaigns, see Bondurant, *Conquest of Violence,* pp. 36–104.

little control over his widespread reputation as a saint; this reputation grew and flourished despite all his denials. On the other
hand, it is also true that Gandhi step by step identified himself
with the ancient Hindu ideal of renunciation and asceticism and
provided the objective ground for that reputation.

Although married, Gandhi took the vow of celibacy (*brahmacharya*) at the age of thirty-seven. He founded an *ashram,* or
spiritual retreat, and although the community he gathered around
him was deeply involved in implementing new social ideals (the
dignity of labor, removal of untouchability, etc.), the traditional
concern for spiritual self-perfection was no less. In 1921 he
changed his mode of dress, discarding the *dhoti* (the Indian lower
garment), vest, and cap, and henceforth wore only a simple loin-
cloth. He announced this step as in part an act of self-suffering
and expiation for the failure of his countrymen to embrace the
khadi (home-produced cloth) movement. Gandhi's followers
pleaded with him not to take this step, for many feared that he
was thus preparing himself to renounce the world and become a
sanyasin.[12]

Gandhi's long fasts were not *merely* dramatic political maneuvers designed to coerce the British government and his followers
into compliance with his wishes, although they frequently accomplished these results. There is every reason to take seriously
Gandhi's own statements that he regarded these acts of self-
imposed suffering as necessary for his self-purification. Behind
Gandhi's public acts lay the ancient Hindu notion of the ascetic
who by the power of his austerities (*tapas*) could bring about
changes in his environment.[13] The Hindu theory was one of
metaphysical forces that gave the ascetic control over nature;
Gandhi applied it to social and political relations. In so doing,
however, he was not simply influencing other men by manipulat-
ing religious ideas that they held. He remained convinced of the
reality of the spiritual forces in the universe that he could tap by
self-suffering and truth seeking.

Gandhi believed that asceticism, and particularly sexual absti-

12. See Krishnadas, *Seven Months with Mahatma Gandhi* (Madras: S. Ganesan,
1928), 1 : 202–203.
13. This theme is well developed in Rudolph and Rudolph, *Modernity of Tradition,* pp. 196–99.

nence, enhanced an individual's potency in all other areas of life. Sexual indulgence involved the loss of a certain amount of "life force" which was then unavailable for higher pursuits. "Without Brahmacharya," he wrote, "the Satyagrahi will have no lustre, no inner strength to stand unarmed against the whole world." [14] Gandhi's asceticism had much in common with the ancient Hindu ideal but with a radical difference: it was a this-worldly asceticism directed mainly at political change, and individual self-perfection was sought in and through service to an entire people.

It is clear that a great deal of Gandhi's political effectiveness lay in his embodiment of a Hindu religious ideal. Over his long years in political life, millions of Indians attended his meetings to see the face and if possible touch the feet of, not a Congress leader, but a Mahatma. As the Rudolphs have written:

> By communicating in a fresh and historically relevant manner the idea that those who could master themselves could achieve serenity, religious merit, and mastery of their environment, he evoked a response that his authority as a consummate and skilled politician could not alone have commanded.[15]

THE AVATAR—DIVINE INCARNATION

The title "Mahatma" did not exhaust the religious meaning of Gandhi for many millions of his followers. As his great campaigns of nonviolent resistance to British rule gathered momentum, many were reminded of the Lord Krishna's statement that he assumes new incarnations from age to age. As stated in the Bhagavad Gita: "Whenever there is a decline of righteousness and rise of unrighteousness, O Bharata, then I send forth Myself. For the protection of the good, for the destruction of the wicked, and for the establishment of righteousness, I come into being from age to age." [16]

Gandhi was widely regarded as an avatar by Hindus of all strata. A follower recorded the words of an old widow who came in search of the Mahatma. "Just as we have had Ram and Krishna

14. Ibid., p. 209.
15. Ibid., p. 159.
16. Bhagavad Gita, IV, 7–8.

as Avatars, so also Mahatma Gandhi has appeared as an Avatar, I hear. Until I have seen him death will not come to me." [17] And a young follower expressed his view: "Gandhi is now marching as Buddha marched through India. . . . When you walk with him a light seems to emanate from him and fills you with its deep radiance. It is a new phenomenon, the present incarnation of Gandhi." [18]

Throughout his entire public career, Gandhi was daily sought out by people who wished to receive *darshan,* the view of a sacred being (temple deity, king, or holy man) that brings merit to the viewer. Undoubtedly, for many the quest for darshan of Gandhi was related to his reputation as an avatar. Gandhi's own frequent protestations that there was nothing in him to make him worthy of giving darshan were completely ineffectual.[19]

Widespread reports that he was a prophet, a messenger from God, or an avatar were strongly rejected by Gandhi. He wrote in 1924: "I lay claim to nothing exclusively divine in me. I do not claim prophetship. I am but a humble seeker after Truth and bent upon finding it. . . . There is already enough superstition in our country. No effort should be spared to resist further addition in the shape of Gandhi worship. Personally I have a horror of adoration." [20] It is doubtful that such statements ever dissuaded any Gandhi worshipper and, in fact, may even have served to confirm the belief that the Mahatma was indeed an avatar!

GANDHI'S IMPACT ON POLITICS

In analyzing Gandhi's political leadership, a fundamental consideration is the extraordinary effectiveness with which he simultaneously communicated with both the Western-educated elite and the tradition-oriented masses. One reason for his success in doing this was that Gandhi embodied and expressed a wide range of symbols, from universalism to Hindu particularism. The first two roles discussed in this chapter—Gandhi as eclectic religious

17. Krishnadas, *Seven Months,* p. 34.

18. Cited in Jordens, "Gandhi's Religion," p. 51.

19. The darshan seekers placed extreme demands on Gandhi's time. See Rudolph and Rudolph, *Modernity of Tradition,* pp. 229–31.

20. *Young India,* 11 September 1924, quoted in Bondurant, *Conquest of Violence,* p. 124.

leader and soul-force mobilizer—locate him at the universalist end of the continuum. The third and fourth religious roles—Gandhi as Mahatma and avatar—place him at the opposite end, that of Hindu particularism. Much of Gandhi's political genius lay in the fact that he communicated relevantly and forcefully at all points along the continuum.

Some of the more secular Western-educated Congress leaders were deeply disturbed by Gandhi's use of religious symbols in politics. Thus Nehru, commenting on events in 1921: "Gandhiji was continually laying stress on the religious and spiritual side of the movement. His religion was not dogmatic, but it did mean a definitely religious outlook on life, and the whole movement was strongly influenced by this and took on a revivalist character so far as the masses were concerned." [21] Nehru consoled himself with the thought that Gandhi used religious language because it was well understood by the masses. But even for the agnostic Nehru, Gandhi provided something that held strong, positive appeal.

> What I admired was the moral and ethical side of our move-ment and of satyagraha. I did not give an absolute allegiance to the doctrine of non-violence or accept it forever, but it attracted me more and more, and the belief grew upon me that, situated as we were in India and with our background and traditions, it was the right policy for us. The spiritualiza-tion of politics, using the word not in its narrow religious sense, seemed to me a fine idea. A worthy end should have worthy means leading up to it.[22]

The more religiously inclined among Western-educated Hindus were generally pleased by Gandhian reinterpretations that placed nonviolence at the center of their tradition. Hinduism, long under attack from the West, now stood forth in a position of moral su-periority vis-à-vis its Western detractors. And Gandhi's universal-ism, his emphasis that all religions are true, further emphasized the enlightened character and validity of Hinduism, as they saw

21. Nehru, *Toward Freedom*, p. 71.
22. Ibid., p. 72.

it. In Gandhi, nationalism and the renewal of Hinduism seemed to coalesce.

If universal ethics and eclecticism formed the most salient religious aspects of Gandhi's appeal to the Western-educated elite, it was *Mahatma* Gandhi, saint and avatar, who led the *masses* into active political participation. M. N. Roy, a lifelong critic, explained Gandhi's political potency in terms of the "religious superstitions" of the Hindu masses. "It is neither a philosopher nor a moralist who has become the idol of the Indian people. The masses pay their homage to a Mahatma—a source of revealed wisdom and agency of supernatural power." [23] Religion was indeed the vital and indispensable vehicle of mass politicization under Gandhi's leadership.

There were important Muslim leaders who were devoted followers of Gandhi and faithful members of the Indian National Congress. However, despite his most determined efforts, Gandhi was never able to attract the Muslim *masses* to his movement. In retrospect, it could hardly have been otherwise, for a different set of symbols was required. [24]

23. William T. deBary, ed., *Sources of Indian Tradition* (New York: Columbia University Press, 1958), p. 912.

24. For a Pakistani historical perspective, note the words of Chandhri Muhammad Ali: "There was a time when the issue hung in the balance and many Hindus and Muslims believed that a truly common nationalism was in the making. But with the growth of mass movements, reliance on specifically Hindu stimuli to action increased, and the fate of Indian nationalism was sealed. The outer aspect of Indian nationalism continued to be secular and noncommunal, but its inner spirit was informed by Hindu inspirations." *The Emergence of Pakistan* (New York: Columbia University Press, 1967), p. 14.

8

Buddhism and Mass Politics in Burma and Ceylon

HEINZ BECHERT

Max Weber, in his famous study of the sociology of religion, characterized early Buddhism as a nonpolitical or even antipolitical religion of highly intellectual mendicants.[1] Buddhism as understood by Weber was "a quite specific soteriology of cultivated intellectuals."[2] Weber described it as "the product not of underprivileged but of very positively privileged strata" of society.[3] Buddhism, therefore, had "no sort of tie with any sort of 'social' movement, nor did it run parallel with such, and it has established no 'social-political' goal."[4]

How, then, could Buddhism in the rather conservative form of Theravada or Pali Buddhism become a factor in the process of political change such as it has been in the history of several Asian countries? To answer this question, we have to begin with a discussion of the basic principles of Buddhist religious organization, which divides the adherents of the Buddha's teaching into the ecclesiastical body, or Sangha of monks (*bhikkhu*) and nuns (*bhikkhuni*), on the one hand and the laity on the other hand. In Buddhism, monastic institutions play a key role, and the higher states of spiritual culture were thought to be accessible only to

1. See Max Weber, *Gesammelte Aufsätze zur Religionssoziologie*, vol. 2, *Hinduismus und Buddhismus* (Tübingen: J. C. B. Mohr, 1923), pp. 217–319; English translation: Max Weber, *The Religion of India*, trans. H. H. Gerth and Don Martindale (New York: Free Press, 1958), pp. 204–90. Weber's opinion is discussed by Heinz Bechert, "Einige Fragen der Religionssoziologie und Struktur des südasiatischen Buddhismus," *Internationales Jahrbuch für Religionssoziologie* 4 (1968): 251–55.
2. Weber, *The Religion of India*, p. 205.
3. Ibid., p. 227.
4. Ibid., p. 226.

monks, though rare exceptions from this rule were believed to be possible. However, it is a misunderstanding to describe Buddhism as a religion in which the laity plays only a marginal role. It was not only that the laity provided the means of subsistence for the monastic community and, therefore, the need arose to convince the lay population that it was right to support Buddhist monks: it is evident that a tradition of lay Buddhism developed side by side with the monastic traditions rather early, though it is much less represented in the existing literary documents that were handed down by monks.

We must, therefore, consider both aspects—monastic and lay Buddhism—to arrive at an understanding of the role of Buddhism in mass politicization.

Traditional Sangha-State Relations

There can be no doubt that the early Buddhist Sangha was a nonpolitical body with purely religious aims. It was, however, organized on the model of a political body, namely, the aristocratic republic of ancient India. The canonical law-book of the Buddhist Sangha, known by the name of *Vinaya Pitaka,* is therefore a mirror of the law of this early period of Indian culture. It is remarkable for its highly developed state: for example, the differentiation of voluntary and involuntary acts, the rule *"nulla poena sine lege,"* the distinctive procedural regulations, and so on. The rationalistic features of early Buddhist law correspond to the rationalistic way of thinking in Buddhist doctrine. The regulations of the Vinaya thus reflect the high standard of education of the classes that formed the origin of the large majority of the early Buddhists. These were the aristocratic Kshatriya clans, but early Buddhists were enlightened enough to make their religious organization open to anybody who was ready to follow the instructions of the founder and thus to build up a purely spiritual aristocracy in their Sangha. This was done in opposition to the Brahmanical hierocracy.

The early Sangha was far from being "unstructured." [5] Its structure was, however, a legal and social structure rather than an organizational one. There was no generally accepted spiritual

5. That "Buddhism persisted in an unstructured state . . ." was held by Weber, *The Religion of India,* p. 223.

succession to the Buddha nor a head of the Sangha organization after him, and local Sanghas could be formed by wandering monks coming together for a limited or unlimited period within a certain "boundary" (*sima*), which had to be agreed upon by a legal act. Unity was guaranteed by the universal acceptance by all local Sanghas of one and the same "dharma and vinaya," that is, procedural law and disciplinary regulations. This basic unity was strong enough to survive dissensions in the early Sangha which, naturally, were not rare and rather difficult to prevent. The legal unity was independent of any territorial limitations. In this respect, its nature was consistent with the nature of Hindu law of all periods and schools—a purely personal law.[6] Thus, under the structure of the early Sangha, splits remained a minor problem for the unity of Buddhism and its Sangha as a universal religious body as long as its legal unity was not destroyed.[7] The formation of organized sects was a rather slow process, compared to what we would expect under the conditions of a religious body without a commonly recognized head. Though we have some information concerning permanent splits dividing larger sections of the Sangha on the ground of different interpretations of rules and discipline in the earlier period, it is only from the period of King Ashoka that we have more reliable records of such developments.[8] Evidently, early Buddhist sects had less individualizing features than the sects of other great religions due to the legal structure of the Sangha.

It is by no means accidental that we can trace distinct "sects" (*nikayas*) in Buddhism from the reign of Ashoka, the great royal

6. See e.g., P. R. Ganapati Iyer, *Hindu Law; A Treatise* (Madras: Thompson, 1915), 1 : 139.

7. On the structure of the early Sangha and early splits in the Sangha see H. Bechert, "Aśokas 'Schismenedikt' und der Begriff Sanghabhedha," *Wiener Zeitschrift für die Kunde Süd- und Ostasiens* 5 (1961): pp. 18–52. See also Gokuldas De, *Democracy in Early Buddhist Sangha* (Calcutta: Calcutta University, 1955).

8. On early Buddhist sects, see André Bareau, *Les sectes bouddhiques du Petit Véhicule* (Saigon: Ecole Française d'Extrême-Orient, 1955). Important contributions to the understanding of the early history of Buddhism are found in Erich Frauwallner, "Die buddhistischen Konzile," *Zeitschrift der Deutschen Morgenländischen Gesellschaft* 102 (1952): pp. 240–61; idem, *The Earliest Vinaya and the Beginnings of Buddhist Literature* (Rome: Is.M.E.O., 1956). For comprehensive information see Etienne Lamotte, *Histoire du Bouddhisme indien, des origines à l'ère śaka* (Louvain: Publications Universitaires, 1958).

patron of Buddhism. No doubt, Buddhism had had royal patrons from the beginning, when the Buddha was a protégé of King Bimbisara of Magadha, but there was not the least political motivation in this patronage, which was based exclusively on the personal preference of the monarch. The Buddha conscientiously observed the boundaries between his purely religious teachings and the order as a community of "homeless" ascetics on the one hand and the sphere of political power and civic interests on the other. This clear distinction was done away with by Ashoka. He did not try to make Buddhism the state religion but developed a particular ideology of a nonconfessional *dharma,* as we can see from his inscriptions, but his experiment of integrating religious bodies into the political structure of the state affected Buddhism, his favored religion, more deeply than any of the other religious communities. It was under Ashoka with his reform of the Sangha that formalized state-Sangha relations originated, and it was in Ceylon where Buddhism was introduced as a consequence of Ashoka's missionary activities that state-Sangha relations were further developed on this basis. Ceylonese Buddhism, which belonged to the Theravada school, later had a decisive influence on the development of state-Sangha relations in the Theravada Buddhist kingdoms of Southeast Asia.

These developments deeply affected the position of the Sangha in society and the relations of the Sangha with the masses. On one hand, integration of the Sangha in the political structure prevented it from becoming an independent political factor itself. On the other hand, state patronage resulted in changing Buddhism from the religion of an elite into the religion of the broad masses of the rural population. This meant, in a sense, "democratizing" Buddhism by increasing the number of monks and inducing persons from all social and educational classes to enter the Sangha. By this, the Sangha grew into a potential power in politics, with direct access to the rural masses and therefore the means to stir up unrest. However, medieval Buddhist states developed a system of integration of the Sangha into the state structure that enabled them to control it and prevent such developments.

This state control of the originally independent religious body was justified mainly by two arguments. First, the monks were prohibited by the regulations of the Vinaya from handling money.

Since under Buddhist canonical law, lay trustees (*kappiyakaraka*) were to be appointed to look after the material property of the Sangha and to provide the monks with their "requisites," it was only natural that the state should also act as the lay trustee of Sangha properties. In this way the state came to control the economic basis of the existence of the Sangha. In addition, King Ashoka's efforts to purify the Sangha, that is, to have those monks expelled who did not keep the monastic rules and were engaged in worldly activities not considered fitting for a Buddhist monk, was an accepted example for later Buddhist kings. It provided the ideological justification for an integration of the Sangha into the state structure to exercise enough control over it to prevent political activities. At the same time, the interests of state were now interwoven with the interests of the Sangha to such a degree that serious conflicts of state and Sangha were rare in precolonial Theravada Buddhist states. In complete agreement with other sources, all accounts of travelers emphasized that the Buddhist monks in these states strictly avoided any meddling in political affairs. This, however, did not mean that they were without political resources, since they helped to provide the charisma that legitimized the traditional Buddhist monarchies.[9]

THE SANGHA, IMPERIALISM, AND NATIONALISM

A breakdown of this system of state-Sangha relations could potentially make the Sangha a mighty force of mass politicization, and such a breakdown was brought about by the colonial regime in Burma and Ceylon when it decided to completely abolish the traditional ties that bound the two. As a result, the Sangha became a powerful factor of mass politics in both countries. This has been described in recent studies of political Buddhism, and it is not necessary to present here another factual summary of the activities of sections of the Sangha in the political field and the results

9. For an analysis of these developments see H. Bechert, "Theravada Buddhist Sangha: Some General Observations on Historical and Political Factors in its Development," *Journal of Asian Studies* 29 (1969–70): pp. 761–78. The importance of the political ideology created by the Sangha for Ceylon is discussed by Bechert, "Zum Ursprung der Geschichtsschreibung im indischen Kulturbereich," *Nachrichten der Akademie der Wissenschaften in Göttingen* (Gottingen: 1969) pp. 35–58. For Burma, see E. Sarkisyanz, *Buddhist Backgrounds of the Burmese Revolution* (The Hague: Nijhoff, 1965).

thereof.[10] Instead, I would like to draw attention to some of the underlying factors as well as to the ideological arguments used in the struggle for and against the political activism of the Buddhist monkhood.

The most conspicuous factor in this development has been nationalism. Undoubtedly, religion was the most effective single factor preserving the feeling of national unity in the Buddhist countries during the period of colonial rule. Thus, to take the example of Burma, the feeling of national self-identity was inseparable from being a Buddhist, and in all stages of the independence movement this fact was equally important.[11] There was never any sizable section of the Sangha or of the Buddhist community at large denying that "to be a Burman is to be a Buddhist." However, the degree of active involvement of the Sangha in politics varied considerably. Buddhist monks were involved in political unrest in Lower Burma already in the last decades of the nineteenth century. In the early years of the modernist movement, however, the participation of monks in the newly formed Buddhist associations was rather exceptional. Again, the politicization of the largest religious organization of the country, the Young Men's Buddhist Association (Y.M.B.A.) in 1917, and its transformation into the General Council of Burmese Associations (G.C.B.A.) in 1920, resulted in the extensive entry of monks into the political sphere. The political monks organized themselves in a large association named Sangha Sametggi Council in 1921 and held key posts in several political parties during the following years. After a period of decline in direct involvement in political action beginning about 1930, we find certain large sections of *pongyis* (Burmese term for Bhikkhus or Buddhist monks) participating again in the so-called "Indo-Burmese Riots" of 1938. However, during the following few years monks were rarely seen in the forefront of political actions.[12]

---

10. For the facts underlying the considerations in the present paper, I refer readers to Smith, *Religion and Politics in Burma;* idem, ed., *South Asian Politics and Religion* (Princeton, N.J.: Princeton University Press, 1966), chaps. 21–24; Heinz Bechert, *Buddhismus, Staat und Gesellschaft in den Ländern des Theravada-Buddhismus*, vol. 1 (Frankfurt: Metzner, 1966), vol. 2 (Wiesbaden: Harrassowitz, 1967).

11. See also Fred von der Mehden, *Religion and Nationalism.*

12. See Smith, *Religion and Politics in Burma*, pp. 86–114; Bechert, *Buddhismus*, 2 : 100–28; von der Mehden, *Religion and Nationalism*, pp. 121–136, 149–50, 167–68.

It is evident that nationalism alone does not explain these facts. Nationalism was the main factor behind Burmese politics throughout the last three decades of colonial rule, and its power was steadily increasing. Thus one could expect the pongyis to be equally active in furthering the nationalist cause throughout the years of the independence struggle. The main factor that we have to consider here is the contradictory position of the Sangha vis-à-vis any political activity, and this leads necessarily to the question of ideological factors furthering or hindering the Sangha in such activities.

The Buddha did not want the members of the Sangha to take part in any form of worldly business, as a necessary consequence of his teachings about the nature of the world and the way to salvation. Therefore, the political activity of the Sangha was excluded by the basic concepts of Buddhism. However, it was always considered a legitimate and even necessary task for a monk to give advice to kings concerning moral precepts and the teachings of the Buddha. Such advice had to be strictly religious. Any identification of the interests of the Sangha with those of a particular political agency was completely out of the question. These facts were well known and reiterated by the leading monks of all times. To quote the Burmese example again, it was the Thathanabaing, the head of the traditional hierarchy of the country, who issued a formal injunction against the political activities of monks soon after the British annexation of Upper Burma in 1886, and admonitions of this sort have been given by highly respected members of the Sangha to their brothers ever since. These monks were joined by influential lay Buddhists such as U Nu.[13] Such admonitions did not prevent political activity by monks, and as noted above, some of them became leaders of political parties. The Sangha was, however, always divided on this issue. It became impossible to make use of the traditional hierarchical organization for political ends, and it was always possible to criticize politically active Buddhist monks by quoting the rules of the order. As a consequence, there was some sense of guilt inside the Sangha caused by the political actions of its members. In this way, the

13. U Nu's well known severe lecture for political monks is found in Thakin Nu [U Nu], *Burma under the Japanese*, trans. J. S. Furnivall (London: Macmillan, 1954), pp. 90–92.

traditional religious rules, based on the goals and principles of original Buddhism and contained in the scriptures that were universally accepted by all Theravada Buddhists as the ultimate authority, represented a strong factor against the politicization of the Sangha.

Not less ambiguous was the position of lay Buddhists in relation to this issue. It was a consequence of the meeting of ideas from East and West that Buddhists formed modern associations after the model of Christian missionary organizations for the revival of their religion and the educational uplift of the Buddhist community after 1890. These activities were led and controlled by lay Buddhists who had in their minds a highly idealized model of the Sangha. They expected a revival of the Sangha as a purely religious organization of a very high moral, educational, and spiritual standard and in complete agreement with the canonical rules. This excluded making any use of the Sangha for political purposes. However, when the Buddhist organizations became politically active in 1917 and later years, their leaders soon came to realize that under the given situation it was impossible for them to organize any mass movement without the active help of the monks. This was justified with the argument that the survival of Buddhism was at stake and that it was the duty of the Buddhist monks not only to teach the law but also to do everything possible for its preservation.

Once called in, the monks were extremely effective in organizing a Buddhist mass movement and in politicizing the rural population. There was a monastery attached to practically every village in rural Burma, and according to statistics published in 1893, more than 2.5 percent of the male population of the country were members of the Sangha. Moreover, the custom of becoming a member of the Sangha for a limited period of time, a practice followed by large sections of the Buddhist population, strengthened the ties of the ordinary villager with the life-members of the order. A united Buddhist movement would have been in a position to activate the whole Buddhist population within a short period.

The Buddhist movement, however, had several weaknesses. There was, first, the previously mentioned resistance of strict monks to this sort of activity. It was clear from the beginning that it would be impossible to make any use of what remained of the former hierarchical administration of the Sangha for the nationalist movement. Consequently, the disintegration of Sangha structure—with all its negative consequences for the discipline within this body—was even accelerated during these years. Such a disintegration of the Sangha was the opposite of what the leaders of the reform movement had hoped for. At the same time, the monks who had been able to activate the rural population were not in a position to build up a lasting, working organization of the movement.

Apart from these organizational weaknesses, another factor proved to be even more disastrous for the Buddhist movement in Burma in that period. This factor was the insufficient degree of modernization in the intellectual sphere. The modernists who had provided the initial impulses belonged to the highly educated and modernized urban elite, but rural Burma had remained largely unchanged. We should recall here that Burma was highly isolated and that its traditional cosmological concepts had remained intact until the British annexation. Thus, the movement started by the modernist elite was taken over by tradition-minded members of a rural society still deeply influenced by nonmodern ways of thinking. The modernists could not in any way agree with these concepts, which provided no way to independence and no practicable alternative to colonial rule. The Buddhism of the modernists did not consist of an indiscriminate revival of traditional beliefs, but it was an effort to understand rationally the world on the basis of the Buddha's words. This understanding could not be expected from the rural majority of the monks.

Toward the end of the 1920s, the Buddhist movement of Burma was deeply divided and many modernists openly and strongly criticized the politically active sections of the Sangha on the grounds that their worldly involvements were not in keeping with either the letter or the spirit of the monastic rule.

The events of 1930–31 in Burma cast light on another factor in the politicization of the Sangha, the so-called messianic expectations that existed in Buddhist countries.[14] Buddhist "messianism" is connected with the concept of the law of cycles in the history

14. See Emanuel Sarkisyanz, *Russland und der Messianismus des Orients* (Tübingen: J. C. B. Mohr, 1955), pp. 327–91.

of the universe according to which another Buddha is expected to be born on earth in the future. Details of the biography of this future Buddha named Metteyya (*Maitreya*) are described in a number of classical Buddhist texts like the well-known Anagatavamsa in Pali and its various translations in the modern languages of the Buddhist countries and also in a large number of popular tracts. Before Metteyya will appear, a Cakkavatti (*Cakravartin*), or world emperor, who will be born in Burma, Thailand, or Ceylon is expected to rule. In the *Parakumba Sirita,* a classical Sinhalese poem composed in the fifteenth century, it is said that such a universal Buddhist ruler will be born 2,500 years after the death of the Buddha, and the Sinhalese king in whose praise this work was written, Parakramabahu VI (1412–67), is identified as being this future universal monarch in a previous existence.[15] Similar beliefs were particularly widespread in Burma, and there are numerous associations formed around these traditions.[16] These concepts merged with several elements of Burmese supernaturalism and superstition. During the nineteenth century, several revolts against the declining Burmese monarchy and against British colonial rule in Burma were led by pretenders claiming to be the expected Cakkavatti.

By far the most violent movement of this kind was the Saya San peasant revolt of 1930–32. Saya San was a Burmese ayurvedic physician who had participated in political activities first as a follower of U Chit Hlaing, the first president of the General Council of Burmese Associations, and afterwards in the militant So Thein G.C.B.A., popularly known as the "Pongyi party" because it was completely under the control of the political bhikkhus. Saya San then started to build up his forces by spreading "messianic" prophecies and was assisted by radical factions of the Sangha. For several reasons rural Burma was ripe for large-scale agrarian unrest at that time. In December 1930, Saya San succeeded in organizing an insurrection that spread over most parts of Lower Burma, some districts of Upper Burma, and even some of the Shan states. It was only after two years that the British

---

15. *Parakumba Sirita,* ed. K. D. P. Vikramasimha (Colombo: Gunasena, 1964), p. 236, v. 116.

16. See E. Michael Mendelson, "A Messianic Buddhist Association in Upper Burma," *Bulletin of the School of Oriental and African Studies* 24 (1961): 560–80.

succeeded in completely suppressing this uprising. Saya San had been consecrated as a "Buddha King" by his followers. The arms of the insurgents were completely inadequate, and they believed in the effectiveness of amulets and magical practices rather than in modern weapons. It was the last great traditionalist uprising in Burma, the last desperate attempt to restore old Burma as it had been. Political monks and ex-monks played an important role in mobilizing the rural population, but in an exclusively traditionalist way. In this period, the Sangha had not yet exercised active influence toward modernization of the independence struggle in rural areas to any appreciable extent.[17]

Buddhism and Mass Politics Since Independence

In Ceylon, mass politicization was at its height approximately one decade after independence. Here the anglicized elite that had come to power following colonial rule was not capable of bridging the gap that existed between itself and the masses of the rural population and the lower middle class. The latter consisted mainly of Sinhalese teachers, ayurvedic physicians, astrologers, and, last but not least, Buddhist monks. The movement of 1956 was, however, not an exclusively traditionalist reaction against Western cultural and economic influence, but a particular compromise of three main trends that existed in Ceylon at that time: Buddhist modernism, socialism, and Sinhalese traditionalism. It was a comparatively small group of highly educated politicians headed by S. W. R. D. Bandaranaike (1899–1959) who were able to build up a powerful coalition and to oust the former ruling party in 1956. Bandaranaike had been influenced by Buddhism since his studies in England, as we know from his own words: "Later I went to England and Oxford. Here I found great opportunity of acquiring a better knowledge of Buddhism. While I was reading classics I used to read in the Oxford library a great deal about Buddhism. There I found some wonderful writings on the life of the Buddha . . ."[18] Another leader of the Buddhist movement was Dr.

---

17. See Sarkisyanz, *Buddhist Backgrounds,* pp. 149–65; Bechert, *Buddhismus,* 2 : 112–16.

18. See S. W. R. D. Bandaranaike, "Why I became a Buddhist," *The Buddhist,* n.s. 3 (1934–35): 7–9; reprinted in *World Buddhism* 11, no. 4 (November 1962): 22–23. Bandaranaike's final conversion dated from 1931 when the Donoughmore

Gunapala Piyadasa Malalasekera (George Peiris), a well-known
Pali scholar who had obtained his doctorate in England. Thus, it
is not surprising to find many traces of mutual influence in the
writings of Sinhalese and European Buddhists. This is particularly
conspicuous in their attitude toward the problem of Buddhism
and science.[19]

The ideology of the Sinhalese Buddhist movement of 1956 is
well known to us from its main documents, the report of the
so-called "Buddhist Commission" [20] and D. C. Vijayavardhana's
The Revolt in the Temple.[21] The latter was "composed to com-
memorate 2500 years of the land, the race and the faith," that is,
of Ceylon, the Sinhalese, and Buddhism. As in many other writings of those years, the hopes of Buddhist messianism that a great
revival of Buddhism would be connected with the 2,500th anniversary of the Buddha's death were given expression. The book
was written and published first in English and later translated
into Sinhalese. Its division into "Nidanakatha or The Introduc-
tory Story," "Kalyana Magga or The Path of Happiness" and
"Rajjan ca Paja ca or Man and the State" is intended to remind
the reader of classical works of Pali literature, and the concluding
verses are taken from the Mahabodhivamsa, the Pali chronicle of
the Bodhi tree composed during the twelfth century. The con-
tents of the book consist of a very peculiar mixture of Buddhist
and European thought. The main purpose of the author is to
justify political Buddhism. Buddhism is described as "a universalist humanism," which is meant not as a way to personal liberation,
but as a way to create a better society. "The Buddha did not call
men to the homeless life in order that they might live totally aloof

---

reforms opened the way to universal franchise; see Smith, *South Asian Politics*, p.
456.

19. A useful study of this problem is Charles A. Moore, "Buddhism and Science:
Both Sides," in Susumu Yamaguchi, ed., *Buddhism and Culture, Dedicated to Dr. D.
T. Suzuki in Commemoration of his Ninetieth Birthday* (Kyoto: Suzuki Daisetz
Hakushi Shoju-Kinenkai, 1960) , pp. 89–125.

20. *Bauddha Toraturu Parikshaka Sabhave Vartava* (Balangoda: Dharmavijaya
Mudranalaya, 1956); English version: *The Betrayal of Buddhism, An Abridged Version of the Report of the Buddhist Committee of Inquiry* (Balangoda: Dharmavijaya Press, 1956). See Smith, *South Asian Politics*, pp. 460–67; Bechert, *Buddhismus*,
1 : 267–79.

21. D. C. Vijayavardhana, *Dharma-Vijaya or The Revolt in the Temple* (Colombo:
Sinha Publications, 1953).

from human society, but in order that they might serve the world by living a life of self-forgetful activity" (p. 584). Traditional Buddhism is strongly criticized as having degenerated and having invented a number of doctrines foreign to the original teaching of the Buddha. "The revolt in the temple" is nothing but the recovery of the original social purpose of the Buddhist law. The way towards a better world is the way of social reform resulting in the realization of the ideals of Buddhist socialism.

The Sangha is exhorted to give up its attitudes of otherwordliness, traditionalism, and passivity. Having in its constitution the spirit of true democracy, the Sangha is destined to serve society as a leader in the way to social progress. In *The Revolt in the Temple,* large parts of which were written before 1946,[22] theoretical foundations were laid for the leading role of the Sangha in politically activating the masses of the Sinhalese Buddhist population.

Alongside the arguments derived from a new interpretation of the purpose of the Sangha, which were not really supported by textual evidence, the historical argument was advanced in Vijayavardhana's book and similar publications. The Sangha claimed that it had the right and the duty to act as the political and social leader of the country, because it had acted in this way in the glorious past of the Buddhist nations. A very important document to be mentioned in this connection is the foreword to *The Revolt in the Temple* contributed by Pahamune Dhammakitti Siri-Saranankara Sumangala, who had been the Mahanayaka Thera of the Malvatta branch of Syama Nikaya and thus held the most prestigious position in the Buddhist clergy of Ceylon from 1927 until his death in 1945.[23] Here, on the authority of the ancient chronicles of Ceylon, it is shown "that the claim of the Sangha today to be heard in relation to social, political and economic problems and to guide the people is no new demand, but a reassertion of a right universally exercised and equally widely acknowledged, up to the British occupation of the country" (p. 19). There can be no doubt that in the history of Ceylon the Sangha

22. This is evident from the extracts from the work published in D. C. Wijewardene [Vijayavardhana], *Here is Kelaniya* (Colombo: Daily News Press, 1946), and D. C. Vijayavardhana, *Menna Kalaniya* (Colombo: Loko Yantralaya, 1946).

23. Vijayavardhana, *Dharma-Vijaya,* pp. 11–20.

had wielded influence on many political decisions, if only by upholding the principles of Sinhalese-Buddhist nationalism which, as the guiding ideology of the Sinhalese nation, can be traced as far back as the first century B.C.[24] Arguments taken from the Mahavamsa ("Great Chronicle"), which was valued equally highly as the canonical scriptures, thus tended to replace discussion of the problem on the basis of the Buddha's words as contained in the scriptures.

A majority of the lay Buddhist leaders had censured the first wave of political activism by bhikkhus in 1946–47,[25] but in 1955–56 practically all the Sinhalese politicians of the Mahajana Eksath Peramuna (People's United Front) approved of the Sangha's large-scale involvement in the election campaign. When one of the leaders of the Sangha participation in the 1956 elections, Mapitigama Buddharakkhita, who had exercised considerable power on the Bandaranaike government from behind the stage, was found to have been the head of the conspiracy to murder the prime minister,[26] public criticism of political monks became widespread in 1959–60. Soon afterwards the report of the government-appointed Buddha Sasana Commission was issued.[27] This report called for a number of structural and disciplinary reforms of the Sangha and for measures to give Buddhism a better place in the educational and social sphere. Among the measures recommended were the prohibition of monks' participation in party politics and the establishment of a separate system of Buddhist ecclesiastical courts.

In the following few years, controversy over implementation of the recommendations of the report deeply divided the Buddhist movement in Ceylon. The great Buddhist lay organizations demanded a reform of the Sangha, considering what had happened a disgrace and harmful to the cause of Buddhism. The reformist minority group and sects of the Sangha joined them in demanding

24. See Bechert, "Zum Ursprung der Geschichtsschreibung," pp. 47–58. Cf. also Wilhelm Geiger, *Culture of Ceylon in Mediaeval Times* (Wiesbaden: Harrassowitz, 1960), pp. 203–07.

25. Bechert, *Buddhismus*, 1 : 311–15.

26. For the career of Buddharakkhita see Smith, *South Asian Politics*, pp. 490–99.

27. *Buddha Sasana Komishan Vartava*, XVIII vani Sasi Vartava 1959 (Colombo: Government of Ceylon, Government Press, 1959). See Bechert, *Buddhismus*, 1 : 279–82.

new legislation to regulate the "Buddhist problem." But the conservative majority of the monks strongly opposed any reform and, finally, the issue died down.[28]

Until today, the political activity of the Buddhist monks is a factor to be reckoned with by all major parties, particularly during election times. But on the whole, the political importance of the Sangha is less than in 1955–56 when it substantially contributed to the downfall of the United National Party government, or in 1964 when it was a major factor in the overthrow of the first cabinet headed by Mrs. Sirimavo Bandaranaike. Today, it is a less weighty political factor.

In postindependence Burma, Buddhism was systematically promoted by U Nu through legislation and administrative measures. These measures were not in any way directed towards giving the Sangha a political role again, for the purpose of U Nu's religious policy was to enhance political and social stability by a revival of religion. He believed that the Sangha had to be reformed and kept aloof from political activities in the interests of a real resurgence of religion. It was the political crisis commencing with the split of the ruling party in 1958, and U Nu's election promise to make Buddhism the state religion, that dragged the Sangha into politics again until the Revolutionary Government took over in 1962.[29]

It is evident that the role of the Sangha as a major factor of political mobilization of the masses depends on the concurrence of a number of circumstances. First of all, there must be a gap between the religious and social ideology of the ruling class and that of the masses. Such a gap was clearly present during the colonial period. Nor did it disappear when Burma and Ceylon became independent, because the ways of thinking of the ruling political and bureaucratic elite remained basically different from those of the large majority of the population. Historically, the political activity of the Sangha was not effective whenever such a gap did not exist. Thus, the so-called "Moladanda Rebellion" of 1760 against the Sinhalese king Kirtisri Rajasimha was not successful even though influential members of the Sangha were in-

---

28. See Smith, *South Asian Politics*, pp. 500–09; Bechert, *Buddhismus*, 1 : 282–93.
29. See Smith, *Religion and Politics in Burma*; Bechert, *Buddhismus*, 2 : 3–178.

volved. The king was prudent enough to abstain from severe punishment of the monks involved, in order to avoid a dangerous open conflict between the secular power and the Buddhist clergy.[30]

Other factors were the breakdown of state control over and monastic discipline within the Sangha. In the traditional Buddhist states, where the Sangha had long lost its original status as a fully autonomous body and had become part and parcel of the socio-political system of the state, preservation of the existing political system lay in the interests of the Sangha. As a consequence, the Sangha in a newly conquered territory was considered as a potential instigator of revolt due to its loyalty to the earlier government. Burmese kings repeatedly had the bhikkhus in countries annexed to their empire (e.g., the Mon territories, Arakan, etc.) deported or even killed.[31] After the British step by step had severed the ties connecting Sangha and state in Ceylon (which had been retained in the first decades of colonial rule in accordance with clause 5 of the Kandyan Convention of 1815),[32] and after they had refused to confirm the juridical authority of the Sangha hierarchy over the monasteries in Burma after annexation,[33] they created what Burmese kings had always tried to prevent—a strong and influential Sangha independent of governmental control in a conquered country. At the same time, monastic discipline declined seriously in a majority of monastic establishments. Reformist sects were formed and revived strictly ascetic practices, but they represented only a minority of the members of the Sangha.[34] As a rule, there was no power to prevent bhikkhus from disregarding the regulations of discipline and no power to expel monks who openly violated the monastic rules. The phenomenon of the politically active monk was, in consideration of the very nature of the Sangha's religious mission, inseparable from the decay of the Sangha and the nonexistence of a working system of ecclesiastical courts.

Under these circumstances, both Buddhist reformers and adversaries of Buddhist resurgence were concerned at this develop-

---

30. See Bechert, "Zum Ursprung der Geschichtsschreibung," p. 49.
31. See Smith, *Religion and Politics in Burma,* p. 35.
32. Bechert, *Buddhismus,* 1 : 231–40.
33. Smith, *Religion and Politics in Burma,* pp. 44–57.
34. For reform movements inside the Sangha see Bechert, *Buddhismus,* 1 : 33–34, 215–19, 257–58; 2 : 22–24.

ment. Buddhist reformers feared that the political activity of the Sangha might destroy the reverence for the Sangha by dragging inexperienced monks into the political struggles of the day and thus harm the Buddhist cause in the long run. Adversaries of Buddhist resurgence, not concerned with long-range develop-ments, were fearful of the power of the Sangha to activate the masses for the cause of Buddhist dominance over other interests. Until today, all efforts toward a reform of the Sangha and the reestablishment of an effective Buddhist ecclesiastical jurisdiction in Burma and Ceylon have ended in failure.[35] Thus, there can be no doubt that the Sangha of these countries will remain a poten-tial factor of mass politicization in the future as it has been in the past.

The potential political power of the Sangha emerges into an active force during a political crisis. This was the case when Burmese nationalism first reasserted the self-identity and self-confidence of the Burmese nation after 1917, when the Ceylonese government headed by Sir John Kotelawala completely disre-garded the expectations of the Buddhist population on the eve of the 2500 Buddha Jayanti, when the government of Ceylon tried to nationalize the press in 1964, and when U Nu decided to make use of the state-religion issue for political ends. In all these situa-tions, the nation was divided not only on political issues but also on the basic definition of self-identity. Thus, criticism of the Sangha's activities in worldly matters was counterbalanced in these situations by the widespread feeling that the Sangha had to act in order to preserve religion and national culture from a serious threat.

The close parallel of developments in Vietnam during the so-called "Buddhist crisis" of 1963 with the observations made of Ceylon and Burma shows that the doctrinal difference between Theravada and Mahayana Buddhism had little relevance to the basic problem involved. It was only the particular form of the Vietnamese monks' political protest, self-immolation by fire, that has to do with Mahayana doctrines.[36]

The view expressed here concerning the particular conditions

35. See Smith, *Religion and Politics in Burma,* pp. 210–24; Bechert, *Buddhismus,* 1 : 267–93; 2 : 54–73.
36. Cf. Bechert, *Buddhismus,* 2 : 331–51.

necessary for the role of the Sangha in mass politicization is confirmed by a comparison of the role of the Sangha in Thailand and Cambodia. Here, government control of the Sangha and support for the authority of the hierarchy was never interrupted. Whereas the Sangha organizations in Burma and Ceylon underwent a process of disintegration and fragmentation beginning in the middle of the nineteenth century, the Sangha of Siam was provided with a modern administration under government control during the same period. Instead of the repeatedly enacted reform measures that characterized the history of Theravada Sangha in premodern times,[37] a bureaucratic system effectively prevented the political activity of monks. Recently, monks under the control of the political establishment have been used for the purpose of furthering the modernization process by participation in development projects, but this could eventually create major problems for the position of the Sangha, if the traditional understanding of the role of the monk is changed too abruptly.[38] In Cambodia too, state control has remained intact. Political activity of the Khmer Sangha made itself felt only during crisis situations, particularly during the last few years of the French protectorate.[39]

BUDDHIST LAYMEN AND MASS POLITICIZATION

A discussion of the Buddhist laity's role in the politicizing process cannot be separated from that of the Sangha. The situation of the Sangha depends on the economic situation and on the social structure of lay society. The laity, however, was not organized in traditional Buddhist societies. Its religious life centered around the "temple," that is, the monastery of the village. It was only as a consequence of the social change effected by the impact of foreign influence and the modernization of the social structure that formal organizations of lay Buddhists came into existence. These organizations did not replace the old informal community of lay devotees contributing to the needs of the monks and the temple.

37. Cf. H. Bechert, "Ways of Sasana Reform in Theravada Buddhism," in Labuhengoda Candaratana, ed., *Rhys Davids Memorial Volume* (Colombo: Dhara Pali Sangara Sampadaka Mandalaya, 1965), pp. 145–57.

38. See J. A. Niels Mulder, *Monks, Merit and Motivation* (De Kalb, Ill.: Center for Southeast Asian Studies, Northern Illinois University, 1969).

39. Bechert, *Buddhismus*, 2 : 236–45.

The Buddhist associations of a modern type were started as discussion groups for the revival of Buddhism and for the application of the teachings of Buddhism under changed conditions and, step by step, several of these organizations grew into political pressure groups.[40] The best-known example to illustrate this development is the already mentioned transformation of the Young Men's Buddhist Association into the General Council of Burmese Associations in 1920. The political activities of these Buddhist organizations to "give Buddhism its due place" in the political, social, and cultural life of their societies were not hampered by conflicting views concerning the political activity of the Sangha. Therefore, the importance of the religious element for political development within the Theravada countries was a rather constant factor since the beginning of the modernist movement. However, the Buddhist lay movement suffered from certain inherent weaknesses, namely, the ephemeral nature of most Buddhist associations and the problems arising from the active involvement of the Sangha in the Buddhist political movement.

The rather short existence of many Buddhist associations is easily understood as a consequence of the nonexistence of any lay organization in traditional Buddhist societies. Thus, these associations were able to draw substantial support only as long as their goals were popular. They never were able to function as institutions representing the Buddhist populace as a whole. For the average Buddhist, the only religious organization that he felt was worthy of regular support was the Sangha. Thus, the Buddhist lay organizations were able to organize a high degree of mass participation only during limited periods of political crisis. And for even this purpose they needed the support of the Sangha.

Using the Sangha as a symbol to raise mass support for the Buddhist political movement could be done in two different ways. First, the Sangha could be used as a purely religious symbol, and the political activity of the lay movement directed to restoring conditions in which a Sangha keeping the rules of Vinaya could exist. This meant that the respective Buddhist lay organizations

40. On Buddhist associations see Bechert, *Buddhismus,* 1 : 300–05 (Ceylon), 2 : 86–95 (Burma), 2 : 196–97 (Thailand), 2 : 235–36 (Cambodia).

took over those functions of a patron of the Sangha that the Buddhist state in precolonial times had performed. Much of the Buddhist motivation of the modern political movements of Burma can be described in this way.

However, many of the leaders of the Buddhist lay organizations felt that they were not capable of generating enough mass support for this end without using the Sangha itself as an activator of the Buddhist masses' political awareness. But in using this second approach the lay leaders created the problems that we discussed before. Apart from the contradictions caused by the religious rules and ideology, the insufficient education of a majority of monks (judged by modern standards) contributed to the negative results that are seen in the recent history of these countries. Traditionally, many of the most talented Sinhalese, Burmese, Thai, and Khmer joined the Sangha, which was the most prestigious institution of the country and the center of learning. Under present conditions, however, though the Sangha is still highly revered and worshipped, it is being replaced more and more by secular institutions as the center of learning and scholarship. Thus, the monks tend to join other underprivileged sections of the Buddhist lay society when they actively enter the political arena, and the activity of the Sangha usually worked as an antimodern factor, though the terminology of socialism and other modern movements is being used.

Thus, the role of the Buddhist laity in the process of mass politicization was not less ambiguous than that of the Sangha. Consequently, reformers accepted the principle of a secular state, in which the Sangha existed as a community with purely religious aims, controlled by an activated Buddhist laity taking the responsibility of providing the monks with the "requisites" and administering the property of the Sangha. They failed, due to the insufficient degree of modernization of the Buddhist masses and, needless to say, due to certain inherent weaknesses of human nature. In practical politics, Buddhist values were used to effect political change, as in Ceylon in 1956, or for the legitimation of a political system, as in Burma under U Nu. The pressure to bring about a unity of "church and state" in Burma and Ceylon—to make Buddhism the state religion of these countries—caused further contradictions, since a Sangha whose organizational structure had disintegrated could not function as a partner in building up a Buddhist state, and the Buddhist laity was even less prepared for this role.[41] The issue of a state religion together with the whole range of religious symbols were employed by political groups who were simultaneously using the terminology of socialism for the purpose of winning power; the parties acting in this way were often basically nonmodern in their ways of thinking.

An evaluation of these observations leads to the question of how far Theravada Buddhism and its institutions are able, not only to politically activate the Buddhist population, but also to help in the development of more modern attitudes among the masses in these countries. Answers to this question given so far by Western observers are predominantly in the negative. I would warn, however, against the usual generalizing statements on this problem. The Buddhist communities of Ceylon, Burma, and Thailand have been able to produce modernistic interpretations of the Buddha's teachings that definitely contribute toward removing obstacles to progress and toward making popular attitudes in these countries more rational. Thus, Buddhism can potentially be a factor supporting modernization, if the education of the monks and of the Buddhist population at large is influenced by a rational and modern understanding. It is with this judgment that lay Buddhists and governments in Theravada countries have built up a system of monastic schools and examinations. No injunction against political activity can completely stop the bhikkhus from influencing the political views of the rural population under the social conditions prevailing in these countries. Thus, modernizaation of the monks' views by raising their educational standard is the only way out of the contradictory position of the Buddhists vis-à-vis the problems of our time.

41. On the state religion issue see Bechert, *Buddhismus,* 1 : 294–300; 2 : 73–86. The state-religion issue was taken up again in Ceylon in 1970–71; see "Buddhism will be State Religion, says Premier," *World Buddhism* 19 (1970–71): 192–93; "Rightful place for Buddhism," ibid. 19 (1970–71): 253.

9

Islam and Mass Politics:
The Indian Ulama and the Khilafat Movement

GAIL MINAULT

The *ulama,* or Islamic religious leaders, were not the principal initiators of the Khilafat movement but played a crucial role in transforming it into a mass movement.[1] As Donald E. Smith has observed: "In traditional societies, religion is a mass phenomenon, politics is not," and thus, "religion can serve as the means by which the masses become politicized."[2] How this occurred in the case of the Khilafat movement is the subject of this chapter.

I propose to examine three separate points: (1) how the ulama got involved in anti-British politics in the first place; (2) how they organized politically and with what ends in view; and (3) what they did to attain those ends during the Khilafat movement. An examination of these points will enable us to understand the ulama's role and assess their effectiveness in politicizing the Indian Muslim masses.

The Emergence of Anti-British Politics

As the custodians of traditional Islamic culture, the ulama could naturally have been expected to oppose any non-Muslim conquest which eclipsed that culture and their role in it. In fact, in the early nineteenth century Shah Abdul Aziz, a leading *alim* of Delhi, issued a *fatwa,* or ruling on a point of Islamic law, that was distinctly anti-British. He called India under British rule *dar al-harb,* or "territory of war," in which all Muslims are bound by their religion to wage holy war (*jihad*) against the usurpers or

1. The Arabic *Khilafat* is generally used to designate the movement, rather than the English word *caliphate* that is derived from it.
2. Smith, *Religion and Political Development,* p. 124.

to resort to emigration (*hijrat*) to escape them.[3] His call to jihad was heeded by the Mujahidin movement of Sayyid Ahmad Brelvi and Shah Ismail Shahid in the early 1830s and by other ulama who took part in the 1857 revolt against the British. Other ulama took the hijrat alternative and migrated to Mecca to escape infidel rule.

But the ulama were by no means united as a class, and thus their response to British rule was not unanimous. By the late nineteenth century, it was apparent that calls to jihad were fruitless and that more could be accomplished by finding a modus vivendi with British rule and concentrating on revitalizing Indian Islamic culture from within. Fatwas were issued modifying Shah Abdul Aziz's ruling that India had become dar al-harb under the British. It was now said that as long as the Muslims were free to practice their faith without interference, Muslims could live in peace under British rule.[4]

One group of divines who sought to reform Islamic culture from within were the ulama of the Deoband school. They were the spiritual descendants of Shah Waliullah and Shah Abdul Aziz, as well as others of the Delhi school who had emigrated to Mecca, but the Deobandis clearly wanted to stay in India and build up their new institution after 1867. Whatever their past feelings about dar al-harb, the Deobandis had turned in their swords for pens. The Deoband administration scrupulously avoided political activity of any kind in order to concentrate on refurbishing Islamic religious education and on spreading the observances of Islamic religion and obedience to the injunctions of Islamic law more widely in the community than ever before. To increase their ties to the community and to avoid undue government influence, they refused government patronage and sought a broad base of financial support among Muslims of all classes. But this move did not reflect an anti-British stance, just good public relations. In fact, many of those contributing to the support of the Deoband school were government servants.[5]

3. Shah Abdul Aziz, *Fatawa-e-Aziziya* [Urdu trans.] (Kanpur: Matba'-e-Majidiya, n.d.), 1 : 35–37.

4. W. W. Hunter, *The Indian Mussalmans* (Reprint ed., Varanasi: Indological Book House, 1969), app. 2, p. 208; Rashid Ahmad Gangohi, *Fatawa-e-Rashidiya* (Deoband: Kutub Khana-e-Rahimiya, n.d.), p. 76.

5. I am grateful to Barbara Metcalf for the information, gleaned from Deoband's

At Deoband, then, the ulama had found at least a means of coexisting with British rule. Other ulama followed suit. The Nadwat al-Ulama in Lucknow went even further in seeking accommodation with the British. The Nadwa not only accepted government patronage but also attempted, with little success, to blend the traditional Islamic and Western curricula.[6]

This situation continued up until 1911–13, when a series of political events that were particularly upsetting to the Muslims combined to drive the ulama closer to anti-British political action. The same events showed the younger generation of Western-educated Muslims the usefulness of religious appeals for political purposes. The Muslims' modus vivendi with the government was seriously affected in 1911 when the British revoked the partition of Bengal. By eliminating the Muslim majority province of Eastern Bengal and Assam, the government removed an important source of administrative posts and political influence for the Muslim community. The government's decision also showed Muslim political leaders that *agitation,* such as that of the Hindu-led antipartition forces rather than pronouncements of loyalty to the British raj now got results. In the same year began the series of Balkan wars against Turkey, another source of Muslim anxiety. The wars were widely viewed as evidence that the Christian powers were conspiring to crush the Ottoman Empire and the Ottoman sultan, who was also the caliph of Islam. This theory of a Christian plot to overthrow the caliphate, and its corollary, a mistrust of British intentions in the Middle East, were to become even more important after World War I, at the beginning of the Khilafat movement.

The political incident that showed both the ulama and the westernized Muslims what could be accomplished politically by appeals to religious emotion was the Kanpur Mosque agitation of 1913. In this, the ulama and the Western educated were united in their religious indignation and together, with the backing of the community, were able to gain concessions from the British

---

Annual Proceedings, that of some 2,500 regular contributors to the school, over one-third were government servants. Thus it would seem that Deoband maintained cordial relations with the administration.

6. Sir James Meston, "Note on the History of the Nadwa," 22 April 1915, U.P. Education Dept. 55, 1914, U.P. Secretariat Records.

government. The trouble began when the Kanpur municipality demolished the washing place of a mosque to make room for a new road. The Muslims of Kanpur condemned the action as desecration of a place of worship and hence a threat to Islam. A group of local ulama issued a fatwa declaring that the washing place was just as sacred as any other part of the mosque and demanding its restoration, but the local government refused. A mass meeting of Kanpur Muslims was held, addressed by Maulana Azad Subhani, a prominent local alim and an accomplished orator. He said that the local government did not believe that their emotions were genuine, that Islam was in danger, and that it was their duty to show the genuineness of their feelings and to sacrifice their lives if necessary. The crowd surged out of the meeting, went to the damaged mosque to pray, was met by an armed police contingent, and a riot ensued in which several Muslims were killed.[7]

At this point, the leading Muslim newspapers of the country, Muhammad Ali's *Comrade,* Zafar Ali Khan's *Zamindar,* and Abul Kalam Azad's *Al-Hilal,* attacked the government for interfering with their religion, appealed for funds to aid the bereaved families, and turned the affair from a local dispute into a confrontation between Islam and the central government.[8] For once, the younger Muslims trained at Aligarh and the ulama spoke with one voice on a political issue. The viceroy, Lord Hardinge, began to look upon the incident as a "stupid blunder" by the local government and decided to go to Kanpur and settle the matter, agreeing to restore the demolished portion of the mosque.[9] The Muslims were jubilant. The combined efforts of politicians and ulama, and their insistence on the religious nature of the issue, had won the day and had given them a pattern for future political campaigns.

On the eve of World War I, therefore, there was already a strong current of anti-British feeling among Indian Muslims as a result of events both within India and without. Political activity among the Muslim masses, characterized by religious ap-

---

7. *Muslim Gazette* (Lucknow), 9, 16 July, 6, 16 August 1913; reprinted in *U.P. Native Newspaper Reports, 1913,* pp. 704–05, 734–37, 815–17. Sir James Meston, "Minute on the Cawnpore Mosque Incident," Home (Pol) A, 100–18, October 1913, National Archives of India (NAI).

8. *Comrade* (Delhi), 9 August 1913; Meston, "Cawnpore Mosque Incident."

9. Note by Hardinge, 8 September 1913, in Meston, "Cawnpore Mosque Incident."

peals by both ulama and westernized Muslims, was still in its embryonic stage. But the concern about the Turkish caliph during the Balkan wars and the effectiveness of the Kanpur Mosque agitation showed that religious feeling was strong and could be harnessed to gain political points against the government. During World War I, however, pro-Turkish sympathy was definitely unfashionable. Those Muslim leaders who advocated it found themselves either silenced by government internment orders or carried away by the tide of pro-British pronouncements. A major political movement utilizing religious sentiments had to wait until after the war.

ORGANIZING FOR THE DEFENSE OF ISLAM

In turning to the question of how the ulama organized for political activity and with what ends in view, it would be well to look at a few examples of their organization prior to the Khilafat movement. At Deoband and other theological schools, or *madrasas*, the ulama were essentially concerned with establishing educational centers to reform and perpetuate the traditional Islamic curriculum and to confirm their traditional role as the cultural and social arbiters of their community. In addition, these madrasas became the focal points for social service organizations led by ulama, also designed to increase their influence in the community at large.

One example of such an organization was the Jamiat al-Ansar, an organization of former students of Deoband begun in 1909 by Maulana Mahmud al-Hasan, the principal of Deoband, and one of his favorite disciples, Maulana Ubaidullah Sindhi. The Jamiat was a religious and cultural organization that openly disavowed any political aims. Some of its activities were the publication of inexpensive religious books and pamphlets, the placement of well-trained *imams* in mosques, and the making of arrangements for teaching Arabic to Muslim students in government schools. Thus the organization acted as a means of communicating religious messages to a wider public than had been reached before by Deoband graduates and also aimed at reaching Western-educated Muslim students, whom the ulama regarded as virtual infidels.

The activities of the Jamiat were, indeed, strictly religious and cultural, but there was more to these activities than was at first apparent. In addition to the above aims, the Jamiat, or at least its leading exponents, Maulanas Mahmud al-Hasan and Ubaidullah Sindhi, made some specific recommendations for reform at the Deoband madrasa itself: The curriculum should be changed to emphasize the reformist teachings of Shah Waliullah and his successors, and there should be a greater emphasis on public speaking and writing. These recommendations are evidence that Mahmud al-Hasan and his followers were seeking to gain control over the curriculum of the Deoband school by means of an alumni pressure group. They sought to challenge the power of the administrative head of the madrasa and his followers, whose insistence on the apolitical nature of Deoband had deemphasized the tradition of activism among the ulama.[10]

This factional struggle at the madrasa was based, I suspect, as much on personalities as on ideological differences but had the effect of reviving feelings favoring the anti-infidel activism of an earlier day. The simultaneity of such factional struggles, their organizational expression at the madrasas, and the political events described above is, I believe, significant and reinforced the trend toward anti-British political activity among the ulama.

The Jamiat al-Ansar also proposed founding branches of the organization all over the country and actively canvassing for funds. It is clear that the ulama associated with the Jamiat were thinking in terms of an enlarged constituency. Their aims were religious and cultural, but their organization was in embryonic form what would eventually become a political party of ulama. At other madrasas, similar organizations were founded by similar factional groupings, one of which was the Anjuman Muid al-Islam, started by Maulana Abdul Bari at Firangi Mahal in Lucknow in 1910.[11]

Another important organization of the pre–World War I period that involved both ulama and Western-educated Muslims was the Anjuman-e-Khuddam-e-Kaaba, or Society of the Servants of the Kaaba, founded in 1913 by Maulana Abdul Bari of Firangi Mahal

---

10. Azizur Rahman, *Tazkira-e-Shaikh al-Hind* (Bijnor: Madni Dar al Talif, 1965), pp. 152–54, 168–72; Jamiat al-Ansar, *Qawaid o Maqasid* (Lucknow: Jamiat al-Ansar, A. H. 1330 [1912]).

11. The Muid al-Islam comprised Maulana Abdul Bari's disciples at Firangi Mahal, organized to propagate the proper observance of the injunctions of Islamic law in the community. Anjuman-e-Muid al-Islam, *Dastur al-Amal o Maqasid* (Lucknow: Anjuman Muid al-Islam, A.H. 1328 [1910]).

and Shaukat and Muhammad Ali. The Ali brothers were the major political activists among the younger Aligarh generation of that day, and they were also religious disciples of Abdul Bari. The Anjuman arose in response to the feeling among Indian Muslims at the time of the Balkan wars that there was a serious threat of a Christian invasion of the holy cities of Islam. The Ali brothers and Maulana Abdul Bari were unquestionably sincere in their concern for the safety of the holy places and the maintenance of the caliph's authority in the area, but they also could not pass up a golden opportunity to organize the Muslims behind their own leadership for the defense of Islam.

The Anjuman's aims were to maintain the honor of the Kaaba in Mecca and the other holy places of Islam and to defend them against non-Muslim aggression, purposes that they proclaimed to be "strictly religious, having nothing to do with politics." But it is very difficult to dissociate politics from religion in such matters. To accomplish its aims, the Anjuman planned to solicit the membership of every Muslim in India and to collect a membership fee of one rupee per year. These funds were to be used for the upkeep of Muslim holy places, for helping destitute Indian *hajis*, and for other social and educational purposes among Indian Muslims.[12]

The Anjuman enjoyed remarkable success in 1913, owing no doubt to the widespread pro-Turkish sentiments among Indian Muslims in the aftermath of the Balkan wars and to religious indignation over the Kanpur Mosque affair. Meetings were held in most major cities; offices of the Anjuman were set up in Delhi, Lucknow, Bombay, and Hyderabad, with smaller branches in U.P. and the Punjab; and some 8,000 members were enrolled during the year.[13] The society also collected a large, if undisclosed, sum of money, thanks to the oratorical skills of the Ali brothers and Maulana Abdul Bari. But though its cause was popular, the Anjuman did not succeed in enrolling all Indian Muslims nor in uniting those it did sign up. On the contrary, its ranks were soon sundered by a factional dispute concerning misuse of the funds. No one is quite sure what happened to all the money, although part of it

12. "Constitution of the Proposed Anjuman-e-Khuddam-e-Kaaba," *Urdu-e-Mualla* (Aligarh), May–June 1913; reprinted in *U.P. Native Newspaper Reports, 1913*, pp. 513–16.

13. Shaukat Ali, "Report of the Anjuman for the Year 1913" (Abdul Bari papers, Firangi Mahal, Lucknow).

went to establish Shaukat Ali in business as a pilgrimage broker in Bombay.[14] The Anjuman was nevertheless a significant step toward cooperation between the ulama and Western-educated Muslims, and it established a pattern of fund raising that was used successfully during the Khilafat movement.

In these early organizations of ulama, the primary aim was to reform or preserve Islamic traditions, including the ulama's importance in Muslim society. To achieve these aims, the ulama sought to establish new lines of communication with the community at large. The Western-educated Muslims were simultaneously seeking ways of broadening their political following in the community. When the two groups cooperated, as in the Kanpur Mosque incident and the Anjuman-e-Khuddam-e-Kaaba, their religiopolitical campaigns emphasized the defense of Islamic holy places and symbols. In their manipulation of these symbols, the ulama were still mainly concerned with guiding the community along correct religious lines, but they were also serving as political middlemen, and this role would become more explicit during the Khilafat movement.

The first overtly political party of Indian ulama, the Jamiat al-Ulama-e-Hind, was founded in 1919 at the beginning of the Khilafat movement. A prime mover in this organization was Maulana Abdul Bari of Firangi Mahal. Throughout 1919, he appealed to his fellow ulama to organize in order to lead the Muslim defense of the caliphate from extinction at the hands of the Christian West. He emphasized that this was essentially a question of defending the faith and hence was a matter in which the ulama were the natural leaders of the community.[15] He also emphasized the need for unity among the various groups and factions of ulama in this matter. Whatever their differences, personal or sectarian, all should be forgotten in the face of this threat to their faith. It was a powerful appeal, though not all were won over to the cause.

The Jamiat first met on 25 November 1919 in Delhi under the presidency of Abdul Bari; it resolved to promote Indian Muslim

14. F. Isemonger, "Note on the Anjuman," 20 February 1914, Home (Pol) A, 46, May 1914, NAI; Shaukat Ali, Leaflet outlining the Anjuman's service to pilgrims (Abdul Bari papers, Firangi Mahal, Lucknow).

15. Abdul Bari, "Presidential Address to the Anjuman-e-Ulama, Bengal, Chittagong," *Al-Nizamiya* 4 (9 December 1918); *idem, Presidential Address to the Anjuman-e-Ulama, U.P.* (Lucknow: Anjuman-e-Ulama, 1919).

unity through the rapprochement of various schools of ulama and to meet again in December simultaneously with the Congress, Muslim League, and newly formed Khilafat Committee. Mufti Kafayatullah, a prominent Delhi alim and a Deoband product, was elected president, but other Deobandis were conspicuous by their absence.[16] The administration of Deoband, long opposed to political activity, maintained its apolitical stance for the time being.

The December 1919 meetings of the Jamiat al-Ulama emphasized two elements in the ulama's political thinking. First was their desire to maintain a separate organization, distinct from the Muslim League or other political groupings of Muslims. Mufti Kafayatullah called for unity among the ulama in an organization of their own, through which they could influence the community in both political and religious matters.[17] The ulama were wary of subordinating themselves to the westernized politicians, whose knowledge of religion they doubted. Secondly, the aims of the Jamiat stressed religious guidance over political activism. Perhaps to promote unity among the factious ulama, the Jamiat's political program was still vague. The aims of the organization included the leadership of the community according to the tenets of Islamic law and the strengthening of ties with the rest of the Islamic world. A more outspoken list of aims, including defense of the holy places of Islam and independence for India, came later. One of their few ideas for immediate political action was to urge the government to pay attention to Muslim opinion in favor of the preservation of the caliphate. If this was not done, they asserted, "the government will have great difficulties." [18]

A RELIGIOPOLITICAL MASS MOVEMENT

The Khilafat movement was begun by the Indian Muslims after World War I to pressure the British and other European powers into maintaining the territories of the Ottoman Empire intact and

16. "Proceedings of the Jamiat al-Ulama Meeting, Delhi, November 25, 1919," *Mukhtasar Halat-e-Iniqad-e-Jamiat al-Ulama-e-Hind* (Delhi: Jamiat al-Ulama-e-Hind, 1920), pp. 2–5.

17. "Proceedings of the Jamiat Meeting, Amritsar, December 28, 1919," ibid., p. 14.

18. S. Muhammad Miyan, *Jamiat al-Ulama-e-Hind Kya Hai?* (Delhi: al-Jamiat Press, 1946), 1 : 10, 2 : 13–14; cf. Ziya-ul-Hasan Faruqi, *The Deoband School and the Demand for Pakistan* (Bombay: Asia Publishing House, 1963), pp. 68–69.

the temporal and spiritual powers of the caliph undiminished. To do this, the Khilafat leaders, most notably the Ali brothers, had to rally mass support among the Muslims, much as had been done on a smaller scale during the Kanpur Mosque incident. Their purpose was not only religious, to preserve the caliphate, but was equally political—to unify the Indian Muslims behind their own leadership and to establish themselves as the political spokesmen for the Muslim community, displacing those who had previously directed Muslim politics from the bar associations of Lucknow and Bombay. There are no compelling reasons to doubt the sincerity of their appeals for the defense of Islam, but it cannot be ignored that religious appeals were also the means of cementing an alliance between Western-educated politicians and ulama and of reaching the pious, still unpoliticized, Muslim masses.

The leadership of the Indian National Congress was similarly confronted at this time with a new type of political leader in the person of M. K. Gandhi. He took political activity out of the Council Houses and into the fields of Bihar and the mills of Ahmedabad, concentrating on local issues to organize massive nonviolent resistance to the British rulers. It was their similar political style and desire for mass support that attracted Gandhi and the Khilafatists to each other. Each needed the support of the other's following, and so they contracted a marriage of convenience: Gandhi supported the Khilafat movement in return for Muslim support for his new political strategy of nonviolent noncooperation.

In examining what the ulama did during the Khilafat movement, it is important to keep in mind the differences in political approach on the part of the divines and the westernized Muslims. For both, religion and politics were inextricably mingled, but the emphasis differed. Broadly speaking, the westernized leaders were involved in the defense of religion for political advantage; the ulama were involved in politics for the defense of religion.

The ulama were important middlemen in spreading the Khilafat and noncooperation messages among the mass of believers, but they were not the only Muslim religious elite involved in the process. In Sindh, for example, the religious leaders called Pirs enjoyed a particularly important position in rural society. The Pirs were the spiritual descendants of the Sufis who had converted the Sindh to Islam, and the shrines with which they were associated not only benefited from large endowments of land (and the influence that implied) but served as habitual meeting places for worship or other purposes. During the Khilafat movement, the Pirs held meetings in shrines and in villages all over Sindh, preaching that their infidel government had taken over the holy cities of Islam and had defiled them by slaughtering pigs, drinking liquor, and walking with their boots on in the sacred precincts. It was therefore incumbent upon every Muslim to adopt noncooperation with the government or else be condemned to eternal hellfire. Among the illiterate rural Muslims, few knew who the sultan of Turkey was or what the Khilafat was all about, but they did know that their religion was in danger and that the government was somehow to blame.[19] These statements certainly aroused interest in the defense of Islam, but whether they were conducive to nonviolent protest is another matter.

One result of this fire-and-brimstone oratory was the Hijrat movement in the summer of 1920. Among the rural Muslims of Sindh and the Northwest Frontier, ideas of organizing to put political pressure on the British government were much too sophisticated. What they understood from their Pirs and local imams was that Islam was in danger, and one of the ways to save themselves from eternal damnation was to migrate to a country where Islam was still safe—in this case, Afghanistan. The idea was given added weight by fatwas in favor of the migration by two prominent Khilafatist ulama: Maulanas Abdul Bari and Abul Kalam Azad. Their pronouncements were qualified, urging hijrat, or migration, only as an alternative to noncooperation.[20] But thousands took their advice, sold their immovable property, and headed for the Afghan border in the blazing heat of July and August. Soon the Khyber Pass was clogged with caravans of bullock carts, camels, and people afoot carrying their few belongings toward the promised land. Tribesmen plundered the column of migrants, and many were felled by hunger, thirst, and heatstroke. As the tide of immigrants reached 30,000, the Afghan amir issued a proclamation urging

19. Fortnightly Report from Bombay, 17–21 February 1920, Home (Pol) D, 8, June 1920; C.I.D. Report from Karachi, 1 April 1920, Home (Pol) A, 342 & KW, May 1920, NAI.

20. Abdul Bari's fatwa in *Independent* (Allahabad), 24 July 1920; English translation of Azad's fatwa in Malik, *Moslem Nationalism*, app. B, pp. 343–44.

that no more attempt to come. Some lucky ones reached a haven in Afghanistan, but several thousand disillusioned and penniless wanderers returned to India, while many others died en route.[21]

The Ali brothers and the Khilafat Committee were caught unprepared for this movement. At first they hoped it would blow over after a few enthusiasts had gone off to Afghanistan, and they urged all Muslims to stay in India and work for the cause of noncooperation. They stepped in and tried to supervise the movement only when the number of emigrants had reached such alarming proportions that some order had to be brought out of chaos.[22] The movement showed the Khilafat leaders the strength of religious feeling among rural Muslims and the energy that could be released by tapping it. It also demonstrated the frequent incongruence between the pronouncements of the Central Khilafat Committee in cooperation with Gandhi and those of many ulama and preachers at the local level.

As the noncooperation movement progressed in late 1920 and 1921, the ulama became even more active both as middlemen and as exponents of their own views. Maulana Abdul Bari busily rounded up 500 signatures for a fatwa in favor of noncooperation. *The Unanimous Fatwa of Indian Ulama,* as it was titled, was the most uncompromising statement of the noncooperation program yet published and was quickly banned by the government. It said that any cooperation whatsoever with the enemy of Islam, the British government, was religiously unlawful. This not only included membership in Legislative Councils, education in government schools, and the practice of law in government courts (all parts of Gandhi's first stage of noncooperation) but also service in the police and military and the payment of taxes, forms of civil disobedience that the Mahatma had scrupulously postponed. Regarding cooperation with the Hindus, the fatwa stated that it was possible for Muslims to take the advice of friendly non-Muslims, but the leadership of an infidel over Muslims was not permissible.[23]

21. Fortnightly Report from NWFP, 14 August 1920, Home (Pol) D, 11, August 1920, NAI; *Tribune* (Lahore), 21 August 1920; *Bombay Chronicle,* 10 September 1920.
22. Secretaries of the Central Khilafat Committee, "Appeal to the Muhajirin," in the *Bombay Chronicle,* 27 August 1920.
23. *Mutafiqa Fatwa-e-Ulama-e-Hind* (Bombay: Central Khilafat Committee, 1920).

The fatwa showed that ulama were not about to let the Mahatma take over leadership of the Muslims. One could accept Gandhi's advice, but Muslims must retain their freedom of action in religious matters. They did not say that the Muslims should also retain their freedom of political action, but this was doubtless implied. Supporting this contention was the campaign by the ulama for a separate system of Muslim *shari'ah* courts. Nationalist arbitration courts to take the place of the boycotted government courts were all very well, but the Muslims should also have their own, and the ulama should head them.[24]

More important than their fatwas for the movement as a whole, however, was the fact that the ulama began to reach audiences previously uninvolved in politics. Village mosques were convenient and inviolable meeting places, and local imams and itinerant preachers could always summon a crowd of believers to hear what they had to say. The Pirs of Sindh had already been active at the village level, and now the ulama of U.P. organized a Khilafat delegation under Abdul Majid Badayuni, a noted orator. He and a group of Abdul Bari's disciples from Firangi Mahal toured villages in U.P. during the winter months of 1921, speaking on behalf of the Khilafat and noncooperation.[25] Here the fine points of Islamic law gave way to the sonorous generalities of Urdu rhetoric. Khilafat grievances were reduced to a simple matter of redemption or damnation. The faithful were told that their salvation was being threatened by their British rulers, and thus they should boycott British goods, schools, and law courts and start their own shari'ah courts. The villagers responded to this "Islam in danger" cry with enthusiasm; money and ornaments poured into the coffers of the Khilafat fund, and officials noted a decrease in attendance at village schools and an increasing boycott of foreign goods.[26] It is doubtful whether a purely political appeal could have called forth the same demonstration of support.

The ulama were effective political agents in rallying support for

24. Fortnightly Report from Bombay, 1 November 1920, Home (Pol) D, 66, December 1920, NAI.

25. *Independent* (Allahabad), 10, 24 February 1921; *Bombay Chronicle,* 1 March 1921.

26. "Brief Resume of Political Activities in each Police Circle, Rai Bareilly District," January–February 1921, U.P. Genl. Administration Dept., 50, 1921, U.P. Secretariat Records.

the Khilafat movement and for the strategy of noncooperation, but they were still basically concerned with the defense of Islam. In this, they tended to outrun the noncooperation program. While not necessarily politic, their point of view had a certain logic: If defiance of governmental authority was a religious duty, why hold back from disobeying the police and refusing to pay taxes? Civil disobedience was the next step in mass noncooperation, and the ulama were impatient for it to begin. The government's banning of the noncooperation fatwa in the summer of 1921 only increased their restiveness.

In August and September of 1921, the Jamiat al-Ulama held a series of public meetings in Delhi that were attended by thousands of the faithful. The meetings were addressed by such leading ulama as Mufti Kafayatullah, president of the Jamiat, and Ahmad Said, a Delhi alim known for his sharp tongue. In condemning the confiscation of the noncooperation fatwa, Ahmad Said said nothing about its content but rather emphasized that since the fatwa was an abstract of God's orders, its proscription was a sacrilege. He called upon the Jamiat al-Ulama to give the word for civil disobedience to begin. Muslims would then quit the army and police, and any violence that ensued would be all the fault of the government.[27]

Gandhi was aghast. The Ali brothers were already on their way to jail on charges of inciting to violence. The ulama too were now ready to risk violence in order to defend Islam and were thus inviting that government repression which the movement had heretofore so skillfully avoided. The ulama had served almost too well as outriders of the movement. If civil disobedience began without proper preparation, nonviolence would be a dead letter and Gandhi's position of leadership severely jeopardized, as would be the Hindu-Muslim alliance.

For all their effectiveness in serving as middlemen during the Khilafat and noncooperation movement, the ulama at times appeared to be working at cross-purposes with their Western-educated coreligionists who were allied with the Congress. However, we must bear in mind their fundamentally different orientation to

27. Fortnightly Reports from Delhi, 16 August, 2 September 1921, Home (Pol) 18, August 1921; Chief Commissioner of Delhi to Home Secretary, Govt. of India, 2 September 1921, Home (Pol) 137, 1921, NAI.

politics. The ulama were still basically concerned with the religious and jurisprudential guidance of the community. The Jamiat al-Ulama scrupulously maintained its autonomy from the other political organizations of Muslims in order to articulate the ulama's point of view, but it nevertheless supported the political strategy espoused by the Ali brothers in cooperation with Gandhi. As long as the westernized Muslims recognized the guidance of the ulama in matters of religion, the two groups could work together. The Ali brothers and their followers offered that recognition, since they needed the support of the ulama to broaden their political influence in the community. They had seized upon the Khilafat issue, among other reasons, because it was an ideal one upon which to build an alliance between themselves and the divines.

In sum, the alliance proved relatively successful. The generality of Indian Muslims participated in political activity as never before, and the Muslim leaders who sought a broader base of political support became the recognized spokesmen for their community in the eyes of the Congress under Gandhi and in the eyes of the British government. They did not ultimately save the institution of the caliphate, but they succeeded in using the symbol to generate wider political participation in their community.

10

Catholic Priests and Mass Politics in Chile

LUCY C. BEHRMAN

That Catholic priests have been a significant political factor might be assumed a priori given the wealth of the Chilean church, its control over educational institutions, the relatively high status of the priests living in the countryside, and the historical interest of the church in matters of social and political doctrine. But the *type* of political role cannot be so easily designated. Indirectly the priests may have influenced politics by shaping the ideas of the elite who passed through their schools. Also indirectly, behind the political scene, the church definitely did contribute large amounts of money to favored politicians. Openly and directly, in addition, the priests sought to politicize the masses in a church-approved direction by organizing Christian trade unions and social groups and by admonishing and threatening their parishioners at election time, backing up their speeches with warnings of ultimate sanctions for those who disobeyed.

The influence of the priests in any of these roles is not obvious; it requires a knowledge of the relative power of other factors shaping Chilean politics before the popular, or governmental, response to the priest's maneuvers can be evaluated. Further, understanding their political impact requires some knowledge of the changes in orientation generally among church leaders over time and the degree of conflict among them, in terms of their temporal objectives and the accepted methods of influencing politics. This study can neither sketch all the relevant background information on church attitudes toward Chilean politics nor present systematically all the evidence bearing on the different types of priestly involvement in politics referred to above. It will, however, suggest some of the major factors that must be considered and some tentative conclusions that others hopefully may investigate more intensively.

Church and Politics in Latin America

The political roles of the Chilean priests are set against the backdrop of the Catholic church's entanglement in politics all over Latin America. More than various other major religions, Catholicism has been concerned with shaping men's temporal existence; even in their most conservative phase church leaders were concerned and involved.[1] When the Spanish and Portuguese colonial regimes were succeeded by highly unstable independent governments, the church remained, changing gradually internally, perhaps, but still the same institution, relatively stable and, in many countries, relatively rich. But the apparent stability of the church masked its steadily declining influence throughout the nineteenth and twentieth centuries. By the time of the Second Vatican Council (1962–1966) its plight was widely recognized. Separation of church and state in many countries had limited the authority of the Catholic hierarchy over the lives of laymen. In some countries, in addition, outright confiscation of church lands and wealth had weakened Catholic power directly. More importantly, the image of the church was increasingly becoming a negative one to the masses of Latin Americans. The church was identified with conservatism and with an emphasis on order and stability rather than on justice and social reform. At no time had the church really had close, intimate ties with the people or been the source of a religious-moral foundation for the growth of an accepted set of values; instead, its authority had been based on political and economic identification with the ruling elites.[2] Thus, even at the apex of its power, there was a wide gulf between the leaders and their parishioners.

The loss of authority was reflected in a period of serious questioning inside the Catholic hierarchy itself. This questioning, which is still not resolved, raised doubts about the organization, authority, and even mission of the church as these were traditionally conceived. Demonstrating the general confusion and doubt,

---

1. See the comparison of the scope of Catholic concern to the scope of other religions in Smith, *Religion and Political Development*, pp. 17–32, 50–56.

2. Ivan Vallier, "Religious Elites: Differentiations and Developments in Roman Catholicism," in Lipset and Solari, *Elites in Latin America*, pp. 193–197. See commentary on the weakness of the church in Mecham, *Church and State*, p. 424.

the ranks of the clergy were decimated. The insecurity of the clergy was reinforced by the loss of status that they suffered as the church itself lost status relative to other institutions in society.[3] In Latin America the resignation and withdrawal of priests was (and is) a severe problem as the ratio of priests to people was very small.

There is, however, a great diversity among the various countries in terms of the influence of the church in politics and the nature of that influence, which the following four examples will illustrate. In Colombia, for example, the church still dominates education and has an important role in other political and social spheres. The church hierarchy is overwhelmingly conservative and identified with the current political regime, although a minority of the clergy have demonstrated their dissatisfaction with this stance and their concern for social reform. In particular, the deceased priest Camilo Torres symbolizes the revolutionary wing of the Colombian church.[4]

In Mexico, in contrast to Colombia, the powerful conservative clergy clashed directly with the revolutionary government in 1926–29. The church was a target for attack by the revolutionary regime and, in consequence, lost much of its land and possessions while anticlerical legislation stripped it of many prerogatives. The current Mexican church, however, remains an important institution in society as it is the focus of a powerful folk religion. Persecution by the government has more or less ceased. The church leaders remain generally conservative, uninvolved in politics and social reform directly, but with continuing contacts with the masses who attend services. A fraction of the clergy, represented by the bishop of Cuernavaca, is more modern, progressive, and concerned with the role of church in society. They are a minority but have taken strong public stands on issues involving church activism and the reform of Catholicism.[5]

3. See David Mutchler, "Adaptations of the Roman Catholic Church to Latin American Development: the Meaning of Internal Church Conflict," *Social Research* 36 (Summer 1969), pp. 231–52.

4. See Ivan Vallier, *Catholicism, Social Control and Modernization*, pp. 123–26; Mecham, *Church and State*, pp. 115–38; Smith, *Religion and Political Development*, p. 18; and also Camilo Torres Restrepo, "Social Change and Rural Violence in Colombia," in Irving Louis Horowitz, ed., *Masses in Latin America* (New York: Oxford University Press, 1970), pp. 503–46.

5. Vallier, *Catholicism, Social Control and Modernization*, pp. 129–30; Mecham,

The socially concerned minority of the clergy is much more visible in Brazil. Here the conservative and liberal wings of the church are more evenly balanced in terms of influence. The well-known archbishop of Recife, Dom Helder Câmara, is a recognized spokesman for those advocating Catholic involvement and dedication to social reform. In addition, the liberal wing of the church supports the program of the Catholic intellectual, Paulo Freire, to "conscienticize" the population, that is, through literacy training to make them aware of the possibilities and necessities of social change. The program of the liberal wing of the church was stopped by the military coup of 1964 but the Catholic liberal faction remains an important pressure group, advocating reform inside Brazil.[6]

In Chile, in contrast to the other three examples, the liberal wing of the clergy dominates the church hierarchy. The Chilean church, indeed, is one of the most progressive in Latin America.[7] This does not mean that all of the Chilean clergy work for social reform. Most of them, in fact, do not. They may be said to be conservative in that they do not want radical changes in society, they do not question the ties between the upper class and the clergy, and they do not want to tamper with the traditional authority of the church hierarchy. Outwardly they accept the emphasis on social reform because it was stressed by the Second Vatican Council and by their own immediate superiors, but social reform is not their primary concern. Even the uppermost rank of the clergy is not solidly liberal. The cardinal of Santiago, Raul Silva Henríquez, for example, occupies a middle position between the most socially concerned prelates and the larger conservative faction that is more concerned with communist threats to the authority of the

---

Church and State, pp. 340–415; Robert E. Quirk, "Religion and the Mexican Social Revolution," in William V. D'Antonio and Frederick B. Pike, eds., *Religion, Revolution and Reform* (New York: Praeger, 1964), pp. 61–71; and Thomas Sanders, "Two Catholic Innovating Elites," Newsletter to the Institute of Current World Affairs, no. 1 (1 June 1967).

6. Vallier, *Catholicism, Social Control and Modernization,* pp. 131–34; Mecham, *Church and State,* pp. 261–83; Smith, *Religion and Political Development,* pp. 166–68; and Thomas Sanders, "The Paulo Freire Method: Literacy Training and Conscientización," Newsletter to the Institute of Current World Affairs, no. 12 (6 June 1969).

7. Vallier, "Religious Elites," p. 220.

church than it is with social reform. Thus, the famous pastoral of the Chilean bishops in 1962, which underlined the importance of social reform, also was preoccupied with the communist threat.[8] In sum, however, the Chilean clergy as a whole appears more concerned with politicization and reform than its counterparts in the other three countries. The amount of influence it has, though, is not necessarily greater as a result. Indeed, Catholicism my be more of an influence in the peasant societies of Mexico and Brazil, where it is associated with a powerful folk religion, or in Colombia, where it is associated with the conservative regime in power, than in semi-industrialized Chile.

The differences among the four examples above indicate the difficulty of assessing the impact of Catholic priests on politics in Latin America generally. Moreover, within any one country a variety of kinds of priests exist, even in traditional, conservative Colombia. And traditional parish priests have greatly different tactics and outlooks from their more socially concerned contemporaries. Nor is it necessarily the older priests or the lowest (or highest) level of the clergy that can be assumed to be traditional or conservative in outlook. Diversity in outlook may reflect personal political predispositions on the part of the priests involved and/or may be a reflection of the level or branch of the clergy. The relationship among personal characteristics of the clergy and type of clerical position are exceedingly complex but have an important bearing on the question of political influence.

The Chilean Church

In Chile as elsewhere, the distinction between secular and monastic clergy is important to keep in mind. The secular clergy, in simplified hierarchical form, consists of the priests, bishops, and archbishops (and the cardinals, an honorary title). Chile is divided into nineteen dioceses and archdioceses, each of which is

---

8. See *El Deber Social y Político en la Hora Presente; Los Obispos de Chile Hablan* (Santiago: Secretariado General del Episcopado de Chile, 1962); Vallier, "Religious Elites," p. 220; Mecham, *Church and State*, pp. 201–24; Vallier, *Catholicism, Social Control and Modernization*, pp. 135–46; and Thomas Sanders, Newsletters to the Institute of Current World Affairs: "The Centro Bellarmino," no. 6 (23 November 1967); "A Typology of Catholic Elites," no. 10 (21 February 1968); "The Priests of the People," no. 11 (24 March 1968); "The Chilean Episcopate," no. 13 (6 July 1968).

headed by a bishop or archbishop. Technically these are all independent or equal dioceses although the archbishopric of Santiago is clearly the most important position.[9] The dioceses are divided into 602 parishes, almost one-third of which are administered by the monastic clergy.[10]

The monastic orders in Chile are technically under the authority of the bishop in the diocese in which they are located, but, historically, the various orders have had more money and power than the secular clergy. The major orders include the Jesuits, Dominicans, Franciscans, and Salesians, among many others. The Society of Jesus (Jesuits) shortly after its arrival in Chile (1593) became the most wealthy and powerful order. It was expelled from all Latin America in 1767[11] but today it again occupies a position of prime importance in politics. The strongest intellectual and financial support for the Christian Democratic party came from the Jesuits.

The differences among the orders and among members of the regular clergy may take the form of disagreements over proper ritual practices or broader arguments over the social philosophy of Catholicism. Some orders by their nature are more conservative than others although there is a diversity of views among the priests in any order. Thus the Jesuits, who are traditionally among the best educated and currently tend to a more liberal religious and political posture, nonetheless have conservatives as well as liberals in their ranks. Traditionally the orders have wrangled over their prerogatives and power; the most serious disagreement recorded was in 1595 when Franciscan brothers burned down an Augustinian monastery.[12] Presently they are more likely to cooperate among themselves and with the secular clergy; this may be seen as a drawing together in the face of the general decline of church authority.

The latter process began with legislation limiting church prerogatives in the late nineteenth century and culminated in the

9. The present archbishop of Santiago is Cardinal Raul Silva Henríquez.

10. There are 1,561 members of monastic orders in Chile and 878 secular diocesan priests. For further information on the composition and characteristics of the Catholic Church in Chile see Renato Poblete, S.J., *La Iglesia en Chile* (Bogotá: FERES, 1962), pp. 68, 82–83.

11. Fco. Frias Valenquela, *Manual de Historia de Chile* (Santiago: Editorial Nascimento, 1963), pp. 150–52, 220–21.

12. Ibid., p. 152.

separation of church and state in 1925. The process has continued gradually to this day as the state assumes many of the responsibilities, such as education, previously discharged by the church.[13] Traditionally the Chilean clergy was identified with the aristocracy. This is less true at present, but the overwhelming majority of the clergy are of middle-, upper-middle-, and upper-class background.[14] A large proportion of the clergy is of foreign nationality —29.7 percent of the secular clergy and 63.3 percent of the monastic clergy[15]—but even the foreign clergy tends not to be of working-class origin. The differences in class origin, national background, relationship to the ecclesiastical structure, age, and education all affect the priests' social views and, therefore, their impact on mass politics. Further, the level and type of position held by a priest will affect the kind of influence he may have. Priests may be primarily responsible for a parish or concentrate some (or all) their attention on teaching, or they may be primarily concerned with scholarly research or administration of church projects. In the latter positions they may have less direct impact on the mass of Catholics, but their influence on politics may be as great or greater than that of their peers since their pressure on members of the political elite may produce changes in the structure of politics.[16]

At some point a study must be made of the relative impact of priests of diverse background in different positions.[17] In the absence of such a study, only scattered evidence, of a largely anecdotal and descriptive nature, on the political efforts of conservative and liberal priests can be produced to suggest the kind of impact achieved. The distinction between conservative and liberal political roles results from the lack of information that would en-

13. See constitutional guarantees of freedom of belief in *Constitución Política de la República de Chile,* Official Edition, 18 February 1925 (Santiago: Government of Chile, Editorial Jurídica de Chile, 1966). References to earlier laws may be found in Mecham, *Church and State,* pp. 201–24.

14. Poblete, *La Iglesia en Chile,* p. 118.

15. Ibid., pp. 99, 148.

16. Thus a single priest is credited with bringing the Christian Democratic party to power (although of course his influence is overrated in such a statement by enemies and sympathizers alike). See Mutchler, "Adaptations of the Roman Catholic Church," and Edouardo Labarca Goddard, *Chile Invadido* (Santiago: Editorial Austral, 1968), especially "El Hombre de las Manos de Oro."

17. See Mutchler's attempt to differentiate between "line and staff clergy" in "Adaptations of the Roman Catholic Church."

able a more theoretically interesting distinction (such as between lower-class upper-level clergy and upper-class upper-level clergy, for example) but also suggests an important policy change in the Catholic church as a whole in regard to political involvement.

This change is related to the process of secularization said to be an important aspect of political development.[18] As the process goes on, the life of an individual becomes more differentiated and compartmentalized. The impact on religion is to limit the sphere of influence of religious groups and restrict the domain of the church to spiritual matters. Thus, the more modern or developed the environment in which the priest works, the less he might be expected to have an important role in politics. Concomitantly, the progressive priests and his lay contemporaries have accepted the logic of the secularization process and no longer think it is the priest's place to pontificate on political issues. The conservative priest in traditional society was not so restrained. Thus it may be reasonable to assume that the largest role of priests in politics is a negative one: when they represent and uphold traditional standards and values and, in so doing, fight change. The more progressive priests, by this logic, should have a more peripheral role in that they take less firm political postures with less direct effect.

In fact, the relative impact of progressive or conservative priests in a congruent or contrasting social order is not so easily determined. For one thing, although modern priests accept a restriction of the temporal role of the church, their own concern for social reform pushes them to advocate political participation and even to side personally with parties or groups that press for reform. Although they would now state that the church should not be identified with any one political party (as it was in Chile with the Christian Democratic party in the early 1960s),[19] they rationalize their own public political activity in terms of their right as citizens. Further, they feel it is still their duty as priests to point out the moral consequences of different political choices. They may no

18. Peter L. Berger, *The Sacred Canopy: Elements of a Sociological Theory of Religion* (Garden City, N.Y.: Doubleday, 1969), pp. 105–71. See also Gabriel A. Almond, "Comparative Political Systems," *Journal of Politics* 18 (August 1956); and Godfrey Wilson and Monica Wilson, *The Analysis of Social Change, Based on Observations in Central Africa* (Cambridge: At the University Press, 1968), p. 89.

19. Comments along this line of reasoning were made to me in interviews with Roger Vekemans, S.J., and with priests working in urban communities in 1969.

longer threaten excommunication, but insofar as their position as priest gives them greater authority and prestige than the average man, their opinions may influence other peoples' actions. Consequently, the examples considered here take into account the conservative or progressive orientation of the priests involved but examine equally the involvement of both groups.

THE POLITICAL INFLUENCE OF CONSERVATIVE PRIESTS

The conservative priests sought mainly to protect Catholicism. They were not deliberately setting out to prevent popular participation in government but were trying to assert their right to dictate how and in what manner people should participate. Thus they attempted to forbid the choice of certain political options, such as supporting socialist or communist movements, although these were major sources of criticism of the current nonparticipatory elitist social order.[20] They tried to force Catholics to support the Conservative party, which was a party of the right identified with the Chilean upper class and with the protection of order and stability. Their pressure took the form of articles in such periodicals as *El Diario Ilustrado* or *Revista Católica* and of public speeches warning of the dangers, spiritual and temporal, of siding with anti-Catholic groups of this kind.

For example, in 1920 the noted conservative bishop of Concepción, Msgr. Gilberto Fuenzalido, in the period immediately preceding the legislative elections, wrote: "you may not support with your votes affiliates of sects condemned by the Church, such as Masonry or Socialism. . . ."[21] In 1923 he stated that the activities of political parties were intimately related to religion and Christian morality and that these are the basis of civil order. Thus, he argued, Catholics should aid the Christian party and vote for its candidates. Bluntly, he announced: "The Church recognizes in the Conservative Party its best sons, who sacrifice themselves for the defense of its rights and who witness in public their Christian faith. . . ."[22]

The church right-wing opposition to change did not cease with the founding in 1938 of the Falange party (renamed the Christian

20. Vallier, "Religious Elites," p. 195.
21. *Revista Católica* 39 (1920): p. 898.
22. *Revista Católica* 44 (1923): pp. 691–92.

Democratic party in 1957). Many church leaders saw this as a
dangerous subversive group, undermining Catholicism and social
stability because it favored reform. One incident over which
disagreement among church leaders was clear was the struggle in
1948 over the Law in Permanent Defense of Democracy, which
was to outlaw communism. In favor of the law were Conservatives
and Radicals principally, while Communists, Popular Socialists
and Falangists[23] opposed. In this instance the higher clergy was
split; some remained silent on the issue while others vociferously
sided with the Conservatives and condemned the Falangists.[24] A
year later, members of the higher clergy, including some who were
considered relatively liberal, still indicated their disapproval of
those who supported an anti-Catholic party. Thus the cardinal
José María Caro proclaimed:

> [you] would be a traitor to God and to your Christian faith
> to give your vote, for whatever human consideration, to per-
> sons who are atheists, that is to say, are hostile to the belief
> in God, or anti-Catholic, that is to say hostile to the Holy
> Church and its teachings and its morals; such as those who
> defend divorce, those who work to end or limit the Church's
> right to teach . . . those who defend social doctrines con-
> trary to the Church. . . .[25]

The activity of parish priests sharing these political and religious sentiments mirrored that of their hierarchical superiors
although their audience was much smaller. Thus, the priest in
St. Luís de Macul, a workers' community on the outskirts of
Santiago, campaigned for the Christian Democratic party in 1964.
He paid house-to-house visits in order to praise this party and to
exhort his parishioners to vote for it and to condemn those who
said they preferred the Socialist or Communist parties.[26] The
priest did not live in the community and did not have occasion
to visit frequently but he still was respected by his parishioners.

23. See the debate between the auxiliary bishop of Santiago, Monseigneur
Auguste Salinas F., and the leaders of the Falange Nacional in *Política y Espíritu*,
nos. 27–28 (November–December 1947).
24. See the *Revista Católica*, 1948.
25. *Revista Católica*, no. 942 (1949), p. 194.
26. Interviews with residents of the community in 1969 and 1970.

They report that they—and particularly their wives—wanted to maintain the old ritual traditions such as church baptism, marriage, and burial. They were, then, concerned when the priest exhibited a flurry of activity in the preelection period, threatening and warning them of the results of their actions. Asked what effect he had on their electoral decision, however, the parishioners tended to shrug and say, "It was too bad, he upset my wife, but he does not know about politics, it is no concern of his." And the community voted solidly for the United Front (a coalition of Marxist and leftist parties).[27]

Clearly the priest in St. Luís de Macul had little impact on the political pattern developing there. To some extent, this example may be exceptional since the community was organized and led in part by Marxist sympathizers. However, this may be typical of the impact of conservative priests on politics at the present time. Priests at higher levels of the hierarchy have more resources at their command, but it is probable that their impact must also be considered marginal. The conservative priests, after all, are working against the twentieth-century Chilean context. The processes of industrialization and urbanization, coupled with the growth of a middle class, have broken down the control of the aristocratic elite. The influx of new ideas of change strongly upheld by socialist groups (and even by Protestant revivalist movements) contradicts the conservative Catholic emphasis on obedience, tradition, and order.[28] No one in Chile can remain completely untouched by the new ideas.

In any case, at no time in the twentieth century has the conservative Catholic clergy been the only vocal portion of the church. Others, representing liberal views more congruent with the changes taking place in society, have challenged the opinions of the conservative group. Paralleling the warnings against communism, also, are statements that emphasize that the church should not be involved in politics and that people have the right to make their own political choices.[29]

In this situation, then, the influence of the conservative clergy appears to be minimal. Indeed, it seems reasonable to interpret

27. Ibid.
28. Vallier, "Religious Elites," p. 195.
29. See the *Revista Católica* for 1948, for example.

the adoption of the conservative Catholic ideology by some small fraction of the population as the use of an ideology to justify a previously held position, a position that may be defined by the economic or social group to which an individual belongs. Such supporters may typically be middle- or upper-class men or women who feel challenged or threatened by proposed changes in the social order. The Catholic clergy cannot be credited with keeping them in opposition to change and reform although Catholic ideology is used as justification.[30] Some lower-class Catholics, of course, may choose not to participate in politics because of admonitions by their priests. Others may continue to support right-wing groups for this reason. But, in general, the conservatives have not apparently had such an impact. The pattern of politicization of Chilean society appears to develop in a form little affected by the best efforts of the nervous conservative priests.

The Political Impact of Liberal Priests

In contrast to their conservative brethren, the more liberal priests who favored social reform in the twentieth century moved with the trend of their era. In favor of improving the position of the poor, they encouraged workers to participate in the politics of their society and middle- and upper-class individuals to be concerned about the plight of their fellow citizens. The best representatives of this liberal group may be found among the church leaders who had a significant impact on the development of the Christian Democratic party and its reform program.

One of the first outstanding figures identified with this party is Padre Alberto Hurtado (d. 1952). Hurtado, a Jesuit, was considered a saint by most who knew him. The great respect engendered by his personal characteristics enabled him to undertake projects that appeared revolutionary to his fellow Catholics, both lay and clergy. Much concerned with the poverty and disorganization of the Chilean masses, he called on the clergy to involve themselves with the problems of the poor.[31] He founded a confederation of labor unions, Acción Sindical Chilena (ASICH)

30. Vallier, "Religious Elites," p. 195.

31. See his pamphlet *Es Chile Un País Católico?*, referred to in Alejandro Magnet, *El Padre Hurtado* (Santiago: Editorial del Pacífico, 1954), pp. 210–26.

and was identified with the Hogar del Cristo, founded by another liberal priest, Jean-Baptiste Janssens, the general of the Jesuit order. The Hogar was to house a variety of charitable institutions but was best known for its program of caring for the abandoned children of Santiago.[32] Hurtado also helped found the Centro Bellarmino, which he and Janssens envisaged as a center in which priests trained to study social problems would do research and teach laymen to help bring about necessary social changes. Bellarmino (which eventually did become such a center) was not fully operative before Hurtado's death, but the journal he founded, *Mensaje,* in which articles on social problems of the day and criticisms of Catholicism frequently appear, quickly became one of the most outstanding Catholic publications in Latin America.[33]

Hurtado himself did not seek to be involved in politics. But he sided at the outset with a group of young Catholics who broke away from the Conservative party in 1938 to form the Falange party. Hurtado, like the liberal priest Fernando Vives (d. 1935) before him, came under severe attack for his advanced social attitudes and, in particular, his criticism of existing society. Vives was sent into exile for approximately eighteen years.[34] Nothing so drastic was done to Hurtado although he was repeatedly attacked both privately and in public forums such as *El Diario Ilustrado* (the newspaper of the conservative Catholic clergy and the Conservative party). In November 1944, however, he was forced by the conservative faction to resign from his post as national head of Catholic Youth. Although severely hurt by his forced resignation,[35] Hurtado remained a national figure with whom the young leaders of the nascent Christian Democratic movement identified until his death six years later.

Perhaps even more identified with social change and the attempt to bring Catholics to act for reform was Manuel Larraín, the bishop of Talco (d. 1966). Larraín led the Chilean bishops

32. Sanders, "The Centro Bellarmino."
33. See Magnet, *El Padre Hurtado,* pp. 351–352.
34. See George Grayson, *El Partido Demócrata Cristiano Chileno* (Santiago: Editorial Francisco de Aguirre, 1968), p. 76.
35. Magnet, *El Padre Hurtado,* pp. 246–74.

in outspoken advocacy of the need for change. Indeed, he is credited with the writing of the liberal pastorals, such as *Los Obispos Hablan,* which his fellow bishops signed out of respect for him. Certainly he educated his peers and other Catholics on many of the problems facing the Chilean poor and the urgency of action by the church.[36] It was Larraín who convinced the archbishop of Santiago to initiate a land reform scheme in 1962 under which the church gave up a portion of its vast estates to tenant farmers, who were allowed to buy the land on easy terms and were encouraged to organize as collectives. Larraín's plan received much publicity and was looked upon as a pilot project for the further land reforms carried out by Frei's Christian Democratic government after 1964. An organization headed by the archbishop of Santiago, called INPROA, was founded to administer the church land collectives. It received money from Catholic organizations abroad and eventually also used its resources to advise the Frei government on conditions for land reform elsewhere in Chile.[37] In addition, on many occasions Larraín took even more radical stands as, for example, when he sided with striking agricultural and mine workers, contrary to the opinion of many conservative church leaders of that time.[38]

The last and most famous example of the liberal church leaders is Padre Roger Vekemans, also a Jesuit. Vekemans is credited with being the major influence behind the reform program adopted by the Frei government and instituted in 1964. Further, it is widely rumored that the funds he obtained from Catholic sources abroad were indispensable to the electoral victory of the Christian Democrats in 1964.[39] Certainly he was a major intellectual figure in Santiago from his arrival in 1957 to his departure in 1970, influencing the Christian Democratic leaders and also bringing about the reform of the Department of Sociology at the Catholic University. In addition, he set in motion numerous re-

36. Sanders, "The Chilean Episcopate."

37. See William C. Thiesenhusen, *Chile's Experiments in Agrarian Reform* (Madison: University of Wisconsin Press, 1966).

38. See Henry Landsberger and Fernando Canitrot M., *Iglesia, Intelectuales y Campesinos (La Huelga Campesina de Molina)* (Santiago: Editorial del Pacífico, 1967).

39. Mutchler, "Adaptations of the Roman Catholic Church," and Goddard, *Chile Invadido.*

search projects on fundamental social problems, such as the plight and prospects of the urban "marginals." [40]

The result of the activity of the liberal priests was an extensive network of reform-oriented Catholic organizations in Chile. On one level there were the research and development centers connected with the Centro Bellarmino.[41] Aside from these institutions were others, funded in part by foreign Catholic sources, such as INPROA, discussed above, or INDAP, in which research and training were dedicated largely to helping train the urban poor in Santiago. On the level of the mass of Catholics, various Catholic organizations were available for membership, in particular those established by Catholic Action. The Catholic Action groups included the Catholic Working Youth, Catholic University Youth, Professional Catholic Associations, Catholic Teachers' Associations, the Christian Family Movement, the Catholic Women's Movement, and many others. There was also ASICH, the Catholic trade union federation mentioned above.[42]

There is no doubt, then, that the liberal priests influenced their society in at least two ways. On the level of mass influence these

40. Sanders, "The Centro Bellarmino." Also see list of publications issued by DESAL, Santiago.

41. Thomas Sanders in "The Centro Bellarmino" schematically presents the centers connected with it in the following fashion:

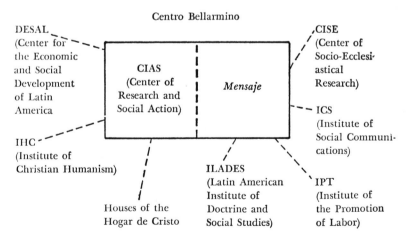

Centro Bellarmino

DESAL (Center for the Economic and Social Development of Latin America)

CIAS (Center of Research and Social Action)

Mensaje

CISE (Center of Socio-Ecclesiastical Research)

ICS (Institute of Social Communications)

IHC (Institute of Christian Humanism)

Houses of the Hogar de Cristo

ILADES (Latin American Institute of Doctrine and Social Studies)

IPT (Institute of the Promotion of Labor)

42. See *Guía Parroquial y Guía Eclesiástica de Chile* (Santiago: Libraria San Pablo, 1969), p. 102.

men had the time, the interest, and the financial backing to provide a forum for the views of the poor. They did successfully institute unions and Catholic Action groups that drew individuals
into organized group participation through which they were
taught to work together to seek social reform. Secondly, the Catholic priest intellectuals had a decided impact on the Chilean elite.
As Thomas Sanders points out, Santiago for all its size (2.5 million) has the air of a provincial city. The members of the elite
(the educated and wealthy) know each other. The socially conscious Catholic lay elite frequently met Vekemans and other
priests like him. And they heard him discussed, as they heard
the ideas of Hurtado, Janssens, Vives, and others debated.[43] As
members of the Catholic Youth organization, Eduardo Frei,
Radomiro Tomic, and other future leaders of the PDC discussed
Christian humanism and the philosophy of Jacques Maritain. The
Falange party itself was formed by them when they were part of
the Catholic Youth movement originally connected to the Conservative party.[44] The ideology of social reform that they adopted
was explicitly Catholic; they saw it as quite distinct from Marxist
or secular liberal programs of reform.[45]

The considerable political influence of the liberal priests in
Chile cannot be doubted. To some extent the location of outstanding liberal, trained men in key positions in the Chilean
church in the post–1925 period was fortuitous. Moreover, the
accident that located Vives, Janssens, or Hurtado in Chile was
one with cumulative results. These men attracted other individuals of like views to Chile. Further, their views coincided with
an increasingly important emphasis in world Catholic forums—
the need for the reform and adaptation of Catholicism to the interests of the masses of the poor. (This emphasis dates back at least
to Pope Leo XIII's *Rerum Novarum* of 1891.) Thus the liberal
priests were increasingly able to bring in outside money and
personnel to carry out their plans.

The rapid urbanization of Chile (with 47.6 percent of its pop-

43. Sanders, "The Centro Bellarmino."
44. See Grayson, *El Partido Demócrata,* pp. 63–146.
45. See Jaime Castillo Velasco, *Las Fuentes de la Democracia Cristiana* (Santiago: Editorial del Pacífico, 1968).

ulation now in towns of 5,000 or more inhabitants[46]) and the lack of a strong Catholic folk religion probably facilitated the incursion of Protestant sects and Marxist movements.[47] The appearance of the latter and the continuously weakening temporal power of the church in the twentieth century contributed to the sense of crisis that made the call for reform and a new Catholic approach increasingly attractive to the clergy. Nonetheless, it is still not obvious why the Chilean church, unlike its sister institutions in other places, allowed the liberal clergy to dominate. Nor is it clear to what extent the clergy shapes or is shaped by the Catholic parishioners with whom they interact.

One final example, drawn from a study of the impact of priests living among poor working class residents of a *población* in Santiago, may be relevant. Thus far, no distinction has been made among types of liberal priests although scholars elsewhere have considered this a vital distinction.[48] Being a liberal may mean that a priest asks to break the traditional identification of the church with the aristocratic elite and the status quo but still places considerable importance on church ritual and hierarchy. It may also mean more, however: some fraction of the liberals may be militant revolutionaries or may simply dedicate themselves to social reform above and beyond any other aspect of their priestly role (just as some fraction of the conservatives may be militant reactionaries). The militant extremes have not been very important in Chile, thus no breakdown of the conservative-liberal dichotomy has been made here. But the priests dedicated primarily to social reform, the worker priests, are active in Chile and do provide a particularly good example of the attempts of priests at direct involvement in the politicization process on the individual, rather than the national, level.[49]

Through a survey it was possible to compare the political attitudes and activities of a community in which worker priests have been active for ten years and more to one in which the infrequent

46. Poblete, *La Iglesia en Chile*, p. 32.

47. See Vallier, "Religious Elites," p. 221.

48. Ibid., pp. 203–10, and Sanders, "A Typology of Catholic Elites."

49. For a discussion of the worker priests in Chile see Sanders, "The Priests of the People."

visitations of a conservative priest provided the only contact with the church. Results indicated that the worker priests had achieved an unusual visibility in their community. They had projected an image of social concern and, as a result, won the confidence of their parishioners that they could and would help workers. Further, they had transmitted new ideas of what should be the relationship of clergy and laymen and of what being a Catholic meant. These results were in striking contrast to the neighboring community where the traditional image of the church, with its negative, status quo, ritualistic orientation, prevailed. But although the worker priests had explicitly attempted to mobilize the population of their community to be active politically, they had not had such an impact. There was no significant difference between the communities in regard to political behavior patterns. Furthermore, the respondents indicated that they clearly did not see the priests as explicit political leaders nor credit them with important political roles.[50]

PRIESTS AND POLITICIZATION

Tentatively, then, we may conclude that despite their position as members of an elite in contact with uninformed masses, the Catholic clergy at the national or the local level have not had a decisive impact on the process of mass politicization. The conservative priests, at the most, may have slowed up the process somewhat but have been swept aside by the current of events in their society. The liberal priests, on the other hand, have sought to mobilize the population for the reform of Chilean society. Thus, the organizations they formed and the advice they gave provided support and encouragement for citizens who were grad-

50. The survey, conducted in 1969–70, was composed of four random samples of property title holders (owners or renters, whichever was resident) including 294 respondents. The secular measures were drawn up with the advice of Alejandro Portes, University of Illinois, while Renato Poblete, S.J., DESAL, suggested many of the questions tapping religious variables. The results were analyzed using chi square and Fisher (exact probability tests). The questions used and results discussed here may be found in L. Behrman, "The Political and Social Impact of the Peoples' Priests in Chile" (Unpublished, University of Pennsylvania, 1971). For general discussion of the survey see L. Behrman, "Patterns of Religious and Political Attitudes and Activities during Modernization" (Unpublished, University of Pennsylvania, January 1972), and L. Behrman, "Political Development and Secularization in Two Chilean Urban Communities," *Comparative Politics* 4 (January 1972), pp. 269–80.

ually involving themselves in the political process. Furthermore, the national liberal church leaders had much to do with the *form* that development programs took in Chile. Despite the success of the Marxist coalition in the 1970 elections, the Christian Democrats remain an important part of the Chilean political scene. The politicians are heavily indebted to the priests for the reform program with which they are identified. But had these priests not been active, it seems unlikely that the general direction of political change in Chile would have been markedly different. The priests' concerns, after all, mirrored concerns already in society. The liberal priests, then, have been an important factor in Chilean politics, but their role in the politicization of Chilean society appears to have been a modest one.

11

Catholic Political Parties and Mass
Politics in Latin America

HARRY KANTOR

Catholic ideology and the hierarchy of the Catholic church have
been prominent in the political life of Latin America since the
conquest of the area by Spain and Portugal in the sixteenth century, but never as a really unified force. Catholic leaders have
been found in all types of political movements, from the most
dictatorial and reactionary to the most idealistic, democratic, and
socialistic, from the most pacifist to the most violent. This participation in the area's political life was natural because the kings
of Spain and Portugal, by pontifical mandate, were the founders,
protectors, and administrators of the Catholic church in America.

THE COLONIAL LEGACY

The distinguished Mexican historian Joaquín García Icazbalceta summarized the situation as follows:

> The Spanish kings came to exercise a power in the ecclesias-
> tical government of America which, except in purely spiritual
> matters, appeared to be pontifical. Without the king's per-
> mission, no church, monastery, or hospital could be con-
> structed and no bishopric or parish erected. No priest or friar
> might go to America without his express license. The kings
> named bishops and, without waiting for their confirmation
> by the Pope, sent them out to administer their dioceses. The
> kings marked out the boundaries of the bishoprics and
> changed them at their pleasure. They could appoint to any
> religious office—even to that of sacristan—if they wished.
> They had the power to reprove severely, to recall to Spain,
> or to banish any ecclesiastical official, including bishops who,

even though they might often dispute with governors, never failed to listen to the voice of the king. The kings administered and collected the tithes, decided how and by whom they should be paid, without reference to bulls of exemption. They fixed the income of the benefices and increased or diminished them as they saw fit. They tried many ecclesiastical suits and, by the use of force, paralyzed the action of church tribunals or prelates. Lastly, no decision of the Pope himself could be carried out in the Indies without permission of the king.[1]

What was probably most important in tying church and state together was the king's power to appoint persons to ecclesiastical office, what came to be known as the *patronato*. This created situations in which the same individual could become an official of both church and state; the practice of appointing churchmen to important political positions was not uncommon.[2]

In colonial Latin America there was no involvement in the political decision-making process by the masses. By law and tradition the overwhelming proportion of the population was effectively kept from political participation. Government was monarchical, with all power centralized in the hands of officials appointed by the crown, and usually the highest positions were given to persons native to the Iberian Peninsula who were sent to America to exercise their functions. In this closely supervised governmental system the Catholic church played an important role, and the introduction of the institution of the Inquisition during the sixteenth century put the church into a prominent position as the guardian of the system created by the conquerors. As Mecham has pointed out, "In the later days of the colonial period the Inquisition came to be used more and more for political ends. In particular, it was used to keep liberal ideas out of America by

1. Joaquín García Icazbalceta, *Don Fray Juan de Zumarraga* (Mexico, D.F., 1881), pp. 128–129, as quoted in Pike, *Conflict Between Church and State*, p. 5.

2. The leading work on church-state relations in Latin America is Mecham, *Church and State*, rev. ed. In the 1934 edition the frontispiece is a picture of Pedro de Moya y Contreras who was archbishop of Mexico, visitor-general, inquisitor-general and viceroy, thus the holder of the highest offices in both church and state in the colony of New Spain. See also "The Church in Latin America," 8 : 448–69, and "Patronato Real," 10 : 1113–16, both in *The New Catholic Encyclopedia* (New York: McGraw-Hill, 1967).

placing a strict surveillance over the importation of books." [3] The church was thus a central component of the colonial religio-political system.

INDEPENDENCE, CONFLICT, AND ANTICLERICALISM

When independence came to Latin America during the first decades of the nineteenth century, the newly emerged independent states were completely unprepared for self-government. Independence brought so many difficulties to the church that it has not as yet recovered from the shock. The church was split during the struggle for independence; some of the key figures in the movement were parish priests, Father Miguel Hidalgo y Costilla and Father José María Morelos of Mexico being among the best known. At the same time, most of the bishops and archbishops tended to oppose the movement for independence.

The leaders of the newly created republics failed in their attempts to create stable political systems, and Latin America then lived through a century of chaotic struggles. Basically, the problem was that independence had destroyed the only symbol of legitimacy the people knew, the crown, and created nothing to take its place. With the crown gone, there was no commonly accepted symbol of authority to hold the polity together. A struggle began, and is still going on, to create viable political systems in the various republics, and the Catholic church was inevitably drawn into the struggle.

When independence came, the church was the holder of vast wealth and in practically every country was the largest landowner. One can get some idea of how wealthy the Catholic church was when we read that:

> in 1800 the four best paid people in Lima were the mother abbess of the monastery of Concepción with an annual income of just over 100,000 pesos, the Dominican provincial with almost 83,000, the archbishop of Lima with about 70,000, and, a poor fourth, the Viceroy with 61,000 pesos. If he had still existed, the provincial of the Jesuits would have headed the list, for according to a secret report of 1748 of the procurator of the Lima province to the Jesuit general in Rome, the

3. Mecham, *Church and State,* p. 35.

province realized in the preceding year from its lands, mills, vineyards, and mines about 602,073 pesos.[4]

Part of the struggle after independence revolved around the question of what to do about the wealth controlled by the church. To this day the struggle continues, particularly about the redistribution of land still owned by the church in some countries.

Even more important in drawing the church into the political struggle was the effort by the new governments of the independent republics to continue the practice of appointing church officials (the patronato). The new leaders of the independent states believed they would not be fully sovereign unless they assumed every single power that the Iberian kings had exercised during colonial days. The popes eventually granted this power, although loath to do so. The church hierarchy was in politics whether it wanted to be or not, because it was appointed by politicians.

The great issue in Latin America during the first century of independence was how the new states were to be organized. Two definite factions emerged, generally known as the Conservative and Liberal parties. The Conservatives consisted of those political leaders who favored the continuation of life about as it had been during colonial days, with the only change being that Spaniards born in America, instead of Spaniards born in Spain, were to hold the most important positions in the new government. The Conservatives upheld the traditional land-tenure system, the continuation of the rights and privileges of the Catholic church, its utilization as a means of controlling the masses of illiterate Indians and Negro slaves, and government protection of economic activity in the old mercantilist tradition of the colony. The Conservatives favored strong central government, with very little or no participation by the mass of the population. The hierarchy of the Catholic church was inevitably tied to the Conservative groups; its composition in terms of class background was virtually identical, as well as its views on the nature of a Catholic state and society.

In opposition to the Conservative groups and the church hierarchy a Liberal movement developed. The Liberals were those who, influenced by ideas coming from England, France, and the

4. "The Church in Latin America," p. 458.

United States, wanted economic development, the improvement of education, a weak central government with local autonomy, a broader suffrage, no restrictions on immigration, and a laissez-faire economic system. Many were strongly anticlerical and favored getting the hierarchy out of politics. They wanted to confiscate and redistribute some or all of the vast lands owned by the church. They wanted to take away the church's control of such things as vital records and the administration and control of education.

As the years went by, the more the church tried to defend its traditional privileges, the stronger the anticlerical movement became. During this struggle, the masses sometimes were involved, usually as soldiers in the competing armies fighting for control of the government. In many cases the masses, influenced by the church, supported the Conservatives. In Guatemala, for example, the Conservative political leader, Rafael Carrera, led an army of devout Catholics using the slogan, "Long live Religion, and death to the Foreigners." He seized power, abolished the United Central America the Liberals were trying to create, and instituted decades of Conservative rule.

In Ecuador, Gabriel García Moreno tried to use the Catholic church as a unifying factor and almost turned Ecuador into a theocracy in which only Catholics could be citizens. He had Ecuador dedicate itself to the Sacred Heart of Jesus and gave the church exceptional privileges that were formalized in a concordat with Pope Pius IX. Ironically, García Moreno was assassinated on the steps of the cathedral.

As these examples demonstrate, the church was one of the most important factors in the political system of the republics during the first decades of their existence and in some this political influence continued into the twentieth century. The Catholic church paid dearly for its support of the Conservative cause in Latin America because eventually the Liberals triumphed in practically every country. Since the church was on the side of the losers, it had to take the penalty handed out to losers in great struggles. Large sections of the population were alienated from the church, although many continued to call themselves Catholics and no other religious organization won wide support. The church lost much of the land it owned. In the majority of the republics, church and state were legally separated. The process has not yet been completed, as in several of the republics the government still has the right to nominate the persons who are appointed to the highest offices of the Catholic church, and the church still maintains a preferred position in some of the republics. In the majority of the republics, however, the church was effectively pushed out of active participation in politics.[5]

This background is essential to understand the position of Catholic political parties in Latin America in 1974. Whenever a party tries to utilize Catholic ideology or is too closely tied to the hierarchy of the church, it is forced to face the accumulated general opinion held by the population about the church. This makes it very difficult for the party, whether it calls itself Christian Democratic or some other name, for it is forced to face an anticlerical sentiment that is very strong in some countries and is present in all.

THE EMERGENCE OF CATHOLIC PARTIES

Although the Conservative parties mentioned above considered themselves to be defenders of the church, they were not really Catholic political parties. They were parties composed of the traditional defenders of the way Latin America was organized; the church hierarchy generally cooperated with and supported the

5. By 1971, church and state were constitutionally separated or the government had returned to the Vatican the powers of the patronato in twelve countries: Chile, Uruguay, Brazil, Mexico, Venezuela, Ecuador, Argentina, Cuba, Honduras, Panama, Nicaragua, and Guatemala. The patronato is still exercised by the governments of Bolivia, Costa Rica, Paraguay, Peru and Colombia. The position is unclear in the Dominican Republic, El Salvador, and Haiti. Although the Argentine government returned the power of the patronato to the Vatican on 10 October 1966, the constitutional clauses in the 1853 constitution are typical of what the situation was during most of the past century and still continues to be the rule in the five countries without church-state separation:

Article 2. The Federal Government supports the Roman Catholic Church.

Article 76. To be elected President or Vice President of the Nation, it is necessary . . . to belong to the Roman Catholic Apostolic Church.

Article 86, clause 8. [The President] exercises his rights of ecclesiastical appointments by selecting bishops for the cathedrals, from three names proposed by the Senate.

Article 86, clause 9. [The President] approves or withholds applications of the decrees of the councils, bulls, briefs, and rescripts of the Supreme Pontiff of Rome, with the consent of the Supreme Court, a law being required if they contain general and permanent provisions.

Conservative political leaders since it too favored the traditional organization of society.

The political parties that were the first truly Catholic parties developed in Uruguay, Argentina, and Mexico. That in Uruguay is the oldest, originating in a Catholic club founded in 1878. By 1911 it was known as the Civic Union and was a formal political party contesting elections. Beginning as a simple defender of Catholicism, it slowly became more reform-minded, especially after 1962, when it merged with another group of reformist Catholics and changed its name to the Christian Democratic party. Although it is an old, well-established organization, with its own daily newspaper and many prominent individuals as members, it has never done very well at the polls, usually winning about 5 percent of the votes in each election.[6]

In Argentina, Catholic social action groups began to appear soon after the encyclical *Rerum Novarum* was issued. In 1902 a Christian Democratic League was organized, in 1911 this became the Christian Democratic Union, and in 1920 the name was changed to Argentine Democratic Union. In 1927 this was transformed into the Popular party, which was modeled on Luigi Sturzo's Italian Popular party. This organization received about 9,000 votes in the 1934 election, then slowly disappeared. After the Peronista regime was overthrown, there was a new attempt to create a Catholic political party, which was formally organized by 1957 as the Christian Democratic party. It won almost 5 percent of the votes in the elections at the end of the 1950s, but the party soon split into quarreling factions. The military government that took power in 1966 banned all parties, and the Christian Democratic movement disappeared.

In Mexico, a group of liberal Catholics organized a Catholic party after Madero came to power. In the 1912 election it won control of the Jalisco state legislature, but the party disappeared during the years of revolutionary war.

Many years later, there developed an important Catholic po-

6. See the chart listing the votes cast in Uruguayan elections, 1925–58, in Philip B. Taylor, *Goverment and Politics of Uruguay,* Tulane University Studies in Political Science, vol. 7 (New Orleans: Tulane University, 1960), app. B. During these years the highest vote received by the Civic Union was 44,255 out of 879,242 cast in 1954. The party elected one senator and three deputies that year.

litical group that was extremely conservative. Known as the National Sinarquista Union, it advocated an organization of Mexico based upon the Catholic faith, the Spanish tradition, the stable home, and a Christian political order. It opposed labor unions and favored censorship of the press by the Catholic church in order to strengthen law and order. The Sinarquista Union was strongest in the 1940s, even having branches among Mexican workers in the United States, because the German Nazis supplied the organization with funds. The Mexican government outlawed the Sinarquista movement during World War II, but it managed to preserve its organization. In 1963, the Sinarquista Union united with the Mexican Nationalist party and dissolved its independent organization.[7]

Another Mexican political party sympathetic to the Catholic church is the National Action party (P.A.N., founded in 1939), which has been the leading opposition party during recent decades. P.A.N. is particularly interested in winning the repeal of Article 3 of the Mexican Constitution, the article that bans religious education in the public schools. The party's vote varies from election to election, generally running around 10 percent of the total cast. Efforts were made to transform P.A.N. into a Christian Democratic party with a reformist program, but they all failed. P.A.N. has been represented by observers at some of the conferences of the Latin American Christian Democratic parties, but it has never joined their organization and is much more conservative than most of the Christian Democratic parties.[8]

The Christian Democratic Movement

The great spurt in the creation of Catholic-influenced parties in Latin America came with the rise of Christian Democracy. This movement developed just before and after World War II. Its creators were the young, devout Catholics who found themselves

7. On the Sinarquistas, see Margaret Shedd, "Thunder on the Right," *Harper's Magazine* 190 (1945): 414–25; and Mario Gill, *Sinarquismo, su origen, su esencia, su misión* (Mexico, 1944).

8. The program of the National Action party is synthesized in "Social Justice and Christian Democracy in Mexico" in Pike, *Conflict Between Church and State*, pp. 218–24. This is a reprint of a statement issued by the youth section of the National Action party in 1960.

without a political home when a great wave of nationalism and reform swept the continent.

By the time of World War I, foreign capital and the effects of the war greatly stimulated the industrialization and modernization of the economic system. At the same time, public health began to improve, modern means of transportation and communication began to be introduced, and a period of rapid urbanization began. As a result, new groups became stimulated to enter politics. In some countries the process of mass politicization was furthered by mass immigration, for many of the immigrants brought their European ideas about politics with them. Soon, European-type political parties sprang up in various countries: the French-type radical parties in Argentina and Chile, Spanish anarchist groups in various countries, and socialist, communist, and fascist-type parties all over the continent.

During the period between the two world wars, another group of political parties developed in Latin America, the indigenous revolutionary type, including such parties as the Uruguayan Colorados, the Peruvian Apristas, Venezuela's Democratic Action, and similar groups in other countries. These parties thought the time had come to stop copying European ways of doing things. They advocated the study of Latin America to discover the true nature of their countries so that political institutions could be built in harmony with the character of the people of Latin America. These parties sought a revolutionary reorganization of society to bring a better life to all people, especially the workers and farmers who had been left out of participation in the political process.

The European-type radicals, socialists, and communists, as well as the indigenous revolutionary groups, were opposed by the traditional holders of power, and most of these new parties developed anticlerical positions. The leaders of the Peruvian Apristas, for example, were the first to find themselves exiled from their country after a struggle with the dictatorship in the 1920s over the question: Should Peru be dedicated to the Sacred Heart of Jesus? Many times the Catholic church became involved in the struggle between the traditional holders of power and the new political parties. In Argentina, for example, the Radical and

Socialist parties became even more anticlerical than they had been previously after the hierarchy of the Catholic church supported Perón in the 1945 election.

As the European-type and indigenous revolutionary parties matured, many became mass movements that won wide support. There was one group, however, whose support they failed to win —the young, devout Catholics who wanted many of the same things the new parties were advocating but wished to remain faithful to the church.

Thus, especially during the 1930s, a decade of great ferment, groups of young Catholics in various countries found themselves without a political home. They began to meet together to discuss the problems of their countries, and slowly they became the organizers of the new Christian Democratic parties.

They were the product of their time—seeking a more equitable organization of society, they were offended by the status quo position of the traditional elitist Conservative parties that generally still had the support of the Catholic hierarchy. The young Catholics were alienated by the Russian orientation of the communist parties and they did not feel at home with the indigenous revolutionary groups because of their anticlericalism.

The young Catholics were greatly influenced by the social encyclicals issued by various popes, especially *Rerum Novarum* and *Quadragesimo Anno*. Luigi Sturzo and Jacques Maritain had great influence on these young people, as well as individual priests with whom they came into contact. There was no real connection between these people during their formative years; that is, it was not a Latin American movement, but stirrings in various countries.

When the Christian Democratic parties began to emerge in the various countries, each reflected its country more than it did any classic Christian Democratic ideal type. All vary greatly in their programs and activities as well as in the success they have had in mobilizing mass support. Programmatically, they vary from the Chilean party, which advocates "Revolution in Liberty" and is practically indistinguishable from the Peruvian Apristas or Costa Rica's National Liberation party, to extremely conservative parties that find it easy to cooperate with military dictatorships

Country	Name of Party	Year Founded	Present Status in National Legislature	Date	Votes in Latest National Election Vote
Argentina	Christian Democratic Party	1955	7 deputies in 1963 election. No legislature functioning early in 1971.	July 1963	434,923 (4.5%).
Bolivia	Social Christian Party	?	None.		Never on ballot.
	Christian Democratic Party	1954	None.		Last on ballot in 1962 when it received about 20,000 votes.
Brazil	Christian Democratic Party	1945	After 1963 election, 20 in Chamber of Deputies out of 409. 1 in Senate out of 66. None in 1971.		The P.D.C. usually was in an alliance with other parties, thus their vote cannot be estimated.
Chile	Christian Democratic Party	Traces to 1935	1969–73 Congress: 55 of 150 seats in Chamber, 23 of 50 seats in Senate.	1970	824,829 votes (27.8%).
Colombia	Democratic Social Christian Movement	1966	None.		Never on ballot.
Costa Rica	Christian Democratic Party	1963	1 in 57-seat National Assembly, 1970–74 term.	February 1970	5,015 out of 562,766 votes in presidential election.

Country	Party		Legislative representation		Electoral results
Cuba	Christian Democratic Movement in Exile	1959	No legislature functioning early in 1971.		Never has been on ballot as no elections have been held since party was organized.
Dominican Republic	Revolutionary Social Christian Party	1962	None.	1966	30,660 votes.
	Progressive Democratic Christian Party	1963	None.		Never on ballot.
	Christian Democratic Party	1966	None.	1966	9,378 votes.
Ecuador	Social Christian Movement	1951	No congress in existence since early 1971.		Never on ballot.
El Salvador	Christian Democratic Party	1960	15 in 52-member House, 1970–72 period.	July 1967	90,089 out of 402,019.
Guatemala	Christian Democratic Party	1955	6 in Unicameral Congress of 55 members.	March 1970	116,864 out of 546,287 votes cast.
Haiti	None in existence				
Honduras	None in existence				
Mexico	National Action Party	193	20 seats in Chamber of Deputies; o in Senate.	July 1970	1,945,070 out of 14,065,820 cast.
Nicaragua	Social Christian Party	Late 1950s	No representation.	February 1967	Social Christian Party was part of a united opposition. Never has been on ballot as yet.

CATHOLIC-INFLUENCED POLITICAL PARTIES IN LATIN AMERICA, 1971

Country	Name of Party	Year Founded	Present Status in National Legislature	Votes in Latest National Election Date	Votes in Latest National Election Vote
Panama	Christian Democratic Party	1956	No legislature functioning early 1971. 1 seat out of 42 in 1964–68.	1964	9,681 out of 305,255 votes cast.
Paraguay	Christian Democratic Party	1960	None.		Never on ballot.
Peru	Christian Democratic Party	1955	1963–69 Legislature: 5 seats in Senate of 45; 13 seats in Chamber of Deputies out of 140.	1962 (last election party was on ballot)	48,792 votes (2.85%).
	Christian Popular Party	1966	No legislature functioning in early 1971.		Never on ballot (split-off from Christian Democratic party).
Uruguay	Christian Democratic Party	Traces to 1878	1966–71 Legislature: 3 seats in Chamber out of 99. 0 in Senate out of 30.	November 1966	3.5% of votes cast.
Venezuela	Social Christian Party (Copei)	1945	1969–74 Legislature: 16 Senators out of 52; 59 Deputies out of 213.	December 1968	1,082,941 out of 3,723,000 votes cast.

and parties that work with Communists and other advocates of violent revolution.[9] This variance among Latin American Christian Democrats is also typical of European Christian Democratic parties, as Michael Fogarty has pointed out.[10]

The International Congress of Catholic Youth held in Rome in 1934 seems to have played an important role in stimulating talented young Latin American Catholics to get active in politics. Among those in attendance who, decades later, were to be among the most important leaders of Christian Democratic parties were Eduardo Frei of Chile, Mario Polar of Peru, and Rafael Caldera of Venezuela.

Christian Democracy in Latin America became vitalized when dynamic organizations arose in Chile and Venezuela after World War II. In 1947, the leaders of Uruguay's Civic Union arranged a meeting in Montevideo where Christian Democrats from Argentina, Brazil, Chile, and Uruguay exchanged ideas. At another meeting in 1949, a formal organization of Christian Democratic Parties of America was created.

A brief review of the status of Christian Democracy in the twenty republics in 1971 is summarized in the accompanying chart. A more lengthy review of these parties will enable a judgment to be made on how successful Christian Democracy has been in mobilizing Latin America's population for effective political action.

The largest and most successful Christian Democratic party in Latin America is the one in Chile. It originated with a group of talented young people, members of the Conservative party, who in 1935 founded the National Falange as a progressive caucus within the party. One of the leaders of the National Falange was Eduardo Frei.

The Falange broke away from the Conservative party to become an independent group in 1938. It grew very slowly, win-

9. The pro–Russian Communist viewpoint of many of the leaders of the Peruvian Christian Democratic party contributed to the split in 1966 that resulted in the creation of a second Christian Democratic party, known as the Christian Popular party and led by the former Mayor of Lima.

10. "One does not have to attend very many gatherings of Christian Democrats to realize that the Dutch approach is of one kind, the French approach very much another." Michael P. Fogarty, *Christian Democracy in Western Europe: 1820–1953* (London: Routledge and Kegan Paul, 1957), p. 15.

ning only 4.7 percent of the vote cast in 1950 and 2.9 percent in
1953. Meanwhile, the Conservative party had split again and one
of the new factions called itself the Conservative Social Christian
party. This new organization competed for membership with the
Falange, but the two often combined their efforts, especially in
elections. Both organizations were Catholic-oriented and interested in reform, and in 1953 they united to form the Social Christian Federation; in 1957 they completely united their organizations to create the Christian Democratic party. After that, the
party began to grow very rapidly until by 1971 it was the country's
largest. From 1964 to 1970, its leader, Eduardo Frei, served as
president. In his 1964 election Frei received 56.09 percent of the
votes cast. In the congressional election of 1965, the Christian
Democratic party won a majority of the seats in the Chamber of
Deputies, the first time in 100 years in Chile that one party had
done this. This was the party's high point at the polls until now.
From 56.09 percent of the votes in the presidential election of
1963 and 42.3 percent of the votes in the congressional election
of 1965, the party's share of the votes cast has gone down to 35.5
percent in 1967, 31 percent in 1969, and 27.8 percent in the 1970
presidential election in which the Christian Democratic candidate, Radomiro Tomic, came in a poor third. The low vote in 1970
was due to a split over the party's attitude toward the Chilean
communists and Fidel Castro.

The Chilean Christian Democrats were as successful as they
were because they had excellent leadership and made determined
efforts to get the support of the workers, the urban poor, and
other groups usually not very active in politics. The party is
particularly attractive to the Catholic members of the middle class,
youth, intellectuals, professionals, and women. Many of the self-
made financiers and industrialists support it. Of all the Christian
Democratic parties in Latin America, it has been most successful
in mobilizing masses of people for its program of "revolution in
liberty." [11]

11. The best source of information on the Chilean Christian Democrats is *Política
y Espíritu* (Casilla 3547, Santiago, Chile), its official organ. See also Leonard Gross,
The Last Best Hope: Eduardo Frei and Chilean Democracy (New York: Random
House, 1967); G. W. Grayson, "Chile's Christian Democratic Party: Power, Factions
and Ideology," *Review of Politics* 31 (1969): 147–71; Ernst Halperin, *Nationalism*

The second most important Christian Democratic party in Latin America is Venezuela's Social Christian party (Copei). This originated with a group of students who were devout Catholics. In 1936 they broke away from the Venezuelan Student Federation because of its anticlerical stand on various issues and formed the National Students Union. This organization wanted to "permeate the structure of Venezuelan society with the teachings of Christianity." Soon the Students Union was in politics and after undergoing a series of changes of name emerged as a political party in 1945, the Independent Committee for Electoral Political Organization, known as Copei from the first letters of the Spanish name. In the late 1960s the name was changed to the Social Christian party (Copei).

From 1945 to 1948, Copei was the main opposition party and thus attracted much conservative support from those who did not like the program of the party in control of the government, Democratic Action. During the 1948–58 period of military dictatorship, the Copei party was radicalized and developed a more reformist Christian Democratic program. It participated in the 1958–63 post-revolutionary government led by Rómulo Betancourt, and this experience seems to have strengthened its reformist views. In December 1968 the leader of the Social Christian party won the presidency of Venezuela for the 1969–74 term.

The Venezuelan Christian Democrats have always been a minority but have improved their vote by a little in recent elections. Rafael Caldera, who has always been the party's presidential candidate, received 21 percent of the votes in 1948, 16 percent in 1958, 21 percent in 1963, and 29 percent in 1968. He was elected president because a large number of candidates split the vote among themselves.[12]

---

and Communism in Chile (Cambridge, Mass.: M.I.T. Press, 1965), "The Christian Democratic Alternative," pp. 178–205; and in Federico Gil, *The Political System of Chile* (Boston: Houghton Mifflin, 1966), "The Christian Democratic Party," pp. 266–76.

12. On the Venezuelan party, see Franklin Tugwell, "The Christian Democrats of Venezuela," *Journal of Inter-American Studies* 7 (1965): pp. 245–67. See also Rafael Caldera, "The Christian Democratic Idea," *America* 107 (1962): pp. 12–15; and idem, "Christian Democracy and Social Reality," in John J. Considine, ed., *Social Revolution in the New Latin America* (Notre Dame, Ind.: Fides Publishers, 1965).

The only other Christian Democratic party in Latin America to win substantial support at the polls is that of El Salvador. This party was organized on 3 December 1960 with an ideology based on Catholic Social Action doctrines. The party has elected a substantial minority of the members of the national legislature during the 1960s as well as many local government officials, including the mayor of the capital city. In the 1967 presidential election the party received 90,089 of the 402,019 votes cast. This party has been active in organizing a Central American League of Christian Democratic Parties.

Other countries with Christian Democratic parties are Guatemala, Nicaragua, Costa Rica, Panama, Cuba, the Dominican Republic, Colombia, Ecuador, Peru, Bolivia, Brazil, and Paraguay, but none has received wide support.[13]

CHRISTIAN DEMOCRACY AND MASS POLITICIZATION

Some observers, particularly a few years ago, saw Christian Democracy as a movement destined to become a great political force throughout Latin America. James D. Cochrane called Christian Democracy "the Latin American political movement growing most rapidly in strength and influence." [14] James Nelson Goodsell of the *Christian Science Monitor* in 1966 thought that "the rise of Christian Democrats in Latin America during the past decade is probably the most significant political development in the

13. Information about most of the parties can be located in the bibliographies on Christian Democratic Parties listed in Harry Kantor, ed., *Latin American Political Parties: A Bibliography,* University of Florida Libraries Bibliographic Series, no. 6 (Gainesville: University of Florida, 1968). See also *Anales del V Congreso Internacional de la Democracia Christiana* (Lima: Editorial Universitaria, 1959); Robert J. Alexander, "The Rise of Latin American Christian Democracy," *New Politics* 3 (1964): 76–84; James D. Cochrane, "The Christian Democrats," subchapter of "Latin American Political Movements," in *The International Encyclopedia of the Social Sciences,* vol. 9 (New York: Macmillan and the Free Press, 1968), p. 45; Alexander T. Edelmann, *Latin American Government and Politics,* rev. ed. (Homewood, Ill.: The Dorsey Press, 1969), "The Christian Democratic Parties," pp. 369–73; Edward J. Williams, *Latin American Christian Democratic Parties* (Knoxville: University of Tennessee Press, 1967); and Rafael Caldera, "El crecimiento de la Democracia Christiana y su influencia sobre la realidad de America Latina," *Política y Espíritu* 19 (1965): pp. 10–19.

14. Cochrane, "Christian Democrats," p. 45.

hemisphere." [15] Another commentator wrote that the Christian Democrats "are on the ascendancy throughout most of Latin America," because "they offer a meaningful alternative to the widespread threat of Communism." [16] And the author of one of the first scholarly books on Christian Democracy written in the United States asserted that "there is little doubt that the [Christian Democratic] movement has emerged as one of the strongest democratic forces in Latin America." [17]

Even from our present perspective of time, however, it is difficult to accept such enthusiastic judgments, for Christian Democracy remains a minority movement in practically all of Latin America, and where it has done best the reason for this is something other than Christian Democracy or the party's connection with the social doctrine of the Catholic church. Much of the enthusiasm for Christian Democracy was generated by its rapid rise in Chile, but as we have seen the party did poorly in the 1970 presidential election.

I would hypothesize that the growth of Copei in Venezuela and of the Christian Democratic party in Chile were the results of peculiar local conditions which it is doubtful will ever be duplicated in the other Latin American republics. The cultural milieu in Latin America is such that a party calling itself Catholic or depending upon Catholic social doctrine has little hope of success. The electoral achievements of the Christian Democratic parties in Chile, Venezuela, and El Salvador, the only countries in which they have done well, had nothing to do with whether or not they were Catholic political parties.

One study of the election in which Eduardo Frei won the presidency concludes that he was elected, first, because Frei was anticommunist and, therefore, the Chilean conservative political parties threw their support to him and, two, because of "the extraordinary appeal and attractiveness of Frei and his program." [18]

15. James Nelson Goodsell, "A New Force in Latin America," *Christian Science Monitor,* 17 April 1966, p. 11.

16. Edelmann, *Latin American Government,* pp. 61, 369.

17. Williams, *Latin American Parties,* p. vii.

18. Federico G. Gil and Charles J. Parrish, *The Chilean Presidential Election of September 4, 1964,* Elections Analysis Series, no. 3 (Washington, D.C.: Institute for the Comparative Study of Political Systems, 1965), p. 50.

All competent observers agree that Frei is a most charismatic individual who probably would have become president no matter
what party he had behind him.

In 1956 Father Albert J. Nevins published an article on the
status of the Catholic church in Latin America in which he divided the twenty republics into three groups. One consisted of
the countries in which the Catholic church was strong (Mexico,
Costa Rica, Colombia, and Argentina); the second, of those where
the church was standing still (Guatemala, Nicaragua, El Salvador,
Chile, Venezuela, Peru, and Uruguay); and the third, those in
which the Catholic church was dying (Bolivia, Brazil, Cuba, the
Dominican Republic, Ecuador, Haiti, Honduras, and Panama).[19]
What is significant is that of the countries in which the Catholic
church was regarded as strong, none has an important or sizable
Christian Democratic party, although two of them, Mexico and
Colombia, have parties that attract many of the active Catholics
(P.A.N. in Mexico and the Conservative party in Colombia). The
most important Christian Democratic parties, those in Chile,
Venezuela, and El Salvador, function in countries in which Father
Nevins thought the Catholic church was standing still. The connection between these two facts illustrates why the Catholic-
inspired political parties have so much difficulty winning wide
support.

Catholic political parties have difficulty because it is a myth
that the overwhelming proportion of the people in Latin America
are Catholics. Mecham thinks that "Roman Catholicism in Latin
America is nothing more than a tradition for the vast majority of
the people." [20] In actual practice, most of the people in Latin
America, if they are Catholics, are Catholics in name only. Various
estimates are that only 15 to 30 percent of the population are
practicing Catholics.[21]

This is well known to the leaders of the various Christian Democratic parties and in their propaganda they try to separate them-

19. Albert J. Nevins, "How Catholic is Latin America?" *The Sign* 36 (1956): pp.
11–18.

20. Mecham, *Church and State,* p. 422.

21. One scholar writes, "Churchmen seem to be the prisoners of their own statistics. The national census reports that about ninety-eight per cent of the population
is Catholic; in reality, only thirty per cent may be active Church members." John J.
Kennedy, quoted by Pike in his *Conflict Between Church and State,* p. 26.

selves from the Catholic church. President Caldera of Venezuela, for example, has written that

> Christian Democracy is not in any way a religious movement; nor does it have a confessional character. Christian Democratic parties include among their members Catholics, Protestants, Jews, agnostics, professing the widest variety of conceptions and creeds. The name Christian does not represent a religious position but the conviction that Christian values and the spirit of Christianity can best fulfill successfully the requirements of social justice and defeat Marxism in the struggle to conquer the soul of the people. We believe that the Social Christian inspiration overflows the boundaries of a given creed.[22]

In the same way, Eduardo Frei, former president of Chile, never speaks of his party as connected with the Catholic church. He emphasizes the party's support of democracy, liberty, economic development, social justice, and nationalism; he was elected on the slogan "Revolution in Liberty." "Christian Democracy, my friends," he said to an International Congress of the Christian Democratic Parties meeting in Peru, "is not a confessional party, it is not the church which we want to involve. The church is out of and above political disputes. Woe to the parties which want to make use of the church! And woe to the church that wants to mix itself into political struggles!" The stenographic report at this point indicates that the thousands of people listening gave Frei tremendous and prolonged applause.[23]

The attempt to win support using the name Christian Democratic, yet avoiding connection with the church, is almost universal. The program of the Progressive Christian Democratic party of the Dominican Republic states: "Liberty of thought, of faith, and of conscience has to be made secure. A religious demonstration or a religious ideology should not be taken advantage of for partisan politics." [24]

The Costa Rican Christian Democratic party speaks of itself

22. Rafael Caldera, "Christian Democracy and Social Reality," p. 68.
23. Eduardo Frei, "Discurso," in *Anales de la Democracia Christiana*, p. 245.
24. *Programa Fundamental Partido Progresista Demócrata Cristiano* (Santo Domingo: El Partido, 1961), p. 18.

as "the party which struggles so that the citizens will come to live in a more just and dignified society in which everyone will be able to develop to the maximum his condition as a human being" and declares that "it is nourished by a Christian conception of man." [25] This is as far as most Christian Democrats will go, yet they fail to strike a responsive chord among the masses. I attribute this to the traditional anticlerical attitude still so prevalent in Latin America.

Another factor which makes it difficult for the Christian Democratic parties to win wide support is the tremendous disagreement among Catholics, both among members of the church and among priests and members of the hierarchy. This means that Catholics are found in all of the various kinds of political parties active in Latin America. In Brazil in 1962 four Catholic priests were members of the National Legislature. Each was elected by a different political party: one by the Christian Democratic party, one by the Brazilian Labor party, one by the Democratic National Union, and one by the Social Democratic party. The Chilean Christian Democratic party lost the 1970 election in part because of a split in its ranks that saw a section of the party supporting Salvador Allende, the candidate of the communist-socialist coalition, running against the Christian Democratic candidate.

Many Catholics remain tied to the traditional conservative parties. Others share the new chiliastic dreams of instantaneous revolution and join one of the Armed Forces of National Liberation. Camilo Torres, a Colombian priest from an aristocratic family, did this and was shot dead in a battle. His name has become a slogan to certain of the followers of the new millenarianism.

What future can be forecast for the Christian Democratic Parties of Latin America? Rafael Caldera thinks that "Christian Democracy constitutes today the best and perhaps the only hope for the people of Latin America." [26] The evidence does not seem to warrant this assessment. Most observers agree that President Frei and his Christian Democratic government succeeded in carrying out most of the program upon which he had been elected. By 1970, practically every child up to fourteen years of age was in school,

25. *Manuel del Demócrata Cristiano*, Ideological Series, no. 2 (San José: The Party), p. 3.
26. Caldera, "Christian Democracy and Social Reality," p. 74.

the housing situation had improved, there was a favorable balance of trade, copper production was up, and the government had gained 51 percent ownership of almost all the copper companies. In addition, agrarian reform had begun and laws legalizing farm workers unions had been passed. These were all measures promised by President Frei's "Revolution in Liberty." Yet when the new election took place in 1970, the Christian Democratic candidate was badly beaten in a fair election, coming in third among the three candidates.

The republics of Latin America are the product of a long, historic development and the Catholic church has played an important role in that history. Unfortunately for the church, it became involved in politics and after centuries of struggle is slowly being pushed out of the political arena. The people of Latin America will probably remain more or less Catholic, but it is very doubtful that the Christian Democratic parties, which draw their inspiration from Catholic ideas, will win the support of the masses who seek solutions to their problems. There is no doubt that there is a desire among some intellectuals to draw on Latin America's Catholic heritage to develop a political philosophy independent of the Russian and North American models. As a result, for the foreseeable future, Christian Democracy will continue to be one of the political forces competing for the allegiance of the people, but it is very doubtful that it will become the predominant force in the area or in any of the individual republics.

PART 4

The Religious Legitimation of Change

12

Hinduism, Sarvodaya, and Social Change

MIRIAM SHARMA AND JAGDISH P. SHARMA

In recent years there has been a serious and conscious attempt to reformulate ways of thinking about the nature of religion, especially with regard to the role it plays in the new nations of the Third World. It is no longer acceptable to see religion as a "completely static and inert complex of beliefs and structures" that can present only a massive obstacle to any kind of desired change.[1] Considerable work has also been done on a reappraisal of Max Weber's hypothesis regarding India's religions and economic development.[2] Hinduism and Buddhism are no longer regarded as being unqualifiedly inimical to modern economic change. Indeed, it has been shown that these religions do contain modes of thinking that are both rational and conducive to economic change.[3]

We acknowledge with gratitude the bibliographic assistance provided by Ernestine Enomoto and Sara Gleaton.

1. Smith, *Religion and Political Development*, p. 201.

2. Max Weber, *The Religion of India* (New York: The Free Press, 1958).

3. See especially Milton Singer, "Modernization of Religious Beliefs," in M. Weiner, ed., *Modernization* (New York: Basic Books, 1966), pp. 55–67, and attached bibliography; idem, "Religion and Social Change in India: the Max Weber Thesis, Phase Three," *Economic Development and Culture Change* 14 (1966): 497–505; Morris D. Morris, "Values as an Obstacle to Economic Growth in South Asia: An Historical Survey," *Journal of Economic History* 27 (1967): 588–607; Robert N. Bellah, *Religion and Progress in Modern Asia* (New York: The Free Press, 1965). As Milton Singer has aptly noted, "this sweeping conclusion of Weber's is frequently echoed and elaborated in recent discussions without benefit of his vast erudition or of contemporary empirical studies of the relation of religious beliefs and practices to modernization. Indeed, this conclusion is frequently converted into modernizing policies and value judgments that would have horrified Weber's scientific conscience." "Modernization of Religious Beliefs," p. 56.

Religion, Culture Management, and Social Change

That religion not only serves to support the status quo but also contains potentialities for change within its varied, and often contradictory, components has been amply revealed in the case of Hinduism. The political potentialities of Indian cultural materials was proved often by new aspirants to leadership. For the past hundred years, religious reformers, poets, and revolutionaries have appealed to aspects of a revitalized indigenous tradition as offering national strength, unity, and dignity. The issue was one of identity, of presenting a national self-definition that could renew a sense of Indian distinctiveness while incorporating ideas suitable for a changing world.[4] Further, not only can a religion contain the seeds of change within its traditional structure, but, like any other aspect of social behavior, it can be consciously contrived, reinterpreted, and managed to make change both acceptable and meaningful to people. Gandhi, one of the most conspicuous "modernizers of Indian politics," showed how old symbols could be managed and changed, if necessary, in order to serve and support new functions.[5]

The Sarvodaya movement[6] provides an excellent example of "culture management"—the conscious and deliberate choosing of values (in this case, religious) to mobilize support for a particular view (in this case, about social change).[7] As exemplified by the *Bhoodan* (land-gift) program, the movement is the direct outcome of Gandhi's thought and is the masterful creation of his protege, Vinoba Bhave. Its self-image is that of an indigenous experiment in planned social change that seeks to bring about a nonviolent social revolution based on the Hindu values of service, nonviolence, equality, and freedom. Expressed almost exclusively in a religious idiom, Sarvodaya uses a reinterpreted Hinduism to legitimize revolutionary change toward a utopian society.[8]

4. McKim Marriott, "Cultural Policy in the New States," in Clifford Geertz, ed., *Old Societies and New States* (New York: The Free Press, 1963), p. 30.

5. Rudolph and Rudolph, *Modernity of Tradition*, p. 157.

6. By Sarvodaya movement or Bhoodan movement we mean both the ideology originally expounded by Gandhi and elaborated upon by Bhave and Narayan and the programs devised by the latter two.

7. Marriott, "Cultural Policy," p. 29. "Culture-Management" was coined by Lloyd A. Fallers, "Ideology and Culture in Uganda Nationalism," *American Anthropologist* 63 (1961): 667–78.

8. Perhaps T. K. Oommen did not consult the writings of Bhave and Narayan

Sarvodaya philosophy, however, has incorporated some basic modern ideals that are contradictory to the actual values governing the behavior of the majority of Indians. This incorporation is achieved by a skillful "managing" of carefully chosen traditional Hindu values and symbols in order to gain support for, or legitimize, the essentially modern ones or, as in the case of *ahimsa* (nonviolence), ancient ones that were never truly actualized. While Vinoba says that the new social order of Sarvodaya is prescribed by the Hinduism of old, he really seeks to demonstrate that Hindu religion can provide the motivation to achieve this goal. Vinoba recognizes that for people to be motivated toward social change, it is necessary to work within, and appeal to, the already existing world view. Since India's is primarily a religious world view, then "changes in the ideas and values associated with that world-view might have a profound impact on motivation and behavior." [9]

SARVODAYA: THE IDEAL SOCIAL ORDER

Vinoba writes that after Gandhi's death he devoted himself to "furiously thinking how in the present state of progressive material and moral deterioration of the country, he could revive hope and confidence in Bapu's way." [10] Gandhi had provided the philosophy; now it was up to Vinoba to provide the action. This led directly to the origin of Bhoodan—Vinoba's program to bring about a social revolution and achieve the Sarvodaya ideal. As this movement is both a continuation and actualization of Gandhian thought, though in some ways altered, the nature of Gandhi's ideas must be examined closely. [11]

---

and could thus state, "Like Gandhi, he [Vinoba] traces the origins of his ideas continually to traditional Hindu sources, thereby suggesting that all he hopes to achieve is to reestablish the traditional order without the attendant manmade evils." This leads the author to conclude that "far from challenging such [rational-legal] authority, however, they want to reinforce appropriate traditions; the idea of modernization is not dear to them. . . . Our evidence is that, while both Gandhi and Vinoba can be legitimately labelled as charismatics, they are at best system-maintainers." "Charisma, Social Structure and Social Change," *Comparative Studies in Society and History* 10 (1967): 98.

9. Smith, *Religion and Political Development*, p. 5.

10. J. B. Kripalani, "An Interview with Sri Vinoba," in P. D. Tandon, ed., *Vinoba Bhave: The Man and His Mission* (Bombay: Vora and Co., 1962), p. 9.

11. The Sarvodaya movement is termed "Neo-Gandhian" by Joan Bondurant and Margaret Fisher, "The Concept of Change in Hindu, Socialist and Neo-Gandhian Thought," in Smith, *South Asian Politics and Religion*, pp. 235–48.

Sarvodaya, most commonly translated as the "welfare of all" or "uplift of all," represents that aspect of self-rule which remained to be fulfilled after independence.[12] It pertained to the freedom of the Indian masses from the bondages imposed by the conditions of their society. Going beyond mere reforms, it calls for a total revolution. In the words of Jayaprakash Narayan, Gandhi always insisted upon a dual revolution, "the internal as well as external; human as well as social. Without the internal revolution, the external one is meaningless." [13] Religion and politics become intermeshed with social change. The internal revolution was to Gandhi a spiritual transformation of the nature of society and its governance; and Sarvodaya pointed not only to a distant utopia but represented a practical way of mobilizing the physical, economic, and spiritual resources of society in the service of all.[14]

Gandhi was greatly influenced by the three postulates put forth in Ruskin's *Unto This Last:* (1) the good of the individual is the good of all, (2) all types of labor are equal, and (3) the life of the laborer (tiller or craftsman) is the life worth living.[15] Gandhi rejected the socialist concept of the class struggle and the violent methods of achieving social change associated with it, but the professed ultimate goals of socialism were not dissimilar to his own. Writers have referred to Sarvodaya as "Gandhian socialism" or "Hindu socialism." [16] That J. P. Narayan, founder of the Congress Socialist party, could join the movement is extremely telling of the commonality between these two doctrines. Narayan himself states, "the Sarvodaya plan contains 80 per cent of the immediate pro-

---

12. Another term used by Bhave is *Samya-Yogi* Society (Society where all are equal), in his *From Bhoodan to Gramdan* (Tanjore: Sarvodaya Prachuralaya, 1957), pp. 4–6.

13. J. P. Narayan, *Dual Revolution* (Tanjore: Sarvodaya Prachuralaya, 1963), p. 18.

14. J. P. Narayan, *Challenges After Nehru* (Thanjavur: Sarvodaya Prachuralaya, 1964), p. 16; see also Adi H. Doctor, *Sarvodaya: A Political and Economic Study* (Bombay: Asia Publishing House, 1967), p. 3.

15. Quoted in Mohandas K. Gandhi, *Sarvodaya: The Welfare of All* (Ahmedabad: Navajivan Publishing House, 1954), p. 3.

16. Joan V. Bondurant and Margaret W. Fisher, *Indian Approaches to a Socialist Society,* Indian Press Digests Monograph Series, no. 2 (Berkeley and Los Angeles: University of California Press, 1956), and Smith, *Religion and Political Development,* pp. 215–17.

gram of the Socialist party, besides sharing the common ideal of a classless and casteless society." [17]

The entire ideology of Sarvodaya centers in the idea of service based on love—an individual ethic that is translated into a social ethic, whereby one serves oneself best by serving others. In order to come to the point at which this is the key value governing men's actions, a moral revolution must take place. This is not an impossible achievement, for Gandhi fully accepted the creative power of the self-suffering of human individuals, the process that lies at the root of social betterment. Through self-suffering (*tapas*) one arrives at the truth (*satya*), which, in turn, is inseparable from nonviolence (*ahimsa*). Added to these personal virtues are those of self-sacrifice and renunciation, extending also to possessions, self-restraint of all the senses, religious tolerance, noncompetitiveness, and Tolstoy's concept of "bread labor" (the moral necessity for all to do physical work).[18]

In Sarvodaya, the basic unit of social interaction is the village. Gandhi portrayed this as a return to an idealized past in which these were autonomous republics, self-sufficient in all their basic wants. Self-sufficiency can be obtained only by decentralization, and this is the basic mode of operation in the economic and political spheres. In the Sarvodaya social order economic decentralization is achieved by the principles of *swadeshi* (homemade goods) and the program of *khadi* (homespun cloth). Economic relations are harmonized and equalized through noncompetitiveness (which for Gandhi meant following one's caste occupation) and the principle of trusteeship. Political decentralization leads to the sovereignty of the people based on pure moral authority. When the state has finally become so decentralized, it will wither away. At that time India will have achieved real *swaraj* (self-rule) and Sarvodaya.[19]

Although it was Gandhi who provided the framework for the concept of the ideal society, it was left to his most prominent disciple, Vinoba, to activate this into an explicit social movement

17. Bimla Prasad, ed., *Socialism, Sarvodaya and Democracy, Selected Works of Jaya Prakash Narayan* (Bombay: Asia Publishing House, 1964), p. 91.

18. Gandhi, *Sarvodaya*, pp. 10–21, 25, 32, 91.

19. Ibid., pp. 35–37, 48, 66–72.

with definite programs. The whole movement bears the imprint of the particular style of this man, essentially that of a saintly ascetic who was thrust into the limelight due to his compelling concern for the well-being of his fellow men. Vinoba's approach to the economic transformation of rural India, however, has differed significantly from that of his master. Gandhi laid great emphasis on the principle of trusteeship, whereby "the rich man will be left in possession of his wealth, of which he will use what he reasonably requires for his personal needs and will act as trustee for the remainder to be used for society." [20] Gandhi's trusteeship was an appeal to the rich to give to the poor on the basis of the traditional virtue of charity. Bhave is more interested in the immediate problem of giving land to the landless and abolishing the instinct to hold private ownership in land. Bhoodan (the land-gift movement) advocates a "dispossession" of those who have property, but dispossession that is free of violence and based on persuasion. As such, it leaves no room for bitterness between the giver and the receiver.[21]

A more striking difference in style and approach can be discerned between Bhave and Narayan. Jayaprakash Narayan came to the movement leaving behind him a very full and noteworthy political career. By 1954, when he was the most important Socialist leader in India, Narayan decided that the country's problems could not be solved through active politics and parliamentary legislation. His conversion to Bhoodan came about because he saw that "politics could not deliver the goods—the goods being the same old goals of equality, freedom, brotherhood and peace." [22] Thus he became a *jivandani,* one who dedicated his life fully to the work of Bhoodan and the reconstruction of society on Gandhian lines.

Despite the certain change of emphasis in the Sarvodaya program as carried on by Gandhi's spiritual successors, the ideal re-

20. Quoted in Jayantanuja Bandyopadhyaya, *Social and Political Thought of Gandhi* (Bombay: Allied Publishers, 1969), p. 130, from *Harijan,* August 25, 1940. See also Phyllis Rolnick, "Charity, Trusteeship and Social Change in India: a study of political ideology," *World Politics* 14 (1962): p. 459.

21. Bhave, *Revolutionary Sarvodaya* (Bombay: Bharatiya Vidya Bhavan, 1964), p. 39; idem, *Gramdan, Villagisation of Land* (Tanjore: Sarvodaya Prachuralaya, 1962), p. 51; and idem, *Bhoodan Yajna* (Tanjore: Sarvodaya Prachuralaya, 1955), p. vi.

22. Narayan in Prasad, *Sarvodaya and Democracy,* p. 156; see also p. 112.

mains essentially the same and represents a continuation of his thought. We now turn to the problem of how society can be changed in order to realize this goal.

THE DYNAMICS OF CHANGE IN SARVODAYA

Planned change is one of the basic social processes of our time and, as has been increasingly recognized by those involved in such projects, it cannot succeed without a definite theory of how social change takes place. In our analysis of their thought we find that both Bhave and Narayan are acutely aware of the fact that any program they propose must be rooted in such a theory.

There are three main points in the Sarvodaya view of the dynamics of social change. As in the case of the ultimate goal of Sarvodaya and the program to implement this, the basic ideas come from Gandhi. The concept of social change that he advocates is essentially the same as that of recent theorists on the subject; namely, that it is ultimately a psychological process by which human action is "motivated—not only motivated but purposeful, since it is guided by a consideration of its consequences, that is, by values." [23] Gandhi insisted upon the need for a total revolution in which transformed values provided the base. Secondly, he believed in the creative power of self-suffering individuals and felt that these incessant efforts for the perfection of individuality lay at the root of progress. He was opposed to all those (i.e., the Marxists) who accepted a "deterministic view and taught a mechanical automatism of human progress by the inevitable working of objective forces." [24] Gandhi's third major contribution to the theory of

23. Ward H. Goodenough, "Introduction," in *Cooperation in Change* (New York: John Wiley, 1966). Also see H. Barnett, *Innovation: The Basis of Cultural Change* (New York: McGraw-Hill, 1953), and A. Wallace, *Culture and Personality* (New York: Random House, 1961), "The Psychology of Culture Change," pp. 120–63. Vinoba's thoughts are also in accord with the views expressed at a conference on "Cultural Motivation to Progress in South and Southeast Asia" held in Manila, June 3–8, 1963. Soedjatmoko writes on the challenge of religion, "What is required then is the activation of more basic and more specific motivations for the acceleration of economic development. And these motivations in our societies are undoubtedly embedded in the cultural religious matrix. In part the problem is one of more effective symbol creation and symbol manipulation." Bellah, *Religion and Progress*, p. 6.

24. V. P. Varma, *Political Philosophy of Mahatma Gandhi and Sarvodaya* (Agra: Lakshmi Narayan Agarwal Educational Publishers, 1965), p. 64.

change in Sarvodaya is the doctrine that only nonviolence can bring about such a revolution, as the means determine the ends. Sarvodaya ideology as expounded by Vinoba and Narayan expands farther upon these premises.

Vinoba believes that human destiny and the dynamics of progress are in the hands of mankind. Narayan also says that man is amenable to change and can progress, but this is impossible without the necessary motivation to do so.

> In days gone by men tried to be good, impelled by some higher moral force in which they believed. Society provided every individual with the motive to be good: it was the command of religion and of God. But in the present society there is no hold of religion and so there are no incentives to goodness left. Thus it is clearer than ever that social reconstruction is impossible without a human reconstruction. Society cannot be good unless individual men are good.[25]

Religion in the past provided the motivation for good action. As motivations consist of mental attitudes and predispositions, it follows that "goodness" and "human reconstruction" cannot be legislated. First "persuasion, change of heart and mind, the creation of new social values and the corresponding climate of opinion, and noncooperation with wrong where persuasion is inadequate— all this must occur before a social revolution can take place."[26] No law can effect a transvaluation of values. Law can only reflect this once the transvaluation has already taken place in the lives of the people. Hence, a Gandhian does not concentrate on capturing the power of the state but goes directly to the people and helps them effect a revolution in their lives and consequently a revolution in the life of the community.

In the speeches and writings of Vinoba and Narayan, India's five-year plans and the Community Development and *Panchayati Raj* (local self-government) programs are often referred to as examples of the inadequacy of attempting to legislate motivation for

25. Narayan in D. MacKenzie Brown, ed., *Indian Political Thought from Ranade to Bhave* (Berkeley and Los Angeles: University of California Press, 1961), p. 180.

26. Narayan in Prasad, *Sarvodaya and Democracy*, p. 124.

change. Development programs in India have failed miserably, they say, due to the villagers' lack of motivation. The original initiative for Panchayati Raj came not from the political desire to broaden the base of democracy but from the anxiety to obtain full public cooperation in the execution of devolpment plans. This served to reinforce the Sarvodaya view that "rural society cannot be changed from above; you cannot change the village without first changing the minds of the villagers." [27] They emphasize that state legislation, in fact, has not even touched upon that aspect of the problem at which Bhoodan aims—the equitable distribution of land in a peaceful manner and by voluntary donation, without the payment of compensation. Such an objective could never be legislated, nor could it ever create the type of peace and goodwill among the masses that Bhoodan establishes.

Sarvodaya also maintains that in order to bring about social growth the tools used must be culturally substantive and relevant to the needs of India's development. While it is acknowledged that the present can be built only within the framework of the past, there is an awareness that the essence of change is essentially a restructuring of the past so that a new pattern emerges.[28] The movement, however, must not be misunderstood as seeking to return to a "Golden Age" of India's past. Bhave's basic premise is that Indian (Hindu) values must be reformulated in relation to modern ideas in order to bring about any meaningful change. He continues, "We have to build our society in accordance with the demand of the age. We must realize old values cannot continue in their old forms. Values and norms obtained when Tulsidas wrote his *Ramayana* cannot be accepted today . . . this is the age of comradely love." [29] Elsewhere he says, "Sarvodaya is a complete revolution. It wants to transform old values and norms and establish new

27. Narayan in Bhave and Narayan, *Gramdan for Gram-Swaraj*, pp. 82–83; Narayan, "Organic Democracy," in S. P. Aiyar and R. Srinivasan, *Studies in Indian Democracy* (Bombay: Allied Publishers, 1965), p. 333. To corroborate this point there is the entire body of literature on Community Development programs in India.

28. The main thesis of Barnett's *Innovation* is that the essence of culture change lies in a recombination of parts; it is the restructuring of the parts so that a new pattern results. As such, it works within the framework of old beliefs.

29. Quoted in B. R. Misra, *V for Vinoba: The Economics of the Bhoodan Movement* (Bombay: Orient Longmans, 1956), pp. 55–56.

ones. Hence it calls for the voluntary surrender of ownership and vests it with the *gram sabha* (village council)." [30]

Throughout history, values have constantly undergone phases of transformation. The basic element of social reconstruction and social engineering is the very quest of values. For India, "the most characteristic and important value" that has developed is spirituality. Under this is subsumed "human freedom—the value of identification, love—the value of enabling every individual to develop itself and personality to the fullest extent, and the wholeness of life—of all the pursuits of man." [31] Sarvodaya seeks to bridge the gap between the old and the new. The old is the mode of spiritualism in Indian thought. The new is the tide of change that has brought new values and great scientific progress in its wake. The aim is to "achieve in our country a synthesis of these basic spiritual values which we have inherited from our forefathers, and science. . . . But science and technology must be subordinate to this pattern of social life, to these values." [32]

If one uses coercive techniques to deal with social problems, these techniques merely postpone the time when the serious work of dealing with the individual's attitudes toward social change will have to be taken up. Vinoba believes that the stimulation of compassion in the minds of people is, not only a more moral, but a more effective incentive to social change than the stimulation of hatred through class conflict. "Practically, the use of violence will produce a result lasting only as long as that force persists. If a permanent change is desired, then peaceful means of persuasion and conversion should be utilized." [33] Vinoba has taken up the specific issue of land ownership to show that nonviolent means can solve economic problems and change society.

ORIGIN OF BHOODAN

Bhave first appeared on the national scene after independence when he went to Delhi to work for the rehabilitation of Muslim refugees. While Bhave was engaged in this work, there occurred an event that shocked him. Some landless Harijans (Gandhi's term for

30. Bhave in Bhave and Narayan, *Gramdan for Gram-Swaraj*, p. 49.
31. Narayan, *Three Basic Problems of Free India* (Bombay: Asia Publishing House, 1964), pp. 19, 25.
32. Ibid., pp. 19–25.
33. J. H. Noyes, "An Example to Mankind," in Tandon, *Vinoba Bhave*, p. 56.

untouchables) had asked for land and he succeeded in getting the Punjab government to agree to give them some. Two days later the government went back on its word. This served only to reinforce the familiar Gandhian principle that all constructive work must remain aloof from party politics and governments. Shortly thereafter, in 1949, Vinoba returned to his *ashram* at Wardha due to ill health.

In April of 1951, the third annual conference of the Sarvodaya Samaj was to be held near Hyderabad City. Bhave decided to walk the 300 miles from his ashram as he felt this would be the only way to adequately determine the condition of the villagers. On the way, in every village through which he passed, he came face to face with the misery of the landless. After the conference was over, Vinoba declared he would tour Telangana, an area of severe peasant disturbances and destructive communist activity. "I wanted to tour the Telangana," he said, "as a soldier of *Shanti sena* [Peace Brigade] in order to propagate the message of peace. . . . After obtaining the blessings of the Lord Rama, I have undertaken this tour." [34]

Vinoba had already come to the conclusion that land was the basic problem—not only in India, but in all of Asia. If it could be solved in a peaceful manner, then nonviolent strength would grow. After starting his march, Bhave came to the village of Pochampelli. Here,

> the Harijans of the place asked for eighty acres of land and on my suggestion that someone should come forward to satisfy their demand, he [a villager] offered them one hundred acres. You can meet this friend and learn from him how and in what atmosphere the whole thing originated in that village. To me this appeared to be a signal from God and I decided to start the campaign. It is evident that in the absence of this pointer I could not have thought of this solution to the land-problem. . . . I could not have made bold to undertake it. . . . All the same I took it up with faith in God and decided to try my hand at it. Thus I began to ask for land.[35]

34. Quoted in Suresh Ram, *Vinoba and His Mission* (Rajghat: Akhil Bharat Sarva Seva Sangha, 1962), p. 51.
35. Bhave, *Bhoodan Yajna*, pp. 109–10.

And so Bhoodan was born. It emerged out of the urgent need to
find a solution to the problem of poverty facing India's millions;
it was based on *satyagraha,* the philosophy of constant revolutionary change through nonviolent methods, and it was motivated by
the deeply religious beliefs of one man. Three months after com-
pleting his Telangana tour, Bhave was called to Delhi by Nehru,
to advise the Planning Commission. Once again he set out on foot
to carry the message of Bhoodan to the people.

Bhoodan is actually a compound of *bhoomi* (Sanskrit for "land")
and *dana* (gift). Bhave wanted to convince landholders that, as
good Hindus and good human beings, it was their moral duty to
donate one-sixth of their land as a gift to the landless. He was not
misled by the initial success in Telangana and on his marches
through Uttar Pradesh he set a target of five million acres to be
collected. This was soon accomplished and he went on to perform
his Bhoodan-*yajna* (sacrifice) on a full scale in Bihar. In keeping
with the Sarvodaya view of social change, Vinoba sought to bring
about a threefold revolution: a change in people's hearts, a change
in their lives, and a change in their social structure. He was convinced that "nothing could be achieved through pressure or force"
and that "if force is to be used, I am not required. My feeble hands
would not be of any use." [36]

Vinoba defined three immediate objectives to help in establishing the Sarvodaya goal: (1) all were to have a right to land and
property, (2) there was to be no distinction in the manner of
wages, and (3) power was to be decentralized to the villages. Once
an equitable distribution of land was achieved and people cultivated indigenous crafts using local materials, the villages would
become truly self-sufficient and bring closer the ideal of village self-
government. Certain general procedures were to be followed in
the distribution of Bhoodan lands. Vinoba's representatives were
to find out about the land to be distributed in advance. The distribution was then to take place in a general meeting of the entire
village. As far as possible, decisions were to be made unanimously,
and at least one-third of the land received should be given to the
Harijans. There were specific rules pertaining to the amount of
land to be distributed according to family size, conditions of its

36. Ibid., p. 24.

sale or mortgage, and taxes to be paid. There was also the condition that if cooperative farming was started, the recipients were bound to join it.

In 1952, when a village in Uttar Pradesh wished to offer all its land for redistribution, a new program was born that became operational three years later—*Gramdan* (gift of a village). All landholders now transferred ownership of their land to the village assembly, and village resources were to be utilized for the good of all. The assembly, in turn, would take part of the land (one-sixth) from the former owner for redistribution, and then reallot the remainder to him. Individual families were allowed to cultivate the farms and also to pass them on to the next generation, provided rents had been paid to the village council. If lands were left uncultivated, they reverted to the village community. One-tenth of the village land was reserved for common cultivation on a cooperative basis, and the proceeds from this were used to meet service expenses such as *panchayat* administration, village school, maternity home, sanitation, cultural activities, and festivals. Holders of smaller plots could also practice cooperative methods in farming, harvesting, using irrigation facilities, marketing, and so on.[37]

In 1955 a revised (*sulabh,* literally "easy") Gramdan program came into effect. It was to provide an intermediate step between Bhoodan and the old Gramdan, whereby it became possible to "identify the instinct of self-interest with that of surrender to society and cement them both." [38] It requested a voluntary transfer of land ownership to the village and distribution of only one-twentieth of a man's land among the landless. The owner did this himself and the rest of the land remained in his possession. The new Gramdan scheme also called for the establishment of a village fund in which landholders regularly contributed one-fortieth of their produce and salaried people or wage earners contributed a day's earning monthly (or one-thirtieth of their income) year after year.

Another avenue of approach was to appeal for donations of money from those without land; this was called *Sampattidan* (gift of wealth). Bhave generally asked for a one-sixth donation to pay

37. Shriman Narayan Agrawal, *One Week with Vinoba* (New Delhi: All India Congress Committee, 1956), p. 14.

38. Bhave in Narayan, *Gramdan for Gram-Swaraj,* p. 22.

for seed supplies and implements for those who had received Bhoodan lands, the publication of Sarvodaya literature, and the expenses of village workers. This plan was considered to be equally important as Bhoodan and Gramdan.

The ideal form of Sampattidan, however, is *Shramdan* (gift of labor). Labor alone is wealth, and Vinoba desired to bring about the attitude that any produce of labor can be had only in exchange for physical labor. No article should be given in exchange for money. The dan of wealth produced by physical labor is *daivi-sampatti* (divine wealth), while the latter is *asuri-sampatti* (evil wealth).

Bhave intended to spread the movement over half a million villages and thousands of cities and towns. Building up from his original program of Bhoodan, he launched several other new ones. In 1953, with Narayan's help, *Buddhidan* (gift of knowledge) and *Jivandan* (gift of life) began. With the donation of such gifts, Vinoba wanted people to share their knowledge and life with society and devote themselves to the service of others.

By 1965, when interest in working for the movement appeared to be waning, Vinoba called for a *Toofan* (typhoon) of renewed vitality to hasten the pace until Gramdan would cover the whole country, some two years hence. This led further to Block-*dan* and District-*dan,* in areas where 70 percent of the villages accepted the movement.[39]

Narayan believes that Bhave has "made the concept of sharing, cooperation, and service of others universal" in India but that the emphasis has been so far on the agrarian sphere. The numbers actively involved in the movement are not many and they "cannot do everything at once." However, he is confident that "we can go forward from sharing of incomes to a new kind of industrial organization where there is human fellowship; and where, instead of impersonal rules and laws, human relationships bind and run the organization and govern its life."[40]

Thus, plans for achieving the Sarvodaya ideal of decentralization—where the village is autonomous politically and self-sufficient for all its needs—have not received the same attention as the program of land redistribution. Narayan also realizes that political

39. Ibid., p. 53.
40. Narayan, *Dual Revolution,* pp. 22–23.

decentralization cannot be effected without economic decentralization. Encouragement of village industries and other constructive work is being carried on, but he suggests that much of this is merely a "support to the status quo or of relief nature only." [41]

The Sarvodaya movement has clearly not achieved the goals defined twenty years ago. Its emphasis on political and economic decentralization goes counter to massive developmental efforts directed by the government. Unfortunately, even the program of land redistribution has lacked effectiveness in some areas, due to the organizational deficiencies of the movement. Possibly the greatest achievement of Sarvodaya, although impossible to measure, has been its contribution to a more general openness to change among the Indian people. Sarvodaya is one of the many influences challenging the traditional assumption that what is should be.

HINDUISM AND THE LEGITIMATION OF CHANGE

In the foregoing pages we have attempted to describe and analyze the way in which Sarvodaya has used a reformulated Hinduism in order to find a motivation for change and to design a program which, it was hoped, would mobilize the masses to implement change. Practically every page of Sarvodaya literature reveals the moral tone of its concepts, activities, and techniques. There is an emphasis on gifts, sacrifice, pilgrimage, penance, nonviolence, pursuit of truth, self-restraint, and so forth. While certain exogenous ideas have been incorporated, one must be impressed with the fact that religion—the ethics, morality, and spiritual values of Hinduism—has provided the fundamental basis for the movement.

Bhave writes of the Bhoodan yajna (sacrifice): "When there is any misfortune or distress in the country a yajna has to be performed. Our country is now in distress. There is suffering everywhere. There is conflict between capital and labor, lack of the means of livelihood, untouchability, communalism. Under such conditions to save the country a yajna has been started." The call to participate in Bhoodan is mediated by equating it with participation in the worship of *Daridranarayana* (God as the poor).

41. Narayan in Prasad, *Sarvodaya and Democracy,* p. 126.

Similarly, the basic principle behind Sampattidan is that no man can be the Lord of bhoomi (earth) or the Lord of *Lakshmi* (goddess of wealth). If someone accumulates wealth, it is not due to his efforts alone but to the collective efforts of all. Hence, wealth belongs to all and one should partake of it as *prasada* from the Lord of All to whom it is offered. Bhave asserted: "Some think that I began by asking for land in charity, and now I have begun to ask for it as a right. This is not so—from the beginning I have asked for justice. But it is God's justice, not legal justice . . . In God's world, I want equality as God wished." The historian of religion may find little that he recognizes in such characterizations of Hindu doctrine, but Vinoba Bhave's religious authority has not been seriously challenged. It is precisely the genius of the man that the most daring innovations have been convincingly communicated by the symbols of sacred tradition.

13

The Sources and Meaning of Islamic Socialism

FAZLUR RAHMAN

The term "Islamic socialism" has gained wide currency in the Muslim world since the beginning of the last decade and has also provoked strong opposition from both orthodox Muslims and Marxists. The former condemn the term on the ground that "socialism" is a fad and that the eternal truth of Islam should not be tied to a fad, that Islam contains within itself a sufficient doctrine of economic justice and does not need any extrinsic adjuncts, and that such an adjunct is liable to encourage atheistic socialism to exploit the term to its own advantage. Some of them also think that Islam is basically capitalistic, although nowadays this opinion is not voiced. Indeed, the term "capitalism" in the Muslim world has become anathema, although terms like "private enterprise" and "free initiative" are quite acceptable.

The Marxists, on the other hand, denounce the term "Islamic socialism" because, they say, Islam is essentially a doctrine of capitalism in the economic field, although it originally contained certain elements of primitive socialism, and, therefore, the adjunct "Islamic" destroys the concept of socialism.[1] Is this triangular con-

---

1. A good summary of these arguments has been given by the late Syrian Dr. Mustafa al-Siba'i in his work *Ishtirakiyat al-Islam* [*Socialism of Islam*], 2d ed. (Cairo: National Publishing House, 1960), pp. 6, 244–46. The orthodox Muslim viewpoint is elaborated in 'Abd al-'Aziz al-Badri, *Hukm al-Islam fi'l-Ishtirakiya* [*The judgment of Islam on socialism*] (Madina, Saudi Arabia: al-Mataba al-'ilmiya, 1965). The Marxist side is stated by Maxime Rodinson in his *Islam et Capitalisme* (Paris: Editions du Seuil, 1966). Muslim Marxists, however, do not abandon Islam, at least openly: "Marxist Algerians accept the existence of Islam, but not a reactionary Islam. . . . There need not be any incompatibility between a socialist state . . . Islam need not fear socialism; the real enemy is capitalism." *Alger Républicain*, quoted in Thomas L. Blair, *The Land to Those Who Work It* (New York: Doubleday, 1969), pp. 129–31, 133. For a general discussion of Islam and communism, see

flict a verbal quibble or does it point to something significant in the situation? If the conflict is significant, what is its nature? And can any long-range trends be deciphered in the present situation?

To understand the significance of Islamic socialism it is necessary, first, to examine the historical forces that produced a natural convergence of Islamic reform, nationalism, and socialism. The pattern varied considerably in different parts of the Muslim world, but I shall analyze this convergence of forces primarily in terms of North Africa.[2] The second task is to examine the theoretical formulations of Islamic socialism in contemporary writings. My analysis of both text and context is based on the assumption that ideas themselves are important but must always be understood in terms of historical process.

Mazheruddin Siddiqui, *Marxism or Islam* (Lahore: n.d.), and Khalifa Abdul Hakim, *Islam and Communism*, 2d ed. (Lahore: Institute of Islamic Culture, 1953).

2. In the Indo-Pakistani subcontinent, Muhammad Iqbal (d. 1938) made powerful socialist statements in his later writings. In his poem *Lenin Before God,* he made a scathing criticism of the then unadulterated European capitalism—and colonialism—and the culture that both supported it and was supported by it. This was followed by *God's Command to His Angels*; see Aziz Ahmad and G. E. von Grunebaum, eds., *Muslim Self-Statement in India and Pakistan* (Wiesbaden: Otto Harrassowitz, 1970) pp. 133–35. In his letter to Mr. Jinnah of 28 May 1937, Iqbal wrote,

> "The [Muslim] League will have to finally decide whether it will remain a body representing the upper classes of Indian Muslims or the Muslim masses. . . . personally I believe that a political organization which gives no promise of improving the lot of the average Muslims cannot attract our masses. . . . The problem of bread is becoming more and more acute. . . . The atheistic socialism of Jawaharlal is not likely to receive much response from the Muslims. The question, therefore, is: how is it possible to solve the question of Muslim poverty? And the whole future of the League depends on the League's ability to solve this problem." (Ahmad and von Grunebaum, *Muslim Self-Statement,* p. 151.)

This is a clear-cut blueprint for Islamic socialism. Iqbal, however, denounced communism in more than one place. The aphorism, therefore, attributed to Iqbal that "Islam equals Communism plus God" is hardly credible. Besides, it goes without saying that with the insertion of God, the entire philosophic fabric of communism must change.

In Indonesia, the close association of Islamic and socialist ideas developed early. The Sarekat Islam, founded in 1912, developed socialist tendencies; in 1918, it pronounced capitalism to be "sinful" (primarily, foreign capitalism, however) and, for several years, even members of the Indonesian Communist Party (PKI) belonged to the Sarekat Islam as well, until the break between the two occurred in 1922.

ISLAMIC REFORM, NATIONALISM, AND SOCIALISM

In the second half of the nineteenth century, Jamal al-Din al-Afghani, a pioneer of Muslim modernism, severely rejected materialistic doctrines about life and man in his treatise *Refutation of the Materialists*. In this treatise, he inveighed against "people who have often appeared among nations since ancient times in the name of removing injustice and calling for the purification of minds from superstitions and enlightening the intellects with scientific facts. Sometimes these people appear in the form of friends of the poor and protectors of the weak." [3] Afghani went on to say that religions have been, in their essence, the main prop of civilization and the cementing force of societies, despite the fact that they have often been distorted and sometimes perverted. Afghani was a populist reformer, he struggled for constitutional forms of government in the Muslim world, he emphasized social justice and, in fact, made probably the first attempt at formulating the idea of Islamic socialism. It is clear, therefore, that in the above statement he was not advocating the traditional status quo in Muslim society but was voicing his protest against the basing of socioeconomic reform on materialistic and atheistic doctrines. Afghani argued for fundamental social, economic, and political reform on a strong religious foundation, a base he thought necessary for the Muslim world—even though these reforms might not materialize—in order to generate the strength and solidarity to challenge European imperialism politically.

Afghani died in 1897, two decades before the Russian Revolution. Developments in the Muslim world have, by and large, vindicated his stand. With the exception of those Muslim minorities that are under communist control in the U.S.S.R. and China, the penetration of Marxism in Muslim society has been relatively small. It is interesting to note that Mohammed Harbi, an avowed Marxist, while drawing up the manifesto of Algerian socialism in 1964, La Chartre d'Alger, had to keep the "Arabo-Islamic" culture as its basis.

3. Quoted by two Azhar professors, Mahmud al-Nawawi and 'Abd al-Mun'imal Khafaji *Baina'l-Shuyu'iya wa'l-Islam* [*A comparison between communism and Islam*] (Cairo: Al-Matba'a al-Muniriya, n.d.), pp. 11–13.

A highly interesting and, to my knowledge, unique example of a socialist viewpoint set forth by a trained religious scholar is the work entitled *Tunisian Workers and the Rise of the Trade Union Movement,* published in 1927 by Al-Tahir al-Haddad, a graduate of Zaituna Seminary in Tunis. Although Haddad rejected Marxist atheism and its materialist metaphysics, he completely accepted the economic interpretation of history in terms of class struggle, a systematic and ruthless exploitation of the weaker by the stronger. He condemned the role not of religion but of the "representatives of religion" in becoming instruments of capitalist exploitation by providing the oppressed with consolation regarding the life hereafter. This work, in which Haddad makes no reference to Islam at all, does not appear to have aroused opposition. It is, however, noteworthy that when three years later he published his book *Our Women in Islamic Law and Society,* which called for reforms in family law and the status of women, he was violently opposed by the *ulama* and Muslim conservatives. He was legally barred from sitting for his final examination in law and died five years later, a disappointed and isolated man. The reason Haddad did not refer to Islam in his earlier work was probably that the French colonial government had already shown itself disposed to suppression of the trade union movement on the ground that it had a religious orientation and drew inspiration from the Qur'an.[4]

The actual sources of Haddad's socialist inspiration were undoubtedly the rise of the labor movement in the West and the success of the Bolshevik Revolution in Russia. In his book he distinguished three levels of the socialist struggle. First, the "lofty ideal" was the revolutionary effort to liberate the earth and make its resources the common property of mankind. At the second level were the socialists and trade unionists of the West who thought that this goal should be achieved by peaceful means, agitation, negotiation, and the education of workers. At the third level it was necessary to take into account the realities of traditional, preindustrial societies. For the Tunisian workers Haddad advised slow, reformist, and evolutionary progress, for Tunisia

---

4. Tahir al-Haddad, *Al-'Ummal al-Tunisiyun* . . . (Tunis: 1927), p. 160.

still needed the spread and acceptance of the message of social reform as well as a sufficient initial level of productivity.

The immediate cause of the appearance of socialist trends in the Magrib was the French policy of "assimilation" pursued in Tunisia and Algeria. In Algeria this policy was pursued with particular vigor. Whereas in Tunisia a traditional social base was allowed to exist, in Algeria an all-out effort was made by the colonial power to destroy that base. The French workers in these countries formed their trade unions as an integral part of the French metropolitan trade union movement. Later, when the Tunisian and Algerian workers formed their own trade unions, the French trade unionists persuaded them to join with them. The presence of strong communist forces within the French trade union movement naturally influenced the Tunisian and Algerian sectors as well. But the existence of an effective traditional Islamic base in Tunisia brought Islam into touch with leftism there and prevented the emergence of a communist leadership in favor of a socialist one. This explains the activity of Haddad in such an early phase of the Tunisian movement. Pure Marxism made much greater inroads in Algeria; these inroads were contained only by the nationalist thrust of the freedom struggle involving the totality of the population.

In Egypt an important socialist influence was not felt until near the end of the first decade of Nasser's revolutionary regime. In the Charter (*al-Mithaq*) promulgated in 1962, which officially declared Egypt to be a state based on Arab socialism, Islam is not directly mentioned except in the third chapter, devoted to history, where it states:

> The Islamic conquest was a light which manifested this truth [that Egypt is a part of the entire Middle Eastern region] and delineated its outlines and gave Egypt a new mold of thought and spiritual consciousness. Within Islamic history and thanks to the guidance of the message of the Prophet Muhammad (peace and blessings of God be upon him!), the Egyptian people ushered in the greatest period of the defense of civilization and humanity.[5]

5. *Al-Mithaq* (Cairo: National Publishing House, 1962), p. 16.

In the important chapter 7, entitled "Practical Applications of Socialism and Its Problems," the opening clause refers to the alleged saying of the Prophet, "Work is nobility." After repudiating Western capitalist methods, the chapter also rejects communism: "In other experiments, a tremendous oppression upon the living generations has resulted in their total deprivation of the fruits of their efforts in favor of a promised tomorrow." The Charter goes on to say that such policies belong to the past and may not be repeated today.[6] Finally, the declaration of the Charter affirms the nation's faith in God and in the truly revealed *shari'ah* and states its determination "to unfold our national character and life-orientation within the framework of our religious and moral-spiritual values." [7]

La Chartre d'Alger of 1962 speaks in much stronger and uninhibited terms. After stating that the Algerian liberation struggle has not been waged in isolation, the Charter proceeds to enumerate the factors that have contributed to the national ideology. These are said to be the doctrines of Jamal al-Din al-Afghani and Shaikh Muhammad Abduh (the former's Egyptian pupil) concerning the renaissance of Islam, the Pan-Arab thought of Shakib Arsalan, and socialist ideas.[8] The opening section of chapter 3, entitled "Ideological Foundations of the Algerian Revolution," states:

> Possessing a profound faith, the Algerian masses have vigorously struggled to recover Islam from all accretions and superstitions that have stifled or distorted it. They have always reacted against charlatans who wished to make of Islam a doctrine of resignation and have spontaneously associated it with their task of putting an end to the exploitation of man by man. The Algerian Revolution must restore to Islam its true aspect—the aspect of progress.[9]

This passage not only affirms the partnership of "real" Islam and socialism in Algerian nationalism but also demands that

6. Ibid., pp. 73–74.
7. Ibid., p. 96.
8. *La Chartre d'Alger* (Algiers: La Commission Centrale d'Orientation, 1962), p. 18.
9. Ibid., p. 35.

Islam be rescued from traditionalist and reactionary forces. This points to a real dilemma in the situation of nationalist Islamic socialism and will, in fact, prove crucial for its future course. In the struggle against the colonial power, it was the poor peasantry that suffered most, but the fruits of independence have primarily gone to urban elites and workers. This contradiction, therefore, has to be remedied. The danger, notes the Charter, is that the conservative and reactionary forces may exploit the national freedom struggle to their own advantage and thus create a contradiction between nationalism and socialism. This underlines the necessity of converting the peasant soldiery to socialism through integration with the workers and thus facilitating the acceptance of a socialist version of Islam.[10] The Algerian revolutionaries were acutely aware that the war of liberation alone was insufficient unless a socialist ideology was attached to it as its goal: national liberation was the means and a necessary step towards the achievement of socialism, which is the end of the struggle.[11]

Besides the moral force generated by Algerian nationalism for socialism, the economic factor that facilitated its acceptance was "autogestion," that is, the workers' ownership and management of those industrial and agricultural estates that had been abandoned by the French *colons* when they left Algeria. This state of autogestion was, in fact, imposed upon Algeria by sheer necessity, but it proved so successful that various communist delegations came to observe and admire it. The Charter of Algeria declared it to be "the characteristically principal gate to socialism in Algeria." With the fall of Ben Bella, however, the new regime abandoned the policy of autogestion in favor of "state socialism" amid loud protests not only from the autogested institutions but from many other quarters. The imperatives of national politics were victorious over purely economic considerations.

SOCIALIST INTERPRETATIONS OF ISLAM

The overwhelming majority of modern Muslim writers on the question of private ownership affirm that ownership in an absolute sense belongs to God alone, that man holds what he possesses

10. Ibid., p. 37.
11. "The Tripoli Program," in Thomas L. Blair, *Land*, pp. 222–24.

as a "trust" or "owns" it in a derivative sense, and that all men
are equally entitled to benefit from what God has created. Jamal
al-Din al-Afghani sought to derive this doctrine from the words of
the very opening verse of the Qur'an, where God is described as
"The Sustainer of the entire World." In his work entitled
Islam and the Solution of Economic Problems, Abu'l a'la Maududi took a similar stand.[12]

It is interesting to note certain shifts of emphasis and nuances
in the interpretation of key Qur'anic verses from the earlier liberal modernist to the new socialist expositions. Mustafa al-Siba'i,
in his *Socialism of Islam,* quotes a whole set of verses from the
Qur'an, for example, "God has rendered submissive for you that
which is in the earth and that which is in the heavens" and "He
(God) has made submissive to you the sun and the moon and
the night and the day." [13] Al-Bahiy al-Khuli, in his work "Socialism in Islamic Society in Theory and Practice," similarly quotes
the Qur'anic verse, "God it is who has made for you all that is in
the earth." [14] Whereas in the earlier liberal modernist commentaries on the Qur'an the stress was generally laid on the
point that God has created the universe *for* man, that is, for his
control and exploitation ("He has made submissive," i.e., ex-
ploitable), the stress in the socialist exegesis falls upon the word
you as well, that is, all of you, the whole of mankind. The fruits
of the earth and of nature, therefore, cannot be the property of
some to the exclusion of others.

Especially instructive and interesting is the socialist interpretation of the last-quoted verse, which al-Khuli interprets as meaning "God it is who has made for you all that is in the earth." The
word "all" was generally construed in previous commentaries as
qualifying "that is in the earth," and the earlier liberal commentators had taken the verse to mean that God had created all
the treasures of nature for the sake of man, thus encouraging Muslims to learn natural sciences and unravel the mysteries of the
universe. Al-Khuli now takes the word "all" to qualify "of you,"

12. Al-Afghani's article is included in G. H. Gardner and S. A. Hanna, eds., *Arab
Socialism: A Documentary Survey* (Leiden: E. J. Brill, 1969). Maududi, *Economic
Problems* (Lahore: Islamic Publications, n.d.).

13. Al-Siba'i, *Ishtirakiyat al-Islam,* p. 81.

14. Al-Khuli, *al-Ishtirakiya fi'l-mujtama' al-Islami bain al-nazariya wa'l-tatbuq*
(Cairo: Wahba Press, 1963).

that is, God has created what is in the universe for *all of you.*
Grammatically, both constructions are possible!

In this connection, Muslim socialists also appeal to a reported
saying of the Prophet Muhammad, "You all commonly share three
things: water, fire, and grass." From this the socialist commentators argue that all basic industries may be nationalized if necessary since "water, fire, and grass" have to be taken only as illus-
trations; the principle is that common utility resources cannot be
restricted to private owners but may be made public property. In
order to strengthen their argument, the representatives of the
socialist school point to the fact that in Islamic law, all mineral
wealth is declared to be national property. This argument lends
plausibility to the general socialist stand.[15] It is clear, however,
that this interpretative activity is made possible by the assumption that one can legitimately elicit general principles from the
injunctions of the Qur'an and the *sunnah.* The conservatives, although they do not deny that principles may be elicited from the
special injunctions of the shari'ah, nevertheless do not agree with
the modernists in the wholesale use of this method. Indeed, this
is the crucial difference between the two.[16]

All protagonists of Islamic socialism accept on principle the
right of private ownership, and their contention that absolute
ownership belongs to God is intended to function as a modifier
of this principle according to need and circumstances. Their
thesis is that whenever private ownership leads to abuse and social
injustice, it may be interfered with to the extent of remedying
this situation and maximizing economic production. But within
the tension of these two terms, private ownership and social well-
being, there is a wide range of possibilities and opinions that may
be held. Thus, Labib al-Sa'id takes a relatively conservative position and allows the socialization of basic industries only if there
is genuine need for it; otherwise maximum liberty to private
initiative should be allowed.[17] Mustafa al-Siba'i and perhaps

15. Al-Siba'i, *Ishtirakiyat al-Islam,* pp. 101–02; Labib al-Sa'id, *Al-Shuyu'iya wa'l-Islam [Communism and Islam]* (Cairo: National Publishing House, 1961), p. 41.

16. See my "Islamic Modernism, Its Scope, Method and Alternatives," *The International Journal of Middle East Studies* 1 (1970): 317–33.

17. Al-Sa'id, *Al Shuyu'iya wa'l-Islam,* pp. 40–41, expresses his opposition to the wholesale nationalization of property and industry.

Mahmud Shalabi (in his *Socialism of Muhammad*) assume a more moderate position, while al-Khuli appears to take a radical stand and encourages assumption by the state of at least all basic utility industries.[18]

All these authors think, however, that natural differences between men in their native endowments and abilities must be taken into due account and equitably rewarded. They reject the principle that "from each shall be taken according to his capacity" as unjust. The two Azhari shaikhs, Mahmud al-Nawawi and 'Abd al-Mun'imal Khafaji, coauthors of *A Comparison of Communism and Islam,* express the same view and emphasize that this principle had to be rejected also by communism, since it destroys the instinct of competition and innovation.

Al-Khuli, however, takes the most radical position: "the ownership of God means ownership of society as a whole"; when an individual works on a part of this property, he works only "on behalf of the community," not on his own behalf. Whatever natural abilities a person has, he has to exercise them for the community of which he is a member, and he cannot deem himself to be the exclusive possessor of those abilities. This is the lesson al-Khuli draws from the stand of Abu Dharr al-Ghifari, a Companion of the Prophet who, during the caliphate of the Third Caliph 'Uthman, revolted against the huge accumulations of wealth in private hands, condemned private wealth as categorically un-Islamic, and was exiled by the caliph from Madina.[19]

The ideologues of Islamic socialism have been quick to appeal to a large number of Qur'anic statements that generally call upon the faithful to "expend the best part of their wealth" for the sake of Allah, which expenditure is a "credit with God." Believers are admonished to desist from hoarding wealth at the expense of the poor, which would bring divine chastisement upon them. They are not to be afraid that they would become poor if they parted with their goods, for it is Satan who whispers such fears into their souls; God, on the contrary, promises them prosperity if they expend their wealth in His cause.[20] Prayers are not

18. Al-Siba'i, *Ishtirakiyat al-Islam,* p. 83.
19. Al-Khuli, *al-Ishtirakiya,* p. 106.
20. Qur'an, III, 92; LVII, 18; LXI, 17; II, 262–80; IX, 34–35.

acceptable if they are not accompanied by spending on the poor, and so on.[21] From al-Afghani until today, the Qur'anic injunction that "wealth must not circulate only among the rich from among you" [22] is used with an ever fresh vigor to support ideals of social justice.

Arguments based upon the Islamic institution of *zakat*, however, have been elaborated with the greatest enthusiasm. Zakat was the tax levied by the Prophet, in fact, the only permanent tax levied by him, upon the wealthy for the general welfare of society. The proceeds from zakat were spent particularly for the relief of the poor but also for *jihad* (holy war), facilities for wayfarers, and, according to many commentators, education and health. It is surprising, however, that no socialist commentator has been bold enough to suggest that zakat be construed not just as a particular tax with specified percentages as laid down by the Prophet (for his own time, no doubt) but as a general principle of interference in private wealth in the larger interests of social welfare and social justice, which it really appears to be.

In Muslim countries generally, zakat has for centuries now been a purely voluntary contribution to the welfare of the poor. If the exponents of Islamic socialism take their task seriously, they will obviously have to interpret zakat not just as an institution but in terms of the principle that underlies it, even though this will undoubtedly assure opposition from conservative quarters.[23] Because zakat is understood in a rigid institutional form, the communists are not slow in attacking and ridiculing it. Zakat, they contend, presupposes the existence of a poor class, but real socialism aims at eliminating such a class from society; therefore Islamic socialism can never be true socialism. To this attack Mustafa al-Siba'i weakly replies that even communists have not been able to get rid of poverty altogether. Although what it states is true, this reply misses the point, and Islamic socialism has to face the task of reformulation and rationalization of zakat in the modern situation.

21. Qur'an, CVII, 1–7.
22. Qur'an, LIX, 7.
23. For a further discussion of this point see my "Islamic Modernism," pp. 327–28.

The Qur'anic prohibition on exploitation through usury, termed riba, is always discussed in writings on Islamic socialism.[24] Although the exact nature of riba is not very clear, it is obvious from the Qur'anic statements and other available materials that it was a method whereby the capital sum (or commodity) loaned was "increased manifold" (the word riba itself means "increase"). It naturally fell heavily upon those who borrowed for consumption purposes as distinguished from trade. The Qur'an calls it "oppression." From this law, which threatened "war from God and His Prophet" against those who did not desist from practicing riba, Muslim lawyers drew the conclusion that all "return of an increment" on the principal sum to the creditor was illegal, and, therefore, Islamic orthodoxy today holds bank interest to be forbidden.

Around the turn of the century several Muslim liberal modernists attempted to legalize certain forms of interest on money advanced for commercial and productive purposes. Shaikh Muhammad Abduh, the eminent Egyptian reformer and disciple of al-Afghani, attempted this in his commentary on the Qur'an, and Shaikh Shaltut, rector of al-Azhar till his death in 1963, also issued a *fatwa* legalizing bank interest. However, he appears to have withdrawn this legal opinion later, probably under pressure from his colleagues. In India, too, several attempts of this nature were made.

With the emergence of new socialist ideologies, however, a clear trend has set in to confirm the classical legal position. In 1967, the Azhar Institute of Research decided at its annual meeting that private insurance and banking were not allowed in Islam but that a government insurance agency was allowed because it belonged to the public. The institute remained undecided on the question of the Islamic validity of government or collective banking. The same indecision was reflected at a meeting of Muslim scholars at Kuala Lumpur in April 1969.

"Poverty is a social disease," said Mustafa al-Siba'i, and he insisted that a major purpose of all religions was to eradicate or minimize poverty, not to console the poor as the communists say.[25]

---

24. Al-Sa'id, *Al-Shuyu'iya wa'l-Islam*, pp. 46–47; see in particular the discussion of *Riba* in Sabir 'Abd al-Rahman Tu'aima, *al-Islam wa-thara al-Ijtima'iya* [*Islam and social revolution*] (Cairo: *Maktaba al-Qahira al-Haditha*, 1970), pp. 178–80.

25. Al-Siba'i, *Ishtirakiyat al-Islam*, p. 82.

The Prophet said, "Poverty leads to disbelief." The most natural and important remedy of poverty is work. Al-Siba'i interpreted numerous verses of the Qur'an that speak about "works and their just requital." While the classical commentators overwhelmingly interpreted "works" in the sense of morally good and pious acts, al-Siba'i understood the word as including both good acts and labor in the economic sense. The Arabic term *'amal* means both.[26]

Emphasis is put on the Qur'anic dictum "man shall not get but that which he endeavors for." [27] Labor is a man's productive effort, "good works" are a laborer's contribution to social insurance and security. The Prophet said, "work is human dignity." [28] This is the expression also used, as we saw above, in Nasser's socialist manifesto, with the further elaboration, "Work is a right, work is necessary, work is life (itself)." The Prophet said, "It is better that a man should take his rope and haul wood on his back than that he should go to a man and beg, whether the latter should give him anything or not." Beggary is therefore a curse, and this curse has been brought on the Arabs largely by the colonial powers who created a few landlords as their stooges and reduced the rest of the people to dire poverty.[29] Finally, the eradication of poverty is a jihad according to President Bourguiba and the Indian Muslim socialist revolutionary, Ubaidullah (d. 1944).[30]

Just as it is unlawful to be a parasite and live on others' labor, so is it a crime to deny labor its just reward. Manual labor is regarded with particular favor in Islam, according to a reported saying of the Prophet, for many prophets were laborers: Noah was a carpenter, Moses a shepherd, Idris a tailor, and David used to manufacture helmets. Muhammad himself was a shepherd in his early life.[31] According to a tradition of the Prophet, workers can demand that the government provide work for them. The Prophet also said, "Pay the worker his wages before his sweat

26. Ibid., pp. 17–19.
27. Qur'an, LIX, 40.
28. All our authors stress this *Hadith* in their chapters on work and labor.
29. This view, expressed by various writers, neatly combines nationalist and socialist themes while overlooking the considerable historical evidence of internally generated inequality in Muslim societies.
30. Smith, *Religion and Political Development,* p. 227.
31. Al-Sa'id, *Al-Shuyu'iya wa'l-Islam,* pp. 53–55.

dries." And again: "Among those people whom God himself shall indict on the Day of Judgment will be he who got full work out of a worker but did not pay him fully for his labor." [32] The great Spanish Muslim theologian and lawyer of the eleventh century, Ibn Hazm, even declared at that early stage of history that the government should compel employers to put some money by as disability or old age payment for the workers. Ibn Hazm also held that if the rich do not provide for the maintenance of the have-nots and the hungry, the latter would be perfectly justified from a religious point of view in wresting from them whatever they needed to keep alive. Furthermore, if a fight should ensue and a have-not is killed by a rich person, the latter shall be accused of murder, but if the rich man is killed, the have-not will not be accused of murder in religious law.[33]

THE SIGNIFICANCE OF ISLAMIC SOCIALISM

In the progression of the Islamic socialist argument, one can discern three broad factors which, in a historical process, can be described as phases but which also overlap and coexist in varying proportions in all situations. These factors or forces can be called reformism, nationalism, and apologetic. In the earliest period, in the work of Jamal al-Din al-Afghani, for example, reformism appears to be the supreme motivation, with certain apologetic strands, even though the context of this reformist thrust is pan-Islamic politics. With the rise of active freedom struggles, nationalism assumed supreme importance, and Islam occupied a significant position in this nationalist current. But since most of those nationalisms were directed primarily against outside powers, at the ideological level a certain element of apologetic was seen to be present, as well as a significant reformist dimension.

The apologetic concern is dominant today, and the main target of the apologetic is the Marxist trend present within these societies. Although Marxism has been officially rejected by all Muslim socialist states in North Africa and the Middle East, the Marxists are a rising factor and are also connected with the framing of actual official policies. In fact, these Marxists inter-

32. Ibid., pp. 2, 16–56.
33. Al-Siba'i, *Ishtirakiyat al-Islam,* p. 122.

pret the official socialist documents of their state policies in their own way and watch for every opportunity to validate their interpretations. Islamic socialist thought, therefore, strengthens the official non-Marxist stand of these states. Particularly noteworthy is Nasser's severe criticism of communism as an "enemy of faith, of the individual and individual freedom, turning man into a mere tool in the vast machine of production." [34] Islamic socialist thought, therefore, plays a double role: in its reform aspect it legitimizes and facilitates socialist reformist policies, in its apologetic aspect it defends Muslim society from the Marxist alternative. It attempts to show that the communist way is not the only way of economic progress; indeed, in the light of the overall needs of man, which include the moral and spiritual aspects of life, it is not at all a desirable way. Communism, they assert, is incompatible with Islam. In Islam's theory and early practices, modern Islamic socialist thought has found an impressive and even moving array of ideas and symbols whose total impact and appeal is very strong. It is significant that several works on Islamic socialism published in the Arab world in the last decade exhausted their first editions within a few months.

The question, however, is: To what extent will this intellectual construction be effective and yield actual results? The ideas of social justice, cooperation, and above all the idea of the "community" and its common goal have a strong religious basis in Islam and are capable of stirring deep emotional and moral chords in the consciousness of an average Muslim. But equally strong is the conservative pull, the pull of "historic" Islam—its formulations and practices endowed with a romantic attachment by the modern Islamic apologetic itself. In most cases, it is not at all easy for the educated Muslim mind to disentangle the historical from the normative. Without the results of a careful, discerning, and purposeful scholarship becoming accessible both intellectually and spiritually to the average Muslim in good time, this whole effort could not only remain fruitless but even prove self-defeating. This explains why al-Siba'i felt constrained to launch a lengthy argument in his book against the conservative ulama.

34. Al-Nawawi and Khafaji, *Baina'l-Shuyu'iya wa'l-Islam.* The foreword to this work contains Nasser's condemnation of communism.

With the appearance of the economic imperative, the socialist argument has entered its final and decisive phase. This development has been made possible by the actual economic situation and is not the result of any nationalism or purely reformist idealism. It is rooted in reality. This situation has been brought about by rising population pressures, by deteriorating living standards, and by simultaneously rising expectations and an openness to change. The logic of the present situation is, therefore, different in nature from the earlier phases, imperatively demands an answer, and applies generally to all developing countries. This economic necessity is both the challenge and the opportunity for Islamic socialism.

It is obvious, however, that the economic demand cannot be met without extensive social change. Population control policies have to be effectively implemented, and education has to be carried out on a mass scale. Family law reforms have been introduced in most of these countries but will have to be strengthened further. Above all, people's attitudes toward work must be transformed by changing actual conditions; preaching and exhortation have decisively failed.

Unless social patterns undergo fundamental change, purely economic reforms will not bear fruit. Socialism is clearly not an overnight panacea for the multiple ills of underdevelopment. Islamic thinking and reform has a vital role to play in this process, a role that will be only gradual and probably not without profound internal conflicts.

14

Nasserism and Islam: A Revolution
in Search of Ideology

GUENTER LEWY

At the time of their seizure of power in July 1952, the Free Officers were virtually without a program that could provide direction to the tasks of government. The general vision of the group was expressed in "Six Principles" that were intimated in the manifestos circulated secretly and privately by the officers before their coup. The Six Principles were incorporated into the platform of the Liberation Rally in January 1953 and they were formulated more clearly in the preamble of the Constitution of 1956: "The eradication of all aspects of imperialism; the extinction of fedualism; the eradication of monopolies and the control of capitalistic influence over the system of government; the establishment of a strong national army; the establishment of social justice; and the establishment of a sound democratic society." [1] Out of these general principles there emerged gradually an ideology that is often

"Nasserism and Islam" is part of a larger study of the Nasser regime's attitudes and policies toward Islam—a chapter in my forthcoming book, *Religion and Revolution*. Important aspects of U.A.R. religious policy such as the abolition of the religious courts, the development of relations with the Muslim Brotherhood, the reform of al-Azhar, and the training and dispatch of Muslim teachers to Africa have been omitted here for limitations of space. I am indebted to Dr. Hatem Ishaq Hussaini, a former student at the University of Massachusetts, for research assistance and to my colleagues, Professors Robert M. Haddad and Leila Meo, for their criticism of an earlier draft of this paper. Support for this research was provided by the Advanced Research Projects Agency under Order no. 883 and monitored by the Office of Naval Research, Group Psychology Branch, under contract Nonr-3357(08), Nr 177–907.

1. Quoted in Fayez Sayegh, "The Theoretical Structure of Nasser's Arab Socialism," in *St. Antony's Papers*, no. 17, Middle Eastern Affairs, no. 4 (London: Oxford University Press, 1965), p. 13.

called "Nasserism"—a mixture of the old and the new that reflects the intellectual turbulence of the Islamic intelligentsia attempting to achieve modernization without being swallowed up
by the West. The uneasy balance of traditional and revolutionary
elements can be seen in two key planks of Nasserism—Arab nationalism and Arab socialism. Both ideas have survived the death
of Nasser on 28 September 1970 and continue, at this writing, to
function as ideological underpinning of Egypt's political life.

ARAB NATIONALISM

Prior to the Egyptian revolution of 1952, the ideological center
of Arab nationalism—a synthesis between pan-Islamism and the
local nationalism of the petty Arab states that emerged from the
ruins of the Ottoman empire after the first World War[2]—was in
Syria and Lebanon.[3] Egypt had played an important role in the
shaping of the cultural aspect of Arab consciousness by being the
seat of several pan-Arab societies, but it was not until the 1930s
that there developed any interest in the cause of Arab unity. To
many Egyptians, aware of the rich Egyptian heritage of the Nile
civilization that predated both the emergence of the Arabs and
Islam, the term "Arab" was a synonym of backwardness.[4] By the
forties the pan-Arab idea had made headway; Egypt took an active
role in the establishment of the Arab League in 1945. But the
defeat of the Arabs in the Arab-Israeli war of 1948 led to a new
strengthening of isolationism. Inter-Arab cooperation had failed a
vital test and the feeling that Egypt should concentrate on its own
affairs and the promotion of Egyptian nationalism was widespread
among opinion makers.[5]

The Free Officers who seized power in 1952, in line with the
political temper of the time, were preoccupied with solving Egyptian problems. Relations with other Arab states for them were
primarily a matter of foreign policy rather than ideology.[6] In

---

2. Elie Salem, "Nationalism and Islam," *Muslim World* 52 (1962): 277.

3. See Sylvia G. Haim, ed., *Arab Nationalism: An Anthology* (Berkeley and Los
Angeles: University of California Press, 1962), introduction.

4. See Anwar G. Chejne, "Egyptian Attitudes Towards Pan-Arabism," *Middle
East Journal* 11 (1957): 254–56.

5. Ibid., pp. 260–61.

6. See Leonard Binder, "Radical-Reform Nationalism in Syria and Egypt," *Muslim
World* 49 (1959): 105–06.

Nasser's *Philosophy of the Revolution*, published in 1955, the term "Arab nationalism" does not appear. Nasser spoke of three circles within which Egypt was located and which determined its life—the Arab, the African, and Islamic spheres:

> It is not without significance that our country is situated west of Asia, in contiguity with the Arab states with whose existence our own is inter-woven. It is not without significance, too, that our country lies in northeast Africa, overlooking the Dark Continent, wherein rages a most tumultuous struggle between white colonizers and black inhabitants for control of its unlimited resources. Nor is it without significance that, when the Mongols swept away the ancient capitals of Islam, Islamic civilization and the Islamic heritage fell back on Egypt and took shelter there. Egypt protected them and saved them, while checking the onslaught of the Mongols at 'Ain Jalut. All these are fundamental realities with deep roots in our lives which we cannot—even if we try—escape or forget.[7]

The Arab circle, Nasser maintained, was the most important, for Egypt was linked to the Arab world not only by the facts of geography and history but also by a common religion. Still, the interests of Egypt clearly ranked first. Nasser spoke of "the tremendous possibilities" to be realized through the cooperation of the many millions of Muslims in the world, but, perhaps to differentiate his priorities from those of the Muslim Brotherhood, he added that such cooperation was not to go "beyond the bounds of their natural loyalty to their own countries." [8]

If Nasser thus was espousing an essentially secular nationalism in 1955, emphasizing the primary allegiance to country before that to ethnic bonds or religion, he was soon to discover that the Egyptian masses could be reached and mobilized only by associating nationalism with Islam. For the urban Egyptian, in particular, the laborers and semieducated who had made up the rank and file of the Muslim Brotherhood and whom Nasser was seeking to draw to the side of his regime, the emotional sustenance for the

7. Gamal Abdul Nasser, *Egypt's Liberation: The Philosophy of the Revolution* (Washington, D.C.: Public Affairs Press, 1955), pp. 86–87.
   8. Ibid., p. 113.

spirit of nationalism derived from an Islamic universalism. For these men to attain national dignity meant to resume the mission that Muhammad had inaugurated; it meant reconstitution of the Muslim community advocated in the Prophet's teachings and achieved by his first followers, the Arabs. Nationalism, in short, meant Arab nationalism with a pronounced religious underpinning. Since nationalism is a force that draws on the achievements of the past and since the only glory the Arabs ever knew was achieved under the banner of Islam, Arab nationalism naturally was driven to lean upon the heritage of Islam and to "find its intellectual stimulus in the great Arab-Islamic culture of the past —a culture which was made possible by Islam." [9]

Sunni Islam recognizes neither geographical nor ethnic boundaries and distinguishes merely between the community of faith, the *ummah,* and the outside world of unbelievers. Upon this concept of ummah, Arab nationalism grafted the idea of nationhood, and this transformation of a religious into a political community by and large was accepted by Muslims.[10] The masses could be enlisted through the appeal to the spirit of Islam; the intellectuals rallied to the standard of Arab unity on account of its potential in standing up to the encroaching West. The notion of an Arab nation thus merged with the Islamic concept of ummah and in this manner Arab nationalism achieved a spiritual ethos and mass support. If we blur the theoretical distinction between the Islamic community and the Arab nation, "nationalism has been able to evolve as a modern expression of traditional Muslim sentiments regarding the unity, dignity, and historic destiny of the Community rather than flying in the face of such sentiments." [11] Arab nationalism has emerged as something close to a "political religion"; it functions as a "Sorelian myth." [12]

The Islamization of nationalism has had many advantages. Islam provided a sense of history, identity, and solidarity, helping to build a heritage distinctive from both Western liberalism and

9. Salem, "Nationalism and Islam," p. 282.

10. See Sylvia G. Haim, "Islam and the Theory of Arab Nationalism," in W. Z. Laqueur, ed., *The Middle East in Transition* (New York: Praeger, 1958), p. 293.

11. Malcolm H. Kerr, "Islam and Arab Socialism," *Muslim World* 56 (1966): 277.

12. Richard H. Pfaff, "The Function of Arab Nationalism," *Comparative Politics* 2 (1970): 158.

communism. Rather than having to oppose the tide of Muslim militancy, manifested in the popularity of the Brotherhood, Nasser's regime was thus able to swim with it. At the same time, this Arab nationalism with Islamic overtones not infrequently created problems for Nasser—domestically as well as in foreign relations. For Egypt's Christian minority, the Copts, the failure to separate nationalism from religion has meant emotional and other more tangible hardships. During the short-lived union of Egypt and Syria, the latter with a well-educated and politically conscious Christian minority (14 percent of the population), the Islamic aspects of Arab nationalism had to be downgraded, especially since Christian Arabs have had a leading part in its formulation and have tended to stress its secular components. The vague nature of Arab nationalism, based upon the longing for a restored Muslim community and dreams of empire, has tended to give an appearance of unity where none exists. Underneath the commitment to Arab unity lie sharp cleavages over the content and means of achieving such unity.[13] The record of Nasser's relations with the rest of the Arab world bears witness to the difficulty of linking a coherent and rational foreign policy to as emotional and undefined a principle as Arab nationalism.

Until 1955 Nasser concentrated on Egyptian affairs and was content with being *one* of the leaders of the Arab world. From 1955 on, he began to pursue an increasingly aggressive foreign policy and to assume the role of spokesman for the Arab people. A number of factors were involved in this reorientation. Iraq's alignment with the West in the Baghdad pact of 1955 threatened the political and military isolation of Egypt; Nasser reacted by actively promoting Arab solidarity and unity—a policy he continued to pursue until his death. Domestically the new emphasis on Arab nationalism and the fight against imperialism helped divert attention from the difficulties involved in social and economic reform. The milestones in this nationalistic and pan-Arab course are well known: In late 1955, following a major Israeli attack on the Egyptian-held Gaza Strip that exposed Egypt's military weakness, Nasser concluded a barter agreement for arms with Czechoslovakia; in 1956 he nationalized the Suez

13. See Hisham B. Sharabi, *Nationalism and Revolution in the Arab World* (Princeton: D. Van Nostrand, 1966), p. 97.

Canal; and in 1957 Nasser emerged from the Suez war as the hero who had defeated two major powers, Britain and France. In February 1958, Syria and Egypt agreed to form the United Arab Republic. Nasser was at the pinnacle of prestige. He had successfully defied the Western powers and he had made a major advance along the road to Arab unity. For the Arab masses all over the Middle East, Nasser was the new Saladin, the hero who was going to fulfill their longings and hopes.

But Arab unity was more easily glorified than achieved. The introduction in Syria of economic and administrative reforms based upon Egyptian rather than Syrian needs alienated wide segments of Syrian society and ultimately led to the secession of Syria.[14] "The Charter of National Action," a lengthy programmatic document adopted by the Nasser regime in June 1962, proclaimed a new formula: Arab unity, to succeed, presupposed the radical and revolutionary transformation of society in a socialist direction. The merger of states with deeply contrasting socioeconomic and political structures could not lead to real and lasting unity. Steps must be taken "to fill the economic and social gaps occurring between various Arab states as a result of imperialist-inspired differences in stages of development"[15] and the U.A.R. had the duty to support all popular progressive movements in the Arab world that sought to close these gaps.

The proclamation of the Charter restored some of Nasser's popularity, but the new tactic could no more nullify and overcome the diversities of environment, language, political experience, and abilities that stood in the way of Arab unity than could the earlier, more direct approach. Egypt no longer was the leading power in the Arab world, which now had several competing revolutionary centers—Syria, Iraq, Algeria, as well as the United Arab Republic. All of the existing Arab nation-states, despite their partly artificial borders, have developed local ruling groups for whom the survival

14. Malcolm Kerr, *The Arab Cold War 1958–1967* (London: Oxford University Press, 1967), p. 31. See also Monte Palmer, "The United Arab Republic: An Assessment of its Failure," *Middle East Journal* 20 (1966): 50–67.

15. *The National Charter of the United Arab Republic,* cited by Sharabi, *Nationalism and Revolution,* p. 135. See also George Lenczowski, "The Objects and Methods of Nasserism," *Journal of International Affairs* 19 (1965): 69.

of these states is a matter of compelling self-interest. One of the few centripetal forces in the Arab world is hostility to Israel. In the wake of the Six Day War of 1967 several Arab countries not directly involved in the fighting agreed to provide financial aid to the U.A.R. and Jordan, and a series of conferences have since taken place to coordinate strategy against Israel. It is too early to tell whether the new federation of Egypt, Libya, and Syria will lead to more concrete results.

The acceptance of Islam by most Arabs, of course, is another force making for convergence. But even the Muslim factor seems unable to provide a basis for a unified ideology as was demonstrated during the controversy over the so-called "Islamic Pact" in early 1966. When King Faisal of Saudi Arabia proposed the idea of an "Islamic conference" of heads of Muslim states in Mecca, Nasser interpreted this proposal as an attempt to build a coalition of conservative states that would isolate revolutionary regimes like the United Arab Republic. Faisal's insistence that he had sought neither an alliance nor an anti-Egyptian campaign apparently was not mere rhetoric.[16] Nevertheless, Nasser reacted with a vigor that indicated that an exposed nerve had been touched. The idea of an Islamic conference, Nasser reminded the Arab world, had been proposed by him as early as 1954, but the creation of the Baghdad pact in 1955 had prevented the conference from convening. Real Islamic solidarity, he insisted, "is the solidarity of the Islamic peoples struggling against imperialism, not the solidarity between reactionary governments which are imperialist agents exploiting and falsifying Islam; reactionary governments that want to stop the march of history and the march of progress." [17] The Islamic Pact was an attempt to use the sacred principles of religion for reactionary ends; it was a forgery of religion aiming to attack and destroy the idea of Arab nationalism, "to stop the progressive Arab revolutionary tide in the Arab countries." [18] Clearly, Nasser was unwilling to let his political

16. See Kerr, *Arab Cold War*, p. 146.
17. Speech on 22 February 1966, in United Arab Republic, Supreme Council for Islamic Affairs, *The Islamic Pact: An Obvious Trick* (Cairo: S.O.P. Press, n.d.), p. 50.
18. Ibid., p. 44.

opponents wear the mantle of Islam. Islam was neither a factor upon which to build a viable pan-Arab unity nor yet an ideological component to be dispensed with.

Arab Socialism

If the appeal to Islam was a useful instrument for popularizing certain goals of Nasser's foreign policy, it was equally important in regard to the regime's social and economic program. Again, the impetus and initial shaping of policy was not and could not be derived from Islamic principles though Islamic loyalties could be enlisted to marshal support for these policies once adopted.[19]

The Free Officers, upon seizing power in 1952, as we have seen, had neither an ideology nor a clear program of social and economic reform. They were revolted by Egypt's gross inequality and poverty, a sentiment that found its expression in one of the Six Principles—the demand for the "establishment of social justice." But the change and the transition from this statement of a general goal to the formulation of a socialist doctrine and a program of action was gradual, pragmatic, and slow. During the early years, in fact, the new regime went out of its way to allay suspicions that it was left-wing in character. "We are not Socialists," insisted Gamal Salem, Minister of National Guidance, in early 1954. "I think our economy can only prosper under free enterprise." [20] Businessmen participated actively in the formulation of a program of development; incentives and private investments were relied upon to spur and encourage growth. The ranks of the Free Officers were purged of leftist elements and most of Egypt's communists were imprisoned. The ringleaders of a strike at a textile plant in August 1952 that had led to the seizure of the factory were summarily tried and hanged. Only the agrarian reform law of September 1952, which limited land ownership to a maximum of 200 feddans (about 200 acres), struck a somewhat different note.[21]

19. Cf. Kerr, *Islamic Reform*, p. 2.

20. *Bourse égyptienne*, 26 January 1954, quoted in Patrick O'Brien, *The Revolution in Egypt's Economic System: From Private Enterprise to Socialism, 1952–1965* (London: Oxford University Press, 1966), p. 68.

21. P. J. Vatikiotis, *The Egyptian Army in Politics* (Bloomington: Indiana University Press, 1961), p. 75.

During the years 1952–56 the Egyptian economy experienced a firm government and the state moved gradually away from a laissez-faire approach. Still, economic and social policy essentially continued to follow the lines initiated before the 1952 coup, and the period has been described as the "free-enterprise phase of the Egyptian revolution." [22] Perceptible changes took place after the Suez war of 1956. Realizing that Egypt's economic problems were far more serious than they had thought at first, the officers gradually were driven to more drastic measures. Certain foreign and later also Egyptian establishments were nationalized, a program of central planning and intensified industrialization was initiated, and the taxation of higher incomes was increased sharply. These measures, extending state control over private enterprise, "were accompanied by a swift break-away from the west in both political alignment and ideological approach and by an increasing use in public pronouncements and the press, of pseudo-Marxist and class-war slogans." [23] The term "controlled capitalist economy," employed by Nasser in 1958, accurately describes this phase of the revolution.

Egypt's first five-year plan, formulated in 1959–60, had envisaged a mixed economy and close cooperation between the public and private sectors of the economy. But the planners soon found that private enterprise was slow to comply with the targets for production, investment, and saving. When exhortations and incentives failed to bring about adherence to the goals of the central plan, the regime decided to inaugurate what is now referred to in Egypt as the "Social Revolution." In July 1961, coinciding with the ninth anniversary of the revolution, a large share of Egypt's industrial and commercial property was nationalized. A new land reform law prohibited any individual from owning more than 100 and any family more than 300 feddans of agricultural land.[24] After the secession of Syria in September of the same year, and in the face of a difficult internal economic situation caused by floods and damage by parasites to the cotton crop, the

22. O'Brien, *Egypt's Economic System,* p. 84.

23. Charles Issawi, *Egypt in Revolution: An Economic Analysis* (London: Oxford University Press, 1963), p. 54

24. The July decrees are described in more detail in Malcolm H. Kerr, "The Emergence of a Socialist Ideology in Egypt," *Middle East Journal* 16 (1962): 128–29.

property of some 850 persons was sequestrated. A vigorous press campaign was launched against "reactionary, feudalist, and capitalist elements" and over 7,000 persons affected by the expropriation laws were deprived of their political rights.[25]

The ideological justification of the Social Revolution by way of a theory of Arab socialism came after the event. Egypt's economic and social system, which had developed piecemeal and by trial and error rather than according to a predetermined plan, now was given a theoretical underpinning: the blueprint of a socialist society was laid out. The socialist revolution, Nasser explained in August 1961, was succeeding in "eradicating feudalism, in destroying the dictatorship of capital, and in establishing social justice, entirely by peaceful means." [26] The goal was the elimination of class distinctions. It was due to the particular circumstances of the Egyptian revolution, Nasser admitted in November 1961, "that the revolutionary application, our revolutionary application, may be prior to the theory. Then what is the theory? The theory is the evidence of the action." [27]

The official formulation of Arab Socialism was presented to the Egyptian people in the Charter of May 1962. This lengthy document attempted to explain the various reforms promulgated since 1961 as well as to outline a program for future action. Socialism, according to the Charter, "is the way to social freedom; social freedom means equal opportunity to every citizen to obtain a fair share of the national wealth." [28] However, the national wealth must not only be redistributed but also expanded. The national income had to be doubled every ten years, a feat that could be achieved only through scientific planning. An efficient public sector was to provide leadership—heavy industry and financing institutions had to be owned by the state. In light and medium industry and in external trade, mixed ownership could prevail. "In the agricultural sector, Arab socialism does not believe in the

25. Issawi, *Egypt in Revolution*, pp. 61–62; O'Brien, *Egypt's Economic System*, pp. 130–31.

26. Speech on 17 August 1961, quoted in Sayegh, "Nasser's Arab Socialism," p. 30.

27. Speech on 25 November 1961, *Battles and Achievements of the Political and Social Revolution* (Cairo: National Publications House Press, n.d.), p. 38.

28. *The Charter*, quoted in Sharabi, *Nationalism and Revolution*, pp. 129–30. Further relevant excerpts from the Charter, based on a different translation, can be found in Hanna and Gardner, *Arab Socialism*, pp. 344–372.

nationalization of land but in individual ownership within limits that prevent feudalism." [29]

The idea of Arab Socialism continued to dominate the ideology of the Nasser regime. The struggle for socialism became the theme for the mobilization of maximum effort and the striving for economic growth. "The Revolution of July 23," Nasser stated in November 1964, "was but an introduction to the Revolution." [30] The achievement of a socialist society, he warned, would be far more difficult than the fight against the external enemy. The gains chalked up by the Social Revolution until now support Nasser's realistic appraisal. Socialist planning, now in its twelfth year, so far has not brought about rapid economic development or a decisive improvement in the standard of living. The extension of public ownership in itself could not and did not work wonders.

In 1952 about 0.5 percent of all proprietors owned 34.2 percent of the land, and 5.2 percent owned another 30.5 percent of all landed property.[31] Agrarian reform has broken the power of the landlords, but most rural families have not benefited from the redistribution of land and remain either landless or with just enough land to produce a meager subsistence. Even at the completion of agrarian reform less than 8 percent of all rural families will have received some land.[32] The law has brought no relief to the landless laborers who in 1958 made up 73 percent of the rural population.[33] Inequality of wealth and income has been reduced through a series of nationalizations, sequestrations, fixing of maximum salaries, and extension of social services. But those who have gained most, concludes one observer, "seem to have been middling peasants, the employees of corporate industry and commerce, and middle-class tenants of rented accommodations, three groups who altogether form no more than a small and

29. Sharabi, *Nationalism and Revolution,* p. 131.

30. Gamal Abdul Nasser, *Addresses at the Opening Meeting of the Second Session of the National Assembly, November 12, 1964* (Cairo: National Publication House, n.d.), p. 36.

31. Anouar Abdel-Malek, *Égypte: Société Militaire* (Paris: Éditions du Seuil, 1962), p. 64.

32. Issawi, *Egypt in Revolution,* p. 161.

33. Ibid., p. 120. See also Bent Hansen and Girgis A. Marzouk, *Development and Economic Policy in the UAR (Egypt)* (Amsterdam: North Holland Publishing Co., 1965), pp. 84–93.

privileged minority of the population." [34] For the masses of the Egyptian people a marked improvement in their lot will depend upon the achievement of a rate of economic expansion sufficient to outpace substantially the increase in population, which at an explosive growth rate of 2.5 percent a year (compared to 1.2 percent in the U.S.A.) threatens to nullify the benefits of even as spectacular a development project as the Aswan Dam.

The scale of Egypt's Social Revolution thus has not been as far-reaching as official statements have depicted it. Still, for Egypt's tradition-bound masses the changes have been revolutionary enough to require an elaborate program of ideological justification that seeks to prove the compatibility of Arab socialism with Islam. Nasser himself took the lead in 1961 when he distinguished Arab socialism from Marxian socialism and insisted that the former not only was not opposed to Islam but actually derived from it. We have said, he explained, that "our religion is a socialist one and that in the middle ages Islam had successfully applied the first socialist experiment in the world." Reactionaries like King Hussein, Nasser continued, allege "that socialism is against Islam. Islam in his conception implies harems and palaces, usurping the people's money and leaving them poor and naked." That was all wrong. "Islam implies equity and justice. The Arab people will never be deceived." [35]

In the years that followed, Nasser time and again stressed the same central theme. A few passages, taken from a collection of Nasser's speeches published in 1964, will have to suffice as a sample: "Islam is the first religion to call for socialism, the first religion to call for equality and the first to call for an end to domination and inequality." "Mohammed, God's blessing be on him, gave us the example of social justice, progress and development, and thus Islam was able in these early days to defeat the strongest nations . . . and spread to all corners of the earth because it was the religion of righteousness, freedom, justice and equality." Our enemies "say that socialism is infidelity. But is socialism really what they describe by this term? What they de-

---

34. O'Brien, *Egypt's Economic System*, p. 213. A similar conclusion is reached more recently by Robert Stephens, *Nasser: A Political Biography* (London: Penguin Press, 1971), pp. 574–75.

35. Nasser, *Addresses, November 12, 1964*, pp. 48, 63.

scribe applies to raising slaves, hoarding money and usurping the people's wealth. This is infidelity and this is against religion and Islam. What we apply in our country is the law of justice and the law of God." [36]

Reinforcing Nasser's speeches, since 1961 the regime has sponsored a large amount of scholarly writing and a flood of propaganda propounding the unity of Arab socialism and Islam. A formal legal opinion (*fatwa*) issued by a canon lawyer (*mufti*) in 1962 dealt with the question whether the socialist laws of 1961 were averse to the spirit of Islam. The Muslim expert, citing the Qur'an and the traditions, concluded that these laws were sanctioned by Islamic jurisprudence: "Private ownership is legitimate in the eyes of Islamic jurisprudence as long as the owner observes the ordinances of Allah concerning his wealth. But if he does not abide by them, the ruler is entitled to devise the laws and regulations which force him to adhere to the commandments of God." [37] The law of agrarian reform and the restriction of landownership aimed at realizing the public good and social justice: "the distribution of wealth between the poor and the rich so that it may not be circulated among the rich only, is a procedure approved of by Islamic jurisprudence." [38] Islam prohibited the monopoly of food and similar resources and "thus we can sanction the nationalization of public institutions indispensable to everyday life such as the institution established to secure water, electricity and easy transport." [39]

Other writers have gone further and have argued, as Nasser himself had done, that Arab socialism not only was not averse to Islam but actually represented the fulfillment of the Prophet's commands. "Arab socialism is the only road to human freedom, it is the only way to social freedom as Islam calls for; . . . our socialist revolution aims with all its strength at building a society of justice and equality, thus receiving its principles and inspira-

---

36. Gamal Abdul Nasser, *Majmu'at Khutb wa-Tasrihat wa-Bayanat* (A collection of speeches, statements and announcements of President Gamal Abdul Nasser—ed.) (Cairo: U.A.R. Information Department, 1964), pp. 560, 407, 210.

37. "The Mufti Answers Your Questions," *Minbar al-Islam: A Quarterly Magazine Devoted to the Cause of Islam*, Eng. ed., vol. 2, no. 3 (July 1962): 58.

38. Ibid., p. 60.

39. Ibid., p. 59.

tion from the pillars of Islam." [40] Under feudalism and capitalism, argued another author, the individual leads a self-seeking existence. Under Arab socialism, on the other hand, the individual was guided to benefit himself and his society.

> Arab socialism is the system that can implement the Islamic concept of requiring the individual to fulfill his duties. In preparing him to fulfill the cooperative duties in which he is a supervisor and a partner at the same time, and in requiring him to consider the interest of the group . . . it thus reflects the Islamic ideal which requires a righteous individual and a cooperative society.[41]

Socialism based upon Islam did not deny the interests of the individual though it did oppose the struggle between classes that results in enmity and hate. "Thus it has made work the basis of distributing wealth and reward, and it forbade excessive wealth and its exploitation of others." [42] Islam did not allow unlimited freedom of ownership but insisted on conditions that would guarantee justice and equality. "Islam allowed the ruler to strike those who do not observe these conditions and allowed him to take property and redistribute it to the people in accordance with the general and public good." [43]

It is not necessary to challenge the sincerity of these writers in order to see that this endeavor of reconciling socialism and Islam raises the same problems as did the attempt to establish a synthesis between nationalism and Islam. The political, economic, and social principles evolved by a society in the seventh and eighth centuries can hardly be expected to fit the complexities of life in the twentieth century. Notions like justice and equality are vague enough to accommodate a great variety of concrete programs. It is

40. Husni Abdul-Majid, "Da'wat al-Mithaq al-Watani min Da' wat al-Islam (The Cause of the National Charter is the Cause of Islam)," *Minbar al'Islam* 24, no. 9 (12 December 1966): 52.

41. Mohammed Mohammed al-Madani, "Al-Ishtirakiyah al-Arabiyah fil-Mizan (Arab Socialism in the Balance)," *Minbar al-Islam* 24, no. 7 (15 October 1966): 22.

42. Hanafi Sharaf, "Al-Ishtirakiyah al-Arabiyah Ruh al-'Aqida al-Islamiyah (Arab Socialism is in the Spirit of Islamic Belief)," *Minbar al-Islam* 25, no. 11 (10 February 1967): 165.

43. Mohammed Mitwali al-Nizami, "Al-Ishtirakiyah fi al-Islam (Socialism in Islam)," *Minbar al-Islam* 24, no. 5 (17 August 1966): 277.

not difficult for modernists to go back to the Qur'an and the traditions and to find there permission for whatever social reform they wish to promote and uphold. "Just as in the second century of Islam the fabrication of hadiths and the elaboration of a system of deductive legal reasoning had sanctified the assimilation of existing local customs and precedents into a unified Islamic system of law, so today the modernist principles may be said to have performed an assimilative function." [44] And yet, it is clear that this search for the endorsement of Islam by way of a highly selective reading and quoting of holy writ has to some extent the same quality of "pious fraud" which Ignaz Goldziher had attributed to the outright forgery of many of the early traditions.[45] Such a romanticizing of the Muslim past can foster national pride and it can help justify and legitimize the contemporary state's actions; it cannot, however, define objectives or provide guidance in solving the practical problems of modernization. Writing in 1945, Sir Hamilton Gibb expressed the hope that Muslim intellectuals would turn to creative thinking, "removed from the intellectual confusions and the paralyzing romanticism which cloud the minds of the modernists of today." [46] This expectation, it appears, has been fulfilled only in part.

The idea of Arab socialism, as Malcom Kerr has noted in a perceptive article, fulfills some of the nationalist and religious desires of the masses.

> It offers advancement, social harmony, equality, public morality, collective self-respect. It responds to the populism of the nationalist, and to the believing Muslim's desire for a straight path to follow amid the uncertainties of modern life. . . . the ummah has taken its affairs in hand, in an assertion of collective will that appeals to nationalists, and simultaneously in a spirit of welcoming of communal duty and a striving for the Right that are the essence of *jihad*.[47]

44. Kerr, *Islamic Reform*, p. 220.

45. G. Ignaz Goldziher, *Vorlesungen über den Islam* (Heidelberg: Carl Winter's, 1910), p. 48.

46. H. A. R. Gibb, *Modern Trends in Islam* (Chicago: University of Chicago Press, 1947), p. 105.

47. Kerr, "Islam and Arab Socialism," pp. 277–78.

At the same time, the Islamic component of socialism, no matter how artificially contrived, may in time create difficulties. Arab socialism, unlike communism, as the propagandists emphasize constantly, rejects class violence and does not attack the institution of private property as such. In the future this conservative element, implying reconciliation rather than a class struggle, could inhibit the forward march of the social revolution. Lastly, Islam is a religion in which precedent and tradition carry great weight— it "tends to place on innovators and individualists the burden of proof of the moral acceptability of their actions." Religion thus reinforces the bureaucratic mentality, the attachment to routine; and it counteracts "the mixture of scientism, experimentalism, Marxism-Leninism, activism, and self-assertiveness from which so far the revolution has acquired much of its momentum." [48] For the time being these different elements in the official ideology live alongside each other; eventually their coexistence may end and break up.

ISLAM AND THE PURSUIT OF LEGITIMACY

The leaders of many developing nations live in two worlds at once. In order to raise their countries from poverty, they seek to modernize and to acquire for their societies education and the advanced technical know-how of the West. At the same time to establish rapport with their tradition-bound people, they have to appeal to native pride, communal and ethnic sentiments, as well as religion. What makes the resulting crisis of identity and ideological outlook more severe is the fact that these leaders often have been unable to clarify for themselves a definite personal attitude to tradition and religiosity. Thus a policy toward religion that on the surface may look like a Machiavellian manipulation of a religious sentiment is what it is, sometimes not only as a result of considerations of expediency, but also because of genuine uncertainty and ambivalence on the part of its originators.

The majority of the officers ruling Egypt, including the late Nasser, seem to fit this description. Well-informed observers of the Egyptian scene continue to report that most of the leaders of the revolution are practicing Muslims. "Of modest country stock, they

48. Ibid., p. 281.

have been unaffected by the wave of modernist scepticism and demoralization which has been sweeping over the Egyptian upper classes for over half a century." [49] "Abdel Nasser's belief in Islam," noted another writer, "appears genuine. He personally follows the rituals of his religion—not just for public display—and he takes part in the community prayer on Friday." [50] Nasser's successor, Anwar Sadat, is considered a deeply religious person. To be sure, when Anwar Sadat in 1953—and Nasser at the height of the Suez crisis in 1956—took to the pulpits to address worshippers, they clearly were motivated not only by religious sentiments. Similarly, the attendance of Nasser with visiting Muslim dignitaries at mosque services obviously served mainly ceremonial purposes. Nevertheless, the appeal to religion is more than just propaganda. Nasser appeared to be sincere when he declared in 1963:

> We boast that we stick to religion, each one of us according to his religion. The Muslim upholds his religion and the Christian upholds his, because religion represents the right and sound way. If we listen to them today telling us from Damascus that they consider our adherence to religion tantamount to our adherence to rotten religious ideas, we pride ourselves on that. We pride ourselves on the fact that since the first day of our Revolution we have adhered to religion. Not only the Revolution leaders, but the people as well. It is the great secret behind the success of this Revolution: the adherence to religion.[51]

Nasser's conception of Islam, as we have seen, was reformist and modernistic. He sought to fit Islam to modern life. In the manner of Muhammad Abduh, Nasser held an optimistic outlook upon life and he emphasized the need for action. Aspirations and hopes cannot be realized, he told his followers in March 1965, by merely relying upon God's help. Sacrifices and persistence are essential. Islam is a religion of struggle. "It is only the way of effort, only

49. Jean Lacouture and Simonne Lacouture, *Egypt in Transition,* trans. Francis Scarfe (London: Methuen, 1958), p. 440.

50. Hans E. Tütsch, *Facets of Arab Nationalism* (Detroit: Wayne State University Press, 1965), p. 59.

51. Speech on 28 July 1963, in *Speeches and Press Interviews: January-December 1963* (Cairo: U.A.R. Information Department, n.d.), p. 188.

the way of work, which is the way for the realization of our hopes and aspirations, it is only the way of construction which is the way of salvation." [52] Nasser's political activism was opposed to the thinking of Muslim apologists who speak of the inherent superiority of Islam and thus encourage a spirit of complacency.

And yet, here again lies a dilemma. Modernists like Nasser feel constrained to point out past errors and outmoded elements in their own culture and to keep open the door to the West. They reject a mere romanticizing of the Islamic past and they stress the need to accept Western ideas and techniques. At the same time, these modernists often seek to hide the extent of their borrowing by asserting that the borrowed elements are actually of Muslim origin or at least a logical development of Muslim elements correctly interpreted. They strive to preserve self-respect and to overcome their sense of inferiority when confronted with the obviously superior power of the West by praising the accomplishments of their native civilization. They encourage pride in the Islamic past, which becomes a warranty of a glorious future. The result of this dualistic set of orientation is intellectual confusion and strain that affects Arab attitudes to the West as well as toward their own history. The decay of the once flourishing Muslim civilization and the weaknesses of today's Muslim world have to be admitted, but, as von Grunebaum phrases the problem, on whom is the guilt for the predicament of the present to be placed?

> Was it the theologians of the Middle Ages whose distortion of the Prophetic message caused the drying up of the Islamic inspiration? Was it the Mamluks whose ruthless rule sapped the strength of Egypt beyond recovery? Or was it Muhammad 'Ali whose precipitate steps toward Europeanisation did more harm than good by creating that psychological confusion that still lies at the bottom of the incessant political unrest of the country? There is no end of questions of this order and they are becoming more burning as it is less possible to brush them aside by pointing to colonialism as the root of all evil. And even if colonialism is impugned, the problem is only pushed back one step, for it would be difficult not to ask fur-

52. Speech on 8 March 1965, *Pre-election Speeches . . . March 1965* (Cairo: U.A.R. Information Department, n.d.), p. 13.

ther: What was it that weakened the Muslim world to such an extent that it no longer could or would resist the intruder?[53]

These questions are raised but the answers given often involve considerable self-deception. "We Muslims," noted Anwar Sadat, "inherited a glorious torch that could have guided us to the road to justice, knowledge and peace. Why then did we become hungry, ignorant, sick and slaves?" Because Western colonialists, in alliance with reactionary rulers and an ignorant priesthood, stole and hid the torch of the true religion that exists to improve human life.[54] This tendency to blame outsiders for present difficulties and past failures is widespread.

Of course, obstacles on the course of modernization are created not only by the lack of intellectual incisiveness on the part of the ruling elite but, at least as importantly, by the continuing strength shown by the traditional Islamic ethos among the masses of the people. The very fact, notes one observer, that those in power feel the need to invoke Islamic ideas for the justification of both Arab nationalism and Arab socialism "indicates the extent to which their assessment of popular opinion has led them to conclude that the Arab Islamic past is far from having spent its force." [55] Among the poorer classes, in particular, religious elements quietly endure. The *fellahin,* the rural proletariat of Egypt who constitute about two-thirds of the total population, still live a life of isolation; reform measures bringing health centers and schools have not yet been able to break down traditional behavior. In 1966, 70 percent of the Egyptian population was illiterate.[56] Interviews conducted in 1957 among rural families who had benefited from land reform revealed that 86 percent were illiterate, 65 percent preferred large families, and 83 percent had never even heard of birth control. Ninety-eight percent of the men insisted on their religious and legal right unilaterally to divorce a wife.[57] The passions and emo-

53. Gustave E. von Grunebaum, "Problems of Muslim Nationalism," in Richard N. Frye, ed., *Islam and the West* (The Hague: Mouton and Co., 1957), p. 27.

54. Anwar al-Sadat, *Nahwa Ba'th Jadid* [Toward a new revival] (Cairo: Islamic Conference, n.d.), p. 14.

55. Abu-Lughod, "Retreat from the Secular Path," pp. 467–68.

56. Tom Little, *Modern Egypt* (New York: Praeger, 1967), p. 245.

57. Saad M. Gadalla, *Land Reform in Relation to Social Development in Egypt* (Columbia: University of Missouri Press, 1962), pp. 83–84.

tional needs of the masses of the population are still tied to Islam. Unlike the guilds, the Sufi orders, though weakened, have not yet disappeared. Offering spiritual and material brotherhood and security in their ranks, they continue to appeal to men craving for a dynamic alternative to the formality of Islamic orthodoxy and to the official trade unions or the Arab Socialist Union.[58] The same factors account for the survival of the Muslim Brotherhood.

Following the attempted assassination of President Nasser on 26 October 1954, the Brotherhood had been outlawed and its leaders imprisoned or executed. Many of the rank and file had been jailed without trial. By 1961 many of these men had completed their sentences or had been released as a result of amnesties, and the secret apparatus of the society was regrouping. Money, it appears, was being supplied from branches of the Brotherhood in Syria, the Sudan, and other Arab countries. In August 1965 a new plot against Nasser was uncovered and more than a thousand Brethren were arrested. Among the accused ring leaders was Sayed Qutb, a prolific author often regarded as the theoretician and philosopher of the Brotherhood, who had called in his writings for the establishment of a truly Islamic society. The problems created by modernization, Qutb had written in 1962, were the result of deviating from Islam. What was needed were not more books, films, and lectures on Islam but the desire to take Islam as charter and law.[59] He was now accused of conspiring to seize power in order to implement these ideas.

In late August 1966 sentences were passed upon the accused plotters. Hodeiby, the former Supreme Guide of the Society, and other leaders released during earlier amnesties were once more given prison terms ranging from three years to life. Seven members of the so-called Sayed Qutb group were condemned to death. The death sentences of three men were commuted by Nasser to life imprisonment; four men, including Qutb, were executed on 29

---

58. See M. D. Gilsenan, "Some Factors in the Decline of the Sufi Orders in Modern Egypt," *Muslim World* 57 (1967): 11–18. In 1964 Morroe Berger found 64 functioning Sufi orders in Egypt that involved hundreds of thousands of primarily poor people. See his *Islam in Egypt: Social and Political Aspects of Popular Religion* (Cambridge: At the University Press, 1970), pp. 67–81.

59. Sayed Qutb, *Al-Islam wa-Mushkilat al-Hadarah* [Islam and the problems of civilization] (Cairo: al-Halabi, 1962), pp. 181–184.

August 1966.[60] By November 1967 the regime felt secure enough
to announce the release of 1,000 imprisoned Brethren,[61] but members of the society living abroad concede only the loss of a battle
and not of the war. Said Ramadan, director of the Islamic Center
in Geneva and editor of a monthly journal, *al-Muslimun,* told a
correspondent of *Die Weltwoche* of Zurich that the Brotherhood
still had two million secret members in Egypt. "Colonel Nasser is
secularizing Egypt and thereby opening the doors wide to atheism
and Communism. He is persecuting religion, killing our brother-
ers." Eventually Nasser will fall: "Tomorrow, the day after tomorrow, whenever it pleases God." [62]

Nasser has died, but unless the Muslim Brotherhood can regain
its influence in the armed forces it seems unlikely that the society
can overthrow the regime established by him. The ruling officers,
as we have seen, have been quite successful in appropriating the
Islamic ethos. Islam, even for westernized intellectuals, is part of
the national heritage and the regime is careful to nourish this
sentiment. The Muslim religion serves as the basis for minimum
agreement between the members of the political community and
it will continue to serve in this capacity until a new and secular
formula for legitimacy can evolve and find acceptance.[63] Meanwhile, a confusion of norms will prevail. The task of nation building within the framework of Islam will be difficult, for Muslims
have never successfully developed a realistic theory of the state.
The original Muslim state under the so-called "Rightly guided
Caliphs" cannot be resurrected nor would the system fit the Arab
nation-states of the twentieth century. During the thirteen hundred years of Islamic civilization there was loyalty to family and
religious community, to profession or trade, but only rarely to the
political unit of city or state.[64] A sense of citizenship was never
born and the emergence of a modern state today is handicapped
by the suspicion with which any central authority has always been

---

60. *Egyptian Gazette,* 30 August 1966.

61. *New York Times,* 11 November 1967.

62. Translation in *Atlas* (May 1966): 299.

63. Cf. P. J. Vatikiotis, "Dilemmas of Political Leadership in the Arab Middle
East: The Case of the U.A.R.," *International Affairs* 37 (1961): 195.

64. Morroe Berger, *The Arab World Today* (Garden City, N.Y.: Doubleday,
1962), p. 295.

viewed. Even though the fellah is more truly Egyptian than many
political leaders, "he is still not conscious of belonging to a nation." [65] These words of Father Ayrout were written in 1938;
change is slow in coming.

The mobilization of mass support for the regime's goal of
modernization and rapid social change as well as the search for a
new source of legitimacy thus take place in an environment that
is conducive to neither. The ruling officers are faced with a para-
dox: "the need to appeal to the 'Islamic Myth' of communal and
cultural identity in order to work for the achievement of a new
formula to supersede it." [66] Hence, the tie between modernization
and legitimacy is cultivated as a crucial means of bridging the gap
between reality and aspiration. A strong leader endowed with
charismatic qualities becomes the focus of loyalty and inspires his
followers with an enthusiastic picture of the nation's future. David
Apter calls the fully developed form of such a system "mobilization regime." It relies on a "political religion" to bolster the
legitimacy of the leadership. Such a regime, he says, "represents
the new puritanism. Progress is its faith. Industrialization is its
vision. Harmony is its goal." [67]

The disruption of traditional patterns at a time when no new
integrating force has yet fully emerged is hazardous. The resolution of rival and divergent views of the world is unlikely to be
accomplished on the theoretical level and the adaptation of Islam
to modernity will continue to defy consistency and philosophical
neatness. A new kind of Islam, radically different from anything
history has known so far, will probably be defined by practice and
in the heat of action. It would be presumptuous to maintain that
such a religion should no longer be called Islamic. "Throughout
its history," notes John S. Badeau, "Islam has been in constant
interplay with the processes of society and the result has been a
working compromise between Muslim and non-Muslim elements
that reflects the conditions of each era. To say that Islam is changing its role today is not necessarily to say that it is on the verge

65. Henry Habib Ayrout, *The Egyptian Peasant,* trans. John Alden Williams
(Boston: Beacon Press, 1963), p. 109.

66. Vatikiotis, "Dilemmas of Political Leadership," p. 192.

67. David E. Apter, "Political Religion in the New Nations," in Geertz, *Old Societies and New States,* p. 78.

of disappearing—only that once more compromise is taking place, the final form of which cannot yet be determined." [68]

68. John S. Badeau, "Islam and the Modern Middle East," *Foreign Affairs* 38 (1958): 61–62.

15

The New Latin American Catholicism

THOMAS G. SANDERS

The analysis and promotion of development and social change in Latin America since World War II have deeply affected the Roman Catholic church, formerly one of the region's most powerful and traditional institutions. The redefinition of its social responsibility has provoked various responses within the church, ranging from hostile resistance to radical advocacy of change.[1] The total effect has been a division of the church into various points of view and a pronounced shift of the official consensus, as expressed in episcopal documents, to support for economic development and new political, social, economic, and cultural structures.

As the 1970s get underway, the basic lines of a new Latin American Catholicism are emerging and becoming consolidated. Despite the apparent diversity of opinion in the church, key groups for the future such as younger bishops, innovating pastoral priests, specialized lay groups, and the more sophisticated publications now reflect a common set of new assumptions about the nature of the Christian faith, the prerequisites for revitalizing the Catholic community, and sociopolitical responsibility. Advanced ecclesiastical documents, such as those produced by the Latin American Bishops Conference (CELAM) at Medellín, Colombia, in 1968,[2] include many of the new views in uncomfortable juxtaposition with other, more traditional ideas.

1. Recent attempts to develop a typology of Latin American Catholicism include David E. Mutchler, "Roman Catholicism in Brazil," *Studies in Comparative International Development* 1, no. 8 (1965); Thomas G. Sanders, "A Typology of Catholic Elites," *Catholic Innovation in a Changing Latin America* (Cuernavaca: Centro Intercultural de Documentación, 1969); and Vallier, "Religious Elites."

2. *La Iglesia en la Actual Transformación de América Latina a Luz del Concilio*, vol. 2, Conclusiones (Bogotá: CELAM, 1968).

The current rethinking of all aspects of Catholic life points to a wide-sweeping "modernization" of the Latin American church that should properly be analyzed as a whole. Theological concepts, pastoral strategies, and modes of political action are interdependent.

This position has been in gestation since the late 1950s. In its political and social expression it was often called "leftist," "socialist," or "radical." Although politics became a prominent part of its activity, such terms give a misleading emphasis to what is fundamentally a total church renewal with derivative political implications. In an article written in 1968, I introduced the word "innovator" to describe the outlook of the participant in this position and also to show the interrelationship of advanced theological and pastoral with political views.[3] The extraordinary strengthening of this general perspective since the Medellín meeting indicates that we are now dealing with a consolidated position moving toward consensus and possibly replacing older approaches. Terms like "new Church" or "new Catholicism" now seem to be more effectively descriptive. The use of "Church" or "Catholicism" emphasizes the fact that a new approach to social and political phenomena is merely a part of a modernized Catholic church in Latin America.

THE EVOLUTION OF CATHOLIC SOCIAL THOUGHT AND ACTION

The new Catholicism represents another stage in an overlapping but clear evolution of the church's social thought and action during this century.

The encyclicals of Pope Leo XIII, *Rerum Novarum,* and Pius XI, *Quadragesimo Anno,* had an important effect in awakening certain Latin American elites to the problem of social justice. By the 1930s, two political philosophies, fascism and neo-Thomism were active, both claiming to interpret the church's position authentically.

The role of fascism in Latin American Catholicism needs reassessment. It appeared as something new and dynamic to a relatively unreflective and socially indifferent church. Although it aimed fundamentally at achieving order and authority in a tumul-

---

3. Sanders, "Catholic Elites," in *Catholic Innovation,* p. 5–8.

tuous world threatened by communism and individualistic capitalism, it made Catholics reflect on new political and social models.
In Brazil, where it was called Integralism, it stimulated in its followers a concern for national significance and dignity, promoted
labor unions and social welfare mechanisms, and established
schools, libraries, and cultural centers in many communities.

Neo-Thomism had a somewhat different effect. It wanted to
maintain democratic political forms against the threat of authoritarianism and fascism, justify religious pluralism rather than the
traditional church-state alliance, and achieve social justice by
applying the papal social teachings through public policies. Neo-
Thomism helped form Catholic elites that were receptive to new
ideas, undogmatic in their social views, and flexible in their political actions. It is difficult to see how Latin American Catholicism could have accepted the innovations of the Vatican Council
and changed so readily in the 1960s without the preparatory
period of neo-Thomism, which helped open the minds of Catholic
leaders to the reality of change.

In his *Religion and Political Development,* Donald E. Smith
divides the church's response into three stages.[4] First, the church,
confronted with the modern world, aims at constructing a "neo-
religious society" by insisting on its role as "the divine authority
in the midst of human society with power to direct, guide, and
judge all temporal institutions." Smith calls the second stage a
"religious socialist society," though in practice it has revealed itself
in Latin America to be more properly a form of reformist society
based on religious inspiration. Here the church retreats from its
pretension to restore some kind of religious order and dedicates
itself through direct and indirect activities to an attempt at solving society's problems on a "humanist" basis. Smith's third stage,
a "secular pluralist society," is now emerging in Latin America,
and the church's response represents the theme of this chapter.

Since World War II and especially since 1960, a form of religiously inspired reformism, the Chilean model,[5] has attracted the
dominant attention not only of those interested in new developments within the church but often of those concerned with eco-

4. Smith, *Religion and Political Development,* pp. 212–45.
5. Systematic discussions of the Chilean model appear in *ibid.,* pp. 204–11, 229–
32; and Vallier, *Modernization in Latin America,* pp. 141–46.

nomic, social, and political development in Latin America. The Chilean model was a progressive and imaginative attempt by the church to use its various forms of influence and organization in promoting a distinctive Catholic solution to the problems of a Latin America in process of change and secularization.

Its theoretical inspiration came from neo-Thomism, the papal social teaching, and the Christian Democratic parties of Europe. Despite the clearly Catholic origins of this thinking, its advocates believed that their program was "pluralist" and "humanist." The organizations for its implementation were open to anyone who agreed with their aims and were based on the natural law, which gave them their quality of "Christian inspiration." The older political vehicles—Catholic conservatism, populism, and anticlerical liberalism—were considered inadequate for several reasons. Catholic conservatism was linked to traditional ruling groups and lacked a sense of social responsibility. Populism was fiscally irresponsible, demagogic, and inclined to dictatorial methods. Liberalism was "individualistic," opportunistic, and, because of its antireligious views, incompatible with the church's outlook.

It was common in the early sixties for Latin American Catholics to speak of the need for an ideological solution to the region's problems and to argue that the church, through its teaching on society and organizations inspired by this teaching, offered the only ideological alternative to Marxism.

The appearance of the Alliance for Progress bolstered the Christian Democratic approach because of the similarity of their aims: economic development through a mixed economy, reformism, and strengthening of democratic institutions and participation. By the early 1960s many Latin American Catholics and Western-oriented observers considered the Chilean model the most promising approach to the region's problems, and the Christian Democratic victory in 1964 seemed to offer an opportunity for implementing it by a wide-ranging and in many ways impressive program.

The Alliance for Progress and Christian Democracy had something else in common: both were programs that came from outside. The alliance represented a progressive effort by the United States government to maintain Latin America within its political and economic sphere of influence. The organizations of Christian inspiration were a similar progressive effort by Catholic clerical and lay leaders to retain a role of moral leadership in the region by offering basic guidelines for institutions and development derived from papal teaching.

The logical next step, which we can already discern, is twofold: the appearance of a new nationalism oriented to development and based on the special characteristics and possibilities of Latin America and of each country, and the emergence of a secular society in which the church exercises its evangelical and moral role among its adherents and as one position along with others.

THE LEFTIST ORIGINS OF THE NEW CATHOLICISM

The wide interest in the Chilean model overshadowed the attempt of other Latin American Catholics to formulate a different approach to the region's problems. Those called "leftists" criticized the theoretical bases of the Chilean model on a number of grounds: its orientation to "Western, Christian culture," its assumption that the church had a special solution or responsibility for Latin America, its implicit paternalism, its natural law orientation, the concept of organizations of Christian inspiration. They tended instead to look with sympathy on a more radical change of structures by cooperating with secular political movements, often of Marxist inspiration.

The earlier organizational manifestations of this position were Brazil's Catholic Left,[6] the program of Colombia's priest-sociologist, Camilo Torres,[7] and the Intercultural Center of Documentation (CIDOC) in Mexico.[8] It is interesting that each of these suffered adversity, if not tragedy. The Catholic Left, whose most interesting manifestation was the organization Popular Action (Ação Popular), was persecuted by the military movement that took power in 1964 and is now disbanded and without public influence in Brazil. Father Torres failed to develop his hoped-for front of the Left, joined a violent revolutionary group, and died in a skirmish. The inspirational genius of CIDOC, Mon-

6. See Thomas G. Sanders, "Catholicism and Development: The Catholic Left in Brazil," in Kalman H. Silvert, ed., *Churches and States: The Religious Institution and Modernization* (New York: American Universities Field Staff, 1967).

7. See German Guzman, *Camilo Torres* (New York: Sheed and Ward, 1969).

8. The Intercultural Center of Documentation publishes a bulletin of documentation called *CIDOC* that often includes materials on innovating movements in Latin American Catholicism.

signor Ivan Illich, encountered criticism within the church, was subjected to a farcical ecclesiastical inquiry, and voluntarily withdrew from sacerdotal functions.

These movements attracted criticism for several reasons. In Latin American Catholic circles, they were disliked because their views were often in tension with the prevailing official consensus of the church; they sympathized or cooperated with radical, non-Catholic political movements; and they criticized the church's attempt at a progressive solution according to the Chilean model. Observers in Europe and the United States, being usually also progressive and well meaning, could not understand their hostility to "imperialist" economic and political policies in Latin America and attempts by the church or the Alliance for Progress to bring in "outside" solutions. The sharpest criticisms were usually directed to the political side of their thinking and action, since in practice they absorbed Marxist ideas (like class struggle), advocated a "revolutionary" and "socialist" program, and cooperated with secular leftists in contexts where the conditions for a leftist program to succeed did not exist.

More fundamentally, however, those called leftists were profound innovators who saw through the deficiencies of the transition stage represented by the Chilean model and began sketching the outlines for a modernized Latin American church. New organizations have sprung up, such as Argentina's Third World Movement,[9] Colombia's Golconda Group,[10] and Peru's National Office of Social Information (ONIS),[11] but a relatively small group of bishops, priests, and laymen has had far more influence. Highly motivated and well informed on the issues under discussion, they discerned the implications of conciliar and contemporary Catholic theology and absorbed the most critical analyses of Latin America. They gave speeches, wrote articles, and participated in commissions to influence clerical and lay groups as well as the official consensus of the church. Their interests varied from new modes of catechism and analysis of popular religion to higher education

---

9. "El Movimiento 'Tercer Mundo' de la Argentina y su Opción por la Liberación," *NADOC*, no. 147 (1970).

10. "II Encontro do Grupo Sacerdotal de Golconda," *SEDOC* 1 (1969): 1454–60.

11. "Conclusiones del II Encuentro Nacional de Sacerdotes de ONIS," *NADOC*, no. 96 (1970).

and ecumenism, to political responsibility and analysis of the power structure in their countries. The aim: a new and more vital church.

The transition stage represented by the Chilean model legitimated change through a variety of mechanisms, such as papal teaching, hierarchical influence in declining Christian cultures, clerical organizations, direct church programs and institutions, lay organizations, and a political party.

In a genuinely secular society, the church will legitimate change in a more modest way, which the new Latin American Catholicism now suggests. The church is expected to accelerate its decline from being the dominant moral and legitimating institution of the nation toward becoming one interest group among others.

The church teaches a religious ethic favorable to change and internalized by those committed to its world view. The effect of this ethic on change is twofold: (1) As an institution and as a community of persons the church provides support and sanction for change carried out by secular institutions. (2) the ethic motivates individuals whose values are shaped by the church to favor and participate actively in change.

THE ETHIC OF THE NEW CATHOLICISM

This religious ethic can be stated in a series of themes.

Change as a given process.   The Medellín documents are entitled "The Church in the Actual Transformation of Latin America in Light of the Council." They open with the affirmation that

> Latin America is . . . under the sign of transformation and development—transformation which is not only occurring with extraordinary rapidity but touching and affecting all aspects of man, from the economic to the religious. This means that we are on the threshold of a new epoch in the history of our Continent, an epoch full of desire for total emancipation, liberation from all bondage, personal maturity, and collective integration. We can discern here the signs of the painful birth of a new civilization.[12]

12. *La Iglesia en la Actual Transformación,* vol. 2, p. 42.

The position of the bishops at Medellín represents the culmination of a long process of redefining change. The church was not opposed to change per se, but it emphasized gradualness, moderation, harmony, and consistency with tradition and permanent values. The alteration of this view comes largely from new ways of thinking about history adopted from existentialism and biblical perspectives, which were legitimated by the Vatican Council, and from an awareness that economic and social changes are a regional destiny.

Two characteristics of this concept of change deserve emphasis. One is its given-ness. This is not something that the church has created but a historical reality of which the church cannot avoid being a part. Second is its open-endedness. In the Chilean model a dominant preoccupation was to guide change according to "Christian principles." The new Catholicism sees the future as open (if rather utopian) and the heritage of the past as being altered in new, uncertain ways.

The theological significance of the process of change. The demise of Thomism in Catholic thought has brought into focus the fact that Catholic Christianity is a historical religion. This means that its principal beliefs are extrapolations or interpretations of historical events. Creation, God's action in biblical history, the incarnation of Christ, the formation of the church are theologically significant events that have not exhausted the divine action.

The important leap in Catholic thought is the recognition that the *secular* history of Latin America must be understood by the church for its *theological* meaning.

> We cannot fail to interpret this gigantic effort for a rapid transformation and development as an evident sign of the presence of the Spirit which conducts the history of men and people. . . . We cannot fail to discover in this will . . . the vestiges of the image of God in man as a potent dynamism. Progressively this dynamism brings him to ever greater dominion over nature, to a deeper personalization and fraternal cohesion, and also to an encounter with Him who ratifies, purifies, and deepens the values attained by human force.[13]

13. Ibid.

The rootage of this vision in the thought of Teilhard de Chardin is evident: growth, development, human realization are manifestations of God.

Participation in historical change.   "The essence of man is his freedom concretely engaged in a project of historical responsibility. There is no metaphysical dualism and consequently no pessimism congenital to the biblical view." [14] With words like these, the Brazilian Jesuit philosopher Henrique de Lima Vaz helped justify the desire of a whole generation of Catholic Action youth to join in the process of transformation that they discerned in the early sixties. Writing more recently, Vaz points out that "the church, as such, will not form a political party nor propose its ideological version for the Latin American revolution. But it must accept as normal and inevitable that political and ideological implications unfold, and . . . that they do not occur in abstract space, but in a concrete historical context, in whose origins and development it is found intimately participating. . . ." [15]

The concept of participation has important implications for the relationship between authority and social action within the Catholic context. Traditional Catholic social thought tried to define how the Christian individual and the church might bring given processes into correlation with predetermined norms. Vaz suggests, and the more thoughtful Catholics agree, that the options and even thinking of the Catholic actor and the church will be defined by the context. The Catholic is oriented by certain values, but their expression is conditioned by the problems and possibilities at hand. One does not shape the context by a preconditioned concept of justice, but the nature of justice is defined by the historical process. The Medellín documents take up this theme, referring to the "search for a form of more intensive and renovated presence of the church in the actual transformation of Latin America." [16]

14. Henrique C. de Lima Vaz, "Consciência Cristã e Responsibilidade Histórica," in Herbert José de Souza, ed., *Cristianismo Hoje* (Rio de Janeiro: Editôra Universitaria, 1962), p. 80.

15. Henrique C. de Lima Vaz, "Igreja-reflexa vs. Igreja-fonte," *Cadernos Brasileiros*, no. 46 (1968), 21–22

16. *La Iglesia en la Actual Transformación*, vol. 2, p. 44.

Radical humanism. The Chilean model defined its humanism through the neo-Thomist concept of natural man as a rational being, the agent of rights and responsibility. Man expresses himself through corporate entities, and his well-being becomes the objective of public policy. While this mode of humanism represents an important opening to secularity within the religious system, its abstractness and essentially Catholic character may be contrasted with the "Basic Document" of Popular Action:

> Our unique commitment is, then, to man. To Brazilian man, above all. He is born with the shadow of early death stretching over his cradle. He lives with the specter of hunger under his miserable roof, inseparably accompanying his uncertain steps, which trudge through life without hope and without aim. He grows up brutalized and illiterate, alienated from the benefits of culture, from creative possibilities, from the authentic human ways of genuine freedom. He dies an animal, anonymous death, stretched out on the hard floor of his misery.[17]

Both views are humanistic. One defines man in the categories of Catholic philosophy; the other is attempting to work out a view of man based on what he is. The difference of mentality is decisive: the latter does not assume that the church has a special wisdom about the way man is or should be.

Conscientization. A number of terms have arisen in Catholic circles to describe how the church views its work among men. Some are loosely used, such as human promotion, popular promotion, and solidarity, but they are usually specifically linked to the formation of effective intermediate structures between the person and the state. These may include the family, professional organizazations, labor unions, and community groups. As such they reflect an older neo-Thomist polemic against individualism and the concern to maintain centers of initiative between the individual and the state.

17. "Basic Document of Ação Popular," in Paul E. Sigmund, ed., *Models of Political Change in Latin America* (New York: Praeger, 1970), p. 127.

The laymen, Paulo Freire,[18] and Brazil's Basic Education Movement (MEB) are the originators of the concept of *conscientização*, developed in connection with literacy training. The term refers to an awakening of consciousness, that is, the transition from an ingenuous, uncritical, and passive attitude toward nature and culture into an awareness of freedom, creativity, criticism, and action. Conscientization implies an awareness of one's situation, its causes, and the possible options for changing it. Conscientization stands in distinct contrast to the traditional Thomist concept of human fulfillment through expression of potential moral and rational capacities. Like radical humanism, it has no predetermined notion of what man is. Only Latin Americans themselves can define their style of emancipation. Conscientization stands at an opposite pole from paternalism or the kind of structure developed in Chile's popular promotion program. Both agree that the masses should be incorporated into the new Latin American society, but conscientization assumes that only the masses themselves can determine how this will occur.

The term conscientization is now so commonly used in Latin America that its radical implications for popular pressure and politicization are sometimes dissipated. The more precise sense, however, is often maintained. The Medellín documents refer to it as "deepening the consciousness of human dignity, favoring free self-determination, and promoting communitarian sense." [19] A statement of Peru's ONIS insists that "social transformation is not merely a revolution for the people, but that the people themselves . . . ought to be agent of their own liberation. In this sense it is indispensable to begin realizing a serious work of conscientización to arrive at popular participation in the process of structural change. . . ." [20]

Movement toward a Latin American interpretation of Latin America. The early stages of leftist Catholicism were marked by the contributions of European thinkers who helped free Latin Americans from the prevailing neo-Thomist and Christian Demo-

---

18. See Thomas G. Sanders, *The Paulo Freire Method*, American Universities Field Staff Reports, West Coast South America Series, vol. 15, no. 1 (1968).
19. *La Iglesia en la Actual Transformación*, vol. 2, p. 59.
20. "Conclusiones de ONIS."

cratic framework. Philosopher Emanuel Mounier was widely read
for his existentialist motifs, and the Dominican sociologist L. J.
Lebret emphasized Latin America's linkage with the Third World
and the distinctness of its problems in contrast with the European-
oriented social teaching of the church. The views of Pope John
XXIII and the Vatican Council gave important institutional support for those who were in conflict with the prevailing theological
views of the church in Latin America.

Little by little Latin Americans have become more innovating
in their theology and have adopted secular categories for diag-
nosing Latin America. According to one of the leading interpreters of the new Catholicism in Chile, "Christianity is evolving
. . . not to the sound of foreign and alien theological and pastoral
problematics and schemes, but responding dialectically and vitally
to the contradictions and internal crises which convulse the Latin
American societies." [21]

The distinctiveness of Latin America is set, first, against the
developed world and, second, in contrast with the rest of the
underdeveloped world. For some years the Third World motif
dominated leftist Catholic thinking, but Latin America's differences are obvious: its relatively advanced level of development
and industrialization, its Iberian religious and social heritage, the
multiracial character of many of the countries, the special relationship to the United States within the Western hemisphere, the
failure to capitalize economically on a century and a half of
political independence. Thus the movement of Catholic thought
has gone from affinity with "Western, Christian values" to a sense
of commonality with the Third World, to emphasis on the distinctiveness of the Latin American problematic and the necessity
of special policies to deal with it.

Dependence. This concept is a relatively recent development in both Latin American and Catholic thought and is tend-
ing to supersede terms like "imperialism" and "colonialism" derived from Marxist and socialist thought.[22] The Medellín docu-

21. Gonzalo Arroyo, "Católicos de Izquierda en América Latina," *Mensaje* 19
(1970): 369.
22. The classic statement of the dependence theory is Osvaldo Sunkel, "Política
Nacional de Desarrollo y Dependencia Externa," *Estudios Internacionales* 1 (1967):

ments refer to "external neo-colonialism" but define it as "the consequences for our countries of their dependence on a center of economic power, around which they gravitate. Consequently our nations frequently are not masters of their possessions and economic decisions. Obviously, this does not fail to have influence in politics, given the interdependence which exists between the two areas." [23] The documents go on to cite as examples of dependence the distortions in international commerce, the flight of economic and human resources abroad, progressive indebtedness of the nations, the evasion of responsibility and taxes by foreign companies, and the influence of international monopolies.

The adoption of dependence represents an evolution from the view, common in the transition, that regarded Marxism as the danger to combat, through Marxism, and to a common and distinctive Latin American analysis that has developed since 1967 and is associated with nationalist thinkers.

Injustice. The awareness of injustice is not distinctive to this position, but it rounds out the analysis. According to the Medellín documents, "many studies exist which deal with the situation of the Latin American man. All of them describe the misery that marginalizes large human groups. This misery, as a collective fact, is an injustice which clamors to the heavens." [24] This "situation of sin" can be spelled out in many ways: the poverty of the lower classes, inadequate opportunities for education, subjection of women, and a lack of "receptive and active, creative and decisive participation in the construction of a society." [25]

Liberation. Liberation is one of the most common terms used in the Medellín documents, but it has been most systematically analyzed by a Peruvian priest, Gustavo Gutiérrez. Father Gutiérrez views liberation as the alternative to dependence and

---

43–75. A recent analysis is Theotonio dos Santos, Tomás A. Vasconi, Marcos Kaplan, and Helio Jaguaribe, *La Crisis del Desarrollismo y la Nueva Dependencia* (Lima: Instituto de Estudios Peruanos, 1969). For bibliography and a presentation of the major themes, see Gonzalo Arroyo, "Pensamiento latinoamericano sobre subdesarrollo y dependencia externa," *Mensaje* 17 (1968): 516–20.

23. *La Iglesia en la Actual Transformación,* vol. 2, p. 67.

24. Ibid., p. 51.

25. Ibid., p. 54.

injustice. It has three dimensions: (1) the liberation of man from sin, (2) the liberation of the Latin American man from the structures that oppress him, and (3) the liberation of Latin America from underdevelopment and dependence. "To procure the liberation of the continent," he says, "is more than to overcome economic, social, and political dependence. More profoundly, it is to see the future of humanity oriented toward a society in which man appears free of all servitude, in which he may be subject of his own destiny." [26]

Father Gutiérrez draws a sharp distinction between liberation and development, which he considers a technological and outside remedy that did not "attack the roots of the evil" and provoked disappointment and frustration. Liberation entails a popular transformation, a social revolution to change radically the situation of Latin America.

Prophetism.   The new Catholicism defines the role of the church as being a prophet or critic of injustice. Prophetism, as a reaction to concrete problems, differs from the usual view of the church's social teaching, which speaks in generalities and applies lines of thought emanating from the Vatican. Not only the institution, but individuals are prophets. The most commonly acknowledged example of an ecclesiastical prophet is Monsignor Helder Câmara, archbishop of Olinda and Recife in Brazil.

Ivan Illich of CIDOC argues:

> Revelation forbids us [the church] from supporting one political tendency against another. But the Church must denounce categorically every injustice, wherever it is found. At the same time it must suffer impotently the injustices done to it, like Christ on the Cross. The Christian is called to condemn the evil, in the name of God, wherever he sees it.[27]

The church's long-time approach to moral and social issues tended to associate it with certain political options, though it rarely admitted this. Prophetism as a criticism and analysis of con-

26. Gustavo Gutiérrez, "Apuntes para una Teología de la Liberación," *NADOC*, no. 137.

27. Werner Harenberg, "Puede ser Cristiana la Violencia? Plática del *Spiegel* con Ivan Illich, católico, experto en asuntos latinoamericanos," *CIDOC*, Doc. 70/214, p. 5.

crete problems, in contrast with advocacy of a generalized set of
social norms, places the church on the side of the victims of injustice and strengthens its postconciliar desire to be a servant and
defender of the poor.

The minority church.   The church throughout Latin American history enjoyed a prominent political position, economic
power, and cultural influence, based on the assumption that the
vast bulk of the people were Catholics. This image has been challenged on several grounds: (1) The secular outlook of many of
the elites, a consequence of the rationalism of the nineteenth century but, even more, of the indifference and lack of serious Christian conviction among many who claim to be Catholic; (2) the
adherence of most of the population to forms of popular rather
than normative Catholicism; and (3) the obstacle to a free and
revitalized church created by its privileges and institutionalized
linkage. Speaking of the situation in Peru, Father Gutiérrez insists that

> the actual regime creates a situation in which the religious
> appears as an integrating element of the political order—an
> element necessary to 'sacralize' certain official acts, including
> legitimating determined political situations and postures. In
> this way it comes to be behavior of simple religious formality,
> bordering on hypocrisy, and a use of Christianity to remain
> within certain social canons. All of this is profoundly alien
> to the evangelical demands of authenticity and interior con-
> viction.[28]

Not surprisingly, the supporters of this position favor a withdrawal of the church from directing schools, hospitals, and other
secular functions.

The most critical Latin American Catholics now believe that
the real church of the future will be a minority. In 1965 the
Jesuits of the Centro Bellarmino, the chief rationalizers of the
Chilean model, admitted, "We must become aware that we do
not live in a society of Christendom and that we constitute a
minority, ever more a minority, in a pluralistic world." [29] The

28. Gustavo Gutiérrez, "La Separación de la Iglesia y el Estado en el Perú,"
NADOC, no. 18 (1969), p. 2.
29. Centro Bellarmino, "Apostolado de Evangelización," *Mensaje* 14 (1965): 163.

church, to be sure, has three dimensions: the people of God, those linked to the ecclesiastical institution by baptism, and those who understand and internalize its message. The latter are few, yet it is of only such persons that one can speak meaningfully of a Catholic participation in society or of elites shaped by Catholic values in the new Latin American church.

Cooperation with secular socialist movements. The political spectrum of Latin America is such that religious individuals favoring change through cooperation with other individuals or through secular institutions almost inevitably have to come into contact with Marxists. The earliest concrete case of this occurred in Brazil, when students of the university branch of Catholic Action (JUC) entered a coalition in 1960 with members of the Communist party and other Marxist groups to capture control of the National Student Union (UNE). Father Torres was one of the first Colombian Catholics to dialogue with Marxists, and he believed that only a political front of the left could solve the problems of his country. The recent breakdown in the Chilean model stems in large part from the question of whether to cooperate with the Marxist left or not. The current division of the Christian Democratic party and the departure of certain members to form the Movement of Unitary Popular Action (MAPU) reflect this disagreement.

Characteristically, movements that begin as organizations of the Catholic left abdicate their Catholic character to become secular organizations. Thus the political activists of Brazilian Catholic Action formed Popular Action as a nonconfessional group; the radicals of Christian Democracy dropped the name Christian to form MAPU; and the Golconda Group changed from an essentially clerical institution into a secular political movement, one of whose major leaders is a Marxist, Germán Zabala.[30]

An interesting question is whether these organizations will inevitably become Marxist. Popular Action by 1967 had become ever more immersed in Marxist theory, while the younger members of MAPU now come close to a doctrinaire Marxism-Lenin-

---

30. Cf. the joint article by a priest and a Marxist, Noel Olaya and Germán Zabala, "En la ruta de Golconda," *Víspera* 13–14 (1969): 36–39.

ism. They have motivated a desire for change more successfully than developed an analysis of such issues as classes, power, and instruments for change. Marxism seems to offer the most cogent interpretations, but the adoption of Marxist themes introduces tension with the Catholic side of their thinking.

An Assessment of the New Catholicism

The religious ethic defined by these themes can be summed up as Christian in theology and values, totally accepting of the role of secular institutions in development and inescapably oriented to change.

Any assessment of its future strength and influence must take into consideration the crisis of the contemporary Latin American church, due in large part to the breakdown of traditional thinking and functions and the transition toward these new forms. The crisis is reflected in a number of ways: the shortage of professional leadership, the disappointment of many young people in the performance of the church, the contradiction between Catholicism and modern thought, and the struggle for consensus amid serious differences of opinion.

Catholicism in a "secular pluralist society" seems certain to be less influential than in the past, but the thought of the new church presumes this without considering it a loss. Its contribution to the legitimation of change, however, will be grounded on a community of people with conviction and a more realistic recognition of the role of a religious institution in a secular, pluralistic society.

Despite the strength of the new thinking among many of the best-known leaders and in the literature of Latin American Catholicism, we should not assume that it dominates the church. Its future seems promising, nevertheless, because of the obvious support by younger bishops,[31] innovating pastoral priests,[32] and lay organizations, especially of students and youth.

31. Cf. Thomas G. Sanders, *The Chilean Episcopate*, American Universities Field Staff Reports, West Coast South American Series, vol. 15, no. 3 (1968): 24–26.

32. Two innovating pastoral journals that reflect the position described in this paper are *Pastoral Popular* (Chile) and *Servir* (Mexico). Documentation services that do so are *NADOC* (Peru) and *CIDOC* (Mexico). *Vispera* (Uruguay) and *Frente Unido* (Colombia) are associated with leftist Catholic and Protestant students and with the Golconda Group, respectively. The now defunct *Paz e Terra* (Brazil) included among its editors many people of the Catholic left. Articles relevant to the

The new Latin American Catholicism must confront certain problems and tensions. One is the conflict between prophetic and conventional religion within the same institution. The new Catholicism is clearly the creation of a small group of sophisticated individuals with profound theological convictions and a free, open way of dealing with the world. Undoubtedly the bulk of those who call themselves Catholic, even in important positions within the church, prefer a simpler, less demanding, and predictable form of religion. Moreover, the new views, if carried out, might entail an alteration of Catholicism beyond what ecclesiastical leaders will tolerate. The cautious stance of Pope Paul VI today reflects his conviction that the church is spawning opinions that endanger its Catholic substance.

The new Catholicism has an almost sectarian quality. It aims at a purification that will make of the real Christians a minority, but it has never satisfactorily indicated what will happen to the other, more conventional Catholics. The church will not abandon them; and to retain them it will have to fulfill many of the functions of a culture religion as it does now. Latin American Catholicism could become, as it almost is now, a comprehensive institution in which most of the people practice a conventional, unimaginative religion, while a "prophetic minority" has a more critical, dynamic way of thinking.

A second tension is that between the contextual and socialist sides of the ethic. As a perspective the new Catholicism has no program except a concern for liberation, the end of injustice, conscientization of the masses, and participation in secular movements leading to change. By deprogramming its thought, it succeeded in freeing itself from the guideline thinking of the Chilean model and opened possibilities for involvement in any kind of economic and political model leading to these basic aims.

In practice, on the other hand, the position supports "revolutionary," "socialist" models that include an emphasis on structural changes and participation of the masses in the political process.

The possibilities for direct influence and participation of this position depend on the modes of change in future Latin America. If the region develops under regimes that call themselves "social-

new Latin American Catholicism may be frequently found in *SEDOC* (Brazil), *Vozes* (Brazil), and *Mensaje* (Chile).

ist," in which new elites break the power of the traditional controlling groups and incorporate the masses, the new Catholicism will play its anticipated role of contributing to the consensus favoring such change and providing individuals to participate in it.

The current situation of Latin America does not, however, suggest that the "revolutionary" vision of the left will be implemented. Rather, segments of the existent power groups recognize that they must "modernize" their countries to fulfill national potential and meet the needs of the population. This requires expanding and diversifying the economy, changing structures that prevent the lower classes from contributing to national development and constituting an internal market, and achieving control of natural resources. The Cuban pattern, in which the power structure collapsed and permitted the entrance of totally new groups, seems unlikely to be repeated. The leading "revolutionary" or "socialist" countries in South America—Chile, Peru, and Bolivia—are developing under the tutelage of the traditional political and military classes.

For the near future, the most difficult problem for the new church will be Brazil, which has had an economic growth rate of 9 percent since 1968 under military technocratic leadership that encourages foreign investment and has as its objective the creation of a modern, internationally competitive industrial capitalism. The model aims at eventual redistribution of income, social benefits, and incorporation of the lower classes, but gradually and without a shift of power or "revolutionary" structural changes.

A planned capitalism, like that in Brazil, can become an instrument for "change," but one which the new Catholicism will have difficulty accepting. It is interesting that in Brazil persons associated with the more radical views have gradually been marginalized, while more moderate leaders in the hierarchy have increased their influence. This has not resulted from mere opportunism but from a recognition that the church, to have any influence at all, must come to terms with the government's concept of development. To propose changes without reference to the options possible within the model means the rupture of dialogue and irrelevance.

If the new Catholicism can legitimate change carried out by secular governments in Chile or Peru that claim to be socialist but cannot legitimate the change achieved by Brazil's more conservative model, it will have lost contact with the Latin American reality. Such words as "socialism" and "revolution" are mere slogans that bear little relation to real development and change. (Even Brazil's government calls itself "the Revolution.") We will mislead ourselves if we think that the dynamic forces now active within the region are socialism and revolution. More fundamental are nationalism and development. All of the major countries are promoting economic development, greater political autonomy, and social change, though with considerable variety of economic programs and political vehicles.

A third problem in the new Catholicism, as in the old Catholicism, is its ignorance of developmental economics and the role of economics in social change.

The Medellín documents have nothing, for example, to say about macroeconomics, except the incredible proposal for the "active participation of all" on "the level of macroeconomics which is decisive in the national and international sphere." They turn instead to a long-time Catholic emphasis on communitarian enterprises as an alternative to liberal capitalism and Marxism.[33] The church is clearly concerned with participation, but the only real contact with the thinking of economic planners is support for industrialization as a means of elevating the living standards of the people and providing better conditions for "integral development."[34] It is clear that the Medellín documents fall within the transitional stage of proposing special Catholic alternatives rather than supporting and understanding economic planning in the modern secular state.

One of the leading theorists of the new Catholicism, Father Gutiérrez, as we have noted, contrasts "liberation" with "development" to the point of seeing a contradiction between them. While the church in a secularized and changing Latin America should not propose an economic program, it could participate with more credibility in the consensus for change if it understood the

33. *La Iglesia en la Actual Transformación,* vol. 2, pp. 55–56.
34. Ibid., p. 58.

role of economics sufficiently to recognize problems like the following:

1. The highly technical character of economic planning under any model makes it the responsibility of specialists.

2. Postponing social benefits so that scarce resources may be allocated for increased production is ethically legitimate. Latin American Catholic social thought continues to have a bias for redistribution and social benefits, which if carried too far in a poor society will lead to economic stagnation by diverting capital from productive investments.

3. Development does not contradict "liberation" but contributes to it. To deny development is to deny political reality, since all responsible governments, no matter what they call themselves, are engaged in economic development, that is, the bettering of the living conditions of the people.

A final problem in the position is the danger of utopianism. The focus on motivational attitudes and ideal goals for humanity has helped free elements in the church from the programmatic pretensions of the religious socialist stage. On the other hand, aims like liberation and conscientization are high ideals of human existence that no society has achieved. The new Catholics must bring their ethical values into correlation with definable economic, political, and power structures and options. Modern statesmen make choices not for liberation but of certain measures that may seem better or more feasible than others. The new Catholicism can legitimate and participate in movements of social change, but its temptation will be to judge the limited possibilities for change by ideal norms. It looks to a "new epoch," when we have no choice but to continue living in this one.

The new Catholicism will make its most important contribution to the legitimation of change, the more successfully it comes to understand the intricacies of the present models of change in Latin America. The 1970s seem to be a time of greater autonomy and diversity by the individual countries in choosing strategies for economic and social development. The political vehicles tend to be authoritarian, because in many situations only strong governments seem able to maintain the continuity of economic growth and mediate among the claims of various social groups in a process of change.

16

The Church and Military in Peru:
From Reaction to Revolution

GEORGE W. GRAYSON

Shortly before 10 o'clock on the morning of 29 June 1969, General Juan Velasco Alvarado, who seized power from democratically elected President Fernando Belaúnde, left the presidential palace with his cabinet, walked across the 400-year-old Plaza de Armas, around which stood soldiers from the Lima garrison, and entered the cathedral where Pizarro's remains are preserved. There he genuflected, prayed, listened to the cardinal's Te Deum mass, and kissed the *lignum crucis de paz* when it was brought to him by a serving canon.[1]

In November 1970, Monseñor Lucien Metzinger, bishop of Ayaviry, in a statement released at the Vatican said of Peru's ruling generals:

> The military government, which is sometimes called dictatorial abroad, is pursuing objectives that coincide with the goals of the Church in Peru. This regime is truly undertaking development in the most exact, most Catholic, and most Christian sense of the word.[2]

These two occurrences reflect the close relationship now found in Peru between the "Revolutionary Government of the Armed Forces" and the Roman Catholic church. The theses of this chapter are that (1) the Peruvian church, attacked by numerous groups, steadily lost influence and legitimacy from independence to the mid-twentieth century, (2) the church, inspired by recent social doctrines, has helped legitimize Peru's military junta by iden-

1. *Expreso,* 30 June 1969, p. 3.
2. Quoted in *Correo,* 25 November 1970.

tifying itself with its actions and programs, (3) the social and economic changes promoted by the generals-turned-rulers have fostered an atmosphere in which the church can implement some of its post-conciliar goals, and (4) church-supported military populism[3] offers a possible model for political development through institution building.

Unless otherwise noted, the term "church" will apply to the hierarchy and formal structure of Peru's Roman Catholic establishment; by "legitimacy" I mean that acts are "accepted and obeyed because they are felt to be justified" by standards common to "both those who command and those who obey";[4] and "influence" signifies the capability of winning allegiance or gaining support. A discussion of the groups which, historically, have set themselves in opposition to the Roman Catholic church introduces this analysis.

ATTACKS ON THE CATHOLIC CHURCH

Colonial Lima appeared as the "Rome of Spanish America" because of the intimate ties between church and state. Under the *patronato,* the Spanish monarch appointed the bishops in Peru and other countries of the New World, while the church enjoyed a monopoly over education, religious practices, and regulation of family life. Further, the church, like the military, established *fueros,* ecclesiastical courts with exclusive rights to hear all cases touching upon persons or property of the clergy and religious. Even civil cases involving a clergyman were tried in a church tribunal under canon law.[5] Such fueros, which made churchmen a privileged class, were deemed necessary to "preserve the dignity

3. "Military Populism" refers, not to the rabble-rousing antics of a Perón or Vargas to elicit frenzied support from the masses by supplying bread, circuses, and symbols of self-importance, but to the attempt of uniformed leaders—frequently acting as heads of military institutions rather than as personalistic saviors—to implement land, educational, housing, and other reforms. These are intended to win favor within the popular sector, thereby fostering a close relationship between the generals and the people, to the detriment of traditional political organizations.

4. Samuel H. Beer, "The Analysis of Political Systems," in idem and Adam B. Ulam, eds., *Patterns of Government,* 2d ed. (New York: Random House, 1962), p. 22.

5. Francis Merriman Stanger, "Church and State in Peru," *The Hispanic American Historical Review* 17 (November 1927): 413.

and sanctity of the clergy." [6] The church also boasted the right to collect tithes from Peru's Indians, a privilege that greatly enhanced ecclesiastical wealth, already the largest fortune in the country because of income from regular tithes, first fruits, parochial fees, business earnings, and property donations. Churches, monasteries, and nunneries festooned Lima's narrow streets, and one estimate reveals that of the city's 3,941 houses, 1,135 of the best belonged to clergymen or religious orders.[7] Sharing functions and authority, church and state stood as the twin pinnacles of absolute power in Spanish Peru.

Attacks on the absolutist and vaunted position of the church began shortly after independence in 1821. Although he found a majority of lower clergymen to be liberal advocates of separation from Spain,[8] liberator José de San Martín suppressed the religious orders that had supported the king, expelled the royal archbishop, and invited to the country James Thompson, a Scottish Baptist minister, to direct the republic's educational system.[9] Nonetheless, Peru's first constitution, promulgated in 1823, established Roman Catholicism as the state religion to the "exclusion of any other."

Simón Bolívar, who generally viewed the church as royalist, supplanted San Martín to become "Supreme Political Chief of the Peruvian republic" and won acceptance of his *constitución vitalicia,* which named Catholicism the state religion with no restrictions on the practice of any faith. This was the most tolerant fundamental law until that ratified in 1915.

Bolívar called for the election of bishops, placed all clergymen under the control of their diocesan bishops, curtailed the number of holy days, continued to repress "disloyal" religious houses, forbade minors to take up monastic vows, and reduced the payments to priests made by the country's penurious Indians. Moreover, he decreed that monasteries and convents would have to be inhabited at least eight months each year and converted vacant church buildings into hospitals and orphanages.

6. Ibid.

7. Carlos Pereyra, *Historia de la América Española* 7 (Madrid, 1925); cited in Stanger, "Church and State in Peru," p. 414.

8. A small minority of the hierarchy, including Chávez de la Rosa, bishop of Arequipa (1789–1805), and Pérez Armendaris, bishop of Cuzco (1809–19), favored separatism. Stanger, "Church and State in Peru," p. 420.

9. Mecham, *Church and State,* p. 162.

Opposition emerged to Bolívar from those who opposed both his projected life presidency and grandiose scheme to unite Peru, Bolivia, Colombia, and Ecuador; and the illustrious general left the country on 3 September 1826. His departure brought the repeal of many anticlerical reforms and the return of Roman Catholicism as the state religion and exclusive church of Peru. Nine years later formal religious relations were entered into with the Vatican, and in 1852 Peru established its first diplomatic mission in Rome, headed by the conservative leader Bartolomé Herrera.

The assault on the church was not renewed until the administration of the liberal Ramón Castilla in the mid-nineteenth century. Under the leadership of José Gálvez, Congress passed a resolution to abolish fueros in 1856 and, three years later, halted the collection of tithes from Indians, providing that monies from the national treasury should support the archbishop, bishops, dignitaries, and canons in service of cathedrals.[10] "These payments persist today, but are so insignificant that they can be interpreted only as a gesture of polite contempt." [11]

Although a revised patronato of 1874 invested the Peruvian president and congress with power to name bishops, liberal reforms continued to erode the church's power and influence: clerical control of cemeteries was broken in 1869, a civil marriage law passed in 1897, religious liberty emerged from the 1915 constitution, and a decree-law establishing absolute divorce was enacted in 1930. The church strenuously fought each of these measures.

Since independence clergymen have always been found in the ranks of those opposing dominant church policies in Peru. Luna Pizarro, a priest from Arequipa who later became archbishop of Lima, was strongly steeped in the ideas of the French Revolution and assumed leadership of the National Liberal party. He opposed San Martín's plan for a monarchy, supported religious freedom, and was elected president of the Peruvian congress, whose most liberal members were priests.[12]

10. Ibid., p. 165.
11. David Chaplin, "Peru's Postponed Revolution," *World Politics* 20 (April 1968): 402. Chaplin added: "They probably function to produce even fewer public contributions than the Church might receive were it [financially] independent."
12. Stanger, "Church and State in Peru," p. 421.

Father Virgil, a liberal priest at the time of independence, adamantly opposed the hierarchical, absolutist, and centralized position of the church in the nineteenth century. And despite criticism and abuse from the Vatican, he continued to express his views openly. His most important work was entitled *Defense of the Authority of Governments and Bishops against the Pretensions of the Court of Rome.* In the opinion of one historian, Virgil's "greatest contribution to liberalism was undoubtedly his furnishing an example of a friar and a Peruvian who refused to be intimidated by ecclesiastical censure." [13]

Legatee of these frocked dissenters is the National Office of Social Information (Oficina Nacional de Información Social— ONIS), a group of priests who, while maintaining communications with the hierarchy, have frequently criticized policies of their bishops, cardinal, and pope. (I will return to the Onistas later in this chapter.)

The American Popular Revolutionary Alliance (APRA), arch-enemy of the Peruvian military because there exist ideological differences between the two and because 6,000 of their members were killed by the army following an uprising in 1932, has incurred the wrath of the Catholic hierarchy by demanding separation of church and state and asserting that "we will guarantee the neutrality of the State in religious subjects." [14] While claiming to be "neither religious nor anti-religious," the Apristas have attacked the church for serving to legitimize dictatorial regimes, giving as an example President Augusto de Leguía's consecration of the nation to the "Sacred Heart of Jesus" in 1923, an idea that originated with the archbishop of Lima. They have also condemned its extensive landholdings, accused the clergy of instilling superstition in the minds of the Indians, and advocated state control of education to curb clerical influence in Peru's schools.[15]

Contributing to the acrimonious relations between the two institutions is APRA's insistence that the church remove itself completely from secular affairs. Meanwhile, *Aprismo* contains the

13. Ibid., p. 430.

14. Harry Kantor, *The Ideology and Program of the Peruvian Aprista Movement* (Washington, D.C.: Saville Books, 1966), pp. 93–94.

15. Ibid., p. 95; and Carlos A. Astiz, *Pressure Groups and Power Elites in Peruvian Politics* (Ithaca and London: Cornell University Press, 1969), p. 98.

four basic elements of a religion: "group identity, societal regulation, ecclesiastical organization, and belief system." [16] Many Apristas live within extremely narrow communications channels —belonging to the party's several youth organizations before becoming full-fledged militants, receiving medical assistance at an APRA clinic, eating in a party cafeteria, reading (until recently) the partisan newspaper, playing on an Aprista soccer team, etc.— and exhibit the close-mindedness of religious zealots.[17] Led by the aging Víctor Raul Haya de la Torre, APRA has developed Peru's only nationwide political organization, and the three structures found in even the most remote towns are a military post, a church, and an Aprista headquarters.

Although membership was illegal until 1939, the Apristas enjoyed relative freedom and toleration during World War II, when they attracted attention as outspoken champions of democracy and strong supporters of the Allies. During the same period, many Peruvian Catholics, "from prelates to the humblest parish priests," [18] embraced fascism as a philosophy to supplant the strife, materialism, and selfishness of liberal capitalism and "to remake society in the authoritarian, hierarchical image of the Church. . . ." As Frederick B. Pike has written,

> Fascism was regarded as the means for restoring and safeguarding the aristocratic, centralized, authoritarian political structure, together with the paternalistic and carefully supervised economic order and the close Church-State relationship that Spaniards were said to have maintained in colonial Peru.[19]

Symbolic of the rise of Aprismo and the decline in importance of organized Catholicism was the decision of President José Luís Bustamante y Rivero, a profoundly religious man who had once looked to the Roman Catholic church and its satellite organizations to provide ideas and leadership to the country, to select the Aprista party as the cornerstone of his government in 1946.

---

16. Smith, *Religion and Political Development*, p. 144.

17. James L. Payne, *Labor and Politics in Peru* (London and New Haven: Yale University Press, 1965), p. 7.

18. Frederick B. Pike, *The Modern History of Peru* (New York: Praeger, 1967), p. 257.

19. Ibid., pp. 257–58.

Marxist ideas began to penetrate Peru after the turn of the century and in the view of a noted historian the Catholic University, founded in 1917, was established to prepare a new elite "that would . . . give precedence to spiritual over material values and arrest the spread of Marxian-inspired class violence." [20]

Peru's Communist party was founded in 1930, the year that it affiliated with the Comintern. It emerged from the Socialist party of José Carlos Mariátegui, a gifted intellectual who advocated replacing the feudalism of the *sierra* with a communal system of land ownership and cultivation similar to that practiced by the Incas. Upon Mariátegui's death, party leadership passed to Eudocio Ravines, a former Aprista, and Ricardo Martínez de la Torre, who called the primary objective of Peruvian communism "the war to the death against the bourgeoisie, against the middle classes, and against all those who fight at their side." He also urged an all-out struggle against property owners—the "insatiable monsters, who suck blood of the working classes." [21]

The emergence of a militant leftist movement strengthened the fascism of many leading Catholics. Pike writes that a "characteristic editorial in the periodical published by the Catholic University made the point that a combination of international Jewry, communism, and Protestantism was trying to take advantage of the Indian issue in order to force alien forms of life and culture on the Peruvian people." [22]

While the Communists used the grim circumstances of the Great Depression to win recruits and advocate restructuring society, the Peruvian church buried its head in the fatalistic sands of the Beatitudes. In 1937, the Most Reverend Pedro Pascual Farfán, archbishop of Lima, said that "poverty is the most certain road to eternal felicity. Only the state which succeeds in making the poor appreciate the spiritual treasures of poverty can solve its social problems." [23]

Ideologically sterile, internally divided, beseiged, financially weakened, defensive, and bereft of allies, the Peruvian church reached the mid-twentieth century in danger of becoming utterly

20. Ibid., p. 208.
21. Ibid., p. 259.
22. Ibid., p. 260.
23. Quoted in the *New York Times,* 14 July 1969, p. 12.

irrelevant to the educated clergy, sensitive laymen, professional middle class, Catholic youth, and impoverished masses. Writing in September 1956, Catholic author Albert Nevins described the state of the church in Peru as "stagnant." [24] And in a pastoral letter, the first bishop of Abancay wrote that "we find that religion even among the most pious consists of vulgar external manifestations, completely unspiritual and valueless, and divorced from the practice of the simplest virtues and obedience to the law of God. We can only lament the proven existence of superstition in such worship." [25]

The "stagnation" besetting the church is reflected in the accompanying table, which relates the number of priests, churches, and convents to the population of Peru.

RATIO OF PRIESTS, CHURCHES, AND CONVENTS
TO POPULATION OF PERU

Year	Population	Number of Priests	Priests per 10,000	Number of Churches	Churches per 10,000	Number of Convents	Convents per 10,000
1935	6,500,000	1,123	1.73	1,109	1.70	51	0.08
1940	7,023,111	1,384	1.97	1,296	1.84	59	0.08
1950	8,605,549	1,189	1.38	1,606	1.86	58	0.07
1956	9,500,000[a]	1,458	1.53	1,615	1.70	78	0.08
1960	11,000,000	1,812[b]	1.65	NA	NA	NA	NA

SOURCE: Unless otherwise noted, these figures have been compiled from various numbers of the *Statesman's Yearbook* (London: MacMillan, Ltd.).

[a] Estimated

[b] Luigi Einaudi et al., *Latin American Institutional Development: The Changing Catholic Church* (Santa Monica, Calif.: The RAND Corporation, 1969), p. 51.

In 1960, there were only 1,812 priests in Peru, more than half of whom resided in the four sees with less than one-third of the population.[26] In this priest-starved country, hinterland parishes embracing upwards of 50,000 faithful are not uncommon. The sharp fall in the number of Peruvian "vocations" provides an index to the decline in church influence. Less than half of the priests serving in Peru are native-born, and the percentage is

24. "How Catholic is America?", *The Sign*, September 1956.
25. "Rome's Lost Stronghold," *Christianity Today*, 19 July 1963, p. 15.
26. Luigi Einaudi et al., *Latin American Institutional Development: The Changing Catholic Church* (Santa Monica, Calif.: The RAND Corporation, 1968), p. 51.

declining each year. This dilemma has been analyzed by J. Lloyd Mecham:

> Since the modern Church lacks the prestige which it enjoyed in the past, it no longer attracts to the priesthood and regular orders the sons of aristocratic Catholic families or even those of modest and middle circumstances. The clerical career, instead of being looked up to with awe and reverence, is scorned today with slighting remarks.[27]

THE SEARCH FOR A SOCIALLY RELEVANT CATHOLICISM

In the 1960s, internal and external forces drove the church toward a more socially relevant role. Among the internal forces were the Christian Democratic party (P.D.C.), the country's social conditions, and the National Office of Social Information (ONIS).

Six years after its founding in 1956, Peru's Christian Democratic party sought the presidency with Hector Cornejo Chávez, a prominent law professor, who came forward with *manos limpias*,[28] free of the political dirt of past administrations. Winning the most votes in Lima and Arequipa, he received about 5 percent of the ballots cast in the 1962 contest, which was nullified by the military. In the 1963 election, the P.D.C. threw its support to Fernando Belaúnde Terry in return for the second vice-presidential position and backing in other electoral contests. Belaúnde was a strong favorite among well-placed Peruvian Catholics, and the support of the Christian Democrats assured his victory.

The Christian Democrats, who considered themselves "revolutionary," entered Belaúnde's coalition. Nevertheless, the party's left wing, headed by Cornejo Chávez and eager to differentiate itself from the moderates who occupy the center of Peru's political spectrum, urged the president to quicken the pace of his middle-of-the-road government, called for sweeping agrarian reform, and demanded the nationalization of the International Petroleum Company, a Standard Oil of New Jersey subsidiary. These proposals strained relations within the Christian Democratic move-

27. Mecham, *Church and State*, pp. 176–77.
28. Rosenda A. Gómez, "Peru: The Politics of Military Guardianship," in Martin C. Needler, ed., *Political Systems of Latin America* (Princeton: D. Van Nostrand Co., 1965), p. 306.

ment, causing conservatives to break away from the P.D.C. to establish the pro-Belaúnde Christian Popular party. Subsequently, Cornejo Chávez withdrew his support of the government.[29]

Although unaffiliated with the church, an overwhelming number of the Christian Democrats are practicing Catholics, and leaders such as Cornejo Chávez are influential laymen who keep in constant communication with the ecclesiastical hierarchy, urging support for advanced social and economic programs.

Peru's grinding poverty became increasingly visible during the 1960s. The platforms of both the Christian Democrats and Belaúnde's Popular Action party focused attention on the plight of those living in the "other Peru" characterized by undernourishment, disease, lack of potable water and sewerage services, a 32 percent rate of illiteracy, and 93.2 deaths per 1,000 babies born— one of the highest infant mortality rates in Latin America. These conditions received added publicity as President John F. Kennedy's Alliance for Progress reached Peru. And in 1962, guerrillas sought to supplant the government with a socialist regime that would address itself to the social and economic plight of the masses. Although the 1962 uprising and another led by Luís de la Puente near Cuzco in 1965 were quelled, many church leaders became convinced that violent revolution was inevitable unless far-reaching social and economic changes took place. This opinion was voiced by Pope Paul VI, when he stated: "The world is sick. The poor nations remain poor while the rich ones become still richer. The very life of poor nations, civil peace in developing countries, and world peace itself are at stake." [30]

Also pressing the church to become more involved with Peru's social problems was the National Office of Social Information, headed by priests who have spent much of their lives living among workers and peasants. ONIS emerged from a 1968 conference in Cieneguilla as a "pressure group for the revolutionary change of the country's economic, social, and political structures." Signed by thirty-five priests and laymen, the Cieneguilla "Declaration" gained widespread attention for its direct, empirical indictment of the poverty and injustice gripping Peru. Conceived as a reply

29. Williams, *Latin American Parties*, p. 213.
30. *New York Times*, 29 March 1967, p. 23.

"to Pope Paul's heartrending plea in *Populorum Progressio*," it pointed out that 24,000 rich Peruvians earn as much as all the twelve million others; that 0.1 percent of the landowners hold 60.9 percent of the arable land, while 83 percent possess only 5.8 percent of the cultivated surface; and that in 1966 only 21 percent of the budget sprang from direct taxes, while 79 percent came from indirect, regressive levies on consumers.

The document further asserted that the landowning oligarchy "perpetuates its power through rigged legislation that prods the frustrated *campesinos* to legitimate revolt," criticized the national wealth lost in repatriated profits to "imperialistic consortia," deplored the "inhumane treatment" given to workers, and noted that "a large number of those responsible for the condition of national life have been educated in Catholic institutions." [31] The Onistas called on laymen, priests, and the hierarchy to promote "an authentic second revolution in Peru, that will emancipate the children of God from their servitude. This independence must take place without regard to religion." [32]

Although urging on the church a more active social role, the Onistas have eschewed demagogy, avoided open breaches with the hierarchy, and kept the cardinal fully informed of their activities, which include convening monthly meetings, drafting detailed reports on social problems,[33] maintaining close relations with Catholic students, and working with the Movement of Christian Syndicates of Peru (M.O.S.I.C.P.), the Catholic labor organization, which is made up of twenty-five small unions. Opposed to a highly institutionalized church, ONIS, now with over 200 members, has neither a headquarters nor a formal organizational structure.

External pressures have also played upon the Peruvian church. Convened by Pope John XXIII in 1962, the Vatican Council II

31. "Declaración de Sacerdotes Peruanos sobre las Estructuras Socio-Económicas del País," in Comisión Episcopal de Acción Social, *Signos de Renovación* (Lima: Editora Universitaria, S.A., 1969), pp. 96–98.

32. Ibid., p. 101.

33. Recent reports prepared by Onistas include a proposal for reconstructing the area devastated by the 31 May 1970 earthquake, "No Reconstruyamos la Injusticia," published in *Expreso*, 27 July 1970, and an analysis of the General Law of Industries promulgated on 27 July 1970, "Propiedad Privada y Nueva Sociedad," also in *Expreso*, 17 August 1970.

stressed the role of national episcopal councils (thereby diminishing papal strength), urged bishops to solicit views of the priests in
church matters, recommended greater lay participation in church
affairs, and affirmed that the church, like Christ, must carry out
its work of redemption "amid poverty and persecution." [34] Moreover, the council explored the possibility of greater communication between Christians and Marxists and condemned colonialism and underdevelopment.

The social involvement of the church continued in Pope Paul
VI's *Populorum Progressio,* delivered in April 1967. In this document, whose English title is "On the Development of People," the
pontiff stated that:

> It is unfortunate that a system has been constructed which
> considers profit as a key motive for economic progress, com-
> petition as the supreme law of economics, and private owner-
> ship of the means of production as an absolute right that has
> no limits and carries no corresponding social obligation.[35]

The pope argued that the "superfluous wealth of rich countries
should be placed at the service of poor nations" [36] and called for
reform to enable the poor to become full citizens of their countries.

These external and internal forces have encouraged Archbishop
Landázuri to speak out on social issues. In his first pastoral letter
after becoming cardinal, he wrote:

> The Church sees that the present economic and social order
> must be reformed and improved. . . . A living wage must
> be paid to workers and there must be a better distribution of
> wealth; private selfishness must be curbed for there is no
> longer an excuse for the miserable conditions in which rural
> laborers and the urban proletariat lives.[37]

34. A detailed discussion of the achievements of the Vatican Council II appears
in the *New York Times,* 4 June 1963, p. 20.

35. *New York Times,* 29 March 1967, p. 23.

36. Ibid., p. 24.

37. Quoted in *El Amigo del Clero,* nos. 1610–12 (July, August, September 1959),
pp. 213–14, and in Frederick B. Pike, "The Catholic Church and Modernization in
Peru and Chile," *Journal of International Affairs,* vol. 20, no. 2 (1966): p. 287.

Upon receiving an honorary degree from the University of Notre Dame in 1966, the cardinal stated:

> For the Church in Latin America, it is the hope, the struggle, the dream that is now becoming reality: to be a servant of society in revolution. Not to dominate, but to collaborate; not to temporize, but to inspire. Not to impede progressive changes, but to promote them.[38]

His most sweeping support for social change came at the Conference of the Latin American Episcopate held in Medellín in September 1968. There he called for the collegial commitment of the assembled bishops in attacking Latin America's poverty and articulated a kind of continental nationalism insisting upon the uniqueness of the hemisphere's problems because of economic "servitude" and sociological and psychological "dependence": "Our pastoral duty—we are bishops of this great Fatherland which is Latin America—impels us toward a unity, transcending racial, cultural, economic, and geographic frontiers, places us, with our own personality, in a world yet to be shaped." [39]

With notable exceptions—the distribution of church lands by the archbishop of Cuzco in 1965, for example—the hierarchy confined its social role to charitable practices and multifloral rhetoric. This does not mean that all clergymen remained uncommitted. Father Ivan Pardo's Rural Education Institute has trained hundreds of Indians and *mestizos* to take part in agrarian reform; by 1964, an American Maryknoll, Daniel McClellan, had set up 365 consumer and credit cooperatives with 130,000 members and a total savings of approximately thirty-five million dollars; a radio school established by the Maryknolls in Puno on the shores of Lake Titicaca has broadcast classes in reading, writing, hygiene, and farming—both in Spanish and Indian languages.[40] Father Salomón Balo Hidalgo became one of Peru's best-known ideologists of revolution and helped found the pro-Castro National Liberation Front.

38. From a speech delivered on 5 June 1966 and quoted in Comisión Episcopal, *Signos de Renovación*, p. 81.

39. "Discurso de Clausura de la II Conferencia General de Episcopal Latinoamericano" in Comisión Episcopal, *Signos de Renovación*, p. 248.

40. Pike, *History of Peru*, p. 277.

LEGITIMATION OF THE MILITARY'S REFORMISM

The military *golpe del estado* of 3 October 1968 toppled Belaúnde's floundering regime and brought to power what has turned out to be Peru's most reformist government,[41] a structure whose legitimacy has been enhanced by support from the church.

Six days after reaching power, the generals seized the International Petroleum Company (I.P.C.), whose claim to own the 416,-000-acre La Brea y Parinas oil fields—not merely to operate them as a concession—had long fired controversy in national politics. Eight months later came an agrarian reform, under which three million hectares had been expropriated and distributed among 95,000 families by mid-1972. According to the agriculture minister, General Enrique Valdez, nine million hectares will be apportioned to 400,000 families by 1975. Next a new code regulating water rights was promulgated, stipulating that lakes, streams, and rivers must be used for the welfare of all, not for the exclusive benefit of a few large landowners.

The government has also nationalized the banking system, extended social security coverage to all citizens, and reformed universities to unify decision making, bridle student activism, provide free admission for students from poor families, and promote studies that will enhance the country's social and economic development. Drastic changes in the primary and secondary schools are now under way, and industrial reforms have been introduced to assure participation of workers in the ownership and management of firms through "Industrial Communities."

The junta has invested its foreign policy with principles of the domestic revolution—nationalism, economic reform, and independence. Specifically, the generals have forged diplomatic relations with Cuba, China, and the Soviet-bloc nations, pressed Peru's claim to sovereignty over 200 miles of coastal waters, and vigorously promoted the Andean Common Market, whose headquarters is in Lima.[42]

The church has warmly supported General Velasco's "Revolu-

41. See George Grayson, "Peru's Military Government," *Current History* 58 (February 1970): 65–72, 114–15.

42. For insights into Peru's foreign policy, see Marcel Niedergang, "Revolutionary Nationalism in Peru," *Foreign Affairs*, vol. 49, no. 3 (April 1971): pp. 454–63.

tionary Government of the Armed Forces." Cardinal Landázuri has frequently appeared in public with the president; he openly concurred with the seizure of the La Brea y Parinas oil fields;[43] regarding Governor Nelson Rockefeller's projected visit to Lima, which was declared "inopportune" by the Peruvian government, he expressed skepticism, stating that "Latin Americans are tired of so many surveys and studies when little is done in practice;" [44] he backed the government when the United States suspended arms sales in May 1969;[45] and on the coastal waters question, the prelate stated that "it is necessary to respect the jurisdiction up to 200 miles from the coast." [46]

Following the government's agrarian reform, Peru's bishops issued a statement declaring that "every Christian must be committed to structural change, and fighting any selfish application of the law, will assure the full and effective realization of the reform process." [47] When in August 1970 the conservative National Industrial Society attacked the proposed industrial communities both as utopian and as a violation of a "right granted unto man, as an individual, by his creator," the cardinal replied that nothing contained in the law offended Christian morality.[48] And Landázuri praised the president's plans to create a "United Economic Front" to draw workers and industrialists into the battle against the country's underdevelopment as "good, since it is designed to help the Peruvian people." [49]

To gain legitimacy, Velasco has emphasized that his regime is one of "action not promises," deluging the public with decree-law after decree-law. His government has manipulated such nationalist symbols as the image and legend of the Indian revolutionary Tupac Amaru II, while identifying itself with the victories of the

43. *La Crónica,* 11 October 1968.
44. Quoted by *Excelsior* (Mexico City). An undated clipping of this 1969 interview with the cardinal was made available by the Centro de Informaciones Católicas, Lima.
45. *Expreso,* 22 May 1969.
46. Ibid.
47. XXXVII Asamblea Episcopal Peruana, *Declaración del Episcopado del Peru Sobre la Ley de Reforma Agraria* (Lima: Centro Arquidiocesano de Pastoral, n.d.), p. 2.
48. *La Crónica,* undated clipping, Centro de Informaciónes Católicas.
49. Ibid.

national soccer team, which won a berth in the 1970 World Cup playoffs; and although no survey research findings are available, the open support of the church and church-related organizations such as the Christian Democratic party, the Onistas, and the M.O.S.I.C.P. has no doubt helped win acceptance for official programs among women, moderate Catholic students, clerics, Catholic intellectuals, and the professional middle class.

IMPLEMENTATION OF POST-CONCILIAR REFORMS

With exceptions already mentioned, the church had limited its social involvement largely to resounding pronouncements of general principles prior to the advent of the Velasco government. The October golpe brought to power a regime committed to sweeping reform and offered an opportunity to pursue many of the social aims advocated by Landázuri and a number of other bishops. These goals were articulated in the "Conclusions" [50] of the thirty-sixth conference of the Peruvian episcopal council, convened in January 1969. The 5,000-word statement encapsulated findings of four committees: justice and peace, the poverty of the church, the apostolate of the laity, and education.

Reflective of this preference for discussion of concrete problems to general social rhetoric was the report of the committee dealing with justice and peace. It condemned unproductive investment of capitalists, foreign exploitation, unjust distribution of property, and estrangement of large majorities from political decision making; promised help to peasants and workers to "create and develop their own organizations . . . to seek their rights and social justice"; and proposed a three-point strategy to liberate the Peruvian masses and create "a new order in which the individual is the agent not the object of his own destiny": (1) to understand that the present structures are unjust; (2) to prepare people to fight against these structures; and (3) to develop new social structures in accord with the needs and aspirations of the people.[51]

Congruent interests on various reforms have opened the way to cooperation—albeit unofficial—between Roman Catholics and the junta at three levels: hierarchy, priests, and laymen.

50. Centro de Información Católica, "Conclusiones de la XXXVI Asamblea Episcopal Peruana," *Noticias,* no. 24 (29 January 1969).
51. Ibid., p. 3.

The presidential palace and the cathedral both front on Lima's Plaza de Armas, and there is significant intercourse between these two citadels of power, prestige, and tradition. Many of the most important reform decrees move across the cardinal's desk, or those of his chief advisors, before they are promulgated. Church intellectuals, such as Monseñor Luís Bambarén Gastelumendi, auxiliary bishop of Lima, enjoy close relations with cabinet members, including the prime minister who is Landázuri's brother-in-law. And the government's programs frequently spark discussion at the weekly meeting of the Permanent Committee of the Council of Bishops, presided over by the cardinal.

Some of Peru's 2,500 priests are heavily involved in the junta's programs. Father Ricardo Morales is a key member of the Central Committee of the agrarian reform and Father Harold Griffith is president of a newly established commission to study the influence of radio, television, and films on Peruvian life.

Many well-known laymen are also participating in the "Revolution." Hector Cornejo Chávez has been appointed head of the newly formed National Council of Justice, which selects lower court magistrates; and two military officers known for devotion to their faith and involvement in the lay organization Cursillos de Cristiandad are cabinet members: General Jorge Fernández Maldonado Solari, minister of Mines and Energy, and General Aníbal Meza Cardena, minister of Communications and Transport.

Nowhere has church-military cooperation been more obvious than in the "Young Towns" program, designed to provide technical assistance and public services to the teeming *barriadas* that curl around Peru's major cities. Three years ago, the cardinal appointed Bambarén "Bishop of the Young Towns," which contain over one and one-half million persons. The 41-year-old bishop, who helped form a Young Towns' association, has persuaded the business community to provide technical training in the communities. One of the bishop's staunchest backers has been his close friend Alfredo Ostoja, president of the conservative National Industrial Society. To demonstrate his commitment to their development, Bambarén himself lives in a Young Town.

By moving from his "enormous and luxurious mansion" in Lima's affluent San Isidro district with its manicured lawns and clusters of fruit trees to a modest dwelling in the working class area of La Victoria, the cardinal has manifested his sympathy for the reforms now taking place in Peru. As he stated in an interview published in *Excelsior* of Mexico City: "I think that a bishop must be a symbol of his time, a testimony of the Church in present day affairs. A dispossessed Church, a poor Church. This has been recommended by the Vatican Council and the Medellín meeting." [52]

THE MILITARY POPULIST MODEL

An increasingly apparent, albeit unpleasant, fact of contemporary Latin America is that so-called parliamentary democracy is ineffective in meeting the social and economic needs of the masses and must be replaced or supplanted by new structures. Militaries have rushed to fill this political vacuum in Argentina, Brazil, Paraguay, and other countries, only to reveal their own heavy-handedness and ineptness in fashioning new political institutions. In Peru, however, military forcefulness complemented by social Christian tendencies has produced a strong, legitimate government committed to both sweeping change and humanistic values.

The similarities between the church and military are striking. Both are led by the middle-class, have functional and geographic organizations, are hierarchical and undemocratic, boast a cadre of trained personnel, enjoy international ties, are heavily involved in inculcating values and beliefs, exhibit occasional self-righteousness, indulge in pageantry, and display a tradition anchored in four centuries of Peruvian history. Such affinities are likely to produce increasingly close cooperation between these two institutions which, by working together, may offer an alternative to the liberal and Marxist models for development in Latin America.

To date, in all of their joint endeavors the church has never threatened the military. For example, when a massive earthquake struck Ancash province on 31 May 1970, killing more than 50,000 persons, the church resisted any temptation to launch an independent relief operation. Rather, it placed its personnel, buildings, and communications facilities at the disposal of the government's rescue effort.

52. *Excelsior* (Mexico City). Undated clipping from files of Centro de Informaciónes Católicas, Lima.

All may not be smooth sailing for Peru's Christian-inspired junta. Conflicts have already erupted between the church and the interior ministry over a police raid that allegedly resulted in "intolerable insults and abuses suffered by the [Catholic] University in the person of its Rector, Authorities, Professors, Students, and Alumni." [53] In December 1969, the cardinal backed the demands for a shorter work week of sixty workers from the Texoro plant, who sought refuge from the special police in the Church of San Martín de Porres.[54] And additional disputes have sprung from a proposed educational reform designed to bring all of the nation's schools—private[55] and public—under government control, to inculcate the country's youth with *Peruanidad* (national consciousness) and to assign religion the status of an extracurricular activity like soccer or scouting. Reducing the role of religious instruction in public schools could attenuate church influence. As J. Lloyd Mecham has written:

> A reverence for the Church and its dogmas, profound respect for its ministers, and a dread of disobeying its authority are cardinal aims of this ecclesiastical instruction. If these aims are attained, and no one can say that the Church has failed, then the political position of the cult is given greater security.[56]

The most serious church-state dispute flared out in May 1971, when Interior Minister Armando Artola charged Bishop Bambarén and an American Maryknoll with inciting the poor to seize private building land on Lima's southern outskirts. Alarmed at the possibility of a break with the church, Velasco reacted to this move by accepting his minister's resignation, making 15,000 housing lots available to the rural migrants participating in the invasion, and offering Bambarén a public apology.[57]

The possibility exists that the church will reinforce the gov-

53. Official Communique of the Arzobishopric, quoted in *La Tribuna*, 15 June 1970, p. 2.

54. *Correo*, 29 December 1969.

55. Almost all of Peru's private schools are operated by the church, which educates about 150,000 children or 8 percent of the primary school enrollment. See Mecham, *Church and State*, p. 172.

56. Ibid., p. 175.

57. *Andean Air Mail & Peruvian Times*, 14 May 1971, p. 3.

ernment's negative aspects: clerical backing could enhance the
messianic tendencies exhibited by Velasco and his colleagues;
neither institution displays much interest in birth control,[58] although Peru's population is increasing at a rate of 3.1 percent
annually; both tend to ignore the leadership contribution that
civilians and women can make to national development; neither
seems anxious to enter a "dialogue" with APRA, despite the fact
that Apristas have upwards of 500,000 followers and any new social
organization is unlikely without collaboration of this party; and
the regime's highly nationalistic economic policy could be reinforced by the fuzzy thinking of some church intellectuals who turn
the air blue with such terms as "oligarchy," "imperialist domination," "exploitation," and "marginality," while forgetting the
"iron law of growth," namely, that savings are needed for investment and investment is prerequisite to economic growth.[59]

Even though military juntas such as Velasco's "are usually passionately devoted to matters of social reform . . . they are frequently indifferent or hostile to the needs of political institution-
building," [60] which is crucial in limiting power that might be

58. On the birth control issue, Landázuri has stated: "In the problem of demographic growth, the Church confides in the Providence of God who will not permit
the lack of material necessities for His creatures . . . and to those who propose
radical remedies contrary to natural law, the Church insists upon an international
sense of responsibility and a spirit of solidarity."

See "Discurso del Excmo. Sr. Arzobispo . . . para la Asamblea Arquidiocesana de
Acción Católica con motivo de conmemorarse el 25 aniversario de la fundación de
la Acción Católica Peruana," quoted in *El Amigo del Clero* 49, nos. 1626–27 (November–December 1960), p. 324, and cited in Pike, *History of Peru*, p. 315.

Dr. Joseph Kerrins, a Catholic gynecologist from Attleboro, Massachusetts, began
in early 1967 conducting responsible-parenthood and family-education training in
10 of Lima's *barriadas*, under the auspices of the Christian Family Movement. By
June 1968, 1,231 women had received regular treatment, which in some cases included prescribing antiovulation pills during the 2-year lactation period following
childbirth. The total cost to each patient was 5 soles (roughly 20 cents) a month,
including pills, when prescribed. Despite the cardinal's approval of the pilot project,
in January 1968 Peru's bishops criticized "foreign inspired efforts at family planning in the country; in their view, these efforts did not sufficiently consider moral
norms, safeguard liberty or treat adequately of the possibilities for the development
of Peru." See William J. McIntire, M.M., "Responsible Parenthood in Lima,"
America 119 (26 October 1968) : 380–82.

59. Robert L. Heilbroner, *The Great Ascent* (New York: Harper & Row, 1963), p.
86.

60. Samuel P. Huntington, "Political Development and Political Decay," *World
Politics* 17 (April 1965) : 423.

employed personally or arbitrarily by rulers, while mediating the participation of the masses in the political system. Zealous in protecting the military qua institution and unschooled in methods of developing new intermediate groups, generals-turned-politicians frequently spur literacy, communications, urbanization, and industrialization without strengthening or creating new structures so that, as de Tocqueville suggested, the "art of associating together" grows and improves "in the same ratio in which the equality of conditions is increased." [61]

Thus far the record of the Peruvian generals on creating intermediate groups—Huntington's agents of political development— is mixed. Although permitted to continue their social and economic activities, parties have ceased to play a political role, and the Committees of Defense of the Revolution, originally conceived to assume a number of party functions, have not flourished.

The government has recently announced creation of the Office of Social Mobilization, headed by a general, to organize civilian support for the regime. Drawing together official agencies that now deal with peasants, Young Town dwellers, and cooperatives, the move has been called a "giant step" toward establishing a corporatist state in Peru. [62]

Still, church influence has lent a certain social-Christian cast to the regime. In rejecting both communism and capitalism, urging the formation of cooperatives, stressing the need to overcome conflict between capital and labor in the work place, and insisting that "marginal" citizens be incorporated into national life, Velasco sounds very much like former Chilean President Eduardo Frei, head of his country's Christian Democratic movement. Whereas Frei, after six years in office, had difficulty creating "communitarian" structures in the economic field, Velasco has already developed the concept of industrial communities, which seem to embrace the aims of communitarianism—namely, the reform of industries to provide for the ownership of the means of production by workers. [63]

He has also stimulated formation of peasant associations and

61. Phillips Bradley, ed., *Democracy in America* (New York: Vintage Books, 1955) , 2 : 118; cited in Huntington, "Political Development," p. 386.

62. *Latin America,* 2 July 1971, p. 209.

63. Williams, *Latin American Parties,* pp. 118–23.

encouraged establishment of representative groups in the Young Towns. It remains to be seen whether the generals, as a part of their corporatist strategy, will seek out church and church-related structures—the Christian Democratic party, unions, youth organizations, women's groups, associations of laymen, and so on—as links between the government and the people. Such a move could strengthen the institutional base of a regime that already enjoys legitimacy and power and serve as a model of creative military-church cooperation for other Latin American countries.

Contributors

HEINZ BECHERT is professor of Indology and director of the Seminar für Indologie und Buddhismuskunde at the University of Göttingen. He is author of the three-volume work *Buddhismus, Staat und Gesellschaft* (Wiesbaden, 1966–72) and of *Singhalesische Handschriften* (Wiesbaden, 1969), among other works.

LUCY C. BEHRMAN is associate professor of political science at Rutgers University. She is the author of *Muslim Brotherhoods and Politics in Senegal* (Cambridge, Mass., 1970) and of articles on secularization and political development in Chile.

DANIEL N. CRECELIUS is associate professor of history at California State College, Los Angeles. He is the author of "Nonideological Responses of the Egyptian Ulama to Modernization" in N. R. Keddie, ed., *Scholars, Saints and Sufis* (Berkeley, 1972), and of articles on the Nasser regime's policies toward Islam.

GEORGE W. GRAYSON is associate professor of government at the College of William and Mary. He is the author of *El partido demócrata cristiano chileno* (Buenos Aires, 1968), and of several articles on the policies of the Peruvian military government.

HARRY KANTOR is professor of political science at Marquette University. He is the author of *The Ideology and Program of the Peruvian Aprista Movement* (New York, 1966), *Patterns of Politics and Political Systems in Latin America* (New York, 1969), and other works.

GUENTER LEWY is professor of political science at the University of Massachusetts, Amherst. He is the author of *The Catholic Church and Nazi Germany* (New York, 1964), *Religion and Revolution: A Comparative Study* (New York, 1974), and other works.

GAIL MINAULT is assistant professor of history at the University of Texas at Austin. She is coauthor with David Lelyveld of "The Campaign for a Muslim University, 1898–1920," in Seal and Gallagher, eds., *The Local Bases of Indian Nationalism* (Cambridge, 1974), and author of several articles on Indian Islam in relation to politics.

FAZLUR RAHMAN is professor of Islamic thought at the University of Chicago. He is the author of *Prophecy in Islam* (London, 1958), *Islamic Methodology in History* (Karachi, 1965), *Islam* (London, 1966), and other works.

LEO E. ROSE is lecturer in political science at the University of California, Berkeley, and associate editor of *Asian Survey*. He is coauthor with B. L. Joshi of *Political Innovation in Nepal* (Berkeley, 1966) and author of *Nepal: Strategy for Survival* (Berkeley, 1971).

THOMAS G. SANDERS is an associate of the American Universities Field Staff who has been reporting from Brazil for the past several years. He is author of *Protestant Concepts of Church and State* (New York, 1964), *Catholic Innovation in a Changing Latin America* (Cuernavaca, 1969), and numerous reports published by the AUFS.

JAGDISH P. SHARMA is associate professor of history at the University of Hawaii. He is the author of *Republics in Ancient India* (Leiden, 1968).

MIRIAM SHARMA is a postdoctoral fellow in the Department of Anthropology at the University of Hawaii. Her Ph.D. dissertation (Hawaii, 1973) is entitled "Rules, Resources, and Decisions: the Organization of Political Activity in a North Indian Village."

DONALD E. SMITH is professor of political science at the University of Pennsylvania. He is the author of *India as a Secular State* (Princeton, 1963), *Religion and Political Development* (Boston, 1970), and other works.

FRED R. VON DER MEHDEN is Albert Thomas Professor of Political Science at Rice University. He is the author of *Religion and Nationalism in Southeast Asia* (Madison, Wis., 1963), *Politics of the Developing Nations* (New York, 1969), and other works.

NORMAN L. ZUCKER is professor of political science at the University of Rhode Island. He is the author of *George W. Norris* (Urbana, Ill., 1966), *The Coming Crisis in Israel: Private Faith and Public Policy* (Cambridge, Mass., 1973), and other works.

Index

Abduh, Shaikh Muhammad: Egyptian Muslim reformer, 67, 80, 87, 275; Pan-Arab thought, 248; decrees on bank interest, 254

Acción Sindical Chilena, 194–95, 197

Achdut ha-Avodah, 96n–97n

Act of Royal Succession, Thailand, 56

Afghani, Jamal al-Din al-: as Islamic reformer, 25, 67, 245, 256; influence on La Chartre d'Alger, 248; on Muslim concept of ownership, 250

Afghanistan, 178–79

AFPFL (Anti-Fascist People's Freedom League), 63

Agricultural development, 53, 55, 240

Agudat Israel, 97–98, 111; relations with government, 99; position in constitutional debate, 100, 108

Ahimsa. See Nonviolence

Al-Azhar, 13–14, 72, 78, 86–87

Alessandri, Arturo, 14, 120–21

Algeria, 247–49

Al-Hilal, 171

Ali, Muhammad and Shaukat, 21, 171, 175, 182; founded Anjuman-e-Khuddam-e-Kaaba, 173–74; in Khilafat movement, 176, 181; in Hijrat movement, 179

Ali Mubarak Pasha, 74

Allende, Salvador, 222

Alliance for Progress, 285, 287, 312

American Popular Revolutionary Alliance, 210–11; relations with Peruvian government, 307, 322; principles and organization, 308

Anatomy and Pathology law, Israel, 111

Andean Common Market, 316

Anticlericalism: Roman Catholic countries vs. Hindu, Buddhist, and Muslim societies, 16; characteristics in Latin America, 23, 116, 118–19, 125; and Christian Democrats in Latin America, 222; in Chile, 285; in Peru, 305

Anjuman-e-Khuddam-e-Kaaba, 173–75

Anjuman Muid al-Islam, 173

Apristas. *See* American Popular Revolutionary Alliance

Aqqad, Mahmud Abbas al-, 88

Arab-Israeli war of *1948,* 260

Arab League, 260

Arab nationalism, 260

Arab socialism, 26, 274. *See also* Islamic socialism

Arab Socialist Union, 278

Arakan, 162

Argentina, 17, 126, 207n, 208

Argentine Democratic Union, 208

Arielism, 124

Armed Forces of National Liberation, Latin America, 222

Arsalan, Shakib, 248

Artola, Armando, 321

Arya Samaj, 34

Ashoka, King, 149–51

Assam, 170

Astrology, 45

Aswan Dam, 270

Ataturk, Kamal, 138–39

Augustinians, 188

Aung San, 58–59, 61

"Autogestion," 249

Ayyubi, Salah al-Din al-, 72

Azad, Maulana Abul Kalam, 171, 178

Azhar Institute of Research, 254

Aziz, Shah Abdul, 168–169

Badayuni, Abdul Majid, 180

Baghdad pact, 263, 265

Bakhit, Muhammad, 83n

Balkan wars, 170, 172, 174

Balo Hidalgo, Father Salomón, 315

Ba Maw, Dr., 58–59, 63–64

Bambarén Gastelumendi, Monseñor Luís, 319–20, 321

Bandaranaike, Mrs. Sirimavo, 161

Bandaranaike, S. W. R. D., 20, 157, 160

Banking, 254, 316

Banna, Hassan al-, 67

Bari, Maulana Abdul, 173–75, 178–80

327